Ambassador Yoshidu Shigeru and his wife Yuki leaving for
Buckingham Palace, 11 March 1937.

The
Japan
Society
Founded 1891

Japanese Envoys in Britain, 1862-1964
A CENTURY OF DIPLOMATIC EXCHANGE

Compiled and Edited

by

IAN NISH
LONDON SCHOOL OF ECONOMICS AND POLITICAL SCIENCE

GLOBAL
ORIENTAL

JAPANESE ENVOYS IN BRITAIN, 1862-1964
A CENTURY OF DIPLOMATIC EXCHANGE
Compiled and Edited by Ian Nish

First published in 2007 by
GLOBAL ORIENTAL LTD
PO Box 219
Folkestone
Kent CT20 2WP

www.globaloriental.co.uk

© Global Oriental Ltd 2007

ISBN 978-1-905246-32-8 [case]

The Publishers wish to express their thanks to the UK-Japan Joint
History Research Promotion Fund for their generous contribution to
the making of this book

British Library Cataloguing in Publication Data
A CIP catalogue entry for this book is available
from the British Library

Typeset in Stone 9.5 on 10.5 point by Bookman, Hayes, Middlesex
Printed and bound in England by Athenaeum Press, Gateshead, Tyne & Wear

Contents

In memory of

Bonnie Williams Berry
(1955-2006)

Member of the Council of the Japan Society 1990-2006
and Vice Chairman
Born in Japan and long-term resident in the United Kingdom

and

Professor W.G. (Bill) Beasley
(1919-2006)
Professor Emeritus, SOAS, University of London
and doyen of British historians of Japan

For their great contributions to relations between Britain and Japan

List of Contributors

Best, Antony (Dr), Senior Lecturer in International History, London School of Economics and Political Science. His latest book is *British Intelligence and the Japanese Challenge in Asia, 1914-41*, Palgrave, 2002

Cobbing, Andrew (Dr), University of Nottingham. His latest book with Masataro Itami is *Kawada Ryokichi – Jeanie Eadie's Samurai: The Life and Times of a Meiji Entrepreneur and Agricultural Pioneer*, Folkestone: Global Oriental, 2006

Cortazzi, Hugh (Sir, GCMG), British Ambassador to Japan, 1980-4; Chairman of the Japan Society (London), 1985-95. His latest publication is his translation of the Crown Prince of Japan's memoir, *The Thames and I*, Folkestone: Global Oriental, 2005

Goto-Shibata Harumi, (Dr), Asst. Professor of International History, Chiba University

Hotta-Lister, Ayako (Dr), the author of *The Japan-British Exhibition of 1910*, Folkestone: Japan Library, 1999

Ishizaka Ayako. Her latest book, published in her maiden name, Ayako Tomii, is *A Japanese Diplomat's Daughter: An Outsider's Childhood in the 1930s and 1940s* (New York: iUniverse Inc., 2004)

Kadota Shozo, former Minister at the London Embassy

Kuniyoshi Tomoki, an expert on postwar Anglo-Japanese relations, London School of Economics

Kuramatsu Tadashi, Asst. Prof of International History, Aoyama Gakuin University, Tokyo

Nish, Ian, Emeritus Professor of International History, STICERD, LSE

Seki Eiji, Japanese diplomat (retired) and author. He served twice at the London Embassy, initially as First Secretary (1965-7) and later as Minister Plenipotentiary (1984-7). He was Ambassador to Zambia and surrounding countries (1981-3) and later to Hungary (1989-92). He has published various historical works in Japanese and, in English, *Mrs Ferguson's Tea-set, Japan and the Second World War. The Global consequences following Germany's sinking of the SS* Automedon *in 1940* [Folkestone: Global Oriental, 2006]

Yoshida Yuki, wife of Ambassador Yoshida Shigeru

Preface

In 2004, the Japan Society published a volume entitled *British Envoys in Japan* with the object of showing the role of senior figures on the British side in Anglo-Japanese relations over the period 1859 to 1972.[1] This is intended as the successor volume which will present some of the senior figures who served as Japanese envoys in the United Kingdom. But there are three differences: we will not take the story beyond 1964; half of the authors are Japanese scholars; and we have included in addition to the biographies a few, regrettably few, sketches of what life was like within the embassy community so as to illustrate not merely policy-making but also some of the factors which affected the life-style of Japanese residents in London.

Since this is partially intended as a work of reference, we have included (chapter 1) an account of the history of the embassy buildings over the years as given by Shōzō Kadota, a minister in the Japanese embassy, in a lecture to the Japan Society in the 1970s. His essay did not originally go beyond the year 1941 and has been updated in order to take in post-war developments and the transfer to the new embassy building in Piccadilly in 1989. We have included a list of heads of mission up to 2007 (Appendix I). It seemed relevant to add perspective by giving an account of the Foreign Ministry itself indicating the major developments in creating a professional service of diplomats (Appendix II).

In essence, the story of Japanese envoys in the United Kingdom is one of steady growth from small beginnings at the time of the Meiji Restoration with a brief interlude from 1941 to 1952. The most convenient breaks in our story come at 1905 and 1952. In December 1905, the Japanese and British governments agreed to raise the status of their legations to that of embassies and to exchange ambassadors. This was an arrangement which Japan had been seeking for a long time. Since it was adopted in all the major capitals of the world, it represented a major diplomatic triumph for Japan won by her undoubted economic achievements and her victory in the war against Russia.[2] In April 1952, after an interim regime which is described in Chapter 21, the mission was technically reopened when the terms of the San Francisco Peace Treaty came into force and was converted into an embassy with the arrival of the first post-war ambassador. Since then there has grown up a large embassy with a full complement of diplomats, specialist officials drawn from other departments of government and consular staff (who are not considered in this volume).

Chapter 2 deals with Japanese envoys to Britain in the 1860s. This covers missions of various sorts which had different sources of authority and funding and met with different degrees of cordiality from the British authorities, whether Sir Harry Parkes, the minister in Tokyo, or the London authorities. Personnel who took part in these expeditions gained valuable experience abroad and were to play an important part in later Japanese history. But for the present Japan had only a limited pool of talent on which she could draw when she wanted to set up her legation in London in July 1872. Young men who had already been abroad and acquired something of the language were at a premium. Such a one was Terashima Munenori (sometimes Terajima) who at the age of forty became the first full minister. He had been associated with the Bakufu mission of 1862 and the Satsuma mission of 1865 and is described by Andrew Cobbing as 'a diplomat in the making' (Chapter 3). He and the other early envoys, Samejima and Ueno, operated legations of family-like proportions. In photographs of the day the envoy is to be seen surrounded by a very few colleagues and a handful of students, dressed in frockcoats, with tile hats, high collars and sporting moustaches. When the Iwakura mission visited the United Kingdom in 1872 (Chapter 2), Prince Iwakura who headed it had made a point of appearing in kimono; but its younger members quickly adopted the sartorial styles of the Victorian period and this fashion was followed by the early diplomats.

In early Meiji Japan there was competition between the Chōshū and Satsuma clans for appointments; and this is reflected in the appointments to London. The early appointees such as Terashima and Sameshima came from Satsuma and were veterans of the domain's expedition to Britain in 1865. But times changed and Chōshū men like Kawase and later Aoki took over. In those days the big issue in Anglo-Japanese relations was treaty revision, by which was meant the revision of the treaties which had been imposed on Japan in the 1850s. This engaged the attention of a succession of envoys, Ueno, Mori and Kawase, for almost two decades while fraught negotiations were conducted partially in London but largely at the Tokyo end. This marathon was brought to a satisfactory conclusion in July 1894 by the Anglo-Japanese Commercial Treaty which had been negotiated in London by Minister Aoki (Chapters 4-7).

The coming of Minister Katō Takaaki (Chapter 8) in 1895 introduced some new features. First, he was the first 'university graduate' to become an envoy (but this claim is disputed). Second, he had previously worked as a businessman in Liverpool and London. Thirdly, he was not from the aristocracy of Satsuma and Chōshū and owed his preferment to his personality and the anti-Satsuma-Chōshū sentiment which was growing in the 1890s. Moreover, the issues with which he had to deal – Japan's war with China (1894-5) and the attempted intervention in it of the European powers – were of a much more important order than any that had gone before. Katō had a strong sense of the dignity of his position and his homeland. He was insistent on improving legation buildings and offering entertainment appropriate to Japan's status in the world. He was anxious that Japan should share in the glittering social life of the Court of St James's, then the diplomatic capital of the world, though he realized that parties and dances did not automatically appeal to Japanese, particularly those still close to their samurai origins.

In 1894, the Foreign Ministry introduced a system of examinations for recruitment to the diplomatic profession and began training courses on a modest scale (Appendix II). Thereafter, diplomats were no longer appointed on the basis of patronage but on the basis of education. They were soon sent abroad for further training, often to London. They were chosen for their promise and the skill of the selection process is shown by the fact that so many early entrants rose to prominent positions later in their careers. Ayako Hotta-Lister (Chapter 10) points out that Matsui Keishiro, Shidehara Kijūrō, Hayashi Gonsuke, Ijūin Hikokichi, Mutsu Hirokichi, Makino Nobuaki, Uchida Yasuya and Yoshida

Shigeru were being trained in the London embassy in different junior capacities over these years.

One of the problems of a professional service based overseas was that those who spent their lives abroad without a posting at home often lost touch with home politics. This was an important consideration for the governmental process because in the prevailing Japanese system the foreign minister was invariably drawn from envoys serving in overseas embassies. But, especially after the coming of the Diet and the growth of political parties from 1890 onwards, it was difficult for diplomats who had spent their careers abroad to adjust.

The Anglo-Japanese Alliance, which lasted from 1902 to 1923, obviously defined a period of relative cordiality between the two countries. But even in those balmy days the staff of the newly-created embassy was small, though its members outshone those of middle Meiji. Katō who had been a successful minister returned as ambassador in 1908. Thereafter, ambassadors like Inouye Katsunosuke, Chinda Sutemi and Hayashi Gonsuke had the task of consolidating an alliance which was slipping in popular appeal, especially in the tense years of the First World War (Chapters 12-14). They were diplomats who had reached the summit of their profession and went into retirement after their London postings. The allies were generally happy that the alliance should survive into the post-war years but recognized that it was distrusted by so many outside powers that it was allowed to lapse at negotiations during the Washington Conference of 1921-2.

The decade between 1926 and 1936, when the envoys were Matsui Keishiro and Matsudaira Tsuneo, had its ups and downs. But the embassy of Yoshida Shigeru (1936-8) was weakened by a double blow: Japan entered into the anti-Comintern Pact with Germany (which Yoshida himself did not agree with); and the undeclared war with China started in 1937. These events generated frenetic diplomatic activity. It was perhaps not surprising that Madame Yoshida should commit her sadness to her book *Whispering Leaves in Grosvenor Square, 1937-8* which was published privately (Chapter 19). On holiday in the Bournemouth area at the end of 1937, she recorded:

> When we went out driving in the afternoon, my husband simply slept the whole way and back for the heavy burden on his shoulders must have been too much for him. . . I tried to get to sleep that night listening to the sound of the waves but it only brought me back again to the thought of the troubles in China. (*Whispering Leaves*, p. 79)

Antony Best (Chapter 18) deals with the critical mission of Ambassador Shigemitsu Mamoru. A sense of crisis prevailed throughout his spell in Britain. Although greatly weakened by the European war, Britain would not give in to Japan's requests in the long term. Shigemitsu, always eminently resourceful, tried to prevent the deterioration of the relationship but had eventually to admit that by 1941 the key decisions on East Asia were no longer being made in London and the focus of power had moved elsewhere. He was recalled to Tokyo in May 1941. The embassy was closed by Minister Kamimura Shinichi with the outbreak of the Asia-Pacific war in December.

*   *   *

The Japanese embassy was re-opened in 1952 with the appointment of Matsumoto Shunichi as ambassador. This followed the coming into force in

April of the San Francisco Peace Treaty between Japan and the wartime belligerents. In preparation for this the Japanese government had sent over Asakai Kōichirō, who had studied at the University of Edinburgh and served in the embassy before the war, to act as the official in charge of the liaison office from August 1951 and from April 1952 as minister plenipotentiary until the arrival of the new ambassador. Tomoki Kuniyoshi describes him (Chapter 21) as popular with the British public and efficient in paving the way for the reopening of the embassy.

The three chapters dealing with the post-war ambassadors Matsumoto, Nishi Haruhiko and Ohno Katsumi cover elements of tension (Chapters 22-4). Since it was already obvious to Britain that Japan would emerge as the most formidable industrial power in Asia, she recognized that it was essential that she should re-establish bilateral relations with Japan without delay. The problem was hostile public opinion on the British side, caused by the POW issue. Apart from this fundamental question, Matsumoto had to deal with the visit of the Crown Prince of Japan in 1953 and the visit of Prime Minister Yoshida in 1954. In turn, Nishi had to cope with Britain's reluctance to admit Japan unconditionally into GATT and to convey Japanese protests against British nuclear tests in the Pacific Ocean area. It was left to Ambassador Ohno to deal with the last phase of the trade negotiations which led up to the conclusion of the Anglo-Japanese Commercial Treaty in 1962, a natural turning-point in relations.

* * *

At intervals in the biographies we have included essays on what life was like in London as seen from the perspective of a Japanese diplomat's family. The first is written by Dr Ayako Hotta-Lister, herself an expert on the Anglo-Japanese alliance, in which she depicts aspects of diplomats' lives between 1884 and 1913. Her essay focuses especially on the remarkable experience of Mutsu Hirokichi who was connected with the Legation in the 1890s and later became Chargé and then Minister in the 1900s (Chapter 10).

Later chapters include extracts from the autobiographical volume on the period 1936-7 by Madame Yuki Yoshida, the wife of Ambassador Yoshida. It gives only a flavour of embassy life in a particularly difficult period dealing with her experiences of travel around Britain and the ceremonial of the Court of St James's. That same period is treated in an essay written specially for this volume by Ayako Ishizaka (Tomii), a schoolgirl in London at the time but now an acclaimed author for her book, *A Japanese Diplomat's Daughter*.[3] She was the daughter of Baron Tomii who was minister under Yoshida and covers contrasting aspects of diplomatic living such as sea-passages to the UK, finding houses and schools in London and recruiting domestic staff (Chapters 18 and 19).

* * *

An enterprise of this kind depends on the initiative and cooperation of many people. The vision underlying this project was that of Sir Hugh Cortazzi and the task of steering it successfully through the Publications Committee of the Society was conducted by him. Thanks are also due to the chairman of that committee, Mr Michael Barrett. As editor of a large part of the *Biographical Portraits* series, Sir Hugh himself collected and edited much of the material on which we have depended for this volume. We were greatly assisted in the early stages by Mr George (Hirahisa) Takeuchi, minister in the London embassy. He was helpful in procuring much material from various sources in Japan which supplemented material available at this end.

We are especially grateful for material made available to Dr Ayako Lister by Mrs Sachiko Mutsu, widow of the late Ian Mutsu, from the papers of Ian's father, Mutsu Hirokichi. We are grateful to Paul Norbury, the publisher of this book, for permission to reproduce extracts from Madame Yoshida's memoir, *Whispering Leaves in Grosvenor Square, 1936-7* which he published in 1997. We are also grateful for advice and material supplied by Dr William Brown and Sir Sydney Giffard. A special debt is owed to one of the contributors to this book, Ambassador Eiji Seki, who went out of his way to collect rare material for this volume quite beyond the call of duty.

The publication of this volume was made possible by a grant from the UK-Japan Joint History Research Promotion Fund, to which we must extend our thanks. In this connection it is necessary to thank the officers of the Japan Society, especially the Executive Director, Captain Robert Guy and Ms Clare Barclay, and members of the Japanese Embassy.

Because some of the essays were contributed to earlier Japan Society publications, the dates of their original publication are added at the end of each chapter. For the convenience of readers subsequent publications in the field are added under the heading 'Further Reading'.

It is unnecessary to add that any errors and misinterpretations are my responsibility. My wife as always has been tolerant of the wide-ranging and demanding historical interests of her husband and is glad that they did not range beyond 1964.

IAN NISH
Suntory-Toyota International Centre,
London School of Economics and Political Science
Autumn 2006

NOTES

1. Hugh Cortazzi (ed.), *British Envoys in Japan, 1859-1972*, Folkestone: Global Oriental, 2004
2. Kajima Morinosuke, *Diplomacy of Japan*, 3 vols., Tokyo: Kajima Shuppan, Vol. II, 1978, pp. 449-52
3. Ayako Ishizaka (Tomii), *A Japanese Diplomat's Daughter: An Outsider's Childhood in the 1930s and 1940s*, New York: iUniverse Inc., 2004

Acknowledgements

As editor, I gratefully acknowledge the help of Suntory-Toyota International Centre of Economics and Related Disciplines, LSE, and its library.

The authors of this volume also acknowledge the cooperation of the following libraries consulted in the course of their research and the help of their staffs:

Archives of the City of Westminster, London
British Library of Political and Economic Science
Gaikō Shiryōkan, Tokyo
Japan Foundation Library, Tokyo
Library of International House of Japan, Tokyo
Library of the Japan Society, London
Library of the Japanese Embassy, London
Library of the Japanese Ministry of Foreign Affairs, Tokyo
Library of SOAS, University of London
National Archives, Kew

Abbreviations

ANZAC	Australia & New Zealand Army Corps.
BDOFA	*British Documents on Foreign Affairs*
CAB	British Cabinet papers, National Archives, Kew
CLO	Central Liaison Office
FO	British Foreign Office papers, National Archives, Kew
Gaimushō	Japanese Foreign Ministry
Genrō	Japanese Elder Statesmen (Meiji period)
GATT	General Agreement on Tariffs and Trade
GHQ	General Head Quarters
NAK	National Archives, Kew (sometimes referred to as 'Public Record Office' [PRO])
NGB	*Nihon gaikō bunsho*
POW	Prisoners of War
RSL	Returned Servicemen's League [Australia]
WO	[British] War Office

JAPANESE NAMES

Ordinarily, the Japanese family name precedes the given name in accordance with Japanese usage. But in some cases in this volume the order of names preferred by the original author has been retained. Any reader in doubt should consult the Index.

1

THE JAPANESE EMBASSY IN LONDON AND ITS BUILDINGS

SHŌZŌ KADOTA

Japanese Embassy, 101-104 Piccadilly

EDITOR'S NOTE

This paper was delivered as a lecture to the Japan Society of London on 9 October 1978 by Mr Shōzō Kadota, then Minister at the Japanese Embassy. It is reproduced here by kind permission of the Japan Society which published it in *Bulletin* 86, November 1978.

The history of the Japanese Embassy can be traced as far back as 1870, when Mr Hisanobu Samejima was appointed as the envoy of the Government of Japan to the Court of St James's at the young age of twenty-four. He resided in Paris and was concurrently Japanese envoy to France and Germany The first Japanese representative to come to Great Britain, therefore, was Mr Munenori Terashima, who succeeded Mr Samejima in 1872.

The first four Japanese envoys to Great Britain, Messrs. Hisanabu Samejima, Munenori Terashima, Kagenori Ueno and Arinori Mori, were all from *Satsuma-han* or Satsuma clan (presently *Kagoshima Prefecture*) which was one of the most powerful and influential provinces and which was largely responsible for the Meiji restoration and the establishment of a new government. It is interesting to note that of these four envoys, three were from among those 15 young men who had been sent to Great Britain in 1865 by *Satsuma-han* in order to learn at first hand the political, economic, and social situation in this country. Mr Terashima later became Foreign Minister and Mr Mori became the first Minister of Education. In contrast, the fifth envoy Mr Kawase was from *Chōshū-han* or Chōshū clan (presently *Yamaguchi Prefecture*), which was the rival of *Satsuma-han*, and which was equally responsible for the creation of a new government. He served as Minister Plenipotentiary of Japan for nearly ten years which is the longest tenure of office in the history of the Japanese Embassy in London. It was Minister Kawase who attended personally the inaugural ceremony of the Japan Society of London in 1891. In his congratulatory address, he conveyed a message from the Emperor Meiji which was sent from Tokyo specifically for that occasion.

The conclusion of a new Treaty of Commerce and Navigation in 1894 marked a significant milestone in the early years of Anglo-Japanese diplomatic relations. The Treaty was signed by Minister Shūzō Aoki who was concurrently Japanese Minister in Germany. This treaty restored to Japan the right of jurisdiction over foreign residents in Japan. Until then, Japan's sovereign rights in this respect were not recognized by major countries of the world. The recognition of this sovereignty by Great Britain, the most powerful and influential nation of the world, had far reaching effects in Japan's favour. About a dozen other nations, mostly in the Western world, followed suit and by the end of 1897, all countries had concluded with Japan a similar treaty.

The conclusion of the Treaty of Commerce and Navigation almost coincided with the Sino-Japanese War. During and after the war, Japanese diplomatic activities in Great Britain were of necessity expanded and intensified. In order to cope with this situation, the Government of Japan appointed as head of mission the youthful, resourceful and brilliantly capable Mr Takaaki Katō, who was then thirty-six years of age. Mr Katō graduated from Tokyo Imperial University as first in his class and was married to the eldest daughter of Mr Yatarō Iwasaki, the founder of the Mitsubishi conglomerate. Up to that time, the Japanese Legation was located at No. 8 Sussex Gardens. Minister Katō moved the Legation to No. 4 Grosvenor Gardens so that he could receive and entertain more people at his residence.

The Anglo-Japanese Alliance can be regarded as a glorious symbol of the happy relations seen in the early years of this century.

After the Sino-Japanese War, Japan was forced to return the Liao-tung peninsula to China by the intervention of Russia, France and Germany. Then, the Russian move towards the south became conspicuous and proved to be a threat to the Korean peninsula which had in turn dangerous implications for the security of Japan. It was therefore the genuine desire of the government of Japan to strengthen her position by entering into an alliance with Great Britain and with such a strengthened position to negotiate with Russia with a view to finding solutions to settle the issue amicably and peacefully. The Anglo-Japanese Alliance was signed by Minister Tadasu Hayashi and Lord Lansdowne, His Majesty's Foreign Secretary, in 1902. When the war broke out in 1904 between Japan and Russia, Great Britain gave valuable support to Japan in every possible way, be it military, financial or otherwise. The great alliance was no doubt one of the important factors which contributed to Japan's victory in that war.

Almost immediately after the Russo-Japanese War, the Anglo-Japanese Alliance was revised and further expanded. In the revised text, ties between the two countries were made yet closer and further strengthened. The revised text was also signed by Minister Tadasu Hayashi and His Majesty's Foreign Secretary, Lord Lansdowne.

In December 1905, the year which saw Japan's victory over Russia and the conclusion of the revised Anglo-Japanese Alliance, the Japanese Legation was elevated to an Embassy and subsequently Minister Hayashi became Ambassador Hayashi. Thus, theoretically speaking, the first Japanese Ambassador to the court of St James's was Mr Tadasu Hayashi. Likewise, the British Legation in Tokyo became the British Embassy and the Minister, Sir Claude MacDonald, became His Majesty's Ambassador to Japan. In this connection, it is of interest to note that Japan was the eighth country with which Great Britain exchanged

Ambassadors. The seven other countries which preceded Japan were: Austro-Hungary, France, Germany, Italy, Ottoman Turkey, Russia and the United States of America.

In the wake of the Russo-Japanese War, Japan's sphere of influence was expanded to the Far East, and Japan's interest conflicted with British interest in that region. Under these circumstances, opinion which did not favour a renewal of the Anglo-Japanese Alliance, began to gain ground in Great Britain.

The restoration of sovereign rights over customs duties was another burning issue of the day for the government and people of Japan. There was a mounting urge in Japan to gain such a sovereign right as soon as possible.

In the light of the situation then prevailing, the renewal of the Anglo-Japanese Alliance for the third time, and the restoration of the sovereign right over customs duties, were by no means an easy task. The burden of discharging this task fell upon the shoulders of none other than Mr Takaaki Katō who had previously been in London as the head of mission. By the time Mr Katō was once again appointed as Japanese Ambassador, he had already been Foreign Minister twice, and a leading figure in Japanese diplomatic circles. With tremendous help from his staff, Ambassador Katō embarked upon his duty. Thanks to the herculean efforts of Ambassador Katō and his staff, the Anglo-Japanese Alliance was renewed once again in 1911 for another ten years, although the nature of its contents had to be somewhat changed. It was signed by Ambassador Katō and His Majesty's Foreign Secretary, Sir Edward Grey.

The Agreement, recognizing Japan's sovereign right with regard to customs duties, was also concluded in 1911, thus fulfilling the cherished hope of the government and people of Japan. I said earlier that it was Mr Katō who moved the Japanese Legation from Sussex Gardens to Grosvenor Gardens. This time Ambassador Katō tried to move the Embassy from Grosvenor Gardens to No. 10 Grosvenor Square. It is said that it took the Ambassador almost two years before he could finally persuade officials in Tokyo to accept his proposal. Had it not been for his extraordinary influence, persistence and perseverance, we would not have seen a Japanese Embassy at No. 10 Grosvenor Square. With his extraordinary financial means, Ambassador Katō must have met a wide range of people and entertained them very hospitably at No. 10 Grosvenor Square. Mr Katō returned to Japan in January 1913 to become Foreign Minister for the third time. In 1914 he became Foreign Minister for the fourth time. Thereafter he entered the political world and finally became Prime Minister. Throughout his public life he was a proponent and defender of the cause of the Anglo-Japanese Alliance. He was a true believer in the value of Anglo-Japanese friendship.

When the First World War broke out, Japan took immediate steps to side with the Entente in accordance with the letter and spirit of the Anglo-Japanese Alliance. Here is an anecdote:

A number of Japanese Imperial Navy frigates were despatched to the Mediterranean Sea in order to escort Allied military transport in case of possible enemy attack. In 1917, one of the frigates, called *Sakaki*, was sunk whilst in action and the captain and crew of the ship were all killed. To commemorate all those who gave their lives so courageously for their country, a piece of land was offered by the British authorities at the Royal Naval Cemetery in Malta, and a memorial was erected by the Imperial Navy of Japan. Years passed. During the last war, this cemetery was bombed and the memorial damaged. When I came to be in charge of West European countries in 1971, as Director of Division, I had the privilege of rendering my humble service in the reconstruction of the memorial. I personally went to Malta and supervised the reconstruction plan. How impressed and touched I was to see the memorial, with epitaphs engraved on the surface in both Japanese and English, standing high together with the tombs of British officers and seamen. I saluted the British authorities for the courtesy and kindness with which they allowed the Japanese Navy to build the memorial. There and then, I bore witness to a marvellous example of friendship and alliance between Japan and Great Britain, which, to our regret, had long been lost sight of.

When it came to the end of its life, the Anglo-Japanese Alliance was not renewed for the fourth time. It was replaced by the Treaty of Washington, to include Great Britain, Japan, the United States and France. The end of the Anglo-Japanese Alliance signalled the waning of the close and cordial relations which had so happily existed between the two countries. It is hardly necessary for me to make a detailed account of what happened in the ensuing years. The State Visit of the Prince Regent of Japan in 1921 must have been seen, therefore, as a great occasion which not only enhanced good relations between our royal families but also between our two nations. Mr Gonsuke Hayashi was the Ambassador who arranged this occasion.

The Great Depression which broke out in the United States in 1929, soon swept all over the world and many countries were plunged into economic distress. Japan was no exception to this. As the 1930s marched on, the domestic situation in Japan became tumultuous and the rise of the military severely strained Japan's external relations.

Mr Tsuneo Matsudaira arrived in London in 1929 and remained Ambassador to the Court of St James's for six and a half years. Throughout this difficult time, he made every effort to maintain and preserve good relations between our two countries. When the London Conference was convened in 1930 to negotiate the limiting or reduction of warships possessed by Japan, Great Britain and the United States, Ambassador Matsudaira was made a representative in the Japanese delegation, and his presence contributed greatly to the smooth conduct of negotiations. With dignity and composure, with courtesy and kindness, the Ambassador won the hearts of many people both within and without His Majesty's Government. Ambassador and Madame Matsudaira were also privileged to receive particular favour from the British royal family. I need hardly remind you that the Ambassador is the father of Her Imperial Highness Princess Chichibu. Ambassador Matsudaira's tour of duty finally came to its end in 1935. Hundreds of eminent people came to the farewell party to say goodbye to Ambassador and Madame. His Private Secretary wrote an article in memory of the Ambassador which described the occasion to the following effect: 'Lights were bright as daylight. The ballroom was full of well-wishers who came to bid farewell to Ambassador and Madame Matsudaira. At the height of the party the Ambassador invited a lady to dance. In spite of his age and of a rather overly dignified physical constitution, he danced so smoothly and adroitly to the music, that everyone there was pleasantly amazed and they kept their eyes wide open in admiration of their dancing. The occasion lasted well nigh to midnight. Parting was indeed sweet sorrow for everyone who was there.'

There was no return of such happy occasions after the departure of Ambassador and Madame Matsudaira. As the 1930s proceeded into the latter half of the decade, Anglo-Japanese relations continued to take a downhill course. Ambassador Yoshida did all he could to save good relations between the two countries, but to no avail. Madame Yoshida, whilst in London, wrote a book entitled *Whispering Leaves in Grosvenor Square* depicting the worrying situation then developing in Japan and expressing her deep concern over Japan's future relations with other countries, particularly with Great Britain. Mr Shigemitsu came to London as successor to Ambassador Yoshida only to witness the remaining crucial period before hostilities broke out.

In the course of 108 years (up to 1978) we have had twenty-three heads of mission, ministers and ambassadors, of which 16 were pre-war and seven post-war. I can proudly say that every one of them was the most experienced and qualified diplomat of his day. To give you some idea of their calibre, in the pre-war era, out of sixteen, one became Minister of Education, eight became Ministers for Foreign Affairs, and two became Prime Ministers. These last were Mr Takaaki Katō and Mr Shigeru Yoshida. There was also Ambassador Sutemi Chinda who is said to have courteously declined more than once the office of Foreign Minister, preferring to follow a diplomatic career. This high calibre is a phenomenon not seen in any other Japanese embassy abroad. Even our embassies in the United States, France or Germany do not compare with our Embassy here in Britain. Apart from heads of mission, we have also had a great number of able and outstanding diplomats who have later assumed important posts at home and abroad. A number of them became ambassadors and foreign ministers and constituted the backbone of Japanese diplomacy. It may well be said that the Japanese Embassy here in London is a Mecca for Japanese diplomats.

EDITOR'S NOTE

In addition to the main legation/embassy it was necessary for its various commercial and other functions to be conducted sometimes in Bishopsgate, in the 1910s at No.1 Lygon Place, Ebury Street S.W. and from 1920 at No.37 Portman Square W.1.[1] When German bombing was stepped up in 1940, the embassy emerged relatively unscathed. But buildings in Portman Square where the chancery was located came under aerial attack from September 1940 and were badly damaged. After that the administration switched to two hotels and later to flats in a new concrete building called Kingston House facing Kensington Road.[2]

An extra insight into embassy life in these war years is that Yoshio Markino, the distinguished painter of London scenes and long-time resident in the capital, was given a small room in the embassy by Ambassador Mamoru Shigemitsu. They had known each other since Shigemitsu was a junior diplomat in London and developed a relationship of mutual appreciation. Markino occupied this until his repatriation in 1942.[3]

Because of the danger of German night-bombing raids in 1940, Shigemitsu took the precaution of renting a house in Ewhurst, Surrey, just as Yoshida had earlier rented a property at Maidenhead for rest and relaxation. Ewhurst was a relatively safe haven; but it presented the difficulty of travelling down to Guildford in the black-out. The military attaché, Colonel (later Major-general) Tatsumi Eiichi, also took a property in the same village before he moved to Henley when Shigemitsu returned to Japan in the summer of 1941.[4]

The first move after the war was when a small team arrived in order to set up 'the Japanese Government Overseas Agency in London' (the official translation of the Japanese title which was *Nippon seifu zaigwai jimushō: Eikoku chūzai*) on 30 August 1951, some days ahead of the signing of the San Francisco Peace Treaty.

It set up its temporary headquarters at Grosvenor House and subsequently moved to permanent office accommodation at 32 Belgrave Square. With the coming into force of the treaty in April 1952, the agency became a diplomatic mission. Following the arrival of the first post-war ambassador on 8 June, the Belgrave Square premises were recognized as the embassy.[5]

When Ambassador Shunichi Matsumoto took over in 1952, the Japanese were unable to return to 10 Grosvenor Square, the Ambassador's residence in pre-war days, and had to buy a new residence. They proposed to purchase one at 23 Kensington Palace Gardens in what was commonly called 'Millionaires' Row'. The street had acquired this description because it had contained the residences of millionaires in Victorian times though it subsequently became a street of diplomatic residences and buildings. Strong arguments had to be advanced along the lines that Ambassador Katō Takaaki had earlier deployed in 1898 and 1911 in order to persuade Tokyo to authorize a new purchase: 'to be in an uncongenial legation where one cannot invite guests is not only shameful but it is also a disaster for our country'.[6]

The purchase was eventually approved by the Tokyo government despite the fact that its economy was only gradually recovering. The decision was doubtless made in the knowledge that the Crown Prince would be coming to London to represent the Emperor at Queen Elizabeth II's coronation in 1953. When he came, he stayed in the residence for a month.[7] The ambassador's residence, having been renovated and enlarged in the early 1990s in the time of ambassadors Kitamura and Fujii, continues to this day at 23 Kensington Palace Gardens.

In conducting the highly specialized negotiations for a trade treaty between Britain and Japan in the late 1950s (Chapters 22 [Nishi] and 23 [Ohno]), the commercial section of the embassy was inconveniently placed in an annex in Eaton Square while the main embassy continued at Belgrave Square. During the prolonged negotiations, the employees who had increased considerably in numbers were required to 'work in cramped and crowded conditions'. When the Anglo-Japanese Commercial treaty was eventually signed in 1962 in Ambassador Ohno's time, the embassy was transferred to 46 Grosvenor Street and the commercial department was integrated into the main building.[8]

In the summer of 1989, the embassy buildings were transferred to 101-104 Piccadilly, W1J 7JT, during the spell of Kazuo Chiba as ambassador. The old embassy had been remarkable for its distinguished ballroom which had a painted ceiling and was said to have been a venue where Mozart had given recitals in London. Social functions and lectures were held there. But the premises had become too small to cope with increases in staff and to accommodate the number of functions which were growing in accordance with Japan's new standing in the world. An elaborate search led to the choice of a historic building in Piccadilly which had first been opened as the Junior Constitutional Gentlemen's Club in 1892, coincidentally in the year following the formation of the Japan Society of London. This was approved by Tokyo.

The conversion of a former residential gentleman's club (which had subsequently been occupied by the International Maritime Organization) was undertaken from 1987 by the Kajima Corporation and Tollent Construction of Newcastle. Parts of the building, especially the stone façade, had listed status. This limited the alterations that could be made to the frontage but it also affected changes to the interior. Ambassador Chiba told the press: 'When you are building inside a façade that is as Victorian/Edwardian as that of our new building, it is only right that parts of the interior should be complementary to the outside'. Thus the ballroom, staircases and the exhibition foyer on the ground floor preserved some of the older features while the rest of the building was restructured on modern lines.

The move to the new, more capacious building took place in July 1989 and it was later officially opened in September. The ambassador, in opening the building, described it as 'a new presence for Japanese culture in British society' and added that it would enable 'a level of cultural output that far exceeds what was possible at the old premises in the Grosvenor Square area'. This move was timely because a nation-wide Japan Festival was due to be held in Britain from September 1991 onwards and was already in an advanced stage of planning. It also fittingly marked the end of the Shōwa era and the beginning of the Heisei reign.[9]

The Japan Information Centre which was formerly situated in a convenient but bomb-damaged building at the corner of Grosvenor Square and Brook Street was similarly transferred to the Piccadilly site where its library co-existed with that of the Japan Society on a temporary basis.

In an interesting contrast to the British Embassy compound which has remained in the same privileged position in central Tokyo since the middle of the nineteenth century, the premises of the Japanese envoy and his staff have moved around the centre of London. As the standing of the Japanese nation in the world has increased, so its buildings have become more spacious.

NOTES

1. Inuzuka Takaaki, 'Zai-Ei Nihon kōshikan no setchi keii to sono hensen' [The Japanese legation in London and its ups and downs]. In Terashima's time the legation was located at 9 Upper Belgrave Street. After a short stay at Notting Hill, it was transferred to 9 Cavendish Square under Minister Mori.
2. Yukawa Morio, 'Rondon ni okeru Nihon taishikan no 100-nen' [The century of the Japanese Embassy in London] in *Meiji bunka kenkyū*, Vol. 4, Tokyo: Nihon kōshō tsūshinsha, pp. 1-19
3. On war damage, Yukawa, pp. 14-15
4. Carmen Blacker in Ian Nish (ed.), *Biographical Portraits*, Vol. I, Folkestone: Japan Library, 1994, p. 185
5. *Katō Takaaki*, vol. 1, Tokyo, pp. 242-5 and 678-80
6. F.S.G. Piggott, *Broken Thread*, Aldershot: Gale and Polden, 1950, pp. 349, 351-2
7. Yukawa, p. 16, quoting Shunichi Matsumoto, *Moscow ni okeru niji*
8. Hanaoka Sosuke in Ian Nish (ed.), *Biographical Portraits*, Vol. II, Folkestone: Japan Library, 1997, pp. 325-6
9. *Nichi-Ei Times*. Kazuo Chiba, *Please! Just let me finish*, Tokyo: Japan Echo, 2005

2

JAPANESE ENVOYS IN BRITAIN, 1862-72

SIR HUGH CORTAZZI

Hori Takayuki (seated) and Godai
Tomoatsu, with Ryle Holme

Japan had no fully accredited envoy in Britain until the arrival of Terashima Munenori in July 1872 at the time of the Iwakura mission. The first Japanese envoys to visit London were the members of the Takenouchi mission from the Tokugawa *Bakufu* in 1862 and they constituted the only Japanese party between 1862 and 1872 which gained acceptance as official envoys.

THE *BAKUFU* MISSION

The first Japanese diplomatic mission overseas had been made to the United States in 1860 to exchange ratifications of the United States Commercial Treaty with Japan of 1858.[1] There was no requirement for exchanges of ratification in London of the British Treaty of 26 August 1858 as the Treaty specified that ratifications would be exchanged at Yedo (Edo, later Tokyo) within a year. However the British Minister at Edo, Rutherford Alcock, thought that another mission to European capitals in 1862 could 'open the eyes of the Japanese to the power and wealth of Great Britain', reveal to them 'the splendour of a Court in Europe' and remove some of the 'erroneous impressions' brought back from America'.[2] Alcock emphasised that the members of the mission 'should see and learn . . . as much as possible'. He did not want them to be restricted, as they had been in the USA, by the protocol required for high-ranking feudal lords. His French colleague, M. de Bellecourt, took much the same line. It was agreed that Britain would provide a naval vessel to convey the mission to Europe while France would look after the return journey.

The *Bakufu* chose Takenouchi Yasunori, a foreign affairs commissioner aged 55, to lead the mission and he was accorded the status[3] of Envoy Extraordinary.

Matsudaira Yasunao, a younger man, and Kyōgoku Takaaki, an inspector[4] (*metsuke*), were selected as the other two delegates and were given the status of Ministers Plenipotentiary. The official members of the party included Shibata Takenaka, who had been involved with affairs in Yokohama. One of the interpreters was the later famous Fukuzawa Yukichi. Another member of the staff who later rose to prominence was Matsuki Kōan (better known as Terashima Munenori, the first Japanese Minister to London in 1872 and later Japanese Foreign Minister). Six of the members had been on the mission to the United States. Alcock and de Bellecourt had to argue strongly to keep the size of the mission down to manageable numbers; even so with various hangers-on the mission totalled thirty-five.

Takenouchi sought the advice of Philipp Franz von Siebold[5] who advised him to visit other European capitals and not confine the mission to Britain and France. They should study military training and equipment as well as industry, science and agriculture. The three envoys proposed in a memorandum to the *Bakufu* that they study any matter which would be 'to our country's benefit', but they put the emphasis on points of diplomatic and commercial practice. The *Bakufu* in its response wanted the mission to investigate how Japan should respond if foreign warships were admitted to ports not officially open. It authorized the mission to hold discussions on the rents and land tax payable by foreigners in the treaty ports. Alcock thought this too narrow a remit and urged that the members of the mission be encouraged to pursue their studies of life in the west.[6]

Alcock, who was due for home leave, had hoped to travel with the mission, but he had had to await a reply from London to proposals which the *Bakufu* had made *inter alia* for postponement of the opening of the ports of Hyogo (Kobe) and Niigata and which Alcock had reluctantly recommended London to accept. The response from London arrived after the Japanese mission had left. Alcock was instructed[7] to make no 'concessions without equivalents, and to demand' indemnities for the injuries done to members of his mission as a result of the attack on the British Legation in 1861, punishment of the assailants and a defensible site for the Legation. As the Japanese were 'wholly unprepared to concede any equivalents' Alcock told the Japanese that the issues would have to be settled in London by the mission and undertook to convey their instructions to the mission. The Japanese agreed to send new instructions to their envoys and sent these with their chief interpreter Moriyama. He and Alcock eventually left Japan two months after the mission.

The mission had left Yokohama on 22 January 1862 on the Royal Navy's steam frigate HMS *Odin* under the command of Commodore Lord John Hay. They were accompanied by John MacDonald, one of Alcock's student interpreters, who had acquired some knowledge of the Japanese language. The departure had been delayed while the party was collected together and conveyed on board. The two hundred pieces of baggage which they brought with them presented a problem on a small ship. The party brought 'fifty crockery tea-pots' and five hundred champagne bottles filled with soya sauce, as well as fifty charcoal-burning *hibachi*. A suite of cabins with sliding Japanese panels and *tatami* mats and Japanese-style bathrooms were prepared for them and a moveable kitchen on wheels was set up on the foredeck to provide Japanese meals.

An account of their voyage, as seen by their British escort, was given by John MacDonald in an article which appeared in *The Cornhill Magazine* in 1863.[8] A

number of Japanese members of the mission kept diaries.[9] One of these by
Ichikawa Wataru was translated by Ernest Satow.[10] Fukuzawa Yukichi devoted a
chapter of his *Autobiography* to the mission.[11]

The members of the mission who were not used to travelling by sea had
many complaints not least about the yellow water which came from the ship's
tanks and the ban on smoking. Lord John Hay was also far from pleased at
having to cope with the mission and the disruption they inevitably caused. The
ship's first overseas port of call was Hong Kong, where the mission was greeted
by a guard of honour. They stayed in a hotel and had their first experience of
western living. They called on the Governor Sir Hercules Robinson and were
entertained to dinner and a ball given by Lady Robinson. They were duly
astonished by Western-style dancing. They much appreciated their first taste of
ice-cream. John MacDonald records their repeated comment of '*naruhodo*'[12] at
whatever they saw. The ship then called at Singapore, Ceylon and Aden before
reaching Suez where Lord John Hay was delighted to be rid of his unwanted
guests. The party boarded a special train for Cairo. This was their first experience
of railway travel and duly astonished them by its speed. At Cairo they visited the
pyramids on donkeys on which the envoys reluctantly agreed to ride. The
mission did not like Egypt with its flies and dust.

At Alexandria the party was accommodated on HMS *Himalaya*. They had a
rough passage to Malta and most were sea-sick. They were duly entertained by
the Governor Sir Gaspard le Marchant and attended an opera performance
despite the fact that, as they said, samurai did not go to the theatre in Japan. The
Himalaya took them on to Marseilles. They then took the train to Paris arriving
there on 7 April 1862. A military escort accompanied them to the *Hotel du Louvre*
where they were given luxurious rooms. On 13 April, they presented their
credentials to the Emperor Napoleon III having been again provided with a
military escort. Their talks with the French Foreign Minister Thouvenel, which
concentrated on postponement of the opening of the ports, made no progress
and the mission decided that there was little point in greatly prolonging their
stay in Paris beyond the end of the month.

The mission reached England on 29 April. They were met at Dover by John
MacDonald who had gone ahead from Marseilles. There they received an
address from the mayor and corporation and were entertained to luncheon. A
special train took them to London where they were accommodated at Claridges
and began to unpack their many boxes. Ichikawa Wataru recorded that a copy of
the New Testament in Chinese was placed on a table in every room. He was not
pleased as knowledge of Christianity 'ought to be hated and disliked very much'.

While their hotel contrasted favourably with that in Paris they were not
accorded a military escort or guard of honour as in Paris and the envoys had to
travel in simple carriages and pairs while the junior members of the mission
travelled in 'four-wheelers'. John MacDonald noted[13] that 'the absence of
ceremony on this their first arrival in England was remarked'.

On the following day, they sent a letter in Dutch to Earl Russell, the Foreign
Secretary, announcing their arrival and asking for an official interview. They
were reluctant to make any visits until after they had seen Lord Russell, but
having been told that the Earl would be present at the opening of the Great
Exhibition at South Kensington, the envoys and four of their senior officials
were taken on 1 May 1862 in carriages to witness the ceremonial opening of the
exhibition. 'The party was very warmly received'[14] and conducted to seats
reserved for them with the rest of the diplomatic corps. 'Having taken their

seats, and produced their indispensable fans, their Excellencies ventured to steal furtive glances' at the other people present and the building. On hearing the music they declared that 'English music would not be understood in Japan'.

They were duly received by the Foreign Secretary on 2 May. 'The visit, however, was purely complimentary, the envoys taking occasion to express thanks for the facilities granted them on their journey. On returning from the Foreign Office, they were taken for a drive round Hyde Park.'[15] Earl Russell agreed to their request to see him on business, although he had told the Netherlands representative[16] in London that he did not intend to propose any negotiation to the Japanese Envoys and that he thought it better to treat the Mission as one of ceremony and of friendly regard for European Powers'. An appointment was made for 16 May.[17] They then spoke on lines which he expected from Alcock's reports. As he had to attend the House of Lords he was unable to hear them out or make any reply that day. So they were asked to return the following day. Shortly before this meeting Russell received a telegram informing him that Alcock had arrived at Suez with Moriyama who had new instructions for the envoys. So he made it clear that it was useless to proceed with discussions until they had received their new instructions and despite an effort on their part to induce him to listen further to their representations he cut them short and recommended them to use the interval before Alcock arrived in looking at places which might interest them. After Alcock reached London on 30 May with Moriyama, discussions resumed and the new instructions sent to the mission formed the basis of their main diplomatic function; this was the conclusion (it could hardly be termed a negotiation) of the so-called London Protocol of 6 June 1862.[18] This provided for the postponement from 1 January 1863 for five years of the opening of the ports of Hyogo (Kobe) and Niigata and of the residence of British subjects at Edo (Tokyo) and Osaka. In agreeing to these changes to the 1858 treaty the British government expected that the Japanese authorities would uphold strictly the other provisions of the Treaty and specifically abolish restrictions as listed in the protocol. If not, the British government would be entitled to withdraw their concessions on the opening of ports and on residence at Osaka and Edo. The Japanese envoys agreed to recommend the opening of the port of Tsushima (this was later rejected by the *Bakufu*) as well as the reduction of duties on wines and spirits and other commercial concessions.

When the Japanese envoys tried[19] to raise other issues including such trade questions as export of copper articles and customs issues, Lord Russell[20] firmly rebuffed their attempts. As a result of the delays in concluding the London protocol the mission had some six weeks to undertake inspections and sightseeing. Their insistence on wearing Japanese costume inevitably hindered their movements[21] and did not impress the *Illustrated London News*[22] which thought that their attire was 'seedy'. 'The spectacle of half a dozen middle-aged parties with half-shaven heads, dingy blouses, brown holland inexpressibles [sic] and paper boots did not exactly come up to our expectation of the magnificent.' Their costume inevitably meant that they were subjected to much gawping by the people whom they encountered, although *The Times* commented favourably on 'the docility, gentleness and politeness of the whole retinue'.

Fukuzawa in his autobiography[23] recorded that their ignorance of European social conventions led to 'no end of farcical situations. . . When one of the lord-envoys had occasion to use the toilet, he was followed to the doorway by one of his personal attendants carrying a lighted paper lantern. The attendant in his most formal dress was to be seen squatting patiently outside the open door, holding his master's removed sword. This happened to be in the bustling corridor of the hotel where people were passing constantly, and the gas was burning as bright as day. I happened to come along and see the incident which I ended by shutting the doors.'

The mission had the help of officials such as Fukuzawa whose knowledge of English was getting better all the time and of John MacDonald. But the envoys themselves only spoke Japanese and when they attempted to use foreign words their meaning was often misunderstood. Fukuzawa, for instance, records that when a servant was sent to fetch sugar he came back with cigars. A greater obstacle to understanding was their lack of understanding of the background to European institutions which were only known to them through the studies of the *Rangakusha* (students of Dutch learning). Another significant problem was the lack of Japanese equivalents for many of the objects and still more of the concepts which they encountered in their enquiries. How, for instance, was the term 'parliamentary democracy' to be translated into Japanese? Fukuzawa found it difficult to understand how life insurance and the postal system worked. These problems and their relatively short stay in Europe made it difficult for the party to prepare the kind of report which the *Bakufu* wanted. Shibata[24] noted that Western institutions were so different from those of Japan 'like ice and charcoal'.

Nevertheless, the members of the mission, even if 'inscrutable reticence seemed to be the most noticeable characteristic in the Japanese'[25] displayed 'striking shrewdness'[26] and they took copious notes. They managed to see a great deal by dividing their efforts and 'during their stay in England regularly forwarded voluminous despatches by every mail to their own country'.[27] They showed particular interest in military and naval matters. At Aldershot they saw 'a grand military display, where the cavalry charges and the flying [sic] artillery especially excited their wonder.' At Portsmouth they watched target practice with Armstrong 100-pounders, which they also saw at Woolwich Arsenal where Sir William Armstrong was the superintendent. At Liverpool on 28 May they saw a warship under construction. But the British were determined that their visitors would also see British industry and members of the mission made a number of visits to the Great Exhibition in South Kensington. During their visit to Newcastle they went to the South Seaton Colliery where Takenouchi and five of his suite descended into the mine. They also visited Birmingham. They saw all the usual sights such as the Houses of Parliament and the Zoo. They admired the Crystal Palace and attended a Grand Ball given by the Duchess of Northumberland. They were also taken to Epsom to watch the Derby.

The section on Britain of the report compiled by the mission[28] was divided into forty sub-sections. Following some general comments on government and society there was a description of British diplomatic structure and an evaluation of British politics in the form of a comparison with France. There were then five sub-sections on military and naval matters, three on society including class structure and three on regulations applying to foreign ships and citizens visiting Britain. There was a section on London hospitals and schools. Other sections covered a wide variety of topics including the Armstrong gun, steam trains, gas-lamps and reverberatory furnaces, government finance, commercial taxation, smuggling and bonded warehouses. The authors had great difficulty in finding the appropriate Japanese words to describe what they had seen. Some words used in the Japanese suggested that the topic under discussion had not been properly understood. The House of Commons was described as follows: 'The country is divided into fifty-two localities [*buraku*]. Men of outstanding talent in the localities are put forward from among the people and made spokesmen [*tōdori*] for their locality. . . 'The reporters 'found it difficult to explain a society in which rank, office and income were not related in the way familiar to them in Japan'.[29] They had difficulty in understanding and explaining how the British economy worked. The report 'hinted at a different kind of society from Japan's which might prove to be one of the secrets of Western strength.' Such thinking was anathema to Japanese leaders at the time and the report was not given wide circulation even among senior *Bakufu* officials. The reports of the mission were probably of some value in opening the eyes of members of the *Bakufu* to the outside world, but the reports were inadequate and had only a marginal impact on the policies adopted by the *Bakufu* whose power was declining. Beasley concluded that 'it was difficult to identify any concrete results'.

The mission was, however, successful in achieving agreement on the postponement of the opening of the ports, although Alcock had in fact agreed to recommend this concession to London before he left Edo. The envoys had been unable to present their credentials to Queen Victoria as she was still in mourning for Prince Albert. There was probably no intention to snub the mission, but there was an element of Victorian arrogance in the British reception of the mission. The contrast with their reception in Paris, and later elsewhere in Europe, was noted by the Japanese who were understandably sensitive about any signs that Japan was not being treated with the pomp and courtesy accorded to other powers.

The envoys left London by the royal train on 12 June and boarded a Dutch warship at Greenwich. Their task now was to persuade the other European powers to accept the terms agreed with Britain.

VISIT TO BRITAIN OF A SPECIAL COMMISSIONER IN 1865

In the final years of the *Bakufu* and the first years of Meiji a few retainers of the *Bakufu* visited Britain on official business. They did not have the status of accredited envoys, but in most cases the British Foreign Office was involved to a greater or lesser degree in response to requests made through the British Legation in Edo/Tokyo.

The most important of these visitors was Shibata Takenaka who had been in charge of the mission secretariat in 1862 and who was appointed in May 1865 to lead a small mission including two interpreters and seven other officials. Their main purpose was to visit France to confirm the arrangements, which had been provisionally agreed in Edo, for French military advisers to train the Shogun's army and French naval engineers to build a dockyard at Yokosuka.[30] It was at first proposed that Shibata should have diplomatic status, but Roches, the French Minister to Japan who had reached Edo in 1864, 'argued that this would be inappropriate for what was really a purchasing mission'[31] and Shibata was given the title of 'Special Commissioner'. The recommendation of the British Chargé d'Affaires at Edo that Shibata should also visit Britain was accepted by the *Bakufu*.

Shibata did not like French food and showed no interest in French culture. He insisted that members of his mission like the Takenouchi mission should wear Japanese costume and should stay indoors in the evenings unless there were official functions.

Shibata's mission eventually left Paris on 8 December 1865 for London where they stayed at the new Langham Hotel. In a letter to Lord Clarendon,[32] the Foreign Secretary, dated according to the old Japanese calendar (9 December 1865 by the Western calendar), he sought an interview saying that he had been charged by his government 'with some affairs to communicate to your government.' He brought a letter from Mizuno Iwami no Kami, a Minister for Foreign Affairs, requesting 'instruction on the military sciences of your country.' Shibata was received by Clarendon on 13 December but there is no record that any matters of substance were discussed. Clarendon replied to Mizuno on 20 December 1865 declaring that Shibata's mission 'gives much satisfaction to Her Majesty's Government' and that he would use his best endeavours to make the mission 'agreeable and advantageous.' Shibata also brought presents[33] for the Queen, the Prince of Wales and the Foreign Secretary.

In his first few days despite persistent fog Shibata revisited some of the sites in London which he had got to know in 1862. He went to the Bank of England, the Royal Mint, the Royal Exchange, the Tower of London, Westminster Abbey and the Houses of Parliament and saw London's new underground railway. The Foreign Office had been told by the British Legation in Edo that the mission's main purpose was to inspect military and industrial institutions. So Major F. Brice of the Royal Engineers was put in charge of their programme. The party were taken to Woolwich, Greenwich, Portsmouth and Plymouth (including the dockyard at Devonport). They raised the question of military training missions to Japan but the British 'reacted without enthusiasm'. Brice also took them to his club, the Army and Navy, but Shibata admitted in his journal that he was 'not clear what a club is'. Before leaving, Shibata gave a dinner to which fifty three men were invited to thank those who had entertained them or acted as escorts. According to Professor Beasley,[34] Shibata and his assistants 'set down a plethora of statistics. . . but do not seem to have made much effort beyond this to investigate. One suspects that the whole operation was window dressing in Japanese eyes, designed to obscure the fact that Edo was already committed to France for military and naval purchases.' Shibata inserted in an appendix to his report opinions allegedly expressed to him by foreigners.[35] 'Their general tenor was that Japan could not trust Western motives, even when countries like France and Britain vied with each other to offer military help. . .' The mission returned to Paris on 4 January 1866.

UNOFFICIAL MISSION FROM SATSUMA IN 1865/6[36]

In 1864, a mission which was appointed by the authorities in the Satsuma fief to buy steamers and develop foreign trade for the domain. The mission left in April 1865. This mission was one of the outcomes of the so-called *Satsu-Ei sensō* of 1862.[37] The Satsuma authorities, while proud of the way in which they had defended their positions against the British fleet, had been forced to recognize that their defences had significant weaknesses. They could not rely on the *Bakufu*. They also reckoned that to cover the costs of buying warships and guns they must expand their trade and improve their knowledge of the West. Matsuki Kōan (Terashima Munenori) and Godai Tomoatsu, who had both been taken prisoner during the British attack on Kagoshima and were active proponents of rapprochement with Britain, were appointed members of the mission which was headed by Niiro Gyōbu, a senior samurai. Godai provided the main inspiration for the mission which stemmed from his written proposal prepared while he was in exile in Nagasaki.[38] Machida Hisanari was put in charge of fourteen students from Satsuma. They took as interpreter Hori Takayuki and were escorted by Ryle Holme who worked for Thomas Glover in Nagasaki who arranged transport. As the *Bakufu* had strictly forbidden any Japanese from going abroad without their approval, the mission was illegal and the arrangements for the mission had to be made in secret.

The Mission reached London on 21 June. Niiro, Godai and Hori stayed at the Langham Hotel while Matsuki and Machida took rooms in a hotel in Queen's Gate. The students stayed in private houses to begin their studies. They sensibly cut their hair in Western style and adopted Western dress.

Laurence Oliphant, who had been a member of the Elgin Mission to Japan in 1858 and of the Legation established under the Treaty in 1859 and who had been wounded in the attack on the British Legation at Edo in 1861, was now a Member of Parliament for a Scottish constituency. They had a letter of introduction to him and he took them to see officials at the Foreign Office to explain their purpose in coming to Britain. At first, they did not receive a very sympathetic hearing, but, following the death of Lord Palmerston and the appointment of Lord Russell as Prime Minister and Lord Clarendon as Foreign Secretary, they made some progress in putting their case that the *Bakufu's* policies on trade might be in breach of the Treaty and that restoration of power to the Emperor would lead to the Emperor giving his approval of the treaties. In March and April of 1866 they had three meetings with Lord Clarendon who sought the views of Sir Harry Parkes, the British Minister at Edo.

In the meantime Niiro, Godai and Hori were busy visiting military and industrial establishments including Woolwich Arsenal and the Royal Gunpowder Factory at Waltham Abbey. They also visited the Britannia Ironworks at Bedford, as well as Manchester and Birmingham. They placed orders for cotton-spinning machinery, rifles, ammunition and books. Visits were also made to other European countries including Belgium, the Netherlands, Germany and France, where there was some contact with junior members of the Shibata mission (see pp. 13-14), although Shibata himself refused to meet members of the Satsuma mission. On his return to England Godai was pleased that the Langham Hotel flew the Japanese flag in honour of his mission. Niiro, Godai and Hori sailed home from Marseilles on 11 February 1866 reaching Kagoshima on 25 April. Matsuki left in May 1866 but Machida, in charge of the students, stayed until 1867. One of the results of the mission was the arrival in Kagoshima in December 1866 of technicians from Platt Brothers of Oldham to set up the cotton mill which the mission had ordered.

Godai was a firm advocate of what came to be known under the slogan *fukoku kyōhei*.[39] Japanese leaders should, he thought, concentrate on unifying the country and developing industry. Trade could be left to merchants.

VISIT TO BRITAIN OF TOKUGAWA AKITAKE, DECEMBER 1867

The French were keen to persuade the Japanese to take part in the French exposition of 1867. Shibata had been non-committal but Niiro and Godai expressed interest in participating. Products from Satsuma and the Ryukyu islands were sent to Paris and a Satsuma mission arrived there in February 1867. Satsuma participation persuaded the *Bakufu* that they had to do something themselves and they decided to send a delegation to Paris which would be larger and higher-ranking than that of Satsuma. It was nominally headed by Tokugawa

Akitake, aged fourteen, the younger brother of the Shogun. Its task would be to confirm the *Bakufu*'s close relations with France. One member of the party who was to play an influential role in Japan in the future was the financier Shibusawa Eiichi. The party reached Paris in April 1867. Tokugawa Akitake had an audience with the Emperor Napoleon III and was present at various ceremonies and entertainments including a race meeting at which European royalty were present. Beasley[40] quotes the *Illustrated London News* (22 June 1867) as recording that Akitake 'said nothing to anybody, and nobody said anything to him'.

Akitake was accompanied as interpreter by Alexander von Siebold, son of Phillipp Franz von Siebold, who had been an interpreter to the British Legation but had been released by Sir Harry Parkes to join the mission. Siebold corresponded with Edmund Hammond, the permanent under-secretary in the Foreign Office in London. Akitake visited Belgium, the Netherlands, Switzerland, Italy and Malta, to which island he was conveyed from Leghorn (Livorno) in a British warship and where on arrival he was accorded full military honours.

On 2 December 1867, Akitake travelled to England by a special boat from Calais to Dover. From there he was conveyed by special train to London and stayed at Claridges as a government guest.[41] Major Bevan Edwards of the Royal Engineers was appointed as his escort. The Prince was received privately by Queen Victoria at Windsor on 4 December[42] and was taken on the usual round of visits to the Houses of Parliament, the Tower of London, Bank of England etc, but according to von Siebold 'military matters and armaments' were 'the only thing he seems really to care for'.[43] He saw reviews at Woolwich, where he was introduced to Prince Arthur, and at Aldershot. At Portsmouth he visited several naval vessels and was entertained by admirals at lunch and dinner. The visit was brief but he had been accorded full honours as a Prince. He returned to Paris on 17 December. Soon afterwards, news of the fall of the Tokugawa *Bakufu* was received and Akitake had to return to Japan.

JAPANESE STUDENTS IN BRITAIN

Japanese students in Britain from the *Bakufu* and domains such as Satsuma and Chōshū never constituted diplomatic missions, but they must be mentioned if only because some of the students[44] later played important roles in the Meiji era and because the Foreign Office became involved with some of the problems encountered by the students.[45] Among the most famous Japanese students in Britain at this time were Inoue Kaoru, Ito Hirobumi, Inoue Masaru, Mori Arinori and Terashima Munenori (Matsuki Kōan).

JAPANESE OFFICIALS VISITING BRITAIN BETWEEN 1868 AND 1872

Although none of the officials visiting Britain between 1868 and 1872 had diplomatic status some had important roles in Meiji Japan. In July 1870 Ueno Kagenori (later Japanese Minister to London) and Maejima Hisoka visited Britain in connection with the loan for the Tokyo/Yokohama railway and to find a suitable printing house for Japanese banknotes. They spent the best part of a year in Britain. Maejima took the opportunity of studying the British postal system[46] and came to be regarded as the founder of Japan's postal organization.[47]

SAMESHIMA NAONOBU, JAPANESE COMMISSIONER ('CHARGÉ D'AFFAIRES'?) IN LONDON

The Meiji government wanted to train Japanese to undertake administrative and technical work. This involved regulating the numbers of students sent abroad whose costs were a considerable burden for the Meiji government.[48] They also wanted to recruit foreign advisers and teachers. Although some of the work of recruiting foreign advisers was undertaken through foreign envoys resident in Tokyo it was clear that Japan needed permanent missions in the major capitals. Sameshima (or Samejima) Naonobu was appointed in November 1870 to cover Paris, London and Berlin.

Unfortunately, Sameshima's appointment to London 'as an Envoy' did not find favour with Sir Harry Parkes, the British Minister at Edo, when he heard of it on 2 December 1870 after Sameshima had left. Parkes[49] had been told earlier that Sameshima 'was being sent to take control of the students and would hold neither a diplomatic nor a consular position'. He was surprised that the Japanese 'had defined his office of *Shōbenmushi* as equivalent to that of a Chargé d'Affaires or Diplomatic Representative of the 4th Rank.' When Parkes remonstrated with the Foreign Minister he was told that Sameshima had exactly the same rank and position as Ueno Kagenori [see p. 16] who had been sent to England as a 'Special Commissioner'. Parkes was told that Sameshima had a commission from the Emperor and was again assured that his mission was to look after the students in England, France and Prussia, but the Japanese government hoped that if it was necessary or desirable to refer any other matters to H. M. Government his representations would be listened to. Parkes said that he must leave it to the Foreign Secretary to decide 'in what character' Sameshima should be received in London. He noted that Sameshima had only recently returned as a student from England. He would be accompanied by Shioda 'an able but pushing man' trained by the French. On 22 December 1870, Parkes reported that the Japanese Foreign Minister had asked him to substitute a new letter of appointment for Sameshima simply saying that he was a *Shōbenmushi* 'without attempting to establish any parallel between this and the Diplomatic titles of Europe.' M.Outrey, the French Minister, had, he said, concurred in his objection to according Sameshima the title of Chargé d'Affaires. Parkes thought that the title of 'Commissioner' would 'probably be found to serve all the purposes of his Mission.' Despite Parkes's remonstrations the revised instructions[50] sent to Sameshima were fairly comprehensive and Parkes's objections to his being received as a Chargé d'Affaires were unreasonable.

Sameshima arrived in London in February 1871 and stayed at the Langham Hotel which seems to have been favoured by Japanese visitors at this period. On 6 February he sent a formal letter to Lord Granville, the Foreign Secretary, enclosing a copy of his letters of credence and requesting an appointment. The letter signed by the Japanese Minister of Foreign Affairs specifically states that Sameshima had the character of Chargé d'Affaires (*Shōbenmushi*) of Japan and requested the Foreign Secretary 'to give full Credence to all the communications he shall have occasion to address to you in my name'. Granville[51] made it clear that Sameshima would only be recognized as a 'Commissioner' and not as a diplomatic agent.

At the end of March 1871 Sameshima,[52] perhaps feeling that the status accorded to him in London was not appropriate, left London to deliver his letters of credence to the foreign ministers of other countries to which he was accredited. In June he took up residence in Paris where he was appointed Japanese Minister Resident in June 1872 in anticipation of the arrival of the Iwakura Mission. Sameshima's principal assistant in Paris was Frederic Marshal[53] (1839-1905), an English lawyer known to Laurence Oliphant. In 1871/2 Sameshima, although not living in London, was involved with the recruitment of British and other foreign experts and in negotiating their terms of service. In February 1871 Prince Higashi Fushimi was in London, but Sameshima does not seem to have been directly involved in arrangements for the Prince.

Sameshima was coolly treated by the British authorities and Sir Harry Parkes behaved arrogantly towards him. This was not a good augury for the development of Anglo-Japanese relations while Parkes remained Minister to Japan.

NOTES

I am indebted to Professor W. G. Beasley's *Japan Encounters the Barbarians*, Yale 1995, referred to in the notes as 'Beasley' on which I have drawn freely supplementing from other sources including FO files in the National Archives.

1.   Article XIV had said that the Treaty signed on 29 July 1858 should come into effect on 4 July 1859 and that ratifications should be exchanged at Washington on or before this date, but that if for any unforeseen reason this was not possible the Treaty would in any case come into force on that date.

2.   Beasley, page 72.

3.   The only term the Japanese had for envoys at the time was *shisetsu* and it was Alcock who determined the equivalent status for the three envoys.

4.   Fukuzawa Yukichi in his *Autobiography*, translated by Eiichi Kiyooka, New York 1966, said the *ometsuke* 'had many retainers with him and consequently during our entire journey we were under the constant eye of the chief or a lesser "eye". This particularly applied to us three translators.'

5.   Phillipp Franz von Siebold (1796-1866) had been physician to the Dutch mission in Dejima from 1823-29, but had been expelled after being accused of spying. He had returned to Japan in 1859. He was an outstanding botanist and scholar of Japan.

6.   The revised instructions which were despatched after the mission had left Japan have not been preserved.

7.   Rutherford Alcock: *The Capital of the Tycoon: A Narrative of a Three Years' Residence in Japan*, London 1863, Volume II page 399.

8.   *The Cornhill Magazine* Volume vii January to June 1863 under the title 'From Yeddo to London with the Japanese Ambassadors'.

9.   Published in *Kengai Shisetsu Nikki Sanshū*, 3 volumes Tokyo 1827, reprinted 1971

10. Published in a series of issues of the *Chinese and Japanese Repository* in 1865, but the final part of the translation, if completed, was not published as the journal ceased publication.

11. Fukuzawa also kept a travel journal *Seikō-ki*. This and the associate notebook were published in his collected works *Fukuzawa Yukichi Zenshū*, Volume 10, Tokyo 1962.

12. Meaning 'Indeed'.

13. *Cornhill Magazine* Volume vii Jan-June 1863 page 617.

14. Ibid, page 618/9.

15. Ibid, page 619.

16. Earl Russell to Baron Bentinck, dated 22 April 1862, FO 410 Confidential Print.

17. Earl Russell to Mr Winchester at that time British Chargé d'Affaires at Edo, dated 26 May 1862.

18. W.G. Beasley: *Select Documents on Japanese Foreign Policy 1853-1868*, Oxford University Press, 1955 pages 216/7.

19. One issue they wanted to raise was that of the cavalry escort provided for the British Legation at Edo. Lord Russell made it clear that any attempt to preclude HM representative from maintaining a cavalry escort would not be acceptable. Among other points they wanted to raise

included burials and limitations on the places of residence in the Treaty ports.

20. In a letter to the envoys dated 9 June 1865 (see FO Confidential print for this period).

21. Dr Carmen Blacker in an article on 'The First Japanese Mission to England' in *History Today* volume vii, number 12 December 1957, noted that the Envoys considered it 'a disgraceful violation of the traditional customs of Japan' to wear Western shoes. So 1000 pairs of straw sandals were shipped with the party but when it became clear that these would not be needed they were left behind at Marseilles and eventually thrown away.

22. As quoted by Dr Carmen Blacker in the article referred to in note 21.

23. *The Autobiography of Yukichi Fukuzawa,* (see note 4) , pp 128/9.

24. Beasley, page 81.

25. Dr Carmen Blacker in *History Today* (see note 21), page 81.

26. John MacDonald, *Cornhill Magazine* (see note 8), page 620.

27. Ibid.

28. Beasley, pages 92-4.

29. As quoted by Beasley.

30. The *Bakufu* had sent a mission to France in 1864 to try to settle bilateral issues including the firing on a French ship in the Straits of Shimonoseki. de Bellecourt, the French Minister, hoped that this mission would provide an opportunity 'to demonstrate to Japan the superiority of French culture.' The mission led by Ikeda Nagaaki signed a convention in June 1864 providing that the Straits of Shimonoseki would be opened within three months, but this was contrary to their instructions and the convention was disavowed by the *Bakufu*. But significantly the mission reported that Japanese envoys should be stationed abroad and students sent overseas to learn about 'western skills in land and sea warfare'. When Roches, the new French Minister, arrived in Japan in 1864 he proposed that a French engineer should be invited to Japan to survey for possible sites near Edo for a naval dockyard. Roches also wanted to develop French trade with Japan.

31. Beasley, page 99.

32. See FO 46/62.

33. A paper in Japanese in FO 46/62 lists these. According to the translation attached, the presents to the Queen consisted of 12 pieces velvet with stripe, 6 pieces white ro described as 'particular kind of Japanese silk stuff' and 6 pieces of white gauze. For the Prince of Wales he brought 2 pieces of breech loading 'carabine[sic]'of the Japanese manufacture ornamented with gold and silver' and 2 pieces of breech loading 'carabine polished in eight angles'. For the 'Minister of Foreign Affairs' he brought 6 pieces of velvet of dark blue colour and 6 pieces of white *ro*.

34. Beasley, page 102.

35. Ibid, page 103.

36. Ibid, pp 105 et seq.

37. See *British Envoys in Japan 1859-1972*, edited by Hugh Cortazzi, Chapter 2 and appendix I. Folkestone, 2004

38. See Andrew Cobbing's *Satsuma Students in Britain*, Richmond, 2000.

39. Literally, a prosperous country and a strong army.

40. Beasley, page 115

41. FO 46/86. von Siebold informed Hammond by letter dated 2 December 1867 that their apartments in *Claridges* were very comfortably arranged. The Prince was accompanied by Hayato no Seko, Japanese Minister plenipotentiary in Paris, 'an officer sent with full powers to treat upon certain political questions in regard to the position of the Tycoon with regard to the Daimios.' In a letter of 4 December he asked about arrangements for delivery of presents for the Queen which consisted of lacquer and crystal. The Prince intended to deliver personally a portrait of the Tycoon. In a letter to Hammond of 14 December he sought permission to remain with the Prince in Europe; 'we should not leave the Prince entirely to the French.' Lord Stanley and Hammond called on the Prince at his hotel on 3 December. Lord Derby also called.

42. Lord Stanley wrote in a letter (FO46/86) to the Japanese Minister Plenipotentiary 'The Queen was much pleased with the opportunity of making acquaintance with the Prince and trusts that His Highness when he may write to the Tycoon will assure him of the interest which she takes in his welfare and in the general prosperity of Japan.'

43. According to the report of Major Bevan Edwards recording the details of the VIP programme prepared for him (FO 46/86), 'The Prince did not care to see many things that Asiatics generally like to see. His tendencies are almost entirely Naval and Military and such places as theatres and the ordinary sights of amusement in London he would not go to see. Thus he never cared to go

out of an evening.'

44. The number has been variously estimated; the highest estimate was 151.

45. In addition to chapter 7 of W.G. Beasley, *Japan Encounters the Barbarians*, entitled 'The First Japanese Students Overseas', see for instance *The Satsuma Students in Britain* translated and adapted by Andrew Cobbing, 2000, chapter 19 of *Britain and Japan: Biographical Portraits*, Volume IV, edited by Hugh Cortazzi, Japan Library, 2002, 'Nakamura Masanao' by Akiko Ohta, and article on 'Baba Tatsui (1850-1888) and Victorian Britain' by Helen Ballhatchet in *Britain and Japan 1859-1991* ed. Hugh Cortazzi and Gordon Daniels, London 1991 plus various items in Wikipedia on Japanese Students in Britain.

46. Mr Tilley at the General Post Office wrote to Mr Hammond at the Foreign Office on 2 March 1871 saying that he would be happy to receive Mr Maejima and Baron von Siebold on 6 March. Arrangements were also made for them to visit the Inland Revenue.

47. See 'Maejima Hisoka (1853-1919) – Founder of Japan's Postal System' in Chapter 5 of *Britain and Japan Biographical Portraits*, Volume I, edited by Ian Nish, 1994.

48. Beasley estimates that between 1870 and 1871 there were some 93 official students in Britain, page 152. In March 1871 Togo Heihachiro and eleven others were selected to go to Britain for naval training.

49. Despatch to Lord Granville from Parkes at Edo, dated 3 December 1870.

50. The revised instructions read: 'You will exercise control on all Japanese subjects resident in England, France and Prussia, in your quality of *Shōbenmushi*. Princes of the blood and nobles also residing in those countries are equally under your control. You will await the decision of the Home Government in all international matters. Matters of slight importance or which do not admit of the delay necessitated for reference home will be decided by you as each case may require. In all international matters, you will distinguish what is just and right. You will give every necessary explanation, and aim at rendering the relations of the two countries more intimate.'

51. Lord Granville (FO 46/148) in his reply to Sameshima dated 9 February 1871 said that he had heard from Sir Harry Parkes that Sameshima did not hold the rank of Chargé d'Affaires but 'only a title equivalent to Commissioner' and 'therefore though I shall be happy to receive you in that capacity I cannot do so as Chargé d'Affaires or any other diplomatic character'. An appointment was made for Sameshima to call on the following day.

52. Sameshima Naonobu was born in 1845. He was the son of a doctor in Satsuma and was sent in 1861 to study medicine in Nagasaki. In 1864 he was chosen to study abroad and was sent to Britain with the other Satsuma students. He went with Oliphant to America to join the community set up by Thomas Lake Harris in Massachusetts. In 1868 he returned to Japan and with Mori Arinori was employed on foreign affairs work, joining the Gaimusho when it was established in 1869. His initial appointment as Minister in Paris concluded in December 1874. He married in 1876 and was again appointed Minister in Paris in 1878, but he died there in 1880 at the age of 35. For details of Sameshima's life and of his correspondence in Europe see *Sameshima Naonobu Zaigaikoshokanroku*, Sameshima Bunsho Kenkyukai hen, published by Shibunkaku, Kyoto, 2002.

53. Marshal was first appointed on a part-time basis by a letter from Sameshima dated 19 July 1871 at È50 a month. In the following year the appointment was made a full time one. Marshal seems to have been very useful to Sameshima in explaining diplomatic practice and in facilitating his work. For details see book referred to in note 52 above.

3

TERASHIMA MUNENORI, 1832-93
Master of Early Meiji Diplomacy
[London, 1872-73]

ANDREW COBBING

Terashima Munenori

On 11 August 1872, Terashima Munenori stepped onto the quay in Liverpool. Sporting a beard like many of his peers at that time, he looked elegant in Western clothes, his slight build and correct bearing lending him a false impression of height. Ozaki Saburō, his travelling companion on the voyage from New York, was struck by his 'good-natured and sincere manner', describing him as a man of 'traditional' views with 'a tendency to be a little stubborn at times'.[1] This was Terashima's third visit to Britain. In 1862 he had been among the party of thirty-six delegates in the Tokugawa *Bakufu*'s first mission to Europe. In 1865 he had spent several months in London as an envoy for his native Satsuma domain. Now at the age of forty he was back as Japan's first resident minister to Britain on behalf of the Meiji government.

On his arrival in London a few hours later, he checked into the Langham Hotel and that evening he received a visit from Sir Harry Parkes, his counterpart in Japan. The British minister, home on leave, briefed him on their plans for the following day. In the morning they were to catch a train to Portsmouth and then cross the Solent to the Isle of Wight. Their destination was Osborne House where, on behalf of the Emperor, he presented his credentials to the Queen.[2]

With his scholarly background and reserved style, Terashima's low profile belied his lasting impact on Meiji politics. Supremely confident in his abilities, he already had considerable experience in diplomatic affairs and held no qualms about confronting envoys of the treaty powers with their own vaunted principles of international law. His arrival in London in the high summer of 1872 marked the onset of a diplomatic duel with Parkes that would unfold over the course of the decade. Conducted generally with decorum, their battle of wills encapsulated the small but significant differences in the broadly cordial relations between early Meiji Japan and Victorian Britain.

'With sunny hair and a sunny smile', Parkes, the spirited champion of British merchants' interests, was a very different personality.[3] The two men had known each other for several years, and previously their interests had largely coincided as Terashima tempted the Foreign Office with assurances of Satsuma's desire for open trade. Now there was growing discord, however, over the issue that would dominate Meiji foreign affairs, the new regime's stated desire to revise the 'unequal treaties' signed under Tokugawa rule in 1858. The combative British minister had been used to getting his way, but in Terashima he found a formidable adversary who calmly refused to be browbeaten into offering concessions like the pragmatic but short-sighted *Bakufu* officials of times past. Considering the weaknesses of the fledgling Meiji State, Parkes found his insistence on invoking Japanese sovereignty whenever possible sometimes difficult to tolerate.

AN OUTSTANDING SCHOLAR OF SCIENCE

Given his family background it was hardly surprising that the young Terashima made a name for himself in the world of Dutch Studies (*rangaku*), and with his sharp intellect and passion for learning, he soon attracted notice as a precocious talent. Born in 1832 near the town of Akune on the East China Sea coast, he was adopted at the age of five by his uncle Matsuki Muneyasu (Juan), a physician with a high reputation. On the orders of the daimyo, Juan had spent several years in Nagasaki studying under Phillip von Siebold, and now he was a leading figure in introducing Dutch-style medicine to Satsuma.[4]

In 1837, Fujitarō, as Terashima was known as a boy, was taken to Nagasaki, where he grew up surrounded by specialists in science and medicine. He and his uncle lived together with Ueno Shunnojō, clockmaker, student of gunnery and father of Ueno Hikoma, later famous as Japan's first exponent of photography. During the six years he spent in Nagasaki, Fujitarō received an intensive training in Dutch from Japanese interpreters employed at Dejima, in those days the focal point of interest for scholars with an interest in the West.

His first excursion into the corridors of power was in 1841 when Matsuki Juan and Ueno Shunnojō were commissioned by Satsuma to help set up a chemical laboratory in Kagoshima. When they were granted an audience on their arrival, the nine-year-old Fujitarō, too, was presented to the daimyo.[5] Two years later, when his uncle was again summoned back from Nagasaki to serve permanently in the castle-town, he enrolled at the Zōshikan, the domain's school for samurai in Kagoshima. By the time Juan died in 1845 at the age of fifty-nine, his own standing was already such that, although just thirteen years old, he inherited his position as head of the family. With head suitably shaven and his physician's status indicated by the new name of Matsuki Kōan, he then received orders to train in Dutch Studies in Edo, an honour practically unheard of as he later recalled with pride.[6]

In the shogun's capital Matsuki went on to attend several private colleges, including the Shōsendō founded by the Dutch-style physician Itō Genboku. There, just as in Satsuma, his academic talents won universal acclaim and by the age of twenty-two he was appointed head of the Shōsendō himself. It was not until his first visit to Europe the following decade, however, that he would fully realize the shortcomings of his education in Edo. Confined to applied sciences, Dutch Studies were largely silent on social disciplines like politics and law. This was why, he concluded, early Japanese overseas travellers were so perplexed by unfamiliar institutions such as parliaments and commercial companies. The experience would persuade him to concentrate more on English, for, after seeing people even in Holland relying on other languages, he declared that he could no longer recommend Dutch Studies to anyone.[7]

In the summer of 1853, when the arrival of Commodore Perry's ships off the Uraga coast heralded a new era of foreign relations, Matsuki was far away from Edo visiting his sick foster mother in Akune. Shimazu Nariakira, the new daimyo, took advantage of his return to enlist his linguistic skills in the service of Satsuma. There the security threat posed by Perry prompted a concerted effort to promote scientific research, especially in the field of gunnery. Dutch texts translated by Matsuki contributed to gunpowder experiments and the construction of Japan's third reverberating furnace.[8] Following his return to Edo the next year, the plans he drafted enabled the assembly of a steam engine. This was then fitted to a ship sent up from Kagoshima to create Japan's first motorized vessel, hailed by on-looking Edo townsfolk as 'the lord of Satsuma's steamship' when she was floated down the Sumida River that summer.[9]

In 1854, Matsuki was also one of several scholars of Dutch Studies appointed by the *Bansho Shirabesho*, the *Bakufu*'s new centre for studies on Western texts. Designed literally 'for the inspection of barbarian books', this was set up to handle the increased load of diplomatic paperwork envisaged following the commercial treaties signed with the United States, the Netherlands and Britain. He spent several years there as a young teacher and translator until, in 1857, the progressive daimyo of Satsuma had need of his expertise once more.

Recalled to Kagoshima, his work on Dutch texts prepared the way for further experiments on gas lighting and telegraphy. When the *Kanrin Maru*, a *Bakufu* training vessel called in at Kagoshima in April 1858, it was Matsuki who drew the attention of the nineteen Dutch officers on board. According to the captain, Willem Kattendyke, 'among the daimyo's retinue was one most intelligent-looking individual; this was the famous doctor Mats'ki Köan, teacher and translator of Dutch. He did not speak the language at all but his writing was impeccable'.[10] Taking copious notes throughout, his torrent of prepared questions tested the visitors' knowledge, and they were astonished by a little steamboat, complete with twelve-horsepower engine, that he had constructed himself. One of them, Pompe van Meerdervoort, was so impressed by his command of both natural and applied sciences that he claimed, 'Satsuma's recent progress is in no small part due to the doctor Matsuki Koan'.[11]

After Shimazu Nariakira's untimely death soon afterwards, Matsuki quickly tired of political affairs in Satsuma without the inspiration of his revered lord, and he was given leave to return to the *Bansho Shirabesho* in Edo. From there he was dispatched to Yokohama, where he witnessed the birth of a treaty port. Assigned to the customs house, he had the unenviable task of processing the declarations submitted by incoming ships from the day imports were first admitted on 1 July 1859. As this fishing village was transformed overnight into an international port, he was well placed to observe the growing prevalence of English in commercial affairs.

A DIPLOMAT IN THE MAKING

In the last years of Tokugawa rule, Matsuki's background as a Satsuma officer trained in Nagasaki and Edo forced him to tread a fine line through a minefield of conflicting interests. In varying contexts he was suspected by *Bakufu* officials of sympathies for Satsuma, by the British of complicity in dealings with the Bakufu, and even by Satsuma compatriots of collusion with the British. Recalling an encounter with him at Satsuma's Osaka residence in 1867, Ernest Satow later admitted: 'I had some suspicion that he was not altogether to be trusted, as he was reported to have been in the Tycoon's service.'[12]

It was certainly in the pay of the *Bakufu* that Matsuki first came to the notice of the British. In 1861, like other scholars at the *Bansho Shirabesho*, he was excited by the *Bakufu*'s decision to commission a team of experts to investigate conditions abroad during its forthcoming diplomatic mission to Europe. His selection made him the first Satsuma officer to visit Europe, and it was again evidence of his standing in Dutch Studies that he was chosen ahead of such eminent colleagues as Nishi Amane.[13]

Matsuki's packed itinerary allowed no time for rest as he set about recording all he saw during the Takenouchi mission's travels in 1862.[14] Although impressed by the power of Britain, he was not so enamoured by the lukewarm reception the mission received from the government. Their hotel in London was 'far inferior to the one in which we had stayed in Paris', and everyone in the party, he noted, compared the two capitals with Edo and Kyoto respectively. Unlike others such as Fukuzawa Yukichi who returned to Japan glowing about the material wonders of Victorian Britain, his gaze fell upon some urban problems of the industrial age, including the conspicuous number of beggars. Distracted by tipsy Londoners who sang and danced below their hotel windows day and night, he laid the blame on brandy (he probably meant gin), adding that 'they would rather beg than live in the workhouse where drinking is forbidden'.[15]

The volatile political conditions awaiting his return to Japan in 1863 next propelled him into direct negotiations with the British, this time on behalf of Satsuma. With the movement to expel foreigners in the ascendancy, the recent assassination of a British merchant by a Satsuma officer had provoked threats of military retaliation. Responding to his domain's call to arms he hurried back to Kagoshima where he was placed in command of three second-hand steamships. He was adamant that fighting was futile, and tried to sue for peace when the expected Royal Navy squadron appeared off the coast in August. As Ernest Satow observed, at the time the steamships were seized and their crews put ashore, 'no attempt was made by us [the British] to take any prisoners, but two remained on board the *Sir George Grey*, who gave their names to me as Godai [Tomoatsu] and Matsugi Kowan'.[16] Their efforts were to no avail, for it was the capture of these vessels that prompted the batteries on shore to open fire, commencing a four-hour engagement in the rain that caused damage to both sides.[17]

Matsuki and Godai were later transported to Yokohama on board HMS *Euryalus* before being released. Now viewed as traitors in the eyes of their compatriots they were forced to spend several unsettled months as fugitives in the nearby Musashi area. Godai later travelled incognito to Nagasaki where, assisted by the Scottish merchant Thomas Blake Glover, he devised an ambitious plan for an overseas expedition to Britain. In 1864 this was approved in Satsuma, for the salutary experience of the Royal Navy's firepower had since prompted the domain to pursue closer links with its erstwhile enemy. Godai was pardoned, and as the only Satsuma officer with first-hand knowledge of Europe, Matsuki, too, was summoned back to join the party of nineteen that set sail from Hashima, a fishing village not far from Akune, on board one of Glover's ships in March 1865.[18]

Following their arrival in London, most of these officers registered as students at University College, but Matsuki was there as an envoy. An introduction from Glover secured him an interview with a prominent japanophile, the Scottish MP Laurence Oliphant,[19] who in turn arranged a meeting for him in July with Sir Austin Layard, the under-secretary at the Foreign Office. The following month, in his first despatch to Sir Harry Parkes, Foreign Secretary Lord Russell expressed growing mistrust of the *Bakufu*, and in a clear reference to Matsuki, revealed sympathy for the initiatives by Satsuma and Chōshū to send 'young men to this Country for education, and Officers to enter into confidential communication with Her Majesty's Government'.[20]

In March 1866, Matsuki accompanied Oliphant to the Foreign Office and made his case in person to the new Foreign Secretary Lord Clarendon. Satsuma's agenda was to harness external pressure from Britain through diplomatic channels to wrest control over the commercial treaties from the shogun. Matsuki's strategy, formed with Oliphant's help, attacked the *Bakufu*'s monopoly on trade and called for a council of daimyo to convene in Kyoto so as to transfer signatory power to the Emperor. This articulated a unified state and an imperial restoration, achieved through peaceful means if possible. The British, with their insistence on an outward appearance of neutrality, could not be seen to support a campaign against the *Bakufu*. Matsuki nevertheless received a sympathetic response, and his overtures reinforced the growing feeling in Whitehall that British merchants' interests were increasingly in tune with the trading aspirations of domains like Satsuma and Chōshū.[21]

It was in July 1866, shortly after his return to Japan, that Matsuki first met Parkes. Although initially sceptical about Satsuma's confidential communications, information from the Foreign Office had since persuaded the new British Minister to make an exploratory visit to Kagoshima.[22] At Parkes's own suggestion he was then transferred to Yokohama where, armed with the Minister's business card, he acted as Satsuma's principal contact with the British Legation. It was also at this juncture that he changed his name to Terashima, from the small island in the bay near his family home in Akune. Having previously served the *Bakufu* as Matsuki Kōan, this name he felt was inconsistent with his new duties working against the interests of the Edo authorities.[23]

In 1867, as the centre of political activity moved to the Kyoto area during the last months of Tokugawa rule, Terashima was transferred to the imperial capital and then to the Satsuma residence in Osaka. He often met with British diplomats like Ernest Satow and Algernon Mitford, and now worked closely with Ōkubo Toshimichi, who valued his diplomatic experience in the preparations for the transfer of power. At Ōkubo's behest it was Terashima who drafted the first document proclaiming the restoration of imperial rule to the envoys of the treaty powers. Significantly, it already indicated the new regime's desire to revise the unequal treaties. [24]

THE TERASHIMA ERA OF MEIJI DIPLOMACY

In the years following the overthrow of the Tokugawa *Bakufu*, Terashima campaigned on behalf of Japan's claims to full recognition as a sovereign state. Under the Ansei Treaties (the so-called 'unequal treaties' of 1858) a semi-colonial situation still prevailed in the treaty ports in the shape of consular jurisdiction, which gave foreign nationals extraterritorial rights, and through controls on tariffs, which suppressed the prices paid for imports. Parkes, however, 'was entirely opposed to any measure of treaty revision in Japan's favour'.[25] Not only was he determined to protect British merchants' privileges in the treaty ports, but campaigned in support of their demands for access to the interior as well. In time the vagaries of the consular court system and the growing capability of Japan's modern new institutions would serve to undermine his arguments, but not before a 'long rearguard action', fought primarily against Terashima.[26]

After joining the new government's Board of Foreign Affairs in 1868, Terashima was appointed governor of Kanagawa. Based in Yokohama, his duties were to supervise the everyday business of a treaty port, from merchants' complaints to charges of smuggling, diseased silkworms and a 21-gun salute from British men-of-war in harbour on Queen Victoria's birthday.[27] The telegraph office he established there also won him a reputation in engineering circles as 'the father of Japanese telegraphy'.[28] When the Ministry of Foreign Affairs was created in 1869 he became vice-minister at the age of thirty-seven, a position that enabled him to exercise his authority over Meiji diplomacy for the next decade. It was his choice of personnel that staffed the ministry with compatriots from the Satsuma expedition to Britain and others with experience of life overseas. In 1870, for example, the first officials to be posted abroad as chargé d'affaires were two former Satsuma students: Mori Arinori, who was sent to the United States, and Sameshima Naonobu, who arrived in London with a portfolio covering Britain, France and Prussia.

In keeping with early Meiji government policy of appointing aristocratic figureheads, the first Minister of Foreign Affairs was a court noble, Sawa Nobuyoshi. He was followed by Iwakura Tomomi and then Soejima Taneomi, but significantly most of the correspondence from the British Legation in these years was also addressed to Terashima.[29] When the question of treaty revision was first broached under Sawa, Parkes stalled by insisting on specific proposals; this was one of the reasons that prompted the launch of an ambitious diplomatic mission, the Iwakura Embassy, which sailed for the United States at the start of its grand world tour late in 1871.

In Terashima and Soejima's view, there was little realistic chance of obtaining advantageous terms so soon, and they were dismayed to hear shortly afterwards that, on the counsel of Mori in Washington, two of Iwakura's vice-ambassadors, Ōkubo and Itō Hirobumi, were hurrying back to obtain credentials from Tokyo for formal treaty negotiations. Terashima joined them on their return voyage across the Pacific, ostensibly on his way to London to take up his new appointment as resident minister to Britain. It was with some relief that, following their arrival in Washington, he heard Kido Takayoshi's admission that negotiations had since foundered and the treaty issue would have to be shelved after all. In his first letter to Soejima from London a month later, he declared that the whole episode had made Japan 'a laughing stock in the eyes of the world'.[30]

Terashima had travelled a week in advance of the embassy on his onward voyage across the Atlantic. The timing of his new portfolio was partly circumstantial but also by design. He was of sufficient rank to placate Parkes, who had taken such exception to the appointment of the twenty-five-year-old Sameshima as chargé d'affaires in London that he had been forced to relocate to Paris.[31] Terashima also conceded that he was there on behalf of the Ministry of Foreign Affairs to monitor the Iwakura Embassy's talks with the treaty powers.[32]

He soon moved out of the Langham to the less expensive South Kensington Hotel, and in September premises were found for the first Japanese legation at No 9 Upper Belgrave Street, a terraced house accommodating an office of four Japanese officials and one British clerk.[33] Now he was busy arranging clearance through the Foreign Office for the embassy's visits to factories, mines and military installations. Also taking up much of his time was the task of securing emergency funds for distressed Japanese students left penniless after the collapse of the American Joint National Bank. In the financial scandal that followed, it transpired that the owners, the Bowles Brothers, had absconded with around £24,000 deposited at their head office in Charing Cross by Japanese students and also some members of the embassy.[34] Terashima met with Itō to discuss the related problem of rationalizing the large number of students left dependent on central government funds after the recent abolition of the domains. The proposals they drafted were incorporated into regulations resulting in the recall of most of them in the course of the following year.[35]

On 22 November 1872, Iwakura was granted the first of three interviews with the Foreign Secretary Lord Granville. He arrived at the Foreign Office accompanied by Sugiura Kōzō (Hatakeyama Yoshinari), a member of staff who took notes, but for subsequent visits he requested the presence of Terashima and one of the vice-ambassadors, Yamaguchi Masuka. Granville, for his part, announced that he would be joined by Parkes. The stage was set for a sharp exchange at the second meeting on 27 November. As expected, little headway was made over Japanese claims for treaty revision. Citing an experiment in Egypt where control over civil tribunals had been ceded, Granville announced that 'in all such cases the policy of the British Government was to yield the local authorities jurisdiction over British subjects in direct proportion to their advancement in enlightenment and civilization'.[36]

This was hardly an invitation to discuss terms. Iwakura, for example, could only respond to enquiries about his government's harsh treatment of Japanese Christians by voicing his 'earnest desires' for religious toleration.[37] Parkes, moreover, was unwilling to accept that the Meiji authorities were capable of managing the treaty ports themselves. He was unreceptive to an official request from Terashima for the removal of the British garrison stationed at Yokohama and pursued the demands of British subjects to be allowed access to the interior. In Terashima's view, inland travel for foreigners with extraterritorial rights was an infringement of Japanese sovereignty. Standing his ground he pointed out a host of 'difficulties' and insisted that in this case it would be necessary 'to make foreigners amenable to Japanese law'.[38]

Terashima did not remain in London for long. Plagued by ill health during the course of the winter, in 1873 he was given permission to return to Japan on leave. He set out from London on 26 August, and in the event he would never come back, for with Ōkubo now at the helm in Tokyo, he was appointed Minister of Foreign Affairs in place of Soejima, who had just resigned over the vetoed plans to invade Korea. This was one of several regional disputes that initially prevented him from embarking on any major diplomatic initiatives. Unlike those who were impatient for military intervention, he opposed the Formosa Campaign launched in 1874 in retaliation against the murder of some Ryūkyū Island natives. He also urged peaceful engagement with Korea, rather than the Perry-style gunboat diplomacy used by Kuroda Kiyotaka in forcing the 'unequal' Kangwha Treaty of 1876. More to his liking were Enomoto Takeaki's talks in Russia that resulted in the Treaty of St Petersburg in 1875, defining the countries' respective interests in the Northern Territories with Japan gaining control over the Kurile Islands in return for Sakhalin.

At home there were also tensions in the administration of the treaty ports. In 1874, frustrated by his insistence on linking access to the interior with the issue of extraterritoriality, Parkes finally lost patience and appealed directly to Iwakura and Sanjō Sanetomi, complaining of the 'unfriendly attitude' shown in recent Meiji diplomacy. Dismayed by these senior nobles' more flexible attitude, Terashima threatened to resign, and after some delay a compromise agreement was reached which provided some limited access, although categorically not for commercial activities.[39] Meanwhile, in spite of the views of R.G. Watson who was in charge of the Legation while Parkes was away, Parkes continued to resist further requests for the removal of the British garrison in Yokohama, and it was not until 1875 that he finally agreed to the troops' departure.[40]

Terashima had now been granted the use of a new inter-ministry bureau for treaty inspection, and he seemed ready at last to launch his own diplomatic agenda. The issue of extraterritoriality remained his first priority, but pressure from Ōkuma Shigenobu, the Minister of Financial Affairs, forced him to concentrate instead on the question of tariff autonomy. As far as Parkes was concerned, this was merely an exercise to raise much-needed funds at the expense of British merchants. Terashima, however, was able to exploit the friction between Parkes and the American minister John Bingham on a range of issues, notably their understandable failure to see eye-to-eye over gun laws.[41] Encouraged by Bingham's more positive response, he instructed Yoshida Kiyonari, Japan's envoy in Washington, to pursue negotiations there. Yoshida reported enthusiastically that there could even be potential for a bilateral treaty with the United States that would restore tariff autonomy in exchange for the opening of two new treaty ports.

Aware that such concessions would doubtless be claimed by the other treaty powers as well, Terashima insisted that tariff matters should be negotiated collectively. This was why the convention that Yoshida signed with US Secretary of State William Evarts in 1878 stipulated that the terms were contingent on similar arrangements being made with the other treaty powers.[42] With one precedent already set, Terashima pressed Britain, France and Germany to follow suit. Hopes were raised when the British agreed to a conference in Tokyo, and in April 1879, Ueno Kagenori, the Japanese Minister in London, even declared: 'I believe that the British Government may finally yield at all essential points if you remain firm with S. Parkes.'[43] Encouraged by the scent of victory, Terashima grandly summoned Ueno back to Japan 'in consequence of Treaty Revision at Tokio'.[44]

Parkes, however, remained deeply suspicious of the Americans' stance on tariffs.[45] Insisting that this was just a policy of self-interest at Britain's expense, he called on the Foreign Office to orchestrate collective resistance together with France and Germany. Eventually, on 15 July, he was able to deliver to Terashima a final declaration from the Foreign Secretary, the Marquis of Salisbury, confirming that 'Her Majesty's Government decline to enter into any new negotiations for the Revision of the Treaties'. The British protested that, 'as a basis for joint negotiations', they were willing to accept specific proposals on 'the amendment or modification of the existing Tariff'. The notion of following Washington's lead and surrendering control, however, was out of the question.[46] This precipitated the total collapse of Terashima's strategy on tariffs, and his abiding concern for 'joint negotiations' meant that even Yoshida's efforts had come to nothing.

His mounting problems were now compounded by clashes over extraterritorial rights. Following outbreaks of cholera in western Japan, Terashima's attempts to impose a quarantine period of ten days on incoming ships were seen by Parkes as an assault on consular jurisdiction, and both the British and German Ministers allowed merchant vessels prematurely into Yokohama. Then there was the furore over the release of John Hartley, a British chemist charged with smuggling opium, who received only a token fine from a consular court on the grounds that his consignments had been for medicinal purposes. The growing liberal rights movement was also raising public awareness of the slights on Japanese sovereignty enshrined in the Ansei Treaties, and in September 1879, facing criticism that he had neglected extraterritorial issues in favour of tariff autonomy, Terashima was forced to resign.[47]

Although not spectacular, he could in fact point to incremental progress. In 1876, for example, Britain's own Law Officers had backed the Meiji government's calls to ban the *Bankoku Shimbun*, a Japanese language newspaper seen as potentially seditious, that had been issued by the British journalist John Reddie Black.[48] Moreover, Maejima Hisoka's efficient new Japanese postal service was already taking over from British and French mail ships in the treaty ports.[49] In the political climate of 1879, however, Terashima had to make way, and with his plans for treaty revision in ruins he left for the vacant post of Minister of Education. Lamenting his wild ambition, Parkes felt that a change of personality could help smooth over differences between their governments. Others may have felt this applied in equal measure to Parkes, who still had not fully grasped the reality that Terashima's stand on sovereignty would remain the benchmark of Meiji diplomacy for years to come.[50]

AN ELDER MEIJI STATESMAN

In Tokyo circles, Terashima still wielded considerable influence, sufficient, for example, to warrant an impromptu visit by the Emperor to his grand home in June 1880. The following day this was the venue of a house party for three hundred guests.[51] As the Meiji government apparatus evolved in the next few years, however, he was largely confined to consultative bodies, first as chairman of the Senate (*Genrōin*) and later as vice-chairman of the new Privy Council (*Sumitsuin*). While these appointments reflected his standing as a senior statesman, they were designed to limit his influence in the central corridors of power, where his rival the younger Itō Hirobumi was consolidating control in the years leading up to the new Meiji Constitution.

Now that the government had responded to pressure from the liberal rights movement and promised a new constitution, debate raged over the form of the proposed new assembly. Terashima's own involvement dated back to 1873 when both he and Itō had received instructions to prepare drafts of their own. As the natural leader of the conservative Satsuma faction since Ōkubo's assassination in 1878, Terashima argued that Japan's political culture was not sufficiently developed to allow much democratic freedom. Ōkuma, however, favoured a radical solution in the manner of an English-style parliament. The more pragmatic Itō, the ascendant figure in the aftermath of Ōkubo's death, saw off both challenges in 1881 when he used a damaging corruption scandal involving Satsuma officials to drive Ōkuma and his liberal allies out of office, while manoeuvring Terashima into a venerable post in charge of the *Genrōin*.

Tired of the factional infighting in Tokyo, in 1882 Terashima volunteered for a brief spell in Washington as minister to the United States, although his real motive was to use the opportunity to conduct research on political assemblies. It was partly on his suggestion that Itō was sent on a similar mission, and in government circles this was even viewed as a joint effort, with Terashima and Itō investigating conditions in America and Europe respectively. He took to his studies with renewed energy and published an English paper entitled 'On the National Assembly', reiterating his conservative beliefs that political representation should be viewed in the context of Japan's political evolution. This perhaps echoed the cautious advice that his compatriot Mori Arinori, currently serving as minister to Britain, was receiving in London from Herbert Spencer, the celebrated Victorian pioneer of social science.[52] Now fifty-one years old, his studies, however, were impaired by illness, and in 1883 Terashima was forced to return to Japan where he cut a sorry figure compared with the younger Itō who was also back after his evidently more productive research in Germany.

When the new Office for the Study of the Constitution was formed in 1884, Terashima was given a remit limited to commercial law as Itō appointed men from his own inner circle to tackle the more central question of the structure for a new assembly. Having just received the title of count (*hakushaku*) in the new Meiji peerage he was still very much part of the ruling oligarchy, but he increasingly took to campaigning against the government and fiercely criticised its fiscal and foreign policies. He became a leading figure among the neo-conservative elements in power, although their challenge was effectively defused when they were transferred en masse to the new Privy Council in 1888. In his position there as vice-chairman, Terashima's continued invectives, often in print, still carried enough weight to pressure Itō, now chairman, into the conciliatory gesture of choosing Kuroda Kiyotaka as prime minister during the transitional period when the new constitution came into force.

In the field of diplomacy he also received somewhat unexpected support from the liberal rights movement for his passionate attacks on Inoue Kaoru, his successor in the Ministry of Foreign Affairs. His defence of Japanese sovereignty resonated with the new spirit of patriotism in the late 1880s as suspicions grew over Inoue's covert attempts to win confidence in Meiji justice by inviting foreign judges into Japanese courts. In 1889 he also scored a notable success when he presented a united Privy Council memorandum to the emperor demanding a halt to similar treaty negotiations under Ōkuma. This was instrumental in bringing down the Kuroda government, although it was the terrorist attack the next day in which Ōkuma lost a leg that effectively forced the issue.[53]

Increasingly bedridden in later years, Terashima was too weak to attend the committee convened in 1892 when a new round of treaty negotiations was announced. He nevertheless summoned the energy to send a memorandum, which contributed to the diplomatic successes later in the decade. Britain's fears over Russian encroachment from the north and Japan's now eminent credentials as the first Asian state with a modern constitution had created a more favourable climate for the negotiations that produced the Anglo-Japanese commercial treaty of 1894. The only irony was that Terashima himself did not live to see the resulting end of extraterritoriality in 1899 and the final restoration of tariff autonomy in 1911.

He died on 6 June 1893 at the age of sixty-one. In the popular memory of subsequent generations he was often viewed as one of several Meiji statesmen,

Inoue and Ōkuma included, who signally failed to release Japan from the subordinate status the country had endured since the days of Perry. Later diplomats such as Mutsu Munemitsu and Komura Jutarō received the accolades of the public as the Ansei Treaties were overhauled, but in many ways Terashima had laid the foundations of their success. During his term as Minister of Foreign Affairs in the 1870s, conditions in East Asia had prevented him from making significant inroads into the agreements originally signed by the Bakufu. The fledgling Meiji regime was still an unknown quantity in a region often viewed as a natural hunting ground for commercial and even colonial expansion. His uncompromising style of diplomacy, most evident in his exchanges with Parkes, nevertheless did much to raise international awareness of Japan's emergence as a modern nation state.

[2005]

NOTES

1.   Ozaki Saburō, *Ozaki Saburō jijo ryakuden* [Short Autobiography of Ozaki Saburō], Vol. 1 (Tokyo: Chūōkōronsha, 1976), p.118
2.   Terashima often appears in English spelled Terajima, the preferred pronunciation of many Meiji government colleagues. The island in Satsuma from which he took his name, however, is Terashima, he was addressed as such in Foreign Office correspondence, and in the letter of credentials he presented to Queen Victoria, his sovereign, the Emperor Meiji, declared: 'We have determined to invest with the character of our Envoy Extraordinary and Minister Plenipotentiary our trusty and well-beloved Shoshie Terashima Munenori, whose zeal, ability and discretion have been well approved in his service as one of our Ministers for Foreign Affairs . . . Mutsuhito, Emperor'. FO 46/160.
3.   Isabella Bird, *Unbeaten Tracks in Japan* (San Francisco: Travelers' Tales Inc., 2000), p.9. Parkes had a reputation for driving a hard bargain but he could be 'a careful and attentive host', notably during the Iwakura Embassy's visit to Britain. James Hoare, 'The Era of Unequal Treaties', in Ian Nish and Yoichi Kibata (ed.), *The History of Anglo-Japanese Relations*, Vol. 1 (London: Macmillan, 2000), p.112.
4.   Inuzuka, *Terashima Munenori* (Tokyo: Yoshikawa Kōbunkan, 1990), pp.8-11.
5.   Ibid., p.14. My thanks to Sebastian Dobson for pointing out that, contrary to a longstanding tradition in Japan, it is highly unlikely that Ueno Shunnojō took a camera with him to Kagoshima on this occasion and photographed Shimazu Nariakira, then the daimyo's 32-year-old heir.
6.   As Terashima pointed out, in the 1840s there had been only two or three previous cases of Satsuma sending officers to train outside the domain, and these were young men in their twenties. Terashima Munenori, 'Jijo nenpu' [Autobiographical Chronology], Vol. 3. Kokkai Toshokan (National Diet Library)
7.   Terashima to Kawamoto. *Ihi nyukō roku* [Record of Ports of Call in Barbarian Lands], Vol. 1 (Tokyo: Nihon Shiseki Kyōkai, 1930), p.250.
8.   Japan's first reverberating furnace was built in 1850 by the Hizen domain in the castle-town of Saga. The second was built by the Tokugawa *Bakufu* at Nirayama in the Izu Peninsula.
9.   Under Shimazu Nariakira's leadership Satsuma made rapid progress in developing its own navy. It was a Satsuma ship that in 1854 first flew the '*Hinomaru*' flag, a red sun on a white background, more familiar today as the national flag of Japan.
10. Willem van Kattendyke, *Uittreksel uit het dagboek van W.J.C. Ridder H. v. Kattendyke gedurende zijn verblijf in Japan in 1857, 1858 en 1859* ('sGravenhage, 1860), p.97.
11. J.L.C. Pompe van Meerdervort, *Vijf Jaren in Japan* (Leiden, 1867): Numata Jirō, Arase Shinkyō (trans.), *Pompe nihon taizai kenbun ki* (Omatsudō Shoten: Tokyo, 1968), pp.259-61, 298.
12. Ernest Satow, *A Diplomat in Japan* (Tokyo: ICG Muse Inc, 2000), pp.185-6
13. Terashima was the first Satsuma officer to be officially sent, but there were notable precedents of others reaching Europe. Bernardo, the first known example from Japan, was a

poor Satsuma samurai who arrived in Lisbon in 1553 and became a Jesuit priest. In 1724 two fishermen, Gonzō and Sōzō were the only survivors of a crew killed when their vessel ran aground in Kamchatka. Taken to St Petersburg to teach at a Japanese language school, Gonzō compiled the first Russian-Japanese dictionary, translating 12,000 words into his native Kagoshima dialect.

14. Terashima recalled: 'Mitsukuri Shūhei and I investigated the treatment in hospitals and education in schools . . . we shared responsibility between our fields, recording it all when we returned to our hotels so that we ended up compiling a large volume'. *'Yōkō ni kan-suru Terashima Munenori jiki rireki shō'* [Extract from Terashima Munenori's Own Account of His Overseas Travels], *Sappan kaigun shi* [History of the Satsuma Navy], Vol. 2 (Tokyo: Sappan kaigun shi kankō kai, 1928), p.935. In Paris he exchanged letters with the japanologist Léon de Rosny, and became the first Japanese member of Rosny's Société d'Ethnographie. Inuzuka, *Terashima Munenori*, pp.67-9. In 1865 they met again when Rosny visited London on behalf of the Comte de Montblanc to establish commercial ties with Satsuma. Cobbing, *The Satsuma Students in Britain* (Folkestone: Japan Library, 2000), pp.78-81, 86-8.

15. Letter to Kawamoto Kōmin, 10 June 1862. *Ihi nyūkō roku*, Vol. 1, pp.237-40.

16. Satow, *A Diplomat in Japan*, p.82.

17. For an account of the Namamugi Incident and the subsequent bombardment of Kagoshima see Hugh Cortazzi's biographical portrait of Lt Colonel Neale and Appendix I in *British Envoys in Japan 1859-1972* (Folkestone: Japan Library, 2004).

18. There is some evidence that Terashima, perhaps in order to keep informed of developments, undertook translation work for the *Bansho Shirabesho* during his months in hiding in Musashi. Cobbing, 'The Nagasaki Information War', *Kyūshū daigaku ryūgakusei kiyō* [Kyūshū University International Student Centre Bulletin], *no.10, October 1999*, pp.57-76. This may have been why Satow later questioned his loyalty after hearing that he had worked for the *Bakufu* even after the bombardment of Kagoshima. Satow, *A Diplomat in Japan*, pp.185-6.

19. Laurence Oliphant had served as secretary to the mission by the Earl of Elgin to China and Japan in 1858 and had been first secretary to Rutherford Alcock at the British Legation in Edo where he had been injured in the first Tōzenji incident in 1861 in which a band of *rōnin* attacked the temple then being used as the legation building.

20. Russell to Parkes, 23 August 1865, FO 262/88. Apart from Terashima himself, it is unclear exactly whom Russell was referring to when he mentioned Satsuma and Chōshū officers sent to negotiate with the British government. He may have been thinking of Yamao Yōzō, a Chōshū student in London, whose views had been reported in detail to the Foreign Office the previous year. Yamao vigorously defended his domain's policy and, much like Terashima, protested against the *Bakufu*'s monopoly on trade. Memorandum by Reginald Russell, 1 July 1864, FO 46/49.

21. Glover's introduction to Oliphant was recorded by one of the Satsuma students. 'Kaigun Chūshō Matsumura Junzō yōkō dan' [Matsumura Junzō's Account of His Overseas Travels] *Sappan kaigun shi* [History of the Satsuma Navy], Vol. 2, p.903. Cobbing, *The Satsuma Students in Britain*, pp.70-1, 94. There was no conscious British policy to 'sabotage the shogun' despite some collusion by merchants and diplomats with domains like Satsuma and Chōshū, notably over mutual commercial interests. Even Ernest Satow's ingenious articles in the *Japan Times*, read in translation as 'Eikoku sakuron', had no effect on official policy. James Hoare, 'The Era of Unequal Treaties', in Ian Nish and Yoichi Kibata (ed.), *The History of Anglo-Japanese Relations*, Vol. 1 (London: Macmillan, 2000), pp.110, 112. In this context it is nevertheless worth noting that Terashima's strategy on Satsuma's behalf, conveyed with help from Glover and Oliphant, did exert some influence on the political outlook of the Foreign Office.

22. Parkes's initial scepticism towards reports of Terashima's overtures reflected his unfamiliarity with Japanese politics in his first year as Minister, apparent in his suggestion that Satsuma had been forced to seek outside help from Britain due only to political isolation at home. Gordon Daniels, *Sir Harry Parkes: British representative in Japan, 1865-1883* (Folkestone: Japan Library, 1996), p.57.

23. *'Yōkō ni kan-suru Terashima Munenori jiki rireki shō'*, p.943.

24. Cobbing, *The Satsuma Students in Britain*, p.129. Inuzuka, *Terashima Munenori*, p.134. Terashima's document was based on a text drawn up by the Comte de Montblanc and also reflected suggestions made by Satow. This received imperial approval on 13 January 1868, as Terashima reported to Parkes the same day. He was again present at Kōbe Customs House on 8 February when Higashikuze Michitome of the Board for Foreign Affairs presented an adjusted imperial proclamation to the assembled envoys of the treaty powers.

25. Hoare, 'The Era of Unequal Treaties', p.112. See also J.E. Hoare: *Japan's Treaty Ports and Foreign Settlements*, Japan Library, 1994.
26. Ibid, p.125.
27. Letters from Lachlan Fletcher, British consul in Kanagawa, to Terashima Tōzō and Eseki Saiemon, *'Bakumatsu yori meiji shoki made no kakkoku tono ōrai shokan eikoku raiō kan'* [Correspondence with foreign countries at the end of *Bakufu* rule and early years of Meiji – letters from Britain], Vol. 2, Gaikō Shiryōkan (Foreign Ministry Archives).
28. Inuzuka, *Terashima Munenori*, p.153.
29. Of the official correspondence from the British Legation to the Ministry of Foreign Affairs in the early Meiji years, 60 out of 94 dispatches to Sawa, 33 out of 35 to Iwakura, and 42 out of 50 to Soejima, were also addressed to Terashima in his position as vice-minister. During Terashima's own term as minister, however, such letters were never addressed to the vice-minister as well. *'Bakumatsu yori meiji shoki made no kakkoku tono ōrai shokan mokuroku – eikoku kōshi yori raikan mokuroku'* [List of correspondence with foreign countries at the end of *Bakufu* rule and early years of Meiji – list of correspondence from the British minister], Gaikō Shiryōkan (Foreign Ministry Archives).
30. Ozaki, *Ozaki Saburō jijo ryakuden*, Vol. 1, p.117. Inuzuka, *Terashima Munenori*, p.179
31. Parkes to Granville, 3 December 1870, FO 46/127.
32. Ozaki Saburō, *Ozaki Saburō jijo ryakuden*, Vol. 1, p.113.
33. It was from the South Kensington Hotel at 19 Queen's Gate Terrace that the first correspondence on the headed notepaper of 'the Legation of Japan' was sent to the Foreign Office. Terashima to Granville, 5 September 1872. FO 46/160. Cobbing, *The Japanese Discovery of Victorian Britain* (Folkestone: Japan Library, 1998), p.112.
34. For details of the Bowles Brothers' financial scandal see Cobbing, *The Japanese Discovery of Victorian Britain*, pp.127-8. Also Cobbing, 'Early Meiji Cultural Encounters' in Ian Nish (ed.), *The Iwakura Mission to America and Europe: a new assessment* (Folkestone: Japan Library, 1998), pp.40-1 48-9 and 'Three Meiji Marriages' by Noboru Koyama p.387 in *Britain and Japan: Biographical Portraits Volume IV*. Terashima's role in resolving the financial plight of Japanese students is related in Ozaki, *Ozaki Saburō jijo ryakuden*, Vol. 1, pp.119-27.
35. Cobbing, *The Japanese Discovery of Victorian Britain*, pp.148-9.
36. Records by W.G. Aston of interviews between Granville and Iwakura held at the Foreign Office on 22 November, 27 November and 6 December 1872, FO 46/160 reproduced in full in Hugh Cortazzi's paper in the *Transactions of the Asiatic Society* 2002. The Japanese records of these interviews appear in *Jōyaku kaisei kankei nihon gaikō monjo* [*Japanese Diplomatic Documents on Treaty Revision*], Vol. 1 (Tokyo: Nihon Kokusai Kyōkai, 1941), pp.223-33. Although broadly similar in content, the Japanese account records, unlike Aston's, that much of the dialogue, particularly in the second interview, was conducted between Terashima and Parkes.
37. For details on Iwakura's stance on freedom of religion see John Breen, 'Public Statements and Private Thoughts: the Iwakura Embassy in London and the religious question', *The Iwakura Mission in Britain, 1872*, Sticerd International Studies IS/98/349, London School of Economics, pp.53-67.
38. In Aston's account this statement is attributed to Iwakura, in the Japanese version to Terashima. FO 46/160. *Jōyaku kaisei kankei nihon gaikō monjo*, Vol. 1, p. 226.
39. Inuzuka, *Terashima Munenori*, pp.193-6. As Isabella Bird pointed out in 1878, passports for travel on specific routes in the interior were obtainable for reasons of 'health, botanical research, or scientific investigation'. In her case, thanks to Parkes's efforts, she had 'practically unrestricted' access 'to travel through all Japan north of Tōkiō and in Yezo without specifying a route'. The bearer of the passport had to 'conduct himself in an orderly and conciliatory manner', could not 'light fires in woods, attend fires on horseback, trespass on fields, enclosures, or game-preserves, scribble on temples, shrines, or walls, drive fast on a narrow road, or disregard notices of "No thorough-fare"'. He was also 'forbidden to shoot, trade, to conclude mercantile contacts with Japanese, or to rent houses or rooms for a longer period than his journey requires.' Bird, *Unbeaten Tracks in Japan*, p.38.
40. Hoare, 'The Era of Unequal Treaties', p.112. R.G. Watson, acting chargé d'affaires during Parkes's absence in 1872-3, argued that the presence of the British garrison was no longer justified and deeply resented by the Japanese population. R.G. Watson to Granville, 19 December 1872, FO 262/225.
41. Parkes refused to accept that Japanese game laws should apply to British subjects. In one dispatch he was scathing of Bingham's response to a communication from Terashima to the foreign envoys canvassing their opinion over hunting laws: 'Mr Bingham is evidently at a loss to

know how unlicensed shooting in Japan by an American citizen is to be punished by American law, but as he holds the theory that Japanese law can be enforced in the United States Consular Courts, he suggests that the insufficient means provided by Congress for the control of American citizens in Japan should be remedied by Japanese legislation.' Parkes to the Earl of Derby, 22 January 1877, FO 262/302.

42. 'The present convention shall take effect when Japan shall have concluded such conventions or revisions of existing treaties with all the other treaty powers holding relations with Japan as shall be similar in effect to the present convention, and such new conventions or revisions shall also go into effect.' Article X of Yoshida-Evarts Convention, signed 25 July 1878, ratified 8 April 1879. *Jōyaku kaisei kankei nihon gaikō monjo*, Vol. 1, pp.467-73, 532.

43. The actual wording of this message reads 'if you refuses [sic] firm with S. Parkes'. Telegram from Ueno Kagenori to Terashima Munenori, 9 April 1879. Ibid., p.642.

44. Ibid., p.543.

45. Soon after the Iwakura embassy's departure from Britain, Parkes had made an impassioned appeal on behalf of British merchants claiming that 'liberty in the hands of the Japanese to alter the Tariff as they like could soon ruin the Trade'. Criticizing US Secretary of State Hamilton Fish who was 'inclined to think that the Japanese Government had a right to claim this power', he warned that this 'would tell chiefly against British Trade, as we are the principal importers. The United States have no import trade in Japan, but would like to become the Emporium of produce of that country and China.' Parkes to Granville, 24 December 1872, FO 46/156.

46. *Jōyaku kaisei kankei nihon gaikō monjo*, Vol. 1, p.658.

47. Inouye Yuichi, 'From Unequal Treaty to the Anglo-Japanese Alliance', in Ian Nish and Yoichi Kibata (ed.), *The History of Anglo-Japanese Relations*, Vol. 1, p.139.

48. James Hoare, 'The Bankoku Shimbun Affair: foreigners, the foreign press and extraterritoriality in Japan', *Modern Asian Studies*, Vol. 9, No. 3 (1975), pp.289-302.

49. See Janet Hunter, 'The Abolition of Extraterritoriality in the Japanese Post Office, 1873-1880', *Proceedings of the British Association for Japanese Studies*, Vol. 1 (1976), Part 1: History and International Relations, edited by Peter Lowe, pp.17-37.

50. In 1881, the *Japan Mail* reported: 'We cannot pretend that Sir Harry Parkes's policy has kept pace with the changes among which his lot has been cast'. Hoare, 'The Age of Unequal Treaties', p.126. The same year, in a letter to F.V. Dickins, Satow even likened Parkes to Napoleon in the eyes of his enemies, describing him as 'the bugbear of the Japanese public; in the popular estimation he occupies much the same position as "Boney" with us fifty years ago'. Daniels, *Sir Harry Parkes*, pp.178, 188.

51. Inuzuka, *Terashima Munenori*, pp.228, 300.

52. Cobbing, 'Mori Arinori: from diplomat to statesman' in Sir Hugh Cortazzi (ed.), *Britain and Japan – Biographical Portraits*, Vol. IV (Folkestone: Japan Library, 2002), pp.3-13.

53. Inuzuka, *Terashima Munenori*, pp.259-60, 273-4.

4

UENO KAGENORI, 1845-1888:
A Most Influential Diplomat
[London, 1874-79]

Ueno Kagenori

ANDREW COBBING[1]

'Speaking English with ease and correctness', Ueno Kagenori in 1869 was a young man with a 'sense of humour and restless energy'. As the British civil engineer Richard Henry Brunton recalled, 'no Japanese I ever encountered had the same flow of spirits or animation'.[2] Ueno would later become the second man to serve as Japan's minister at the Court of St James's, following in the footsteps of Terashima Munenori, his Satsuma compatriot and mentor. Terashima had described him as an 'extremely intelligent youth' when they first met in Nagasaki some years before.[3] Although he was often cast in the role of Terashima's trusted agent, he was also something of a pioneer himself, using his linguistic skills to champion Japanese sovereignty in the early years of Meiji diplomacy.

Such was the influence of Satsuma in the Ministry of Foreign Affairs that the first four men nominated to represent Japan in London all came from this one domain. This is to include Sameshima Naonobu, whose credentials were refused in 1871 as the British considered him too young and junior in rank, and Mori Arinori who became the third minister at the Court of St James's in the 1880s. With the exception of Ueno they were all veterans of the 1865 expedition to Britain, when a party of Satsuma officers was covertly sent to study in London in defiance of the Tokugawa ban on overseas travel.

Although no older than Sameshima when he was appointed minister in 1874, Ueno clearly had the requisite experience for this key post in Anglo-Japanese relations. He had played an active role as a hands-on diplomat during the transition from Tokugawa rule to the Meiji regime, assigned on numerous occasions to resolve pressing issues concerning foreigners in Japan. He often worked with *oyatoi* experts employed by the Meiji Government, and through his contacts with British engineers like Brunton he was closely involved in the early days of building Japan's modern infrastructure. He was invariably present at high-level negotiations, and was well known to ministers of the treaty powers resident in Tokyo. And, despite never rising to the post of Minister of Foreign Affairs himself, he was often left effectively in charge in a caretaker role.

SATSUMA'S FIRST SCHOLAR OF ENGLISH

Ueno Kagenori was born in Kagoshima on 8 January 1845. Known to all as Keisuke during his childhood, he was groomed from an early age to follow in his father's footsteps as an interpreter in the service of the Satsuma domain. At the age of four he was sent off to Nagasaki to begin his training in Chinese. With interest in the West on the rise following Perry's missions to Japan, he was ordered to learn Dutch in 1856 and shortly afterwards he became the first person from Satsuma ever to train in English.

Growing up in the treaty port of Nagasaki, the young Ueno was soon tempted to venture abroad himself, even though the longstanding Tokugawa ban on travelling overseas was still in force. Late in 1863 at the age of eighteen he stole aboard a ship bound for Shanghai together with three intrepid fellow students from Aki, Bigo and Hyūga. They had more spirit of adventure than money and contacts, however, and within days of their arrival they were forced to throw themselves on the mercy of Ikeda Takaaki, the Bakufu leader of an official delegation passing through Shanghai en route to France. Ikeda considered taking them with him to Europe until he was reminded by his advisers to observe proprieties, and arranged instead to send them back to Nagasaki. They were returned under the description of 'castaways', a ruse that spared them from facing the penalty, in theory death, for breaking Tokugawa law.[4]

Ueno expressed deep remorse over his Shanghai escapade and was ashamed of his dependence on Godai Tomoatsu, the senior Satsuma officer in Nagasaki who had to fit him out with clothes and swords when he was then summoned back to Kagoshima.[5] He returned there to take up an appointment as the first English teacher at the Kaiseijō, Satsuma's new college of Western Studies which opened in July 1864. Still only nineteen, his students included young men such as Mori Arinori, who would later become celebrated experts in English themselves.[6] Other staff subsequently arrived, among them Maejima Hisoka, the 'father of the Japanese Postal Service' and the famous castaway Nakahama 'John' Manjirō, but in these early days Ueno was probably the only English teacher on site.[7]

As the domain's first scholar in English Ueno was a conspicuous absentee from Godai's expedition of students that travelled to London in 1865. Godai, who was now the moving force behind Satsuma's ambitions to promote trade and industry, may have left him behind because his language skills were needed at home. Ueno received orders instead to accompany Thomas Waters, a British architect engaged to help develop the islands to the south of Kagoshima, and they spent the best part of two years constructing and running a sugar refinery on Ōshima Island.[8] Then in 1867 they were both called back to the mainland to develop the Kagoshima Spinning Mill, Godai's latest scheme and the first Western-style textile mill in Japan. It was Waters who built the residence for a team of three engineers sent from Manchester, while Ueno helped them set up a textile works nearby.[9]

The political upheavals in train, however, soon took Ueno to the centre-stage of Japanese diplomacy. Early in 1868, after Saigō Takamori's coup d'état in

Kyoto ushered in the return of imperial rule, he and Terashima boarded the Satsuma vessel *Kasuga Maru* and sailed for Osaka. He briefly saw action there when the ship was involved in fighting as civil war broke out against Tokugawa forces.[10] His first post in the Meiji regime was as an interpreter under Itō Hirobumi at the new treaty port of Kōbe but he soon transferred to the Osaka Customs House to help Godai in his new plans to transform the city into a modern commercial centre. It was during this time that he supervised proceedings at Myōkokuji Temple in nearby Sakai, where twenty Tosa officers had been sentenced to commit ritual suicide (*seppuku*) after their security force fired on and killed some French military personnel.[11]

Within a month Terashima summoned Ueno to rejoin him and help him manage the Customs House in Yokohama, now Japan's main hub of international trade. It was an apprenticeship that would result in his following in Terashima's footsteps as minister to Britain. During these early Meiji years he spent much of his time overseas on business and helping *oyatoi* engineers in landmark construction projects. Later in 1868, for example, he was sent to Hong Kong for several months to finalise the Meiji Government's arrangements to purchase machinery for the new Imperial Mint. A report back from Ueno effectively determined the mint's location when he pointed out the need for a good water supply. This featured in Thomas Waters' plans when he built what was to be his most famous work in Japan on the banks of the Yodogawa River in Osaka.[12]

It was in 1869 that Ueno accompanied Brunton on a tour of projected sites for lighthouses along Japan's southern coasts, including Cape Sata in his native Satsuma. Brunton was clearly grateful to him for making the voyage 'so pleasant and free from childish disputes with petty officials'. For the local officials it was a less comfortable experience as Ueno 'poured out undiluted ridicule on the antiquated methods of his compatriots, and startled them by the vigour of his methods'. Brunton considered these to be effective, though, as he recalled that 'no department in the Government service made such good progress as did the Lighthouse Service, while Inouye [sic] was connected to it'.[13]

His next assignment was across the Pacific when, at the age of just twenty-four, he was granted full plenipotentiary powers to lead a diplomatic delegation to Hawaii. The aim was to negotiate the return of 150 Japanese labour migrants who had been shipped out of Yokohama under a deal struck with the Tokugawa authorities by Eugene Van Reed, an American merchant who was now US consul to Hawaii. The Meiji Government rejected the arrangement primarily because Hawaii, still an independent kingdom, had no treaty relations with Japan. Since there was no direct passenger service, Ueno was away for eight months including extended stays in San Francisco on both outward and return voyages. On meeting the King of Hawaii in December 1870, he secured a return passage for those labourers who wished to leave, while the others who chose to stay were guaranteed medical care and transport back to Japan at the end of their contracts.[14]

Following his own return in 1870, Ueno next helped with the construction of Japan's first public railway line between Yokohama and Shinbashi in central Tokyo. Among the numerous difficulties the project faced were the growing suspicions over the terms for raising a loan of £1,000,000 arranged by a British entrepreneur intriguingly called Horatio Nelson Lay (no relation). Anxious not to lose the confidence of British financiers, the Meiji Government sent a delegation under Ueno to London with orders to cancel the contract with Lay and finalise arrangements for the Oriental Bank to raise the capital instead. Ueno was accompanied by Maejima Hisoka during the year he spent on this, his first trip to Britain, and he used the opportunity to investigate the latest minting equipment in Europe as part of the Treasury's campaign to protect Japan's currency from forgeries.[15]

In 1872, Ueno was promoted to the third highest rank in the Ministry of Financial Affairs before transferring to the equivalent post in Foreign Affairs later in the year. It was in 1873 that he first deputised for the Minister Soejima Taneomi, who was in China when a Peruvian delegation arrived to protest against Japan's handling of the *Maria Luz*. In an early test of Japanese sovereignty the previous year, the ship's captain had been found guilty by a Yokohama court of illegally confining Chinese coolies after two of them had escaped and complained of inhuman conditions on board. Despite the Peruvian delegation's demands for compensation and an apology, this decision would be upheld in 1875 after mediation by Alexander II of Russia, confirming Japan's equal status under international law.[16]

In June 1873, Ueno was again involved in central politics when he attended the first meeting by the Central Chamber of Councillors to discuss Japan's strained relations with Korea. When questioned he delivered a report pointing out that 'either we evacuate the Japanese residents in Korea or we apply pressure to secure commercial relations, even if this means using military force'. It was a strategy that not only prompted the controversy which forced Saigō Takamori to resign from the government later that year, but also paved the way for the gunboat diplomacy that culminated in the Treaty of Kanghwa in 1876.[17]

AS MINISTER AT THE COURT OF ST JAMES'S

For some time there had been talk of Ueno taking up a post as a resident minister abroad. Although initial plans to serve in Washington fell through, he was the natural choice to succeed Terashima when his term as minister to Britain was cut short by illness. Still just twenty-nine years old, in October 1874 he set out for Britain together with his Satsuma compatriot Nakai Hiroshi, a noted poet and writer who was also on his way to join the legation staff. Travelling via Rome and Paris they reached London in late December. Most officials were already out of town for the holiday season and it was mid-January before he was able to meet the Foreign Secretary, the Marquis of Derby. Queen Victoria, moreover, had spent the winter at Osborne House so it was not until 3 March that Ueno presented his credentials in morning dress at Windsor Castle, having travelled by train together with Derby from Paddington Station.[18]

The Japanese Legation had recently moved into a new building at No. 9 Kensington Park Gardens. This was larger than the residence Terashima had used in Belgravia, which although situated conveniently near Buckingham Palace was too small for the growing legation's needs. Shortly after Terashima's departure, therefore, the acting chargé d'affaires Motono Morimichi had arranged a contract to move to this new location near Ladbroke Square. With the arrival of Ueno and Nakai there were now eight staff on site, and their numbers increased late in 1875 when Ueno's wife Ikuko travelled from Japan with their two-year-old son to join him. Ueno pointed out, however, that the house was physically isolated from other legations, badly in need of repair and situated in an area populated by day workers. In spite of his exhortations the Ministry of Foreign Affairs refused to sanction a move during his term in

London, and it was not until his successor Mori Arinori arrived in 1880 that the legation moved to a grander and more expensive location in Cavendish Square.[19]

While he may not have been an architect of Meiji diplomacy in the mould of Terashima, Ueno certainly made his stamp on the Japanese Legation. If it was Terashima who laid the foundations of the Japanese consular system in Britain it was Ueno who installed its structure. He persuaded the Meiji Government that in addition to the legation's diplomatic portfolio a separate office should handle commercial affairs. In 1876, this resulted in the appointment of Minami Tamotsu in charge of the new Japanese Consulate located in the heart of the city at Mildway House in Bishopsgate Street.[20] Ueno also proposed to extend the term of resident ministers abroad to ten years like those of diplomats from other countries at the Court of St James's. At this early stage, however, the Ministry of Foreign Affairs did not yet have enough experienced personnel to spare their senior staff for more than a few years abroad.[21]

For Ueno, everyday business at the legation consisted largely of arranging permits for Japanese students and visiting government officials to inspect military installations, often Woolwich Arsenal and the naval dockyards in Portsmouth and Plymouth. Growing numbers of Japanese naval cadets received their training in Britain at the time, among them Tōgō Heihachirō, the future 'Nelson of the Orient'. These were formative years for the Imperial Navy. On 14 April 1877, for example, Ueno's wife Ikuko launched the *Fusō*, Japan's first ironclad warship, and two other vessels in this class followed also from British shipyards later in the year.[22]

Extra duties for Ueno included a special mission to Spain and Portugal. During its grand tour of Europe in the early 1870s the Iwakura Embassy had cancelled a visit to the Iberian Peninsula due to the unstable political situation there, but ministers of both countries in Tokyo expressed dissatisfaction at being the only treaty powers not to have received an official delegation from the Meiji Government. It fell to Ueno to redress the situation when he travelled to Madrid and Lisbon for two months in the spring of 1876, and his detailed account of the conditions he saw en route provide a valuable supplement to early Japanese observations of Europe such as Kume Kunitake's official chronicle of the Iwakura Embassy's travels.[23]

It was in the field of diplomatic negotiations, however, that Ueno devoted much of his energies in Britain. Much of this dialogue arose from the agenda set by Terashima who, as the new Minister of Foreign Affairs, had received powers in 1874 to address the issue of revising the 'unequal treaties' imposed on the Tokugawa Bakufu. One key issue was the extraterritorial rights stipulated by the Ansei Treaties of 1858, which gave foreigners in the treaty ports immunity from Japanese law. Another was the tariff rate fixed at five per cent under a convention orchestrated by the British in 1866, which prevented the Meiji Government from raising duties on foreign imports.

New technology allowed Terashima to pull the strings from Tokyo. With a submarine telegraph cable now laid between Shanghai and Nagasaki, telegrams could reach Europe within a day, albeit in Roman letters. High-ranking Japanese diplomats took to writing urgent communiqués in English, with related documents in Japanese arriving the following month by mail. Although working under Terashima's instructions, Ueno showed plenty of initiative in marshalling arguments to draw the Foreign Office out of its shell regarding British merchants' rights in Japan. In the long letters he exchanged with the

Foreign Secretary he was certainly helped by Stuart Lane, the British employee at the Japanese Legation, but the Foreign Office, too, was guarded in its approach and key points were carefully discussed before replies were despatched from Whitehall.

The first real skirmish began late in 1875 when Ueno delivered an announcement from Terashima proposing a ban on foreigners shooting game around the treaty ports. The Foreign Office delayed for several months and only sent a formal reply when pressed on the issue. The Earl of Derby told colleagues in Whitehall, 'I do not think we can trust the Japanese sufficiently as yet to alter our judicial arrangements', although he hoped for a settlement 'in as conciliatory a spirit as possible'.[24] In his official response he explained that 'the principle at stake involves in fact the question of extra-territorial jurisdiction, with which, as you yourself state, your Government has never claimed to interfere while the present Treaties are in force'.[25]

Ueno, however, had a further argument up his sleeve:

> Your Lordship states that British subjects have a perfect right to shoot under the Regulations drawn up by the Japanese Government, and agreed to by the foreign representatives. This no doubt would be so if any such Regulations had really been agreed to . . . but it has not, to my knowledge, been done, and the right of shooting, therefore, does not exist at all.[26]

Moreover, as he pointed out, 'the only Regulation to which my Government is a party, so far as I am aware, is the recent Regulation absolutely prohibiting shooting by foreigners'. As soon as Ueno's reply reached Whitehall, Under-secretary Lord Tenterden drafted a note defending British merchants' licence to roam:

> The foreign residents in Shanghai go up the river great distances on shooting excursions and are absent sometimes for weeks – no suggestion has ever been made by the Chinese Government that they should be amenable to Chinese jurisdiction on these occasions. I am not aware that their case is dissimilar in any way as regards Treaty obligations to that of Foreigners in Japan.[27]

Apart from illustrating some of the prevailing customs in Shanghai, this comment reflects the extent to which Japanese diplomats, rather more than their counterparts in China, had begun to deconstruct the small print of the treaties. As Derby was forced to admit, 'the letter of the Japanese Minister is well written, and contains some arguments with which we have not dealt'.[28]

To the chagrin of Sir Harry Parkes, the British Minister in Japan, foreign diplomats in Tokyo were unable to present a common response to Terashima's proposals on shooting. In fact, the Japanese were so encouraged by US Minister John Bingham's more receptive approach that in 1878 they opened a new bilateral dialogue on tariff reform as Terashima despatched Yoshida Kiyonari, also from Satsuma, to Washington to negotiate a commercial convention with Secretary of State John Evarts. In London, meanwhile, Ueno wrote to the Marquess of Salisbury, the new Foreign Secretary, on 4 May justifying the Meiji Government's proposals to set its own tariffs. In this he pointed out that 'though the obligation to admit foreign goods at a maximum duty of five per cent was imposed on Japan, no Power accorded to her any reciprocity'.[29]

Reluctant to engage in dialogue on treaty revision, the Foreign Office insisted on the need for collective negotiation among the treaty powers. It came as a surprise to learn in the summer, therefore, that a separate tariff treaty had already been signed in Washington, albeit subject to ratification by all the powers involved. In an attempt to placate the British, Ueno despatched Lane to the Foreign Office on 4 October to present the text of the Yoshida-Evarts Treaty. Assistant Under-secretary Sir Julian Pauncefote was persuaded to study the document, although he admitted that 'the whole proceeding has created a bad impression here' and he found it 'unintelligible why there should have been all this secrecy'. Lane was adamant that Japan was not to blame and pointed out that it was 'the United States, apparently for some reason best known to themselves, [who] wish their arrangement to remain private at present'.[30]

Central to Terashima's strategy was his promise that Japan would never charge tariffs higher than those of any of the treaty powers. In Whitehall, however, there were suspicions that this could pave the way for protectionist policies like those in force in the United States and Russia. Some dispute followed over the figures involved as Parkes in Tokyo and Ueno in London challenged each other's statistics on customs receipts over the last few years.[31] Nevertheless, by the end of 1878 there was enough common ground for negotiations to begin. Salisbury reminded Ueno that 'the letter which you did me the honour of addressing to me on the 4th of May last does not constitute such a notice of Revision as Her Majesty's Government are entitled to receive'. Nevertheless, the Foreign Office was now persuaded to the extent that he announced, 'Her Majesty's Government are disposed to waive their objections and to accept the letter above referred to as a notice'.[32]

In his efforts to bring Salisbury to the negotiating table, Ueno had even entertained the idea that Britain might host a conference on treaty revision in London. In a telegram in February 1979 he informed Terashima that the 'British Government is proposing to open [the] Conference in London in view of [its] moral obligation to [the] joint powers signing [the] Tariff Convention [in] 1866'.[33] Parkes, however, succeeded in sabotaging this initiative by informing the Foreign Office that Japan's intention was to host such a conference in Tokyo. Terashima, indeed, had to reproach Ueno for exceeding his instructions, although he added the advice, 'try to withdraw your statement by explaining that it was only your personal view'.[34] By this stage the Foreign Office had already sent out invitations to the other powers, but on 1 April Salisbury was able to inform Ueno that 'Her Majesty's Government have decided to abandon the Project of a conference in London and they are willing to accede to the desire of your Government that the negotiations for the Revision of the Treaty should take place in Tokio'.[35]

Even so, Salisbury still maintained that Terashima's insistence on Japanese autonomy over tariff rates was 'not in harmony with the present view of Her Majesty's Government'.[36] In March, Ueno had also warned in a joint communiqué with Sameshima Naonobu, his counterpart in Paris, that 'most of [the] European Powers particularly [the] English and [the] Germans are manifesting [the] opinion that revision is impossible as long as Japan maintains [its] claim to fix her own tariff freely'.[37] Now he seemed more optimistic, and even claimed, 'I have good reason to believe that the British Government may finally yield at all essential points if you remain firm with S. Parkes'.[38]

Clearly encouraged, Terashima told Ueno that, 'in consequence of Treaty Revision at Tokio you are ordered to return as soon as possible leaving the secretary in charge'.[39] Ueno duly informed Salisbury that he would be 'absent for some time from this Country' and that during this time the Legation's business was to be 'left in the care of Tomita Tetsunos[u]ke, first-secretary, as chargé d'affaires ad interim'.[40] His recall may also have been influenced by suggestions that he was overspending on the legation's budget and not reporting back to Japan with sufficient regularity, although Suematsu Kenchō, a recent arrival in Britain, defended him against such accusations in his letters to Itō Hirobumi.[41] Ostensibly, however, he was summoned back to Tokyo to assist Terashima in his plans for a conference on tariffs; and it was not until December after a hiatus of several months that Tomita informed the British of Mori Arinori's appointment 'as the next minister in the place of Jushie Wooyeno Kagenori'.[42]

A SHOOTING STAR IN TOKYO SOCIETY

Ueno set out for Japan with his family on 9 June 1879, but this was to be a sad voyage as his infant son died in Athens en route. Moreover, by the time he reached Japan in late July, Parkes had persuaded the Foreign Office to pull out of the planned negotiations in Tokyo altogether. Instead the British now insisted, just as Ueno and Sameshima had feared, that they could only accept 'specific proposals on amending the existing tariff'.[43] The collapse of the Tokyo conference precipitated Terashima's resignation shortly afterwards, and Ueno must have been acutely aware of the role he himself had played in his mentor's downfall. He remained a valued figure in the Ministry of Foreign Affairs nonetheless, and after Inoue Kaoru was appointed in place of Terashima he was promoted to the post of vice-minister early in 1880. Ueno deputised for Inoue on several occasions and in 1882 he was involved in preliminary talks on tariff reform with the treaty powers in Tokyo. These, however, followed a European agenda and little was gained from a Japanese perspective, despite the Western-style hospitality lavished on the guests.

Inoue's tenure as Minister of Foreign Affairs, indeed, is often associated with the 'Rokumeikan' or 'Deer Cry Pavilion' culture of the 1880s, a reference to the French-style château built in Tokyo by the British architect Josiah Conder to entertain foreign diplomats in style. The building's poetic name was coined by none other than Nakai Hiroshi, who had served at the Japanese Legation in London. Ueno, too, was an advocate of 'Rokumeikan' diplomacy and a leading figure in introducing Western fashions. His birthday party in January 1880, for example, became the talk of Tokyo society as he invited several hundred guests, including luminaries such as Fukuzawa Yukichi. It may be hard to credit claims that this was the first time foreign guests had ever attended such a soirée, but it was certainly a grand occasion complete with a military band.[44]

At thirty-five years old, Ueno was at the pinnacle of his career, and could look forward to filling senior posts in the Meiji government. Tragically, however, the pressures of his work took their toll on his health. This first became apparent in the autumn of 1882 when he was appointed Minister to Austria and embarked for Europe via America together with Terashima, who was also bound for his new post as Minister to the United States in Washington. During the voyage Terashima noticed that Ueno did not look well and he later commented that the condition which later afflicted him probably took hold at around this time. In Vienna the following year the symptoms became severe and Austrian physicians diagnosed a nervous disorder that was later identified as a form of brain disease. On doctor's orders Ueno spent some time resting in the country, although he broke his convalescence on the occasion of Itō Hirobumi's visit to Vienna.

The following spring, his enforced rest continued with a leisurely journey through Italy, but his condition only deteriorated and on his voyage back to Japan later in the year he found the passage through the heat of the Indian Ocean unbearable. Following his arrival in Tokyo he was examined by Dr Erwin Baelz and other noted physicians but he was never able to return to his full duties. In 1885 he was appointed to the Genroin, the Chamber of Elders, but he was rarely able to attend. He died on 11 April 1888 and was buried four days later at Zuishōji Temple in the Shirogane district of Tokyo, following a grand funeral attended by senior government figures. He was just forty-three years old.[45]

As Minister to the Court of St James's, Ueno had been in the vanguard of early negotiations on treaty revision. To some extent he was complicit in the diplomatic crisis of 1879 which heralded an end to the Terashima era at the Ministry of Foreign Affairs. Nevertheless, he was among the very first Japanese diplomats to expose cracks in Britain's stance on extraterritoriality, and the Foreign Office for its part began to realize that it was now dealing with something very different from the authorities in China. As such, the increasing hesitancy of British officials to 'dismiss Japan as a backward nation' was due in no small part to Ueno's assiduous efforts during these early skirmishes with Whitehall.[46] Ultimately, failing health prevented him from fulfilling his early promise and he never won the notoriety of compatriots such as Mori Arinori, his outspoken successor at the Court of St James's. Nevertheless, through his connections at various levels with architects, engineers, bankers and diplomats, he was a most influential figure in developing relations with Britain in the early years of Meiji Japan.

NOTES

1.   I wish to place on record my debt to Professor Inuzuka Takaaki for his generous help in tracing and providing me with Japanese source material. I am also grateful to Professor Ian Nish for his kind support.
2.   Richard Henry Brunton, *Building Japan 1868-1876*, Japan Library, 1991, p.78.
3.   'Ueno Kagenori Rireki Honkoku Henshū' [Transliterated Edition of Ueno Kagenori's Curriculum Vitae], *Kagoshima Tanki Daigaku Chiiki Kenkyū Kenkyūsho Kenkyū Nenpō* [Kagoshima Junior College Regional Research Centre Research Bulletin], no.11, 1982, p.28.
4.   Ibid., pp.5-6.
5.   Ibid., p.29.
6.   Cobbing, *The Satsuma Students in Britain*, Japan Library, 2000, p.23. 'Ueno Kagenori Rireki,' p.7.
7.   Kadota Akira, 'Nihon Kindaika to Ueno Kagenori' [Ueno Kagenori and the Modernization of Japan] *Kagoshima Kenritsu Tanki Daigaku Chiiki Kenkyū Nenpō*, no.19, 1990, pp.3-4.
8.   'Ueno Kagenori Rireki', p.7. The Ijinkan or 'Foreigners' House' built by Waters is now part of the Shūseikan Museum complex in Kagoshima.
9.   Ibid.
10. Ibid., p.8.
11. Ibid. In this, the so-called Sakai Incident, the French had called for the death of twenty Tosa officers. In addition to the four commanders these were chosen by drawing lots, but on the occasion of the ceremonial suicide one was allowed to live when the French official present called a halt to the proceedings after nineteen deaths.
12. Ibid., pp.9-10.
13. Brunton, *Building Japan*, pp.78-9. Brunton recorded Ueno's name as Inouye, inviting confusion with Inoue Kaoru. He also attributed Ueno's brash manners to his misconception that he had been educated in the United States. He also noted that in 1878 Ueno attended a lecture he gave at the Institute of Civil Engineers in London on the subject of Japan's lighthouses.

14. 'Ueno Kagenori Hawai-koku Tokai Nikki', *Kagoshima Kenritsu Tanki Daigaku Chiiki Kenkyū Nenpō*, no.11, 1982, pp.33-63.

15. 'Ueno Kagenori Rireki, pp.13-5. Gordon Daniels, *Sir Harry Parkes*, p.100. On 14 October 1872 Ueno was in the sixth carriage of the train laid on for the official opening of the Yokohama-Shinbashi Railway.

16. 'Ueno Kagenori Rireki', p.16. Kadota, 'Nihon Kindaika to Ueno Kagenori', p.8. When the Peruvian ship *Maria Luz* docked in Yokohama in 1872, two Chinese coolies on board absconded ashore and lodged accusations of slavery and torture. Questions were raised over who exercised jurisdiction to examine the case, especially since Japan had no treaty relations with Peru, but in an early test of sovereignty a Japanese court tried and convicted the captain.

17. Mori Toshihiko, *Meiji 6-nen Seihen [The 1873 Governmental Crisis]*, (Tokyo: Chūōkōronsha, 1979), p.110.

18. FO 46/187/46, Derby to Wooyeno, 1 March 1875.

19. Inuzuka Takaaki, 'Zaiei Nihon Kōshikan no Setchi Keii to sono Hensen – Nichiei Gaikō no Ura-butai [The Establishment and Development of the Japanese Legation in Britain: the backstage of Anglo-Japanese diplomacy], *Seiji Keizai Shigaku*, no.330, December 1993, p.10. Motono Morimichi's career is also notable in that, shortly before he arrived in Britain, he founded the *Yomiuri* newspaper. In a series of essays entitled *Manyū Kitei [Record of My Wanderings]*, Nakai Hiroshi, his colleague at the Japanese Legation, enhanced his reputation as a writer during his stay in Britain with a colourful but critical account of London society. See Cobbing, *The Japanese Discovery of Victorian Britain*, pp.93-4, 105.

20. Ibid., p.12, 14.

21. Ibid., p.13.

22. The *Fusō* is often referred to as the Imperial Navy's first battleship, but although this was the fleet's first ironclad vessel she was more of a frigate in terms of scale and fighting strength. The two other vessels in this class were the *Hiei* and *Kongō*.

23. Yasuoka Akio, *Bakumatsu Ishin-ki no Ryōdo to Gaikō [Territory and Diplomacy in the 1860s]* (Seibundō. Tokyo, 2002), pp.229, 231-2, 241, 245.

24. FO 46/212/188.

25. Ibid.

26. FO 46/212/224, Ueno to Derby, 22 August 1876.

27. FO 46/212/236, FO Memo, Tenterden, Derby, 22 August 1876.

28. Ibid.

29. *Jōyaku Kaisei Kankei Nihon Gaikō Bunsho [Japanese Ministry of Foreign Affairs Records; Documents on the Treaty Revision Issue]*, Vol. 1 (Tokyo: Nihon Kokusai Kyōkai, 1941), pp.544-8

30. Ibid., p.573, Interview between Sir Julian Pauncefore and Mr. Stuart Lane. 18 October 1878.

31. Ibid., pp.591-9, 605, Wooyeno to Salisbury, 2 November 1878; Wooyeno to Salisbury, 18 December 1878.

32. Ibid., p.603, Salisbury to Wooyeno, 21 December 1878.

33. Ibid., p.607, Wooyeno to Terashima, 6 February 1879.

34. Ibid., pp.629-30, Terashima to Wooyeno; Gordon Daniels, *Sir Harry Parkes*, p.178.

35. Ibid., p.639, Salisbury to Wooyeno, 1 April 1879.

36. Ibid.

37. Ibid., pp.626-7, Sameshima and Wooyeno to Terashima, 10 March 1879.

38. Ibid., pp.642, Wooyeno to Terashima, 9 April 1879.

39. Ibid., p.654, Terashima to Wooyeno, 30 April 1879.

40. FO 46/252/122, Wooyeno to Salisbury, 3 June 1879.

41. Ian Ruxton, 'Suematsu Kenchō, 1855-1920: Statesman, Bureaucrat, Diplomat, Journalist, Poet and Scholar', Sir Hugh Cortazzi (ed.), *Biographical Portraits*, Vol. V, Global Oriental, 2005, pp.64-5.

42. FO 46/252/176, Tomita to Salisbury, 19 December 1879.

43. *Jōyaku Kaisei Kankei Nihon Gaikō Bunsho*, p.658.

44. 'Ueno Kagenori Rireki, p.22. Although Ueno's birthday party has been described as the first dinner party to be held in Japan to which foreign guests were invited, Clara Whitney, an American resident in Tokyo, recorded how she and several diplomats attended a similar occasion at Mori Arinori's house the previous summer. Ueno and his wife were also there, having just arrived back from Britain. Whitney's account of Ueno's party does not feature in the abridged publication of her diary. Clara Whitney (edited by William Steele and Tamiko Ichimata), *Clara's Diary; an American girl in Meiji Japan* (Tokyo: Kodansha International, 1979).

45. Ibid., p.25-8.

46. Daniels, *Sir Harry Parkes*, p.177.

5

MORI ARINORI, 1847-89
From Diplomat to Statesman
[London, 1880-84]

ANDREW COBBING

Mori Arinori

I n January 1880, Mori Arinori arrived in London as the third resident minister from Japan to be appointed to the Court of St James's. Still only thirty-two years of age, he brought with him a reputation as an outspoken champion of radical social reform. Enlisted by the new government after the Meiji Restoration, he had quickly gained notoriety in 1869 for his infamous proposal to remove the samurai's traditional right to bear his swords.Then, in his time as Japan's first minister to the United States from 1870 to 1873, he had advocated religious freedom and even suggested adopting English as the official language. On his return from Washington he had gone on to found the Meirokusha, Japan's first modern intellectual society, which spread progressive ideas through the distribution of its *Meiroku Journal*. This was the man whom the indefatigable Victorian traveller Isabella Bird described as an 'advanced liberal' when she met him on a visit to Tokyo in 1878.[1]

Once likened to a 'lone pine atop a winter mountain', the young Mori frequently cut an isolated figure in the world of Meiji politics.[2] Four years of diplomatic service in London, however, were to effect a profound change in his outlook and bring him closer to the mainstream of government affairs. He returned in 1884 as a statesman in the making, and went on to impose such a centralized and elitist structure on Japan's education system that he was even suspected of forsaking his radical past. Ironically, perhaps, the catalyst in Mori's apparent transition from liberal to conservative was none other than Herbert Spencer, the celebrated Victorian pioneer of social science. It was under his guidance that Mori would consciously set about diagnosing the prevailing maladies in the body politic of Japan and devise his own prescriptions to revitalize the Meiji State.

On their arrival early in 1880, Mori, his wife and their two young sons moved into the Japanese legation building at No. 9 Kensington Gardens in Notting Hill.

Clara Whitney, an American friend of the family passing through, observed: 'We found them luxuriously situated and very well pleased with London.' Equipped with an 'elegant barouch [sic]', Mori, it seems, felt quite at home, as he escorted his guests to city sights from the Tower of London to St Paul's. Some weeks later, Clara recorded how, on one occasion at dinner, 'Mr Mori regaled us with tales of his boyhood and what a savage he was when he first came to London some fourteen years ago.'[3]

Mori's appointment as minister to Britain thus marked something of a nostalgic return. Born in 1847 in Satsuma, Japan's southernmost domain, he received a traditional Confucian education in his early years under the strict supervision of his parents – he told Clara over dinner they were 'real ancient Samurai'.[4] He was sixteen years old when the Royal Navy bombarded his home-town of Kagoshima in 1863, an experience that prompted Satsuma to try and learn from Britain rather than challenge the military supremacy of the Treaty Powers. Two years later, he was one of the nineteen young Satsuma officers who were sent abroad to study as a result, smuggled out of the country in defiance of the Tokugawa regime's ban on overseas travel. He spent two years at University College, London, including trips to Russia and France. Increasingly short of funds, however, he and his five remaining companions were persuaded by their mentor, Laurence Oliphant, to cross the Atlantic for a further year abroad at a Utopian Christian colony in New York State. There, in the company of the eccentric Thomas Lake Harris's 'Brotherhood of the New Life', he pursued his studies on life in the West to the extent that, when he returned to Japan in 1868, he brought with him not just polished English skills but also a passionate belief in the powers of rationalism and an almost Western-style persona that set him apart from other young leaders in the new Meiji government.

Twelve years later, back in London, the Mori family spent the first few months of their stay in England entertaining guests, attending diplomatic functions, and travelling abroad on short holidays to Holland and Switzerland. By now they were accustomed to the social side of diplomatic life, as Isabella Bird had noted when remarking that 'his wife dresses tastefully in English style, and receives his guests along with himself'.[5] Perhaps the most singular development in these early months was on 1 June, with the removal of the Japanese Legation to a new location at No. 9 Cavendish Square. Costing more than double the rent of their former residence, Ernest Satow thought it 'a fine house' when he called on Mori for lunch some time later. He found 'his wife as bashful as ever', and commented that the boys were now speaking English 'quite naturally', having 'entirely forgotten their Japanese'.[6]

MORI AS MEIJI DIPLOMAT

Mori's new surroundings were in keeping with his keen awareness of outward appearances. In practice, his everyday duties consisted largely of correspondence relating to the Imperial Navy, from purchasing and refitting cruisers to training Japanese cadets and preparing visits to dockyards. As one attaché at the legation later recalled, the diplomatic staff also spent much of their time polishing their social skills and refining their knowledge of current affairs so as 'to show what a fine impression the Japanese could make on foreign soil'.[7] This was all part of the Foreign Ministry's new initiative to try and raise Japan's profile in the eyes of the Treaty Powers. Ultimately, the objective was to win support for a fundamental revision of the 'unequal' Ansei commercial treaties of 1858, which the Meiji government had inherited from the Tokugawa regime. Now the strategy was to attain recognition for Japan as a 'civilized' state by conforming to Western standards in institutional development and the trimmings of diplomatic protocol. As an imposing house at a central location in London, No. 9 Cavendish Square was eminently suited to the task.

Japanese hopes of revising these treaties had initially foundered in 1872 during the Iwakura Mission's visit to Washington, when Mori himself was there as minister. The issue had then pursued him in successive diplomatic posts, as minister to China from 1875 to 1877 and subsequently as assistant to the Foreign Minister, Terashima Munenori. There were some encouraging signs, particularly when Yoshida Kiyonari obtained a promise of support from the Americans in 1877. This was conditional on the blessing of the other Treaty Powers, however, and came to nothing when Britain insisted that it endangered free trade, prompting the resignation of both Terashima and Mori the following year.

When Mori was next dispatched to London by Terashima's successor, Inoue Kaoru, his assigned mission was to solicit British approval for a Tokyo conference on treaty revision. Convinced that justice was on his side, he arrived full of confidence and impatient for success, but unprepared for the blithe indifference of the Foreign Office. As Hall has pointed out, 'Britain, with the greatest vested interest in her treaty rights, was least responsive to Japanese hopes for revision'.[8] Now in the grip of a major economic slump, the British were guarding their overseas interests with jealous care. Moreover, in the mind of the ageing Foreign Secretary, Lord Granville, Japan's affairs paled in significance in comparison with more pressing matters like the Afghan War, French expansion in Africa and the Khedive appeal for British protection in Egypt. Mori's overtures also met with suspicion from Sir Harry Parkes, his counterpart in Japan, who was now back in Britain on leave. In recent years, in fact, Parkes had frequently been at loggerheads with Mori in Tokyo over the growing menace of cholera, for he saw Mori's efforts to impose quarantine controls in the treaty ports as an underhand attempt to reassert Japanese jurisdiction and undermine the commercial treaties.[9]

The response of the Foreign Office was to seize the initiative by sending circulars to other Treaty Powers behind Mori's back calling for a conference to be held in London instead.[10] Mori reacted by confronting Granville with Japan's demands for some fundamental changes to the treaties. In April 1881, he called on him at his Walmer Castle home with Parkes also in attendance, only to be told that Japan should concentrate on nothing more than partial amendments.[11] Granville then rejected Japan's agenda altogether and proposed a summit in Tokyo to address the limited issue of tariff reform alone. Convinced that the European Powers were orchestrating a campaign to dictate their own terms to Japan, a furious Mori complained to Itō Hirobumi in October that Britain, now in league with Bismarck, was simply trying to protect her reputation and commercial power. His efforts were to no avail, however, as the following month Inoue accepted the Europeans' plan and a Tokyo summit was opened in January 1882. The talks lasted for several months with little tangible result, in spite of Inoue's attempts to impress his guests with lavish Western-style receptions. It was to be another decade before the British, prompted by fears of Russian expansion in the East, showed genuine receptivity to the Meiji government's crusade against the unequal treaties.

Mori felt that Japan had simply caved in to European pressure, but with the centre stage of negotiations moving to Tokyo there was little he could do. Later, when the summit was over he would feel vindicated enough to remind Britain of Japan's claims to be treated on equal terms with the other Western powers. The Foreign Office, however, either ignored his letters or delayed for weeks or months before sending any reply. When he finally did manage to meet Granville in person, he found it impossible to conceal his frustration. Granville, under fire, considered his tone 'dictatorial and presumptuous', and on more than one occasion, Inoue Kaoru in Tokyo was called upon to try and soothe the British by reminding them that Mori was still 'a very young man', or that his language was 'unauthorized'.[12]

Mori, in truth, was not a natural diplomat. He owed his posts in Washington and London rather to his undoubted intellect, his command of English and his clan affiliation. After all, the Foreign Ministry in these years was filled with Satsuma compatriots such as Terashima, Yoshida and Sameshima Naonobu, all of them veterans of the domain's expedition to Britain in 1865. Now in 1882, with negotiations out of his hands, he found relief from his ordeals with the Foreign Office in the more relaxing atmosphere of the Athenaeum Club in Pall Mall. His status as minister carried with it the privilege of honorary membership, which not only enabled him to indulge his passion for billiards, his only known hobby, but gave him the opportunity to meet some of the most prominent Victorian intellectuals of the day.[13] As a somewhat scathing article observed the following year, 'It cannot be said that Mr Mori has achieved signal success as a diplomatist,' but it did concede that 'his reputation as a philosophical disputant is quite formidable,' even if this was 'scarcely quite what Japan expects of her Minister in London'.[14]

ATHENAEUM DAYS WITH SPENCER

Soon the Athenaeum was 'the pivot of Mori's social life'.[15] This allowed him to renew his acquaintance with another member, Herbert Spencer, who spent much of his time there whenever he was in London. Mori had first met him during a brief trip to Britain in 1873, having read his works extensively in his years as minister in Washington. This in itself was not unusual, for Spencer was something of a cult figure among progressive thinkers in Japan, where some of his works were already available in translation. Spencer had set about applying Darwinian theory to the world of human relations in order to chart organic models of social and political evolution. By distinguishing between the Knowable (Science) and the Unknowable (Religion), this offered Japanese readers a refreshingly accessible approach to Western civilization, uncomplicated by the mysteries of the Christian tradition.[16] Moreover, his emphasis on minimal government interference was welcomed by many in the growing campaign for liberal rights in Japan who found their interests effectively marginalized by the authoritarian approach of the Meiji government.

Mori's visits to the Athenaeum were also of more than passing interest to Spencer, as he frequently cited the case of Japan in support of his own theories and was now seeking a reliable source of information for his new project, Part V (Political Institutions) of his major work, 'Principles of Sociology'.[17] Usually highly selective in his choice of acquaintances, he actively cultivated Mori's company, once hosting a dinner party held at the club in his honour. Mori returned the compliment by introducing him to a number of his own contacts including Ernest Satow, Itō Hirobumi and Itagaki Taisuke, founder of the Jiyūtō (Liberal Party), Japan's first genuine political party.[18]

The intellectual climate of the Athenaeum served to reinforce Mori's general optimism for the future. At the time, prominent thinkers like Samuel Smiles and Spencer, originally doctors and engineers by training rather than men of letters, were expounding 'an enlightenment of steam locomotives and gas-lit streets'.[19] Now at the height of the age of Jules Verne, they were confident that nothing was beyond the capacity of man and machine, a message that appealed to the radical side of Mori's nature and his belief in human progress. Impressed by the utility of electric power, for example, he displayed 'a typical mid-Victorian faith in the unlimited peaceful potentialities of scientific discovery'.[20]

In the field of political ideas, however, the Athenaeum experience served to temper Mori's radical spirit. By Spencer's own admission, in fact, the counsel he gave him was considerably more cautious than the views he espoused in his written works. As his diary record of the very first meeting with Mori back in 1873 reveals, 'he came to ask my opinion about the reorganization of Japanese institutions. I gave him conservative advice – urging that they would eventually have to return to a form not much in advance of what they had and that they ought not to attempt to diverge widely from it.'[21] In future years he would recall his talks with Mori in London in a similar vein: 'I gave him very conservative advice, contending that it was impossible that the Japanese hitherto accustomed to despotic rule, should all at once become capable of constitutional government.'[22]

Spencer's guarded response to Mori was not an isolated case but just one example of a marked tendency by Western liberals to shy away from their beliefs when dispensing advice to prominent Meiji politicians. It seems they feared that their own theories might lead to chaos should they be misconstrued and applied out of context in Japan. Victorian paternalism may also have featured in their thoughts as they tried to help nurture political development in the fledgling Meiji state. What men such as Spencer perhaps did not foresee was that their cautious advice might contribute to an authoritarian reaction instead by 'inducing political conservatism' in men like Mori.[23]

Spencer's influence, however, certainly helped to bring Mori's thinking closer in line with some of the more pragmatic minds within the Meiji government. Significantly, for example, his ideas won the sympathy of Itō Hirobumi, now the ascendant figure in Japanese politics. In 1881, Itō had emerged triumphant after a government purge featuring an open confrontation on the question of a modern constitution for Japan.[24] Now in 1882, he had arrived in Europe to study under legal experts in Vienna and Berlin with a view to realizing the government's resulting pledge to deliver a new constitution within ten years. Mori promptly requested an interview and, after some delay, they finally met in Paris. There, over the course of three days, he explained his growing conviction that a centrally controlled system of education would be a key element in any new constitutional structure. The talks proved to be a turning point, for Itō was so impressed by Mori's argument that he wrote to him shortly afterwards announcing his intention to make him the first Minister of Education in the new Prussian-style cabinet he was planning to create following his own return to Japan.[25]

A PRESCRIPTION FOR MEIJI JAPAN

Enthused by Itō's vote of confidence, Mori returned to London determined to draft his own proposals for educational reform. These took the form of two papers, *'Shintai no Nōryoku'* [Physical Capacity] and *'Gakusei Hengen'* [Educational Administrative Reform]. Spencer's influence was evident here in Mori's growing tendency to use the human body as a metaphor for Japanese society as a whole. Later, in a clear reference to Spencer's guidance, he even revealed how he had been 'taught' about Darwinian concepts such as 'natural selection' and 'survival of the fittest'.[26] He now showed a deep concern for historical continuity, evolutionary development and balance. Spencer's advice enabled him to plot his vision of progress within a gradualistic framework that reconciled his own radical disposition with his growing awareness of the need for pragmatism. Moreover, by approaching Japan as a complex social organism, he also felt empowered to diagnose ailments and identify potential remedies.

When he arrived in Britain in 1880, Mori had still been advocating a radically decentralized system of education. Now he saw educational administration as critical to the general health of the national polity (*kokutai*), and supported a more active role for the state. Japan's current weaknesses, he thought, were symptomatic of more than two hundred years of Tokugawa rule. In his mind, centuries of Confucian culture had exercised a morally debilitating effect, and he claimed that the Japanese people now lacked any sense of 'internally regulating principles'.[27] The Tokugawa social environment, he felt, was also responsible for what he saw as the relative frailty of his own generation, for he insisted that 'there are few, even in fact amongst the warrior class, who have managed to avoid falling into an inferior physical condition.'[28]

Mori thus held out little hope for older people raised under these conditions, so the prescriptions he devised concentrated on educational programmes aimed at raising the moral fibre and physical vitality of the younger generation. He drew encouragement from his belief in the people's innate spiritual strength, notwithstanding the impact of the Tokugawa years. This fortitude, he suggested, might be related to the historical continuity fostered by an imperial line unbroken since ancient times. Drawing on his own experience of living abroad, he observed: 'Go all over the world, take any Japanese you like, no matter how Americanized or Europeanized he may be, and you will find in him the same stout heart which beats in the breast of every native of Japan.'[29] He was also confident in the people's capacity for progress in the modern industrial world since, as he pointed out: 'I don't know how it is, whether from the genius of our nation, or from whatever other cause, the Japanese have ever been prompt to appropriate whatever is best in foreign nations.'[30]

The intensive course of physical training that Mori also recommended was conceived in 'a quasi-moral sense', for he thought this would be beneficial for 'cultivating the character of the people.'[31] His own fixation with physical vitality was nothing new. In his letters to his brother from Britain nearly twenty years before, he had described how his own regime of daily exercises was helping him to survive the rigours of student life in London.[32] His year of devotional labour in America, too, had reinforced his belief in physical training, but what began as a personal interest had now developed into a blueprint for Japan as a whole. By the end of his stay in Britain, it had become something of an obsession.

During his last few months in London, Mori went on to work in consultation with Spencer on developing his own proposal for a new constitution. Spencer recalled: 'My advice to Mr Mori was that the proposed new institutions should be as much as possible grafted upon the existing institutions, so as to prevent breaking the continuity.'[33] The resulting paper, 'On a Representative System of Government', reflected this influence, and even included Spencerian terms such as the 'engrafting' of representative government on the national polity of Japan.[34] Mori was again at pains to strike a balance in order to guard against any abuses of power, but the representation he outlined was in fact extremely limited. Arguing that a system of popular representation was essentially unsuited to Japan, he suggested limiting any franchise rights to patriarchal family heads, with only consultative powers for the first few generations at least.

Mori also expressed a deep mistrust of factional politics, insisting that 'popular representation' did not necessarily reflect the 'popular will'. Like Spencer, he was somewhat disenchanted with the in-fighting at Westminster where individuals like Parnell and Churchill could practically hold Parliament to ransom as they struggled for personal advantage with their 'spoiling politics'.[35] Moreover, the early development of political parties in Japan in the wake of the 1881 purge hardly gave him cause for encouragement. Mori, in fact, confessed that he had little faith in parliaments, for he doubted 'whether parliamentarism can be successfully grafted on Japanese habits of thought'. In his mind, the real barrier was that 'it is hardly in the natural line of our historical development'.[36] While he considered a parliamentary system unavoidable in Britain, he added that 'I doubt whether we shall find it equally inevitable in Japan'.[37]

MORI AS MEIJI STATESMAN

Mori left London for the last time on 26 February 1884, and returned to Tokyo where he took up a new post in the Ministry of Education. As planned, he was then appointed minister when Itō Hirobumi formed Japan's first modern cabinet the following year. This gave him the chance to put into practice some of the theories he had formulated in Britain. His thoughts on a new constitution may have made little impact, but the sweeping reforms he introduced in the field of education during his brief time in charge were to have a profound effect on Japanese society for decades afterwards.

Mori applied his educational theories in two phases, the first reminiscent of his dialogue with Itō and the second more indicative of the influence of Spencer. In 1886, during his first year as minister, he established the New Educational Ordinance, which reasserted central control over Japan's colleges and schools by stipulating objectives and structural frameworks from university to primary school level. At the top, Tokyo University was renamed the Imperial University and came under the direct control of the Ministry of Education, guaranteeing civil service posts for an elite rank of graduates from the faculties of Letters and Law. It was the realization of an idea he had pondered years before in Britain, when he had favoured a strict examination system for entry to the civil service.

The second phase targeted cultural integration through a series of reforms aimed at standardizing the school curriculum and choice of texts. These introduced the moral and physical training that Mori considered necessary to strengthen the character of the people. Ever the patriot, his notion of moral education was based on the ideal of national service. He stressed, for example, that the people should be 'taught to the very marrow of their bones the fervent spirit of loyalty and patriotism'.[38] In 1888, the Ministry of Education published the *Rinrisho* [New Ethical Handbook], incorporating many of the ideas to be found in Spencer's *The Data of Ethics*, which had appeared in Japanese translation four years before. It was entirely secular in content, for Mori harboured no agenda to impose Western religion and, as Isabella Bird had noted a decade earlier, he saw Shinto 'only as a useful political engine'.[39] The *Rinrisho* revealed instead his desire to nurture what he called a 'common sense morality'.[40]

Concerned as ever with physical vitality, he also introduced a military-style training programme into Japan's schools. In years to come this initiative would earn him something of a reputation as the Meiji statesman who mobilized the Japanese population into a national militia. He was certainly not militaristic in outlook, however, for he expressed some ambivalence about the suitability of such a scheme from the start, conscious that it could be prone to abuse. Nevertheless, he was convinced that this was the only way to restore the Japanese people to full health after generations of Tokugawa rule, and concluded that his national physical training programme at least deserved a trial.[41]

Mori's reforms were later described by Inoue Kowashi as 'a philosophy of education based on the national polity'.[42] In some ways they started a trend, for his strong emphasis on national service was reinforced by the unity between ruler and subjects that Inoue and others stressed when they drafted the '*Imperial Rescript on Education*' in 1890. Between them they appeared to lay the foundations for the institutionalized loyalty to the Emperor that became such a feature of Japanese colonial expansion in the early twentieth century. It is only natural, therefore, that he should have been denounced in some circles as a reactionary after World War II, and that his educational reforms should be labelled orthodox, authoritarian and even statist. Mori, however, was never a statist in the mould of some Meiji oligarchs who consolidated their authority through a static system of political control. His was a more progressive conservativism, with an open-ended Spencerian vision of social evolution.[43] Moreover, even in his last years as a Meiji statesman, he could still come across to his contemporaries as a highly Westernized radical who threatened the bastions of traditional Japanese life.

Mori never did have the chance to find out whether a parliamentary system was 'inevitable' in Japan. He was assassinated on 11 February 1889, the inaugural day of the Meiji Constitution. A victim of the tide of ultra-nationalist reaction sweeping across the country, he was shot as he made his way on foot that morning from his government residence towards the Imperial Palace. His assassin, a Shinto fanatic called Nishino Buntarō, left a suicide note justifying his action by claiming not only that Mori was a Christian but also that he was guilty of insulting the Emperor. During a visit to Ise Shrine in November 1887, he had apparently neglected to take off his Western shoes on entry, and used his walking stick to lift the curtain that veiled the inner sanctum. It was an ironic end for a man who was such an inveterate patriot himself. As he confessed to a London reporter on the day before he left Britain in 1884: 'I am Japanese by blood[:] I cannot be impartial.'[44]

One of the most outspoken politicians of the Meiji period, Mori Arinori remains an intriguing figure, conspicuous as much for his radical views as he was for his later conservative agenda. Paradoxical though it may seem, he never consciously betrayed either approach, for his aims remained broadly consistent throughout as he struggled for a balance between his liberal nature and his concern for stability. To some extent these characterized successive stages in his career, from the impetuosity of youth to the pragmatism of middle age. His encounter with Herbert Spencer in London, however, was undoubtedly a critical factor, encouraging him to believe in the possibility of a gradualist compromise incorporating both. The counsel that Mori received at the Athenaeum was, in fact, a heady concoction of conflicting signals, so it is hardly surprising that his own ideas have also defied easy categorization ever since. In this light, his career as a diplomat and statesman perhaps reflects traces of underlying tensions in the Victorian world as well as some of the essential dilemmas of political life in Meiji Japan.

[2002]

NOTES

1.   Isabella Bird, *Unbeaten Tracks in Japan*, 2 vols. (London, 1880) II, p. 202.
2.   Alistair Swale, *The Political Thought of Mori Arinori* (Richmond, 2000), p. 1.
3.   Diary entry for 15 April 1880, 'Clara's Diary' in Okubo Toshimichi et al (ed.), *Mori Arinori Zenshū*, Vol. 4 (Bunsendō, Tokyo, 1999), pp. 288-9, 304.
4.   Ibid., p. 304.
5.   Bird, II, pp. 202-4.
6.   PRO, Satow Papers, PRO-30-33-15-7, 'Diary January 1882-March 1884', entry for 5 April 1883.
7.   Makino Nobuaki, *Kōkai Roku* (Tokyo, 1977) cited in Inuzuka Takaaki, 'Zaiei Nihon Kōshikan no Setchi Keii to sono Henkan' in *Seiji Keizai Shigaku*, no. 330, December 1995, p. 16.
8.   Ivan P. Hall, *Mori Arinori*, (Harvard, 1973.) p. 283.
9.   On one occasion Mori had even refused Parkes' representative, Endymion Wilkinson, entry to a meeting on the cholera quarantine issue by insisting that he was uninvited.
10. Inuzuka Takaaki, *Mori Arinori* (Tokyo, 1986), p. 212.
11. Ibid., p. 214.
12. Granville Papers, PRO-30-29-312, Further Correspondence, Part 5, cited in Hall, *Mori Arinori*, p. 285.
13. Ibid., p. 290.
14. *Japan Weekly Mail*, 1 September 1883.
15. Hall, p. 289. Mori may have come across Oliphant again at the Athenaeum, although there is no record of such a meeting. In addition to this club, he also joined the Royal Asiatic Society in time for its first gathering, where he freely criticized a paper by Professor Friedrich Max Mueller of Oxford on a 'Sanskrit Text Discovered in Japan', a subject he knew practically nothing about. Hall, pp. 291, 293.
16. Swale, p. 13.
17. Hall, p. 289. See Spencer, *Principles of Sociology*, I, parts II and III, and II, part V.
18. Itagaki's interview with Spencer was not a success. Mori reported to Itō early in May 1883 that 'Itagaki had his interview with Spencer – the idol of his researches – three days ago. He went into it as though approaching the Emperor, but in the actual discussion master and pupil traded places, with the disciple doing all the sermonizing and putting forward his usual empty and unfounded theories. Finally, the central idol lost his patience, got up in the middle of the conversation muttering 'no, no, no' [English in original] and took his leave of Itagaki, just like that.' Hall, p. 292.
19. Swale, p. 4.
20. Hall, p. 288.
21. David Duncan, *The Life and Letters of Herbert Spencer*, (London, 1908), p. 161.
22. Ibid., p. 319. Letter from Spencer to Kaneko Kentarō, 21 August 1892.
23. Hall, p. 323. A decade later, for example, Spencer felt compelled to inform another Japanese contact, Kaneko Kentarō, that 'I give this advice in confidence. I wish that it should not transpire publicly, at any rate during my lifetime for I do not desire to arouse the animosity of my fellow-

countrymen.' Duncan, p. 323. Letter from Spencer to Kaneko Kentarō, 26 August 1892.
24. Another major cause of this political purge was the financial scandal over the sale of the Hokkaido Development Agency's assets. See Cobbing, *The Satsuma Students in Britain* (Richmond, 2000), p. 128.
25. Swale, p. 17.
26. *Pall Mall Gazette*, 26 February 1884.
27. Swale, p. 102.
28. *Pall Mall Gazette*, 26 February 1882.
29. Ibid.
30. Ibid.
31. Swale, pp. 105-6.
32. Cobbing, *The Satsuma Students in Britain* (Richmond, 2000), pp. 90-1.
33. Duncan, p. 319. Spencer to Kaneko Kentarō, 23 August 1892.
34. Only the first four parts of *'Representative Government'* survive in English, but there is a complete Japanese version in nine parts entitled *Nihon seifudaigai seitairon*.
35. Swale, p. 86.
36. *Pall Mall Gazette*, 26 February 1884.
37. Ibid.
38. Swale, p. 20.
39. Hall, p. 294.
40. Mori Arinori, Letters to Yokoyama Yasutake, No.10, *Mori Arinori Zenshū* Vol. 2 (Tokyo, 1972), p. 46.
41. Mori Arinori, *'Shintai no Noryoku'* in *Mori Arinori Zenshū* Vol. 1 (Tokyo, 1972), p. 328.
42. Olive Checkland, *Britain's Encounter with Meiji Japan 1868-1912* (London, 1989), p. 131.
43. For an assessment of Mori as a Spencerian 'progressive conservative' rather than a 'statist' in the mould of Stein, see Swale. pp. 184-7.
44. *Pall Mall Gazette*, 26 February 1884.

6

KAWASE MASATAKA, 1840-1919
The Longest-serving Envoy
[London, 1884-93]

Kawase Munetaka

AYAKO HOTTA-LISTER

INTRODUCTION

K awase Masataka was the Japanese Minister at the London Legation between 1884 and 1893; it was an unusually long period to occupy such a position. This was the period, particularly after the return of the Iwakura Mission, when Japan's wholesale transformation was being vigorously carried out by the new leaders. Internally, Itō Hirobumi had just returned to Japan after a year's study abroad in search of an ideal constitution for the new Japan, which was eventually enacted in 1889. However, the new objective of successive governments in this period in relation to Western countries was to conclude successfully a satisfactory revision of the so-called 'unequal treaties', which had been of the utmost importance since the first year of the Meiji period. Britain was one of those countries which had been negotiating with Japan: indeed, she was, in the eyes of the Japanese authorities, the most intransigent of all the treaty nations in refusing the Japanese proposals. While Kawase was in London, negotiating tactics changed according to the different preferences of foreign ministers in post. The Minister in London, therefore, held one of the most important posts in this period, requiring a competent man to carry out the instructions of his home government and to liaise tactfully between the two countries.

It is striking to find that, amongst all the Japanese envoys to Britain in the Meiji period, Kawase is conspicuous in two respects: there is no writing about him and he never attained any prominent job after his return from London unlike other diplomats who served in London. There is no biography about his life, nor is there a single article on him. To most Japanese people, even to historians of the nineteenth century, the name Kawase Masataka seems to be quite unfamiliar, indicating his shadowy profile. Even to established diplomatic historians, his name has hardly been heard of, despite the fact that Kawase did serve for nine years in London. Even a Japanese scholar such as Inuzuka Takaaki, whose interest is, among other things, in Japanese overseas students in the Tokugawa and early Meiji periods, and has written biographies of Japanese envoys in London, Mori Arinori and Terashima Munenori, Kawase's predecessors, has not written a book about Kawase. Again, there are biographies and memoirs of his successors, Aoki Shūzō, Katō Takaaki, Hayashi Tadasu and Komura Jutarō. Many prominent men in the Meiji and Taishō periods, with some exceptions, such as Komura, left some sort of memoirs of their own to posterity, revealing glimpses of their inner thoughts. There are no such writings left by Kawase himself. In Komura's case, there are at least a few biographical portrayals of him written by those who had been close to him, but no-one has written about Kawase. To find out anything about him, therefore, one is confronted with a shortage of material, particularly in respect of writings which would give us an insight into his inner thoughts, leaving the historian a difficult task. There are of course official printed documents and unprinted archives. Several brief profiles of him are available, equivalent to *Who's Who*, but they are often copied out from previous information without much research and thus are not necessarily accurate. Some of them only cover leaders from Chōshū (Yamaguchi prefecture), his birth place, which are often very brief and tend to emphasise the early adventurous and heroic period of Kawase's life.

In addition, there is another problem that many researchers of Japanese men in the late Tokugawa and early Meiji periods face: the use of several different names by Kawase, typical of this turbulent period. Therefore, this short paper, focusing mainly on his appointment as Minister at the London Legation, has to rely heavily upon memoirs, diaries, autobiographies and the like of Kawase's contemporaries which occasionally mention him. There is no doubt that my information on Kawase may not be exhaustive and there may still be some interesting data on him buried somewhere.

EARLY PERIOD

Kawase Masataka was born in 1840 as Ishikawa Kogorō, in Hagi, Chōshū, the son of a Hagi *Hanshi*, a retainer (*Samurai*) of the Hagi Clan. Later, his name was changed several times to Otomi Seibei, Ubeda Saburō, Kawase Yasushirō, and then to Kawase Masataka, a common practice at that time, particularly amongst those who travelled abroad under false names before the Meiji Restoration. He was educated at *Meirin Kan* in Hagi, an exclusive clan school for its employees' sons, where he is said to have sworn allegiance to the royalist group *Son-nō*.[1] His contemporary, Aoki Shūzō, also from Chōshū, harboured a bitter memory of not being allowed to study at *Meirin Kan*, as his father was not a retainer.[2] Almost every profile of Kawase in the pre-Meiji period describes his adventures in more detail than his later life. According to those records, Kawase joined Takasugi Shinsaku's internal coup in 1864 in protest against his own divided clan's decision to yield to the Tokugawa regime, thus determining the future direction of Chōshū's relation to the regime and raising Kido Takayoshi's position in the domain. In this internal battle, Kawase acted as the chief commander of a reserve army, while Itō Shunsuke (Hirobumi) also joined him leading another army. Kawase was prominent in supporting the Chōshū army against the Bakufu army until the ceasefire between them was arranged by Katsu Kaishū in

September 1866.[3] Henceforth, he enjoyed a close relationship with Kido Takayoshi (who became one of the prominent leaders at the beginning of the Meiji period), and by his influence, Kawase's fortunes improved considerably.

After being deeply involved with events which partly led to the collapse of the Tokugawa regime, he was granted leave to study abroad as many of his fellow samurai were around this time. In May 1867, Kawase was fortunate enough to be chosen to go to England to study with funds provided by the Chōshū clan alongside others who went with their own funds. Encouraged by Godai Tomoatsu, the foresighted Kido had been planning to send some mature samurai of middle-rank from Chōshū to England for the sake of the new nation and had recommended Kawase, amongst other candidates, to the authorities. After travelling to Nagasaki, supposedly to study military training, Kawase and a few of his fellow samurai sailed for England on board a ship belonging to Thomas Glover, the influential Scottish merchant, arriving in London in August.[4]

As to exactly what he did in England during his stay of about four years, we know little. We have only some sporadic references to him given by others. We know what some of his fellow travellers did after their arrival in England. For example, Mōri Tōshirō (Dohi Mataichi) studied for two years at the Gymnasium School, based on a German system, in Aberdeen, where Thomas Glover had been a student, and Fujimoto Hanzō is believed to have attended University College in London. It seems certain at least that Kawase and his three fellow students stayed with Glover's friends, the Harrisons, at Kennington in Lambeth between the end of 1867 and the beginning of 1868. Inuzuka speculates that there might have been an agreement between Chōshū and Glover that the Harrisons would look after the students after their arrival in London and that Kawase might have stayed there for some time.[5]

One document states that Kawase 'concentrated on reading and learning English after arriving in London without studying any special subject'. The paper adds that 'one year before his departure from England, he was engaged in supervising Japanese students in Britain and received regular payment from the government'.[6] Another document proves that, in May 1870, on account of his long stay in England, Otomi Seibei (Kawase), was granted some funds by the new Meiji government to continue further study, on condition that he would take on duties such as distributing public funds to government-sponsored students there, overseeing their conduct and supervising them.[7]

From one source, there was a prospect of his going to America in 1867 with Fujimoto, his fellow traveller. They were persuaded by the ever-scheming Laurence Oliphant, who seems to have worried about these naïve Japanese students being exploited by commercial entrepreneurs and tried to send them to America under the protection of the leader of a new religion, Thomas Lake Harris. They wrote a letter to Oliphant in March 1868 saying that they were willing to go to Harris. It was only a last-minute warning letter sent in the summer from the Satsuma students who suspected Harris's trickery that prevented them from leaving Britain and in the end they decided to continue to study there.[8]

From another source, we know that Kawase and his fellow Chōshū students went on 19 June 1868 to greet Sanjō Kimiyasu, son of Sanjō Sanetomi, the lord of Tokuyama, who had just arrived in London. They did so in such a fashion, the old Japanese way of bowing to the floor, that English gentlemen nearby were amazed to see such a scene and an article about it appeared in a newspaper the following day, commenting that the prince who had just arrived must have been of high rank.[9] These are some occasional traces of his activities in Britain during his first four year's stay in Britain and there is no doubt they are not exhaustive.

According to the diary of Kido Takayoshi, with whom Kawase often corresponded, Kawase returned to Japan on 30 August 1871 (Meiji 4), having being ordered by the government in April to be recalled.[10] He was at once appointed as *Kōmu Shōho*, a junior position in the engineering department, then as Lord Chamberlain (*Jijūchō*). However, each appointment must have been only for a brief period, as Kawase is supposed to have travelled back to England again later in the same year with government funding, staying there for about another two years. It was during his brief return to Japan, according to Kido's diary, that Kawase married Kido's adopted-daughter, Kiyo, on 22 November 1871.[11] However, there are two puzzling points relating to the Kawases. The first is the name of Kawase's wife; all collected documents describe her as 'Hideko', not 'Kiyo' as in Kido's diary, suggesting that the father was identified as Egawa Tarozaemon, so presumably they are the names of the same daughter. Her name may have changed at some point, as her husband's had done. The second point concerns Kawase's whereabouts at this time. The same sources tell that he was in England again between the end of 1871 and 1873, overlapping with the Iwakura Mission's stay in England. However, so far, there is no evidence of Kawase's presence there at the time. Nor is there any indication that his wife accompanied him. A few letters from Kido to Kawase, sent from England during this period, show no indication of his being in England, with one letter of 3 November 1972 congratulating him on the birth of their first child.[12] Considering their close relationship, had Kido and Kawase been in England at the same time, they would certainly have been in touch with each other, since Kawase, who presumably spoke adequate English, would have been useful to Kido and the mission. These two points need further investigation.

In a period when there was a shortage of trained diplomats, the experience of living abroad for several years was recognised as a great asset by the new Meiji government, which was mainly formed of former Chōshū and Satsuma samurai who were inclined to appoint their fellow countrymen to prominent posts. As a Chōshū man who had partly helped in bringing about the Tokugawa regime's fall, Kawase had a privileged position with more opportunities in finding many jobs of high status in the new Meiji government than other samurai without these advantages. Kawase seems to have been qualified on both counts, and was given a series of overseas appointments thereafter. Between 1873 and 1877, he was appointed as Chargé d'Affaires in Italy, covering Austria as well; then, between 1878 and 1879, he was sent back there, this time as the Minister Plenipotentiary. On two days before their departure to Europe on 6 December 1873, Kido organised a farewell party at his home for the Kawases and their family, including some entertainments for them.[13] It was during his stay in Italy that his wife, Hideko, seems to have earned high respect amongst diplomats in Rome. She is believed to have spoken to King Victor Emmanuel directly without the aid of an interpreter, which was regarded as unusually brave for a Japanese woman at the time.[14] On 3 December 1879, Kawase was awarded an honour from the King for arranging the hospitable reception for members of the Italian royal family visiting Japan in November.[15]

While he was in Japan between his overseas appointments (1879-1884), Kawase was appointed to a variety of posts in government. He was appointed as a Privy Council official, a committee councillor in crime prevention, an examiner for the army criminal code, an associate judge in the Supreme Court, a secretary to Privy Council etc.[16] We can assume that, however impressive these job titles are, they must have been superficial, as each post he took appears to have been on a short-term basis and did not result in significant achievements.

AS MINISTER IN THE LONDON LEGATION

In May 1884, Kawase was appointed as Minister to the London Legation, in succession to Mori Arinori, serving as Minister Extraordinary and Plenipotentiary of Japan in Britain. He arrived in London at the end of November with Tokugawa Yoshiakira, who came to study. Katō Takaaki, who happened to be in London for business studies, had to look after Tokugawa and his suite at the beginning of their stay, arranging for their accommodation and English teachers.[17] The London Legation, which had been moved in 1880 during his predecessor's time, was located at 9 Cavendish Square, a more central position than the previous offices in Notting Hill.

Kawase was given the rank of Viscount (*Shishaku*) in 1887 for his work. We do not know whether he was happy with the job and his life in London, or what kind of private life he led in London. As in his stay in Britain earlier on, we do not know what he was involved with in Britain other than his official duties, except that now and then Kawase's contemporaries refer to him in their private writings and articles in newspapers and other papers, reporting that either Kawase himself or he and his wife together were attending official and royal functions.

For foreign envoys in the Victorian period, there were many occasions arranged by the royal family, often by command of the Queen, such as functions, banquets and parties when attendance was a matter of obligation. Kawase and his wife were invited to most of these, like most representatives of other countries in Britain. *The Times'* Court Circular was often filled with information of events like the regular Levées, Garden Parties, Marlborough House etc and reported the names of those who attended. The names of Kawase and his wife are seldom absent from these lists.[18] It is surprising to find that one of the Japanese versions of *Who's Who* allocated Kawase's wife almost the same space as her husband, briefly describing her life in London and saying 'she was highly regarded as "Madame Kawase" amongst diplomats in Britain'.[19] However, there was no special reference to her in *The Times* newspaper.

The most spectacular royal event during Kawase's tenure as Minister in London was perhaps Queen Victoria's Golden Jubilee celebration in the summer of 1887, and Japan was one of the nations which sent notable representatives to attend the occasion. Kawase was naturally involved. Mutsu Hirokichi, the son of Mutsu Munemitsu, who had arrived in London earlier in 1887 for study, noted in his diary on 19 June that he and his Japanese friend visited Consul General Sonoda at his home in Holland Road and met Prince Komatsu, representing the emperor for the jubilee, who was there for dinner. On 21 June, the jubilee day, Mutsu and his Japanese friends went to see the grand procession, describing how crowded central London had become.[20] But many Japanese leaders and diplomats believed that not enough attention had been paid by the British to the Japanese delegation, headed by Prince Komatsu, and 'adequate honour had not been paid to him as the symbol of their state'. The blame was placed at the door of the imperial government itself for not taking the event seriously and its un-preparedness, and at that of the minister in London, who 'had not done much to create an impression by only holding a modest reception in the iegation buildings.' Not allowing a similar slight to that of 1887 to happen, Katō Takaaki, Aoki's successor, made strenuous efforts ten years later on the occasion of the Queen's Diamond Jubilee to communicate with the British authorities, succeeding in attaining from them special treatment of the Japanese delegation and its head, Prince Arisugawa, to a greater extent than Katō had expected. Katō also organised, at great expense, an extravagant banquet which impressed the world dignitaries gathered in London.[21]

It does not seem entirely fair solely to blame the British authorities and the Japanese Minister, Kawase, for the apparent failure in 1887 and to compare the occasion with the similar one in 1897. Firstly, to the mighty British Empire, the Japan of 1887 was still a country of relative insignificance. Secondly, Prince Komatsu, an uncle of the Meiji Emperor, and his suite were not sent to Britain for the exclusive purpose of celebrating the Queen's Golden Jubilee. In fact, he had been sent by the Emperor in the previous year, arriving on 22 November in Liverpool, for the purpose of investing the Prince of Wales with the First Class Order of the Chrysanthemum, as well as carrying out similar duties elsewhere in Europe. Prince Komatsu's duty had been duly carried out on 7 December 1886 at Marlborough House and those who were present at the investiture included Minister Kawase, Madame Kawase, T. Sasaki, the Consul-General for Japan and T. Nakada, attached to the Japanese Legation, as well as Sir Julian Pauncefote, Sir Philip Currie and Sir Henry Bergne, all of the Foreign Office. After his arrival in Britain, his activities were closely reported in *The Times*, which commented that Prince Komatsu's stay in England was 'evincing considerable interest in military matters.'[22] The British government had therefore been well acquainted with Prince Komatsu's presence and his task in Britain by the time of the preparations for the Jubilee. It seems likely that, Prince Komatsu, knowing of the forthcoming celebration in the summer of 1887, came back to London in time for the event after his tour of Europe. The Japanese government must have found it convenient for him to represent the Meiji Emperor. Thirdly, by 1897, Japan's standing in the world had changed and she commanded certain respect from the great powers. By then, Japan had successfully concluded part of the treaty revisions with Britain and other nations and had won the war against China. These factors probably played a significant role in Katō's success at the 1897 jubilee in obtaining world-class treatment of Japan by Britain.

During Kawase's tenure in London, at least two official societies were inaugurated, the Japanese Club at Cambridge in 1888 and the Japan Society in 1891, for both of which he became the first president on account of his official position. This was the period of the establishment of a linkage between Japan and Britain in the form of official societies by like-minded people. By this time, a sufficient number of people in both countries had been involved with the other country, one way or another, to form such societies for mutual understanding. The exact time of founding of the former club seems uncertain, but it is assumed to be in November 1888, when its first meeting was held. The members of the Japanese Club at Cambridge were drawn from the small number of Japanese students studying there and members of the London Legation. It is believed to have lasted until 1895. In 1905, the club was amalgamated with the Oxford Society of Japan to form the Cambridge-Oxford Society, as there were more Japanese graduates from Cambridge than Oxford. The Society has continued to this day, with a break during the last war.[23]

The Japan Society held its first meeting to organise the council on 8

December 1891 and its inaugural meeting was held on 29 April 1892, chaired by its first president, Kawase. He delivered the greeting from the emperor who donated the sum of 10 guineas to the society and made a speech. He said 'As regards my countrymen, I can assure you that your work will be highly appreciated by them. Their wish is for these things to be better known to the outer world and they will regard the members of the society as friends to themselves and to Japan.' It already consisted by then of 190 members. One year later, in December 1892, it had 365 members, including Kaneko Kentarō, Ernest Satow, Mutsu Hirokichi and many others, and, by December 1893, it had a membership of 430, forty of which were Japanese and twenty were French, sixteen German etc. The members of the society were therefore mostly British. Kawase was the president until his departure and now and then attended the society's meetings, often accompanied by the Viscountess, who was once reported as dressed 'in magnificent Parisian evening dress and diamonds'.[24] Mutsu, who was elected as councillor in June 1892, often noted in his diary his involvement with the society and, amongst other things, reported the Japan Society's proceedings to the Japanese newspaper *Jiji Shimpō* as its London correspondent.[25]

It was also during Kawase's period in 1885 that two popular public events related to Japan were held which seemed to offend the Japanese community's feeling in Britain: the Japanese Village and a performance of the Mikado. The Japanese Village was opened on 10 January 1885 in Knightsbridge by Sir Rutherford Alcock, the former minister to Japan, and is reported to have been very popular. The Mikado opened on 16 March at the Savoy Theatre and was again popular. The opening of the Mikado seems to have been deliberately coordinated with the popular Japanese Village. Diplomatic circles and Japanese residents, mostly students and business people, and the Japanese government are said to have deplored such events on the ground that they would greatly affect the image of Japan, presenting it as backward.[26] The entry of 16 April 1887 in Mutsu's diary simply jotted down that he '. . . dropped in at the Japanese Village with Rokugō and walked through Kensington Gardens'. He did not write any comment on what he saw. It would be interesting to find out whether this was the same Japanese Village which had originally opened in 1885 or a separate one.

Kawase, while in post, appeared to be prominently active in carrying out one particular duty during his long stay in London: this was his responsibility for the Japanese students in Britain. It may be recalled that, in 1870, towards the end of his first stay in Britain, he was unofficially asked to take on such a duty with payment from the new Meiji government. There is plenty of evidence that shows this through his correspondence with his superiors. For example, several of Kawase's letters to Inoue Kaoru are his reports on some Japanese students, often in detail, how they are getting on in their study and life in Britain, consultation, and some problems etc.[27] Most students he looked after were, after initial education elsewhere in Britain, sooner or later to study at Cambridge University, which was generally preferred to Oxford, as it was more 'practical' than 'philosophical' and thus more attractive to Japanese students.

It seems that Kawase performed these duties quite well in his dual capacity as the minister in London and the chairman of the Japanese Club at Cambridge. It seems to have suited him. Indeed, some parents in Japan of those students in Britain must have found Kawase's existence indispensable. For example, Mutsu Munemitsu, whose son, the aforesaid Hirokichi, was initially studying at

Cambridge, though not as a fully registered university student, consulted Kawase on his son's health problems whilst studying and followed Kawase's recommendation against his son's return to Japan.[28]

According to Mutsu Hirokichi's diary, after having learnt that his return to Japan was inevitable upon his father's appointment as Foreign Minister, he too consulted Kawase in November 1892. He wanted to stay in Britain as long as possible for a personal reason, so he enquired about the possibility of getting a job at the Legation. On this occasion, Kawase, apparently not knowing the reason, suggested to him that it was better to ask his father to send some more money to enable him to stay in Britain longer. It is quite possible that other parents of students might have consulted Kawase similarly.[29] Mutsu Hirokichi sometimes even borrowed money from Kawase. According to Mutsu's diary, Kawase seems to have rented a summer residence on the Isle of Wight called Rose Bank where they spent part of the summer, and they seem to have invited legation staff, students and others to stay there during the summer. Mutsu was one of those to have had this privilege of being invited by them for a couple of weeks in summer. He and his friends were taken around the island and entertained not only by Kawase himself but also Kawase's wife, whose warm personality is said to have been popular among Japanese students. Viscountess Kawase is believed to have looked after them well. For example, when Mutsu was ill, Viscountess Kawase sent a member of the legation staff, Takasaki, to see if she could do something for him. Shortly before Mutsu's departure to Japan in November 1893, she gave him a letter box as a farewell gift.[30] It is assumed that the Kawases might have treated other students similarly, though Mutsu may have been treated better than others, due to his influential father.

As the minister of the Japanese Legation in London, Kawase was expected to do a mountain of other duties. Thus, he was busy dealing with daily tasks such as liaising between home and host governments, just as any minister abroad would do. The Foreign Office's archives at the National Archives at Kew are full of letters exchanged between Jushie/Jusammi Kawase and the British authorities relating to such tasks.[31] It is striking to find that most of those were requests to the British authorities to arrange for Japanese personnel, particularly those in the Japanese Navy and naval students, to visit various British naval dockyards, factories, schools and medical schools etc. Their visits included the Royal Arsenal at Woolwich, the Royal Dockyard at Portsmouth and Chatham, the Royal Naval College, Greenwich, the Gunpowder Factory at Waltham Abbey, the Royal Naval Hospital and Army Medical School. Some requests were to get permission for them to go on board Her Majesty's ships to be trained. Most of the requests were granted, so the next stage for them was for Kawase to follow them up. Kawase seems to have been well acquainted with the procedure for such arrangements. This was the period when Japan was preparing to create a formidable Japanese Navy and Britain was generous enough to provide her pupil with the necessary facilities to learn.[32]

In August 1891, the legation office was moved to 8 Sussex Square near Hyde Park. We do not know the reason for the change and how they found the new place. Uchida Yasuya, who was posted as a secretary to the legation, arrived in London in January 1893 and described the legation: '. . . there were only three of us apart from the Minister Kawase and the Military Attaché and it was so ill-equipped that we were not able to entertain any dignitary there.'[33] The situation did not seem to change at all when Katō Takaaki took over as minister in January 1895 and complained about it to the home government, requesting its move to a more decent place: '. . . the location was wrong . . . and the offices were old and small, and their layout was inconvenient.'[34]

Kawase appears to have kept a low profile during his tenure in London, yet he surprises us with one notable thing. Other than normal official correspondence, Kawase wrote an article entitled 'Tekkō' ('Iron Industry') in 1886, which, together with articles of other contributors, was later compiled by the Ministry of Finance in 1892 in a paper called *Tekkō* ('Thoughts on Iron'). His phrase, 'Our next door neighbour is China, which has plenty of iron' was quoted by the author, Shinobu Seizaburō, of *Mutsu Gaikō* ('Diplomacy of Mutsu'). Unfortunately, we do not know the article's contents and what circumstance prompted him to write it. So far, he never gives us the impression of his being a China expert. It would be interesting to find out more about this and whether or not this was an isolated one-off publication.[35]

Kawase took a long leave of one year between November 1888 and November 1889, during which time Okabe Nagamoto was acting Chargé d'Affaires. We do not know why his leave was exceptionally long and what he did in Japan.

Kawase's posting in Britain for a total of nine years was unusually long by any standards. Since he had stayed in Britain twice before for a total of approximately six years, the government may have found him the most suitable man available at the time. Probably he may initially have been appointed for a normal term and had his stay extended later. Evidence suggests that there was a time when his return to Japan was postponed for the time being. He reported to Inoue Kaoru on July 1889, while he was on leave in Japan, on possible changes.[36] This suggests that he could have initially been appointed to the post for a length of time shorter than he actually stayed. The change could have happened during his leave in Japan. As was a common practice in this period, some Chōshū leaders such as Itō and Inoue may have suggested that he should stay in Britain longer than the period initially proposed. But it is not clear who was responsible for the ultimate decision.

There was a time that the appointment of Kawase to a more prominent post was considered while he was in London. After the collapse of Foreign Minister Inoue's proposal for treaty revision followed by his resignation, Prime Minister Itō took up the post as well as his own. He considered sending Aoki, with whom he was not on good terms, to Germany, and promoting Kawase from London to the post of Foreign Minister. However, Inoue objected to such an idea, saying in his letter to Itō on 29 October 1887 that Itō should either keep the post himself or choose Enomoto Takeaki, who was, to him, more suitable than Kawase for the post, and insisting that Aoki should be given Enomoto's post, Minister of Communication.[37] The impression given is that Kawase was not a man of forceful and assertive personality as were his predecessors and successors in London such as Mori Arinori, Aoki Shūzō and Katō Takaaki. They seem to have known what they wanted and tried hard to have their voice heard by their superiors and often succeeded in influencing the home government's policies.

AS MINISTER IN LONDON LEGATION – DEALING WITH TREATY REVISION

In this period, the issue of treaty revision was given the highest priority by Japan. Kawase's stay in London coincided with Japan's important negotiations for treaty revision with Britain, the most intransigent of all nations. He dealt with the question under Foreign Ministers Inoue, Ōkuma, Aoki and Enomoto, and witnessed one failure after another until Mutsu's period in charge.

Was Kawase a competent man in London who was able to deal with this most important issue? The position of minister or ambassador in London was regarded as the most respectable and important in the diplomatic world before the First World War, due to Britain's standing in the world. Therefore, it was natural for a government to select a suitable man. Did Kawase live up to the expectation of his superiors in this respect? Many questions were raised during the course of this research. With the benefit of hindsight and despite the lack of information, one can see clearly that there was a low-profile period in the London position, sandwiched between the prominent and influential men who later took high and important positions in governments, such as Mori, Aoki and Katō. Despite the fact that their stays in London were much shorter than that of Kawase, they are inclined to boast about their achievements on treaty revision negotiations and other matters in their writings, particularly in Aoki's case. But Kawase, on the other hand, seems to be left in oblivion because he did not publish any account of his career.

Kawase was expected to be at least a good liaison officer between the British and Japanese authorities on the issue of treaty revision: as far as official documents and archives are examined, indeed, he seems to have done what he was instructed to do by his superiors, just as his predecessors had done. He visited British Foreign Office staff to explain his home government's views, requesting some clarification of points in question and negotiating and corresponding with them. According to diplomatic documents, he seems generally to have reiterated what his superiors had instructed him to do and acted on behalf of them. Moreover, although he was not as expert on the subject and as eloquent as his fellow diplomats, he was able to state his case where necessary, as he did to Sir Julian Pauncefote, Deputy Under-Secretary at the Foreign Office, on 17 November 1886. Referring to the period beyond the expiration of the seventeen-year-treaty, Kawase said to him, 'I fully understand the British desire to employ foreign judges in Japan. However, the Japanese government regards this point as the most important aspect of this issue and, personally, I feel rather strongly about it, quite different from other mundane instructions I receive from my government, thus I have my own opinion on this matter. Therefore, I can not agree to your proposal.' Kawase went on to explain the reason why he disagreed, the result of which, after some exchanges of opinions between them, was an agreement on the issue under discussion between Kawase and the British Foreign Secretary on 30 November.[38]

Such cases appear to be rare, however. Evidence suggests Kawase may not have been a competent negotiator for such a sensitive issue as treaty revision. It has been noted earlier that Inoue and Itō referred to his ability in a negative way and Mutsu certainly seems to have thought him unsuitable for the job.[39] According to the limited evidence available, he might have been a good liaison officer, but not an experienced diplomat of high calibre, particularly when dealing with sophisticated and experienced British diplomats. A slap in the face for Kawase came in 1893 when Mutsu Munemitsu appointed Aoki Shūzō, the then minister in Germany, to take over Kawase's position and start negotiating with Britain over treaty revision, combining it with his existing post as minister in Berlin, despite the fact that Mutsu, and indeed some other leaders, disliked Aoki.[40] However, there was one main reason that can clearly be seen: the urgency of his decision. It was a time when the British Minister to Tokyo, Hugh

Fraser, was staying in England on leave and Mutsu considered Aoki indispensable for negotiating with him. When Aoki had taken up the post of Foreign Minister in December 1889, it was with Fraser that he had negotiated on treaty revision in Tokyo, thus both were well acquainted on the issue. On that occasion, Aoki came close to success in agreeing with Fraser. Signature was only prevented by the Ōtsu Incident, which caused the dissolution of the government. It seems that the idea of giving a second chance to Aoki derived from the regret Itō and Inoue had long felt about Aoki's misfortune. As soon as Mutsu completed his plan, which the cabinet unanimously approved in July 1893, he sent letters first to Kawase explaining his intention of carrying out treaty revision with Britain and asking him to assist Aoki who would be the main negotiator and then to Aoki informing him accordingly. Whether Mutsu had any intention of replacing Kawase with Aoki as minister to London at this stage is uncertain. However, to Mutsu, it was vital not to miss this opportunity of Fraser's leave in London, which preoccupied him at the time. He requested Maurice de Bunsen, Chargé d'Affaires in Tokyo, to persuade the home government to keep Fraser in London until the negotiation with Aoki had been completed.

It was around the middle of September 1893 that Mutsu finally decided to replace Kawase with Aoki as Minister in London when there was a prospect of moving the negotiations from Tokyo to London, as had been proposed by Mutsu as his strategy, away from disturbance at home. After having discussed the matter with Kawase, Aoki started preliminary studies and held an exchange of views with Fraser in the autumn.

Although Mutsu may not appear to have been much concerned with sparing Kawase's feelings, he did show some sympathy towards him. As soon as Mutsu officially decided to replace Kawase with Aoki as the minister in London, he sent a letter to Sone Arasuke, then the minister in Paris, asking him to talk it over with Kawase in the hope that Kawase would not resent such a decision. According to the letter, Mutsu seems to have been concerned with Kawase's feelings. Sone was also from Chōshū and they were of the same generation. Although no communication between Kawase and Sone has been found, it is quite possible that Sone did try to soften the blow.[41] Moreover, Mutsu arranged to honour Kawase with a post in the Privy Council upon his return to Japan in order to save Kawase's face, as though this was the reason for his return to Japan. One brief *Who's Who* source clearly describes this as the case.[42]

With regard to the treatment of Kawase, it has to be borne in mind that it was not an isolated case. The minister in Washington at the same period was also treated similarly by Mutsu, solely in order to conclude treaty revision with the U.S. Tateno Gōzō, who is believed not to have been trusted by the Americans, was replaced in August 1894 by Kurino Shinichirō, who succeeded in signing the new treaty on 22 November of that year.[43] We all know that Mutsu's overall strategy worked well and Japan finally extended the unequal treaties revised with Britain in July 1894, to treaties with other nations.

Kawase and his wife left London on 20 December 1893 arriving back to Tokyo on 4 February 1894. Upon his return to Japan, he took up the post that had been offered as Privy Councillor and later in 1897 he combined the post with Gitei-kan until his death. He died on 29 September 1919 at the age of eighty, suffering from stomach cancer.

EPILOGUE

When Mutsu, with his strong personality, who knew the London scene, took charge as Foreign Minister and wished London to be the centre of the negotiation for treaty revision, it appears to have been obvious to him that Kawase was not up to the job. However, it is more likely that, to Mutsu, whether Kawase was a competent diplomat or not was not as important as the fact that Aoki was the right man for the job at the right time. It is remarkable, therefore, that, apart from being a go-between, Kawase was involved very little with treaty revision negotiations, which were being handled mainly in Tokyo until Aoki took over.

As far as the collected and available materials are examined, Kawase Masataka kept a low profile, almost to the point that he was in London as a liaison officer, rather than a diplomat. If he were a diplomat indeed, as in truth he was, he must have been one of those stereotypical 'cardboard figures', the term often used of Japanese by the West, rather than those whose personalities affected policies. It seems to me that Kawase was one of those diplomats who, 'being under very strict orders from the Gaimushō, has little personal discretion or independence'.[44] He seems to stand out in this way because he was sandwiched between diplomats with strong personal characteristics, Mori and Aoki. Nonetheless, there is no doubt that he had the longest tenure in London and was the longest serving envoy in the whole of Japanese legation and embassy history to date.

NOTES

For this paper, I am especially grateful to Mr Haruhisa Takeuchi, a former minister in London who had collected some materials on Kawase, particularly his earlier period before his appointment to London. Furthermore, I acknowledge the help of Mrs Sachiko Mutsu, the wife of late Mr Yōnosuke Ian Mutsu, the grandson of Munemitsu Mutsu, who kindly lent me the diary of her father-in-law, Hirokichi Mutsu, during Kawase's stay in London.

1   Yoshida, Shōsaku, *Kinsei Bōchō Jinmei Jiten* (Dictionary of Names in Chōshū Region (Yamaguchi Pref.), (Tokyo, 1976) p.82;

Yamaguchi City (ed.), *History of Yamaguchi City*, (Yamaguchi, 1982), pp.807-8;

Nihon Rekishi Gakkai (ed.), *Meiji Ishin Jinmei Jiten* (Dictionary of Names in the period of the Meiji Restoration), (Tokyo, 1981);

Nihon Shiseki Kyōkai, *Hyakkan Rireki* (Brief Profile of Hundred Officials), (Tokyo, 1927), p.197-8 (Hereafter *Hyakkan*).

2.   Sakane, Yoshihisa, *Meiji Gaikō to Aoki Shūzō* ('Meiji Diplomacy and Aoki Shūzō'), (Tokyo, 1985), p.4 (Hereafter *Aoki*).

3.   Suehiro Kinko (ed.), *Bōchō Jinbutsu Hyakunen-Shi* ('Hundred years history of Men from Chōshū'), (Tokyo, 1967), pp.183-4 (Hereafer *Bōchō*).

4.   Inuzuka, Takaaki, *Meiji Ishin Taigai Kankeishi Kenkyu*, (1977, 7), pp.150-3, (Hereafter Inuzuka);

Dajō Ruiten, Vol. 1, No. 61, p.46 (National Diet Library, Gikai Kanchō Shiryō-shitsu).

5.   Inuzuka, pp. 170, 180.

6.   Mōri Family Collection, *Han Shin Rireki* ('personal history of Mōri Clan, the Lord of Chōshū'), *Shoshin Jiseki Gairyaku* ('brief information on the Clan's employees'), Vol. 2.

7.   Inuzuka, p.179.

8.   Ibid. pp.170-3.

9.   Ozaki Saburō, *Ozaki Saburō Jijō Ryakuden* ('Ozaki Saburo's Brief Autobiography'), Vol. 1, (Tokyo 1976), p.104.

10.   Brown, S.D, & A. Hirota (transl.), *The Diary of Kido Takayoshi*, Vol. II (1871-4), (Tokyo 1985), p.67 (Hereafter *Kido Diary*);

Dajō Ruiten, Vol. 1, No. 119, 3 April Meiji 4 (1871) at the National Diet Library, Gikai Kanchō Shiryō-shitsu ('the archive room for the Diet and public office').

11. *Kido Diary*, p.100.
12. Kido-Kō Denki Hensansho, *Kido Takayoshi Monjo* ('Letters related to Kido'), Vol.4, (Tokyo, 1930), pp.391-3, pp.416-20.
13. *Kido Diary*, p.404.
14. *Nihon Jinmei Daijiten* ('Who's Who'), (Tokyo 1979), p.212 (Hereafter *Jinmei*).
15. *Hyakkan*, Vol. 1, p.197.
16. *Bōchō* p.184.
17. Itō Masanori, *Katō Takaaki*, Vol. 1, (Tokyo, 1929), pp.177-8 (Hereafter *Katō*).
18. *The Times*, 1884-1893.
19. *Jinmei* (Tokyo 1979), p.212.
20. *Mutsu Hirokichi Diary*, 1887, 19 and 21 June 1887 (Hereafter *Mutsu Diary*).
21. Nish, Ian, 'Itō Hirobumi's Overseas Sojourns' in *Collected Writings of Ian Nish*, Part 2, (Richmond 2001), p.41;
    Katō, Vol. 1 pp.340-5;
    Kimizuka, Naotaka, *Jyōō Heika no Blue Ribbon* ('Her Majesty the Queen's Blue Ribbon'), (Tokyo 2004), p.122.
22. *The Times*, 28 August, 22 November, 1, 3, 8 December 1886, 4 July 1887.
23. Koyama Noboru, *Meiji Ryugakusei-den* ('Meiji Japanese students'), (Tokyo 1999), pp.16, 173.
24. *The Queen*, the Lady's Newspaper, 8 July 1893.
25. Japan Society, London, *Transactions and Proceedings*, Vol. 1-2 (1892-93), pp. viii,1; Mutsu, Hirokichi, 'The Japan Society in London' in *Jiji Shimpō*, 7 July 1893.
26. Checkland, Olive, 'Japanese Life in Britain' in *Britain's Encounter with Meiji Japan, 1868-1912*, (London 1989), pp.162-3.
27. Foreign Ministry, *Inoue Kaoru Kankei Monjo*, 'Kawase Masataka', ('documents related to Inoue Kaoru'), Letters from Kawase to Inoue, 15 July 1889, 18,26 Nov. 1890, 5 May 1891.
28. *Mutsu Diary*, 19 April, 20 July 1890.
29. Ibid, 24 November 1892.
30. Ibid, 30 July-16 August 1887, 24 July 1890, 4 Nov. 1893.
31. Foreign Office's official letters to Kawase were addressed as 'Jushie Kawase', 'the fourteenth rank', or later 'Jusammi Kawase', 'the thirteenth rank'. Officials in early Meiji liked to be addressed by their rank and Foreign Office followed this form of address. Mori Arinori was often addressed, likewise, 'Jushie Mori'.
32. Foreign Office, *Foreign Office Documents*, FO46-340, 374, 392, 403, 413. Another task which Kawase was required to perform was the recruitment of experts to join the cadre of foreigners who were assisting Japan in the Meiji period. We know that Imperial University of Tokyo sought a professor of sanitary engineering in 1886 and instructed Kawase to canvas expert opinion in Britain and conduct the necessary interviews. It was a responsible task. He chose W.K. Burton who joined Imperial University as Professor in 1887 and served there until his death in 1899. This was an administrative task of responsibility for Kawase. Inaba Kikuo, 'Life of Professor William K. Burton', pp. 15-16.
33. Ikei Masaru, *Uchida Yasuya*, (Tokyo, 1969), pp.17-8.
34. *Katō*, p.243.
35. Shinobu Seizaburō, *Mutsu Gaikō, Nisshin Sensō no Gaikō Shi-Teki Kenkyu*, ('Diplomacy of Mutsu: the Sino-Japanese war'), (Tokyo 1935), pp.104-5.
36. *Inoue Kaoru Kankei Monjo*, No. 355-2, 15 July 1889.
37. Itō Hirobumi Kankei Monjo Kenkyukai (Ed.), *Itō Hirobumi Kankei Monjo*, Vol. 1, (Tokyo 1973), pp. 223-224 (Hereafter sited as *Itō*);
    Aoki, p.63.
38. Foreign Ministry, *Nihon Gaikō Monjo*, Vol. 19, No. 32, 35, 36;
    Kajima, Morinosuke, *Nihon Gaikō-Shi* ('Japanese diplomatic history'), pp.89-90 (Hereafter 'Kajima').
39. *Itō*, p.224;
    Okazaki Hisahiko, *Mutsu Munemitsu* (Tokyo 1988), p.200.
40. Perez, Louis G, *Mutsu Munemitsu and the Revision of the 'Unequal Treaties'*, (Univ. of Michigan, 1986), p.200;
    Nish, I. H., *Japanese Foreign Policy, 1869-1942: Kasumigaseki to Miyakezaka*. (London 1977), pp.45, 56-7.
41. *Mutsu Munemitsu Monjo*, No. 153-22, on 22 September 1893.

42. Hata Ikuhiko (Ed.), *Nihon Kin-Gendai Jinbutsu Rireki Jiten* ('Who's Who in modern Japan'), (Tokyo, 2002), p.172;
    Umi o Koeta Nihonjinmei Jiten ('The dictionary of the Japanese who crossed the seas'), (Tokyo 1985), p.212.
43. Kajima, p.208.
44. Ian Nish, 'Diplomats in Japan', p.174.

7

AOKI SHŪZŌ, 1844-1914
Brief Encounter
[London, 1894]

IAN NISH

Aoki Shūzō

W hen Commodore Perry visited Japan, Aoki Shūzō (1844-1914) was nine years of age. He was born in Hagi in the western part of Honshu island and went in his teens to the Chōshū clan academy, Meirinkan, and then to medical school, Kōseidō. As was the common practice at the time, he was adopted by a prominent family, in this case that of the famous president of the school, Aoki Kenzō. Taking the name of Shūzō, he moved to Nagasaki in 1867 to complete his studies in medicine and was instructed to go to Prussia for three years for further study at the expense of the Chōshū clan. He reached Marseilles in December 1868 and proceeded to Berlin. Aoki soon found himself in a country at war and became 'intoxicated' (as he said) with the Franco-Prussian War and the contrast between the performances of the Prussian and French armies.[1]

Because of Aoki's first-hand observation of the conflict, his career pattern changed. He began to study politics and his status changed to that of a *ryugakusei* (student abroad) for the central government of the New Japan in the New Germany. In 1873, he became a first secretary in the Gaimusho (Foreign Ministry), and entered the central government bureaucracy for the first time. In August of the following year he was appointed minister to Germany at the absurdly early age of thirty and was to spend much of the first half of his working career there.

While still a student acquiring the German language and the know-how about the most progressive nation on the continent of Europe at that time, he was much in demand from the Iwakura Mission which visited Europe in 1872-3. One of the influential members of that star-studded mission was Aoki's clansman, Kido Takayoshi (Kōin). In August 1872, Aoki visited the commissioners soon after they reached London and briefed Kido about what the mission might expect on the continent. He obviously had an insatiable curiosity and his enthusiasm clearly impressed Kido. When they reached Berlin in March, Aoki's help was indispensable both because of his fluency in German and his sheer knowledge of the country.[2] Moreover the group of those studying in Germany had already acquired a circle of foreign friends who admired 'the fast progress that the 70 or so Japanese studying in Berlin had made'. They praised their high motivation and their good examination results. As a reward for Aoki's enthusiasm he was allowed to accompany the mission on its travels to Russia in April. Presumably his ability as an interpreter in German was deemed to be useful on the long rail journey to St Petersburg.[3]

After a spell of leave, he returned to Germany as minister in the autumn of 1874. He had from time to time additional responsibilities as minister to Austria, Holland, Denmark and Norway. In 1877 he married Baroness Elizabeth von Rade and this was useful for his diplomatic activities in Germany where court diplomacy was important. Two years later his daughter Hanako (Hanna, sometimes Hanni) was born. From this point Aoki's life-style became increasingly Europeanized; and it was said that the language which was most frequently heard in his household was German. This makes it strange for him to be included in this book. But, if Aoki was a Germanophile, there is a strong current running through his diplomatic career of concern with Britain. This was only to be expected in the light of Britain's dominance in world affairs and the large number of British nationals who lived and traded in the treaty ports of Japan.[4]

It was a sign of Aoki's standing that during a period of leave he had a memorable talk in Inoue's residence with Sir Harry Parkes, shortly before he left Tokyo. In 1880 he returned for another five-year stint in Berlin. At the end of his life he wrote an incomplete memoir of part of his career which was not published during his lifetime. In it he tells of a memorandum he wrote, arising out of discussions with the redoubtable Lord Ampthill, who as Odo Russell served as the British ambassador in Berlin from 1871 till his death in 1884. Aoki ruminated that Japan, if she were to grow as a nation, needed an alliance with either Britain or Germany. France, he wrote, was not in the running after she had been defeated in the Franco-Prussian War and while she was engaged in war with China, though she had made approaches to Japan with that in mind. He gives an account of conversations he had with Bismarck, the German chancellor, on this point. He was conscious that Japan could become a most useful ally to a European power in the east. Above all, he wanted Japan to attain equality with the powers. His long-term objective was to align his country with Britain and Germany and prevent Russia's southern expansion.[5]

Since this was a time of alliances centring on Bismarck and the New Germany, it was not unnatural that Aoki should address the problem of how Japan should fit into the European alliance system. It was to remain a great political concern for him right down to the turn of the century. It is of course very relevant to the later Anglo-Japanese Alliance that experienced Japanese diplomats like him were already in the 1880s acknowledging the need for Japan to have an ally or allies. It may seem odd that a person who was so Germanophile should consider the merits of a British alignment so seriously at this time. But that, I believe, was a mark of the Realpolitik with which Aoki had become imbued during his stay in Germany.

On his return to Japan in 1885, Aoki assisted in the ministry. It was at this time that he penned the above memorandum and spoke along these lines to Inoue Kaoru as foreign minister. He was appointed vice-minister in March 1887.

His main task was to assist in pushing ahead with plans for treaty revision. While Inoue resigned in July, Aoki continued to serve under his successor and concerned himself with the treaties.

FOREIGN MINISTER

On 24 December 1889, Aoki was promoted to foreign minister in the first cabinet presided over by Yamagata Aritomo. This appointment was due to his clan connections. There were various factions associated with the Chōshū clan and Aoki belonged to the Yamagata branch whose moment had now arrived. This was in itself a notable development because Aoki was the first foreign minister who came from the corps of diplomats rather than what could loosely be called 'politicians'. It was to set a trend that was to be followed in cabinets down to 1945 with remarkably few exceptions, namely that the foreign minister would come from a background of diplomatic service.

It was the renegotiation of the treaties of early Meiji that had the highest priority in Japan's diplomacy at the time. The subject had been discussed from time to time over the previous two decades without any results; but it took on a new urgency with the coming of the new Imperial Diet which was due to open in 1890. In the elections which were held that summer, the new opposition parties latched on to the populist issues and attacked particularly the failure of the previous government to make any headway over treaty revision. The first Diet was convened on 29 November and attacked the government on many issues. The Diet had powers which forced the administration to act cautiously in adopting new approaches in diplomatic negotiations. Constitutionally it became necessary to obtain the approval of a majority of Diet members in order to bring new treaties into force. So it was essential for any government negotiating agreements to remember that they would in due course have to obtain ratification by the Diet.[6]

Aoki hated and feared the Diet. He did not enjoy appearing before it. Yet as a good diplomat he emphasized its xenophobic attitudes over treaty revision to his own advantage. He left the powers with the impression that, if they did not give concessions, the treaties would be denounced as a result of the new strong parliamentary opposition which was spreading to public opinion and that the foreign communities would stand to lose everything.

Aoki decided to concentrate initially on Britain which had a bad reputation for holding up treaty revision in previous decades and abandoned the multi-national approaches which had hitherto been followed. His aim was to recover for Japan judicial and tariff autonomy simultaneously. He approached Britain first because it was she who held the most pronounced views on the need for reforming the judicial system before she would give up extraterritorial rights for her nationals and on the need for assurances over tariffs because she was Japan's largest trading partner.

A few days after taking up office, Aoki passed on his personal plans to Hugh Fraser, the British minister in Tokyo. After he had secured cabinet approval he presented the proposals formally on 28 February 1890. On 15 July after the complex matter had been scrutinized in London, Fraser responded by passing over the draft of a treaty of commerce and navigation and a protocol drawn up in Whitehall.[7]

In the tense political atmosphere of the early Diet period, the Yamagata cabinet adopted on 3 March 1891 a comprehensive government policy on a

possible revised Anglo-Japanese treaty. It was passed on to Fraser who rather
optimistically expected negotiations with London to proceed smoothly since the
British draft of the previous July seemed to have met the Japanese demands
halfway; but domestic political turmoil in Japan prevented the matter being
settled so quickly. Yamagata resigned on 9 April and, though Aoki continued
under his successor, he too resigned on 29 May assuming responsibility as
foreign minister for the violent knife attack on the Russian Crown Prince at Otsu
during a visit to the Japanese countryside. Whether Aoki need have assumed the
responsibility for the notorious Otsu incident is a moot point; but he was a man
of conscience and the Foreign Ministry was one part of the administration
involved with the tsarevich's reception. Although the incident was small, it was
the symbol for a lot of anti-foreignism and violence against foreign nationals
which followed the opening of the Diet.[8]

These incidents led the British and Japanese governments to identify a
common interest. Both wanted to hold the negotiations away from the
penetrating and predominantly hostile gaze of the new Diet members and the
urban crowds which supported the political opposition. On 26 May 1892,
Minister Fraser took the initiative to suggest 'a resumption of negotiations in
London through Viscount Kawase, rather than in Tokyo'.[9] While the Japanese
certainly wanted to avoid negotiating in Tokyo, they regarded Kawase who had
been minister in London since 1884 as unsuitable to steer through talks of this
complexity. They replied that Viscount Aoki who had just been posted to Berlin
on 27 January as envoy had more knowledge of the matter than his colleague in
London and would be transferred for this purpose. Kawase who had served as
the first president of the Japan Society of London following its foundation in
1891, was now recalled and became adviser to the Privy Council (*sumitsu
komonkan*).[10]

BRITISH TREATY REVISED

Mutsu Munemitsu, who became foreign minister in August 1892 was ready to
build on Aoki's earlier talks with Fraser on this subject. On 15 September 1893,
Aoki was instructed to go over to London for talks on treaty revision. Fraser and
the other stalwart of the treaty negotiations at the Tokyo end, John Harrington
Gubbins, had by prior arrangement returned to Britain on leave. From his initial
talks with Aoki, Fraser concluded that Japan was not yet ready to make enough
concessions and felt that Britain should not accept the radical terms which she
was proposing. Mutsu had therefore to go back to the drawing board and present
fresh proposals in November. Aoki visited Britain again in December in order to
have further discussions with Fraser before the latter departed again for Japan at
the end of the year and convinced him that the revised proposals were a
sufficient basis for negotiations. When it looked as though these preliminary
parleys would succeed, Aoki was appointed as temporary minister to Britain with
plenipotentiary powers to discuss treaty revision on 5 December. He finally
presented his credentials on 22 February 1894.[12]

Aoki was active at the London legation from February onwards. The legation
was at that time so small that Aoki had to do most of the negotiation himself,
ably assisted by the young Uchida Yasuya behind the scenes.[13] By the very
nature of the subject Aoki had a considerable discretion and on a few occasions
acted against the wishes of Minister Mutsu and Vice-minister Hayashi Tadasu in
Tokyo. On the British side, the main negotiator was Francis Bertie, assisted by

Gubbins. The official negotiating sessions began on 2 April and were held in secret at roughly fortnightly intervals through to July. After six months the negotiations were complete. The new Anglo-Japanese Treaty of Commerce and Navigation was signed on 16 July. Extraterritorial jurisdiction by consuls was abolished; Japan beyond the treaty ports was to be opened to British and foreign traders; and new legal codes were to be introduced before the treaty came into force, perhaps in five years' time. Ratifications were exchanged with great expedition on 25 August.[14]

Although Aoki had made a decisive contribution to the revision of the British treaty, the ultimate accolade for achieving the treaty with Britain went to Mutsu Munemitsu.[15] There is some justice in this. Aoki rightly deserves the credit for conducting the tricky negotiations on a highly technical subject in London where things were made difficult by the known opposition of the British merchants in Japanese ports who wanted to preserve the status quo. In recognition of his endeavours, Aoki and his colleagues, Baron von Siebold and Uchida, were awarded Japanese decorations.[16] On the other hand, Mutsu had to face Japanese politicians and the public who were unhappy about many of the aspects of the new treaty which they chose to interpret as 'a Japanese concession'. At both ends it was a most difficult political operation.

Perhaps its acceptance in the Japanese Diet was eased when war broke out between Japan and China at the beginning of August. Since all the European powers had advised Japan against going to war, it suddenly became important for Japanese diplomats to try to win friends for their cause and influence public and press opinion abroad. Aoki with his vast experience of European courts was, like his amanuensis Baron von Siebold, adept at this as the following telegram to Tokyo will indicate:

> Daily Telegraph friendly; Times and other leading papers changing tone on last information being judiciously employed; secured the cooperation of several press and telegraph agencies beside Reuter. English authority Westlake expressed publicly Naniwa was right by international law. . . .
> You should supply me with about £1000 sterling for secret service.

When one considers that £1000 in 1894 is equivalent to £70,000 today (1998), it is apparent that Aoki had mastered some of the gentle arts of persuasion in the London press world.[17]

Aoki was ordered to return to Germany at the end of the month after one year's responsibility in Britain. His appointment as minister plenipotentiary to Britain terminated on 23 November. This was partly because of the war crisis and partly because Germany was next on the list of powers with which treaty negotiations were to be taken up. Mutsu found that the reactions of the European powers to the war were very difficult to interpret and depended greatly on the advice and good judgement of his representatives overseas. The powers which called on Japan for restraint against China during the war tended to be Britain and Russia. Russia was allied with France which was likely to support her ally. Was it likely that Britain or Germany would ever consider intervening on Russia's side?

These speculations came to practical reality after 17 April when China and Japan signed the Treaty of Shimonoseki. Some of the powers because of sympathy for China and their national interest felt that Japan was demanding too much. Mutsu, who had been expecting outside intervention all along, felt confident from his success over the British commercial treaty (1894) and other evidence that Britain would not join Russia and guessed that Russia would not act on her own. What he had not bargained for was the strong support which Germany decided to give to France and Russia in making up the *Dreibund* or Triplice of intervening powers. When asked his views on the likelihood of Germany's intervention, Aoki gave Mutsu a very conceited answer to the following effect: 'So long as I stay here I will never allow Germany to stand against Japan. Please do not worry yourself so much about it.' As it turned out, Germany took a leading part in the intervention. Soon after the German protest was made in Tokyo in very forceful terms by her minister, Freiherr von Gutschmid, Mutsu sent Aoki a telegram saying teasingly: 'What did you mean by your previous message reading. . . .?'[18]

To be sure, Aoki changed his tune at the very last minute on 13 April and conceded that Germany was inclined to be more interventionist. But his optimistic reports over the previous months appear to have seriously misjudged the situation; Germany's overtures to join Russia and France in intervening had already been underway since mid-March. This illustrates the self-confidence and rashness of Aoki and the hostility underlying his relationship with Mutsu.[19]

Meanwhile, Aoki was busy negotiating the German-Japanese treaty which was based on the British model. It was signed on 4 April 1896. To his consternation Aoki was on 1 September 1897 ordered to return to Japan because he had exceeded his authority on the occasion of signing the German treaty. On 8 February 1898 he left his posts as minister to Germany and Belgium (where he had also been responsible for concluding a new commercial treaty).

The British and German treaties formed the core of treaties with all the trading powers whose revision was celebrated in Tokyo in the summer of 1899. These were the culmination of a quarter-century of hard work and determination. Aoki's contribution to resolving this, the most important issue of the first half of the Meiji period, was substantial and has to be recognized at three levels: his period at the Foreign Ministry where the ground plan was sketched; his personal negotiations with Britain which were tenacious (from the British perspective); his negotiations elsewhere in Europe.[20]

Nonetheless, Aoki's diplomatic career in Europe ended unhappily. At this exalted stage of his career, Aoki found it very hard to accept directions from Tokyo where he felt that those in charge were his juniors. The telegrams he sent from Berlin to the Foreign Ministry were often couched in a rather superior tone. But Mutsu had as a result of the Japanese victory in the war with China been made a Count. When he received an over-confident telegram from Aoki who had the misfortune to be still only a Viscount, he responded by sending him a telegram saying that Counts did not expect counter-instructions from mere Viscounts.

FOREIGN MINISTER AGAIN

On Aoki's return to Japan, he again benefited from a strange reversal of fortune. On 8 November 1898 he was appointed foreign minister in the second Yamagata cabinet, the same position that he had occupied in the first. It must be assumed that he was again favoured because of his Chōshū connections and the goodwill of Yamagata. He brought to the task a fervent hatred of Russia and a predisposition towards Russia's rivals. Also he became in 1900 head of the *Dai Nippon Butokukai* (Great Japan Martial Arts Association), which may suggest that he was recognized as belonging to the right-wing.[21]

His frequent conversations with Sir Ernest Satow, the British minister in Tokyo, show that he – and Japanese opinion – was watching every move by Russia in Korea, the Liaotung Peninsula in China and the East generally. He appeared anxious to act along with Britain. His notion was that the powers were anxious to take advantage of Britain's entanglement in the South African War and were likely to try to capitalize on the uproar in China connected with the Boxer Rebellion from 1899 onwards.[22]

Britain, embarrassed at the simultaneous outbreak on two fronts, took the lead in asking for Japan's assistance by sending troops to north China to join the international expedition for the relief of the foreign legations in Beijing. Aoki was inclined to be positive. He supported the sending of a Japanese expeditionary force to China on 15 June 1900. But, when Britain asked for the Japanese force to be increased, he faced substantial disagreement in the Japanese cabinet which decided that Japan should first take soundings among the world powers. They responded half-heartedly, on the whole urging Japan evasively not to take independent action.

On 8 July Britain, thinking that Japan's reluctance was caused by financial constraints, took the unprecedented step of offering to defray Japan's necessary expenses in sending a division of troops to take part in the international force. Aoki was swayed by Britain's appeal but also by his acute suspicion of Russia's actions if Japan alone were to send such a large force. He often judged things in European terms and appears to have thought that Britain's enemies were forming a continental coalition and that these enemies were the same enemies that Japan had faced in the 1895 Dreibund. He again proposed that Japan should respond favourably to the approach, urging that she would become 'a partner in world history and in the progress of the world'. In spite of serious disagreements within the cabinet and words of caution from Yamagata and General Katsura Tarō as minister of war, reinforced by the *Genro* (Elder statesman) Itō Hirobumi, Aoki's approach surprisingly prevailed. The Japanese decided to mobilize the 5th Division for sending to China. The British money was, however, not accepted. While Japan was serving her own national interest in joining Britain and the powers in their endeavours in saving the legations, she was also responding to a rather special vote of confidence from Britain for powers only distribute largesse to trustworthy partners. And Aoki acknowledged that fact.[23]

The Boxer Rebellion ended with much recrimination between those powers who had troops on Chinese soil, puffed up with the success of relieving the Peking legations. Britain and Japan were at one in distrusting the actions of the Russian armies in the north. In this Britain found an unexpected ally in Germany and concluded an Anglo-German agreement on China (known to the Germans as the *Yangtse Abkommen*) on 16 October 1900 which proclaimed the territorial integrity of China and the importance of the Open Door there. We can imagine that Aoki liked this treaty between the two countries closest to his heart and would as foreign minister have wanted his country to join in it. But the Yamagata cabinet which had only stayed in office to see through the Boxer emergency offered its resignation on the 19th. It was left to Aoki's successor to adhere formally to this agreement on 29 October, which was to prove a most significant stepping-stone on the way to the Anglo-Japanese alliance. But possibly Aoki made his views known before he left office.[24]

Aoki became a privy councilior in November 1901 but was offered no other posting straightaway. He lived in aristocratic style which reflected the nature of diplomacy at the time. He had houses at Kami Nibancho in Tokyo and in

Chuzenji. His daughter Hanako, at the age of twenty-five, married Count Hatzfeldt, a diplomat at the German embassy in Tokyo, in one of the great social events of December 1904, though it was at the height of the Russo-Japanese War.[25]

CODA OF DISENCHANTMENT

The status of Japan's major legations around the world was raised after the Russo-Japanese War on a reciprocal basis. The allocation of the new embassies was worked out during the final weeks of the Katsura ministry and on its recommendation. On 7 January 1906, Aoki was appointed as ambassador to Washington. He might have expected to be promoted to the senior post of ambassador to London but that was being reserved for the retiring foreign minister, Komura Jutarō. Sir Claude MacDonald who was also promoted to British ambassador at this time wrote: 'Viscount Aoki will be much missed by Diplomatic Society in Tokyo where he has dispensed hospitality on a most generous scale.'[26]

It cannot be said that Aoki's new assignment was an easy one. When he reached Washington in April, he found that relations with the United States were soured because of disputes over the Open Door in China but, more significantly, over the various problems associated with Japanese immigration into California. Tokyo, proud of its achievement in defeating Russia, bombarded him with demands to call on the US administration for a speedy end to discrimination against Japanese. Public anger in both countries was running high, though both governments were conscientiously trying to work out some settlement. Aoki often found it necessary to tone down his superior's instructions.[27] Immigration legislation was passed with the Root amendment. The anti-Japanese Californian riot of May 1907 was answered throughout Japan by anti-American outbursts. After Aoki had been in the US for eighteen months, he reported that he had in his personal capacity suggested to President Theodore Roosevelt a solution to the problem by way of an American-Japanese treaty along certain lines and that this had been favourably received. In Tokyo, Foreign Minister Hayashi noted that the proposal did not take account of the immigration issue which was, in his view, the sole issue requiring attention. The matter was presented to the Japanese cabinet who rejected Aoki's personal initiative. Hayashi, therefore, replied to Aoki, dishonouring his approaches and ultimately recalling him to Tokyo for taking the law into his own hands without receiving instructions.[28]

Aoki's remorse was great and he sent three strongly worded defences of his position though not denying that he had taken an initiative not mandated by his government. But in vain: Hayashi had not forgiven him for some of his actions in Europe in 1894.

Aoki's humiliation was widely-known. Commenting on his return from Washington, the British embassy reported that '. . . he is being recalled owing to his having exceeded his instructions in the Immigration question having accepted the principle of reciprocity in the matter of immigration without consulting his Government' and that he '. . . sometimes wrote in the most overbearing tones to his Chief.[29] In high dudgeon Aoki left his post at the end of 1907 and resigned from the diplomatic service at the age of sixty-three. He was again appointed a privy councillor (*sumitsu komonkan*). This seems to have given him some retirement income. At one level, it was the case of a senior man being dismissed for exceeding his powers and failing to accept the discipline of his appointment. At another, it seems to have been part of the bitter personal feuds in which Aoki, probably the seniormost member of Japan's diplomatic service, frequently got involved.

But Aoki was able to mobilize the support of influential friends who sympathized with their clansman. Soon he was able to turn the tables on his political enemies as he had earlier done in 1898. A Chōshū-based cabinet came into power under Katsura on 14 July 1908. Katsura himself became the main force in policy-making and, in effect, adopted Aoki's line. He immediately agreed to conclude a treaty with Washington, the so-called Root-Takahira pact, which generally follows the ideas put forward by Aoki. The latter could take some comfort in his disheartening retirement from the fact that he was not without support in the clan-ridden politics of the day.

Aoki was not happy in retirement and leaves little account of his doings in his fragments of autobiography. But these fragments, which were not published in his lifetime, reflect a little of his thinking. They contain a chapter on religion written late in life in which he praises Protestantism to which he turned from Catholicism towards the end of his life. Not unexpectedly, therefore, he was a believer in 'kojinshugiron' (individualism) to which he devotes a chapter appended to that on religion. Unusually for a Japanese, he extols the merits of personal freedom.[30]

Aoki died on 16 February 1914 aged seventy-one just before Japan declared war on Germany, which he described as his 'second country'.[31] Ambassador MacDonald summed up Aoki by writing that he was '. . . unpopular with the authorities at the Foreign Office [Ministry] owing to the independent position he takes up vis-a-vis that department, and also to his somewhat dictatorial manner and his distinct but sometimes indiscreet pro-foreign proclivities'.[32] Yet he had great achievements. He had served overseas as minister countless times and as ambassador once and had twice been foreign minister. He was a good negotiator as his performance in 1894 showed. But he was a bad parliamentarian: he lacked the politician's capacity for public debate. In the early days of the Diet, he attended reluctantly and left when the going got rough. Perhaps he was not a perfect diplomat because he was too independent-minded. He was more attuned to formulating high policy for himself than to consulting his superiors. As we have seen in this essay, he had, on two occasions at least, 1894-6 and 1907, taken risks and been punished for his transgressions. On the first occasion, he managed to vault back, becoming foreign minister. The second time, he was pushed into oblivion prematurely. He felt it deeply and bore a grudge till his death.

Like many of the distinguished sons of Chōshū and men of Meiji, Aoki was a highly individualistic Japanese. He did not come within the front-rank of Meiji leaders. He was basically an official and politician who never rose to the commanding heights of Meiji political leadership.[33] But he seems to represent some of the characteristics that Japan has lost. The interest of his personality lies in the fact that he was so independent-minded and so direct. Of course, these qualities led to accusations of arrogance, self-importance and, as some thought, indiscipline. Perhaps his marriage and his long service abroad made him unusually international in his approach and sympathies. To some Japanese he seemed to have been out of the country too long; he did not seem to be fully at ease with his own people. Yet his positive qualities are refreshingly similar to contemporaries elsewhere in the world.

Aoki's place in Anglo-Japanese relations was historically significant. At many crucial junctures, he seems to be pointing the way to the Anglo-Japanese Alliance. Although his residence in London was comparatively short, he did affect relations beneficially in 1894. For twenty-five years in the Meiji period, Britain had not appeared to be a friend of Japan over revising their treaties; indeed, she was the major obstacle among the powers. Yet Britain was the big fish who had to be caught if Japan was to win back her international self-respect. And Aoki was the lucky fisherman.

[1999]

NOTES

1.   Sakane Yoshihisa, *Aoki Shūzō jiden* (Tokyo: Tōyō Bunko, 1970), pp. 117-227.
2.   S.D. Brown and Akiko Hirota, *The Diary of Kido Takayoshi*, 2 vols. (Tokyo: Tokyo University Press, 1985), Vol. 2, pp. 199, 301, 317.
3.   Ulrich Wattenberg in Ian Nish (ed.), *The Iwakura Mission* (Richmond: Japan Library, 1998), p. 120.
4.   Sakane, *Aoki Shūzō jiden*, p. 73ff; *Gaimushō no 100 nen*, 2 vols (Tokyo: Hara Shobo, 1969), Vol. 1, p. 335.
5.   Sakane, *Aoki Shūzō jiden*, p. 111ff.
6.   Andrew Fraser et al. (ed.), *Japan's Early Parliaments, 1890-1905* (London: Routledge, 1995), pp. 1, 7; Sakane, *Aoki Shūzō jiden*, ch. 23; Ian Nish, 'The Japanese Constitution of 1889' in *International Studies* (STICERD, LSE), 208(1989), pp. 1-11.
7.   Ian Nish (ed.), *Asia, 1860-1914*, Vol. 3 Japanese Treaty Revision, 1878-94 in the series *British Documents on Foreign Affairs*, (Maryland: University Publications of America, 1989), (hereafter cited as '*BDOFA*'); Sakane, *Aoki Shūzō jiden*, p. 172ff.
8.   Sakane, *Aoki Shūzō jiden*, Chs. 17-19, indicates how seriously Aoki took this incident.
9.   *BDOFA*, Vol. 3, No. 111.
10. Hugh Cortazzi and Gordon Daniels (eds), *Great Britain and Japan: Themes and Personalities* (London: Routledge, 1991), p. 10.
11. *BDOFA*, Vol. 3, Nos 127, 132-6; Ian Nish, 'J.H. Gubbins' in Nish (ed.), *Britain and Japan: Biographical Portraits*, Vol. II, (Folkestone: Japan Library, 1997), pp. 108-12; Sakane, p. 201ff.
12. On Aoki's reluctance, see Sakane, *Aoki Shūzō jiden*, pp. 218-19. *BDOFA*, Vol. 3, Nos 150-2.
13. Ikei Masaru (ed.), *Uchida Yasuya* (Tokyo: Kajima, 1969), pp. 17-20.
14. Ian Nish, 'Japan Reverses the Unequal Treaties' in *Journal of Oriental Studies* (Hong Kong), 13(1975), 137-45; *BDOFA*, Vol. 3, Nos 185, 256, 259.
15. Mutsu Munemitsu, *Kenkenroku*, trans. Gordon Berger (Tokyo: Tokyo University Press, 1982), pp. 238-40.
16. *Meiji 'news' jiten, 1893-97* (Tokyo: Mainichi Communications, 1985), p. 276.
17. *Nihon gaikō bunsho, 1894*, No. 720. I am grateful to Dr Janet Hunter for elucidating the financial equivalent of the publicity budget.
18. Sakane, *Aoki Shūzō jiden*, p. 238; Mutsu, *Kenkenroku*, p. 283.
19. *Gaimushō no 100-nen*, Vol. 1, pp. 340-7 deals with the exchange of Aoki-Mutsu messages in great detail.
20. Sakane, *Aoki Shūzō jiden*, Ch. 21.
21. Tokutomi Iichirō, *Kōshaku Yamagata Aritomo-den*, 3 vols (Tokyo: Minyusha, 1933), Vol. 3, pp. 342-3.
22. George Lensen, *Korea and Manchuria between Russia and Japan, 1895-1904: Observations of Sir Ernest Satow*, (Tallahassee: Diplomatic Press, 1966).
23. Sakane, *Aoki Shūzō jiden*, p. 330. Aoki refers to 'sengo shōri', thereby implying that he saw it as a war. *Meiji 'news' jiten, 1898-1902*, pp. 348-51; *Yamagata-den*, Vol. 3, pp. 413-14.
24. *Nihon gaikō bunsho, 1900*, pp. 51-4.
25. F.S.G. Piggott, *Broken Thread* (Aldershot: Gale and Polden, 1950), p. 30.
26. MacDonald to Grey, 9 Jan. 1906 in (British) Foreign Office 371/85 (Public Record Office, Kew).

27. Akira Iriye, *Pacific Estrangement: Japanese and American Expansionism, 1897-1911* (Cambridge: Harvard UP, 1972); and R.A. Esthus, *Theodore Roosevelt and Japan* (Seattle: Washington UP, 1966), p. 145, 178.
28. Esthus, pp. 205-8.
29. Tokyo embassy report for the year 1907 in Foreign Office 371/472.
30. Sakane, *Aoki Shūzō jiden*, ch. 27 and appendix.
31. *Gaimushō no 100-nen*, Vol. 1, p. 335.
32. *BDOFA*, Vol. 9, p. 172.
33. R.H.P. Mason, 'Foreign Affairs Debates, 1890-1' in Fraser, *op. cit.*, p. 180.

FURTHER READING

Louis G Perez, *Japan comes of age: Mutsu Munemitsu and the Revision of the Unequal Treaties*, Madison: Fairleigh Dickinson, UP, 1999.

8

KATŌ TAKAAKI, 1860-1926
A Remarkable Diplomat and Statesman
[London, Minister 1895-1900; Ambassador 1908-12]

IAN NISH

Katō Takaaki

K atō Takaaki (1860-1926) had a remarkable record as diplomat and foreign minister. He spent about a quarter of his career overseas and was foreign minister four times. He had the good fortune to be able to combine diplomatic service abroad with high office in Tokyo. Since his only overseas postings were in Britain, he occupies a special place in the diplomacy of Anglo-Japanese relations. Among Japanese he was one of the greatest admirers of the institutions of Victorian-Edwardian Britain. Both in the Japanese Embassy in London and in Japan he achieved many of the goals he set for himself. But his temperament was brusque, puritanical, straight-talking and individualistic. Perhaps for that reason he is not generally given the credit for his achievements as one of Japan's greatest diplomats.[1]

Katō was born in Owari outside the area of the clans who had engineered the Meiji Restoration in 1868 and therefore without any special connections in government. In December 1882, after graduating from Tokyo Imperial University, which had just been established, he took up his first employment with Mitsubishi. He joined the sea transportation department, the main branch of the company at the time. After postings at Kobe, Osaka and Otaru, he was sent to London in April 1883 for study abroad (*ryūgaku*). He stayed at 33 Kings Road, Finsbury Park, north London.[2] But much of his time was spent in Liverpool, which had the reputation as the hub of global shipping at the time. In order to learn the technicalities of his trade, he was assisted by James Bowes, a prominent merchant who is described in Katō's biography as a Japanophile (*'shin-Nichi'*). Returning to London, Katō studied customs procedures and the shipping and insurance market, staying at 190 Stanhope Street, NW. There he got to know Mutsu Munemitsu, later to become foreign minister, who was spending 18 months in Europe for study and was based in London for most of that period. Katō developed a great respect for Mutsu which had much effect on the direction his career would take. It was Mutsu who persuaded him on two occasions to join the Foreign Ministry. Katō left London in April 1885 and travelled around Europe on his way back to Japan. These early experiences of Europe were to influence his career deeply.[3]

At the end of his overseas stint he married the eldest daughter of Iwasaki Yatarō (of the Mitsubishi house) who had died shortly before. This gave him wealth and valuable connections. He was charged with planning the merger of his company and the state-owned shipping line. Soon, however, he chose to desert the private sector and entered the Foreign Ministry in January 1887. He became private secretary to Ōkuma Shigenobu as foreign minister and was to play an important part both as interpreter and negotiator in the talks on treaty revision. After Ōkuma's fall from grace, he switched to the Finance Ministry. This double-barrelled experience in the bureaucracy was to prove helpful in his career, though he was later to claim that he was a non-bureaucratic politician.

His old friend and senior, Mutsu, became foreign minister in the Itō ministry from August 1892. When the Sino-Japanese war began in August 1894, Katō gladly returned to the Foreign Ministry and was appointed temporary chief of the political affairs section (*seimu kyokuchō*). He attained the rank of minister plenipotentiary and negotiated the conclusion of the Japan-Korea Defence Agreement. In October he became attached to the General Headquarters (*Daihonei*) at Hiroshima, an indication of his importance to Mutsu. With Hayashi Tadasu and Hara Takashi, he made up a strong team of young officials who supported Mutsu during the travails of wartime diplomacy.[4]

SINO-JAPANESE WAR, 1894-5

The military and naval aspects of the war swung in Japan's favour; and the Chinese were forced to sue for peace. The Sino-Japanese peace negotiations were convened at Shimonoseki on 20 March 1895. But China had already been canvassing for the support of the Powers, hoping that they would intervene or exercise some influence on her behalf. It was vital, therefore, for Japan to preempt any desire they had for intervention.

Foreign Minister Mutsu had been expecting action by the Powers since early in the war. He recognized that Japan was unpopular with Britain because she had not taken up British offers of mediation before and during the war. Mutsu assumed that this frigidity was also due to Britain's friendship with China and made it his objective to win over Britain to goodwill towards Japan. Japan found herself, as happened all too often, under-represented abroad for the task. The existing incumbent who superintended the legations in Berlin and London, Aoki Shūzō, could not cope with the two posts during wartime and had in any case antagonized Mutsu. With great urgency Katō was appointed Minister to the Court of St James's on 23 November. He set off by way of Canada one month later, reaching London on 23 January 1895. For Katō to receive this responsible assignment at the young age of 35 was a sign of Mutsu's confidence in him. He was naturally overjoyed to take over Japan's top diplomatic post at a critical time for his country.

From his first meeting with the foreign secretary of the Liberal government, Lord Kimberley, on 4 February, Katō felt that they established a fine personal rapport but perceived that Japan had still much persuasion to do.[5] Japan passed over the draft of her peace terms to China, which were leaked by the Chinese to most of the powers including Britain. Katō reported to Tokyo his impression that

Britain had no firm position and was watching the movements of Russia and France over eastern developments. When the commercial terms reached him on 6 April, Katō assured Britain that all trading nations would enjoy equal rights under them. The London government received no complaints from commercial circles about these terms and broadly accepted them.[6]

In the crisis atmosphere on 6 April Kimberley asked the Prime Minister, Lord Rosebery, whether Britain should give advice to Japan as the continental powers were proposing to do. 'If that advice is not followed, are we prepared to enforce it? . . . We could advise Japan not to press the cession of Liaotung etc or we might ask that the cession shall not extend beyond the actual peninsula. My mind inclines to non-interference as presenting the least objection'.[7] Rosebery replied that the Japanese terms were not unreasonable and 'we could not therefore interfere by force to reduce them . . . If we are not prepared to back the representations by force, it is useless in the present state of Japanese feeling to make any.' The view that Britain could not go to war with Japan unless she directly and immediately threatened British interests was endorsed by the cabinet on 9 April.[8] From this it would appear that Britain's attitude was not as yet cut and dried and that Katō's persuasiveness was still much needed.

When the treaty of Shimonoseki was signed on 17 April, the Rosebery cabinet on 23 April confirmed its former decision not to advise the Japanese 'without knowing the ulterior measures to which it is in contemplation to have recourse [sic] in the almost certain event of Japan refusing to yield to the desires of the Powers.' Clearly Katō had given the British ministers the strong impression that Japan would reject any outside 'advice' and resist.[9]

Meanwhile, the Tokyo representatives of Russia, France and Germany on the same day gave Japan their friendly 'advice' to reverse the clauses of the treaty of Shimonoseki, asking in effect for Japan to return the Liaotung peninsula to China. Britain did not join this Tripartite (Dreibund) intervention in spite of her desire for a rapprochement with Russia. She recognized that, while Japan's political demands on China were severe, she could not apply any diplomatic pressure on Japan because she was not willing to back it up by force or threats of force. Katō was worried that Britain, in spite of her assurances, might still join as a late-comer. In the end she declined to do so.[10]

Could Katō then persuade Britain to lend her support to Japan against the coalition of European powers? Kimberley had almost daily meetings with Katō over this period. At the meeting on 27 April, which was probably the critical one, Katō asked how far Japan might count on Britain's support against the Dreibund. While Kimberley was in Katō's view 'very cordial', he defined British policy as being one of non-interference, his principal interest being the restoration of peace in the area. Though this was not said, the British cabinet felt that China should accept the terms and that there was no practical way in which it could influence the situation.[11] Britain did not want to depart from neutrality; but Kimberley who was regularly in touch with the three Powers did tell Katō that they too were in earnest and were not likely to be fobbed off by unacceptable compromises.

On receipt of this report, Tokyo replied to Katō in English: 'Your telegram gave us a good guide in determining our action'.[12] Japan would have to handle the problem without positive external support. That meant a climb-down which she eventually made on 5 May and was thankfully accepted by the three Powers. It resulted in an agreement to retrocede all mainland territory granted under the treaty in return for monetary compensation.

When the Rosebery ministry collapsed on 24 June, Katō had a final meeting with Kimberley at which he expressed his appreciation of the actions of the cabinet and the friendliness of the foreign secretary. But his judgment may have been over-optimistic. From the British archives it would appear that Britain did not budge during the crisis from her policy of safeguarding her national interests and observing strict neutrality. Katō received lofty and accurate advice from London but no practical offers of assistance.

If Britain was circumspect during the crisis, there can be little doubt about the importance of Katō's own role. Japan's worry was about Britain's supposed alliance with China and Katō's task was to wean her away from that. In fact, Britain soon lost any confidence she had formerly had in China. It is probably true to say that Katō had great success in improving relations from the low level they had reached in 1894. Then all Britain's initiatives for peace had been firmly repudiated by Japan and Britain was in serious contention with her over the *Kowshing* incident, the undertakings over Shanghai and the Korean customs. The situation improved dramatically during 1895, largely due to the energetic activities of Katō. By the time the crisis had passed, Britain's cordiality towards Japan had been restored.

FOUR YEARS IN LONDON

Katō drew comfort from the thought that a favourable turn in Anglo-Japanese relations had taken place as a result of the ambitions the continental powers had shown during the crisis over the Triple Intervention. With the coming of peace he wanted to continue his collaboration with Britain. But the ministry changed in London and Katō had to cope with Lord Salisbury as foreign secretary – a more distant figure than Kimberley. Indeed Katō's contacts tended to be with Joseph Chamberlain, the colonial secretary, and younger members of the cabinet.

When Ōkuma Shigenobu came to office as foreign minister in the Matsukata ministry in September 1896, he addressed his ministers overseas about the new age (*shin jidai*) on which Japan was embarking after her massive victory in the war and called on them for their reactions.[13]

Katō gave a lengthy response on the steps he wanted to take over relations with Britain. In particular Katō called for an increase in expenditure on the London legation and a change of location for its building. He wanted the legation raised to an embassy. He saw these as essential to project a new image of Japan as a victorious Power. After Ōkuma's visionary approach, Katō's response was down to earth. Under his leadership the quality of diplomats at the London legation improved thereafter; and the number increased. They paid much more attention to hospitality and took the Japanese Legation to a new level of popularity by offering lavish entertainment. Katō never failed to turn up for the annual dinner of the Japan Society. Peter Duus makes the point that perhaps one of the reasons for Katō's appointment to London was his ability to pay the hospitality expenses of the legation from his private fortune. Katō also attached much importance to cultivating relations with the London press. He also succeeded in moving the legation from Sussex Gardens to more prestigious Grosvenor Gardens on 27 August 1898.[14] Still the subjects which engaged most of Katō's attention were the humdrum affairs of an overseas legation with a special emphasis on the consequences of Japan's revised treaties which came into effect in 1899 when all the other Powers had agreed. There were, too, the financial dealings over the large indemnity which Japan was to receive from China.

The highlight of Katō's term of office was Queen Victoria's Diamond Jubilee in June 1897 celebrating her accession to the throne sixty years earlier. This was a most exhausting issue for him. It also offers the historian many insights into Japan's world-view at the time. It occurred when Ōkuma was serving as foreign minister. An invitation to attend the celebrations was sent to the Japanese court and it was decided to send a delegation headed by Prince Arisugawa (Takehito Shinno no Miya), who had completed his education as a naval officer in England, being the first prince of the blood to study abroad.[15] The problem was that the Japanese leaders had the feeling that their delegation had not received proper recognition at the ceremonies ten years earlier to mark the 50th anniversary of Victoria's accession to the throne. It was important to reverse this. All the more so because Japan had in the interval defeated China in the war of 1894-5 and had claims to be regarded as a Great Power.

The prince, therefore, proposed to the throne that he should be accompanied by Itō Hirobumi who was Japan's most senior statesman and the closest adviser to the Emperor but was then out of office. The Emperor (temporarily in Kyoto) was reluctant to allow Itō to leave the country for an extended period but ultimately gave in under the combined pressure of the prince and the cabinet.

In order to understand Katō's position in London, it is necessary to quote some of the correspondence, which was being exchanged between the leaders in Tokyo at this time. This illustrates the high expectations, which the Tokyo government had from Itō's visit to London and European capitals. Foreign Minister Ōkuma wrote:

> I am very satisfied that Itō is going to Britain. We cannot escape from dissatisfaction over the way that country treats our royal family, which may be because of religious considerations in the national character. If she knows that Itō is coming with the delegation, she will treat it more favourably. This would, of course, be important for Prince Arisugawa and for Japan as a whole. In addition I think Itō's journey would be useful both in broadening his views and in improving his health. Moreover the fact that he is not connected to officialdom would be useful in making contact with major statesmen and allowing him to speak more freely than those who have official responsibilities There are many points, which I cannot mention openly to diplomats and where I want to rely on Itō's help. So, when Itō goes travelling from Britain to the continent, I shall send Nabeshima Keijiro to accompany him with the telegraphic codes.
>
> Though Itō is merely one member of the delegation, he is well known around the world as the former Prime Minister of a victorious country. It is natural that he will incur expenses while he is travelling. I would ask you to give him 560,000 yen. I believe that it is necessary for Itō and me to be able to communicate with one another on diplomatic affairs without going through Japanese ministers or secretaries [kōshi mata wa shokikan] overseas. In this way secret exchanges which are difficult to explain to others can be passed over by you to Itō.[16]

Ōkuma's proposal was endorsed by the cabinet as the following letter from a top politician of the time shows:

> . . . at the cabinet the other day, Count Ōkuma said that Prince Itō's

proposed journey was, of course, crucially important from the point of view of Japan's diplomacy and he relied greatly on Itō's help. Though Itō is not in any way in government service, it goes without saying that Britain will accord him considerable respect both as Japan's front-ranking statesman and as the former prime minister of a victorious country.[17]

Katō's skill as a diplomat was sorely tested by Tokyo's ambitious scheme and he insisted that the over-large delegation, which Japan was intending to send, should be slimmed down. On the other hand, he argued effectively the need for receiving more funds in order to entertain as many of Britain's elite as possible since Japan was more prosperous than she had been during the royal visit ten years earlier.

Itō left Tokyo on 7 May and reached Britain after joining up with Prince Arisugawa in Paris in time for the opening ceremonies on 21 June. We need not detail the ceremonial duties which the prince had to endure because the correspondence quoted shows that the cabinet set most store on the activities of Itō. This placed a special burden on Katō who had to try to get introductions to Britain's major statesmen. This was a task he shared with Sir Ernest Satow who happened to be on leave from his post in Tokyo at this time and was often in contact with Katō. It was not easy to secure interviews with the elderly Prime Minister and Foreign Secretary, Lord Salisbury (1830-1903) who was never keen to fulfil his social obligations by glad-handing foreign envoys. He was happy to hide behind the excuse of his jubilee preoccupations. In the end it was arranged that the two should have a conversation and Itō claims that they discussed China at length. More detailed discussions were left to Itō's and Katō's talks with George Nathaniel Curzon, the Parliamentary Under-secretary, whom Itō knew already. The Itō connection at this time was to prove important for Katō's later career.[18]

In the middle of Katō's spell in London, there occurred the serious Far Eastern crisis of 1898 when the stability of the area was threatened by the actions of European powers. It was always Katō's bent to want to influence high policy. In days before the examination system began for entry to the Foreign Ministry diplomats were really politicians. Katō in spite of his youth felt strong enough to urge policies on his home government. When his patron Mutsu left office, he still continued this under his successors Ōkuma and later Nishi. In particular he consistently urged the necessity of an arrangement with Britain. But in Tokyo there was an influential contrary view that a deal should rather be done with Russia over Manchuria and Korea (*Man-Kan kōkan*). In a memorandum of March 1898 Katō stepped in to criticize the view of his seniors, which he considered to be weak (*nanjaku gaikō*), and advocated a more robust policy of cooperation with Britain.[19]

Katō was aware that Britain shared the anxieties felt in Japan about the actions of Russia in the east in particular. It was in this context that he proposed to such as Joseph Chamberlain, the colonial secretary, the idea of an Anglo-Japanese alliance. Japanese sources tell us that Chamberlain at one of his dinner parties spoke in favour of some sort of alliance. But it has to be said that there is no mention of it in British sources or in the private papers of the nation's leaders.

From 1898 onwards, Katō made several attempts to get permission to return to Japan. Japan was however raising a public loan on the London money market and wanted him to stay because of the skill he had shown in clinching the

China indemnity payments. Katō, however, wanted to leave for family and health reasons. Tokyo found the London market difficult because of the deteriorating situation in South Africa and would not give permission. After a dispute with Foreign Minister Aoki, Katō took off for home via the USA and Canada. Arriving in Tokyo in May 1899, he did not attempt to clear his name. In July after consultation with Aoki, he formally handed in his resignation from the diplomatic establishment. Being married into the Mitsubishi family, he was financially independent and was not inclined to be ordered about. He went on an extended trip to Korea and China. Aoki wanted him to go back to London. When he visited Itō Hirobumi who was acting as adviser to the Foreign Ministry Itō asked him to go on transfer to Russia or Germany for a while but Katō refused on family grounds. His visit abroad, however, suggests that he was not distancing himself from foreign policy issues.[20] [See below, p. 144.]

Katō was already taking some part in journalism. Though it cannot be proved, it seems likely that he inspired the following article in the *Nichinichi* on 5 May 1900 from which the following is an extract:

> That Great Britain took the lead in the revision of the Treaties, that she held aloof from interference after the Sino-Japanese war, that she showed her good-will in the matter of payment of the indemnity and of the occupation of Weihaiwei and that her political relations with us have year by year become more intimate – these are facts which cannot be concealed . . . We consider that the great increase in friendship existing between our two countries is largely due to exertions of these two gentlemen in the past [Satow and Hayashi] and that our friendship will depend more and more upon them in future.[21]

This account served as a farewell message both for Sir Ernest Satow as he left the Tokyo legation at the end of April and for Hayashi Tadasu who was about to take up Katō's post as minister in London.

SPELLS AS FOREIGN MINISTER

Katō was appointed Foreign Minister by Itō Hirobumi in October 1900 in the aftermath of the Boxer rebellion. His former associate in the crisis of 1895, Lord Kimberley wrote to congratulate him and received the following reply:

'I feel grateful for your kind expression and also for your assurance that you have not forgotten our pleasant relations while I was in London, which indeed live vividly in my remembrance. I beg to condole with you on the death of your beloved Queen whose loss is, I assure you, sincerely regretted by my countrymen.'[22]

There are puzzles about this appointment. There was no doubt that Katō was experienced and fully competent. He was the first Foreign Minister who had been to university. Itō seems to have preserved good relations with Katō during his resting-period and had discussed beforehand the possibility of giving him a cabinet seat, if Itō returned to power. But Katō had resigned from the Foreign Ministry and his appointment has to be seen as a political one. He was known to have different views from the new prime minister on a number of issues such as dealing with Russia. It is strange, given Itō's own attitudes, that such a hard-liner on Russia as Katō should have been appointed. Indeed, it was rumoured that Itō might have preferred to appoint Katō's contemporary, Hara Takashi, who was probably less strong-minded.[23]

No sooner had Katō come to office than an opportunity came to advance causes which he had cherished while he was attached to the Court of St James's. In October 1900 an agreement was signed between Britain and Germany for an application of the Open Door principle to all Chinese territory 'as far as they can exercise influence' and Katō sought to convert it into a three-sided Anglo-German-Japanese treaty by announcing Japan's adherence to it. Alas, the treaty was so vaguely worded that there were basic misunderstandings between the signatories. While Britain and Katō considered it applied to Manchuria, Germany was not willing to turn it into a challenge to Russia there. Almost inevitably Katō became highly suspicious of, and disillusioned with, Germany. Katō's hawkish policy towards Russia was in tune with the increasingly vociferous domestic opinion. In the aftermath of the Boxer movement where Russia took advantage of her position in Manchuria, Katō looked vigilantly at everything Russia did. He protested at the terms Russia imposed on China and Manchuria and resisted Russian proposals for the neutralization of Korea.[24] When Eckardstein at the German Embassy in London floated the idea of a more elaborate agreement in March, it is scarcely likely that Katō or his colleagues could have taken it seriously.

After the collapse of the Itō cabinet in May, Katō's vision of an exclusive agreement with Britain was carried forward by the Katsura cabinet and came to fruition in the Anglo-Japanese Alliance of 1902. Katō became a reluctant member of the Diet (*daigishi*). Thanks to help from Mitsubishi, he was able to become the owner of the *Nichinichi Shimbun*, and his hands-on involvement with it made him someone who had to be wooed by the political parties.

His second stint as foreign minister came in the Saionji cabinet. But it only lasted for two months as Katō offered his resignation in March 1906. It was a case of *tatemae* and *honne*. In the *tatemae*, one of the reasons for his resignation was his objection to the government's railway nationalization plan, which was valid enough. But the *honne*, the real reason, was almost certainly the unstated one: his failure – and that of his ministry – to implement the policy of the Open Door in Manchuria to which he felt the Japanese were committed. This was primarily caused by his two *betes noirs* – the elder statesmen and the army. But he also failed to convince the majority of the cabinet to his views. Katō was preaching in Tokyo the views on the Open Door held in Washington and London.[25]

While he was out of line with his cabinet colleagues, Katō was in fact attacking the *genro*, the elders in the political world, for their unwillingness to exercise any control over the military who were occupying Manchuria. It was one of the instances where he stood up to protest against *genro* and military interference in foreign policy-making and uphold the Foreign Ministry's independence and autonomy.[26]

AMBASSADOR TO LONDON (1908-13)

Another surprise in Katō's career comes with his appointment to London in 1908. This was in accordance with the recommendation of the retiring ambassador there, Komura Jutarō, who had become foreign minister. He thought that there had been so much ill feeling between London and Tokyo over Manchuria that Japan needed to have there someone who could revive relations with Britain. He recognized that Katō was the person best suited for the London post and recommended him to Prime Minister Katsura as his successor. Komura himself who had had the reputation of shunning social occasions recognized Katō's social aptitudes.[27]

Katō held the post from February 1909 to January 1913, presiding now over a much larger staff than in 1895. He was ultimately responsible for many historic developments: the revision of Japan's commercial tariffs; Britain's acceptance of Japan's annexation of Korea; conclusion of loans in the London money market; and the Great Japan Exhibition of 1910. But the highpoint was the continuation of the Anglo-Japanese Alliance. Katō who regarded himself as one of its authors believed deeply that the alliance, which had been revised in 1905, needed to be resuscitated (fukkatsu) after some of the disagreements of the intervening years. The idea of revising the alliance four years before it was legally necessary was in fact being considered quite independently in inner circles both in Britain and Japan. It is interesting that the revision was being sought by the Japanese (largely because of the Korean clause) as much as by the British. Eventually, the renewal of the alliance took place in July 1911. Katō was acknowledged by being made a Baron (danshaku) for his role in negotiating the third treaty.[28]

After his exertions, Katō took leave in Tokyo from September 1911. During the course of this he met Katsura whose thinking over parliamentary institutions and political parties differed widely from his own. The two got on unexpectedly well together. After Katō's return to London, Katsura was invited to form his third ministry on 21 December but he could no longer choose Komura who had hitherto been his partner as foreign minister as he had died in the previous month. To everyone's surprise Katō was offered the post. Katō accepted, having reconciled himself with someone who had hitherto been regarded as his political adversary. The British Ambassador remarked that he had 'for reasons not clearly discernible thrown in his lot with the new party and accepted the portfolio of Foreign Minister'. Katō left the London embassy, which had moved to Grosvenor Square in September 1912, early in January.[29]

When Katō took up his new post, Britain rather preened herself on being close to the seat of power in Tokyo. Dr Peter Lowe in his study of this period has emphasized the special empathy, which existed between Katō and Sir Edward Grey, the foreign secretary in the Liberal administration (1906-16). In almost their last encounter Katō mentioned that, when the Japanese lease of twenty-five years on the Liaotung peninsula expired in 1923, no Japanese government would be strong enough to give back the territory to China: 'after the great and bloody war which Japan had fought with Russia, she could not cede Port Arthur and the leased territory'.[30] It was a telling warning about the views of Katō and Japanese generally; and Grey did not appear to be too antagonistic in his response.

Katō's tenure at the Foreign Ministry was again short-lived, not on this occasion because of any intemperate resignation but because of the downfall of the ministry. Katsura resigned in February and died in October. His successor asked Katō to stay on as foreign minister but he declined. Instead Katō cautiously entered the Rikken Dōshikai, the political party which Katsura had been building up and left behind leaderless. Eventually Katō became its first president when the Dōshikai held its inaugural meeting in December. This was a remarkable transition. Doubtless he considered that he had reached the top of his profession while he was in Britain for such was the standing of the London embassy at the time. He now saw the opportunity presented by a new career in party politics at the age of 53.[31]

It was in this new capacity as a party leader that he was admitted to Ōkuma's cabinet as foreign minister during the first two years of the world war – his fourth and longest period in the office. The course which Japan steered in becoming a belligerent in the First World War, was greatly influenced by him. He seems to have got his way in cabinet to take Japan into the war against Germany. He was, he thought, acting consistently with the spirit of the alliance but did not claim that Japan was carrying out the letter of the treaty. There were many contrary voices which claimed that the start of the European war would present an opportunity to leave the alliance or at least to diversify by associating with Russia and France. But Katō declined to consult the *genro* or public opinion. The same applies to Japan's wartime policies towards China launched by the so-called Twenty-one Demands, which were the responsibility of the Foreign Ministry. Whether Katō personally bore the major share of blame for them or whether he was merely the tool of the military is still a matter of dispute among historians.[32] Whatever the feeling about his policies, Katō's term at the Foreign Ministry left it in a stronger position than ever before. He had established the autonomy of the cabinet and ministry and challenged interference by the *genro* in state affairs.

*   *   *

Katō never returned to Britain after February 1913. One may therefore ask what influence his three sojourns there had on his later career as a party politician, as party president and ultimately as Prime Minister between 1924 and his death in office two years later. His London years established his reputation for intellect and leadership. He was universally regarded as an Anglophile statesman thereafter. He saw himself as the author of the Anglo-Japanese Alliance and was its most consistent advocate. Even though he took Japan into the Treaty of London with France and Russia in 1915, he still insisted on the primacy of Japan's links with Britain. In 1921 when the Anglo-Japanese Alliance was about to lapse, Katō wrote that the two countries had 'up till now acted together like relatives; this should continue. It is vital that we should not end up as utter strangers'. In any case, the German influences, which had existed in Japanese politics and society since Meiji times, also lapsed after Germany's defeat in the First World War.[33]

Katō's dedication to party politics in the latter part of his career may also have come from Britain. Of course Meiji-Taisho political parties differed widely from those of Britain; but he was still in favour of the cut and thrust of debate and the electoral process. Thus, in January 1914 he spoke in favour of the concept of 'His Majesty's Opposition' – a concept of adversarial politics at odds with bureaucratic politics as were then widely favoured in Japan. Many of his acts as Prime Minister such as the universal franchise act (*fusenhō*) which expanded the franchise to include almost all adult males may reflect his respect for Britain's way of doing things which he had seen there before 1914.

Yet his 'British connection' should not be exaggerated. Just as he was extending the franchise in 1924, he was also responsible for clamping down on demonstrations and left-wing political parties and for repressive police legislation (*jian ijihō*). As Katō became increasingly embroiled in domestic party politics, his ties with Britain became attenuated. He was, after all, a most independent, individualistic Japanese and an opportunistic statesman.

[2002]

NOTES

1. Biographical accounts of Katō are to be found by Hosoya Chihiro in *Nihon gaikōshi jiten*; Itō Masanori, *Katō Takaaki*, Tokyo, 1929, 2 volumes [hereafter cited as 'Katō']; Peter Duus, *Party Rivalry and Political Change in Taisho Japan*, Harvard, 1968; Frederick Dickinson, *War and National Reinvention: Japan in the Great War, 1914-1919*, Harvard, 1999; Hara Kenichirō and Yamamoto Shiro (eds.), 'Katō' in *Hara Takashi wo meguru hitobito*, Tokyo: NHK Books, 1981, pp. 177-98; Omura Tatsuzo, *Nihon no gaikōkan 300-nin no jimmyaku*, Tokyo: Yomiuri, 1975. Obituaries in London *Times* for 23 January 1926 by C.J. Sale (Japan Society).
2. Katō, i, 151-79.
3. *Mutsu Munemitsu haku*, Tokyo: Kasumigasekikai, 1967, pp. 50-1. Hagihara Nobutoshi, 'Mutsu Munemitsu in Europe, 1884-5' in Louis Perez (ed.), *Mutsu Munemitsu and Identity Formation of the Individual and the State in Modern Japan*, Lampeter: Mellen Press, 2001, pp. 77-9.
4. Katō, i, 235-8.
5. I.H. Nish (ed.), *British Documents on Foreign Affairs*, Part I, Series E, 'Asia', Maryland: University Publications of America, 1989 (General editors, K. Bourne and D.C. Watt), Vol. 5, doc. 24 (hereafter cited as 'BDOFA'). Katō, i, 241-2. For a more general treatment, see Ian Nish, 'Japanese diplomats and the Sino-Japanese War' in *The Sino-Japanese War of 1894-5 in its International Dimension*, STICERD International Studies pamphlet, LSE, IS/94/278, pp. 61-72.
6. Note by Kimberley, 14 April 1895 in British Foreign Office (Japan), FO 46/460; Giffen to Foreign Office, 17 April 1895 'Memorandum on Commercial Aspects of the Treaty between China and Japan' in *BDOFA*, Vol. 5, doc. 353.
7. Kimberley to Rosebery, 6 April 1895 in Rosebery papers 10243 (which are to be found in the MSS room of the Scottish National Library, Edinburgh).
8. Rosebery to Kimberley, 9 April 1895 in Rosebery papers 10243. The *Dreibund* intervention is handled in more detail in Ian Nish, 'The Three-power Intervention of 1895' in A.R. Davis and A.D. Stefanowska (eds.), *Austrina*, Sydney: Oriental Society of Australia, 1982, pp. 204-25 and 'Britain and the Three-power intervention, 1895' in *Proceedings of the British Association of Japanese Studies*, vol. 5/1(1980), 13-26.
9. Katō, i, p. 250.
10. Katō, i, pp. 249-52.
11. Kimberley to Rosebery, 27 April; Rosebery to Kimberley, 28 April 1895 in Rosebery papers 10070.
12. Katō, i, 250.
13. Okuma to Katō, 12 Nov. 1 896 in *Gaimushō no 100-nen*, 2 vols, Tokyo: Hara Shobō, 1969, i, 379ff.
14. Katō to Okuma, 11 Dec. 1896 in *Gaimushō no 100-nen*, i, 386ff; Duus, *Party Rivalry*, p. 55.
15. Ian Nish, 'Itō's Overseas Sojourns' in *Bulletin of the European Association of Japanese Studies*, 55(2000), 7-15.
16. Okuma's statement in Kaneko Kentaro (comp.), *Kōshaku Itō Hirobumi den*, 3 vols (Tokyo, 1941), iii, 306-7.
17. Oishi Masami's statement in *Itō den*, iii, 308.
18. Katō, i, 340-8.
19. Omura, p. 35; I.H. Nish, *Anglo-Japanese Alliance, 1895-1907*, London: Athlone Press, 1964, pp. 59-60; Tsunoda Jun, *Manshū mondai to kokubō hōshin*, Tokyo: Hara Shobō, 1968, pp. 30-32.
20. Katō, i, 360-72.
21. Foreign Office (Japan), FO46/527, D. 57.
22. Katō [Surugadai, Suzuki-cho, Tokyo], to Kimberley, 3 February 1901 in Kimberley papers 10249 f. 106 [to be found in the MSS room of the Scottish National Library, Edinburgh].
23. Barbara Brooks, *Japan's Imperial Diplomacy, 1895-1938*, Hawaii: University Press, 2001, *passim*; Katō, i, 373ff; Okazaki Hisahiko, *Komura Jutaro to sono jidai*, Tokyo: PHP, 1998, pp. 133-4.
24. Hosoya in *Nihon gaikoshi jiten*.
25. *Gaimushō no 100-nen*, i, 496-500; Nish, *Anglo-Japanese Alliance*, pp. 104-11.
26. Brooks, p. 22; *Katō*, i, 582-6.
27. Ayako Hotta, *Japan-British Exhibition of 1910*, Richmond: Japan Library, 1999, pp. 43-9.
28. Peter Lowe, *Great Britain and Japan, 1911-15*, London: Macmillan, 1969, ch. 11. G.P. Gooch and H.W.V. Temperley (eds), *British Documents on the Origins of the War 1898-1914*, viii, ch. LXIX, pp 466-540 *passim*, covers the activities of Baron Katō during this period.
29. Katō, i, 685-97; Tsunoda, pp. 627-9; *BDOFA*, Vol. 9, p. 354.

30. Nish, *Alliance in Decline, 1908-23*, London: Athlone Press, 1972, pp. 88-93; *BDOFA*, Vol. 9, pp. 354-5.
31. Katō, i, 708-26.
32. Lowe, ch.7; Duus, pp. 92-6; Dickinson, pp. 91-2; Katō, ii, 1-14; 71-102.
33. Katō in Tokyo *Asahi Shimbun*, 20 July 1921, quoted in K. Bourne and D.C. Watt (eds), *Studies in International History*, London: Longmans. 1967, p. 380.

9

HAYASHI TADASU, 1850-1913
Working for the Alliance
[London, 1900-06]

Hayashi Tadasu

IAN NISH

Hayashi Tadasu was born in 1850 in Edo, the son of a doctor practising Rangaku (Dutch-style) medicine. He was quick to take up the study of the English language in Yokohama. Thanks to his father's prestige at the shogun's court and the patronage of Sir Harry Parkes, the British envoy, he was sent by shogunate officials with a group to England in 1866. He stayed in London from January 1867 and entered University College School in the autumn. Before long he and his companions were recalled to Japan as the Bōshin civil war approached. Hayashi was just in time to join the last stand of Tokugawa supporters and went north to Hokkaidō to serve that cause with Admiral Enomoto Takeaki. He was captured after the battle of Hakodate and languished in prison for two years, expecting execution. Although he had been on the defeated side and did not have useful clan affiliations, Hayashi was released because he seems to have been regarded as useful by the officials of the Emperor Meiji by reason of his knowledge of English. He was allowed to enter the service of the post-Restoration government in 1871.[1]

In the following year Hayashi accompanied the Iwakura Mission as second secretary, serving in effect as interpreter. He visited the United States and went on to act as advance party to prepare the ground for the Mission in Britain. There, he committed an indiscretion and had to return to his homeland early in the company of Kido Kōin.[2]

In 1873, he entered the Kōbushō (Industrial Affairs Bureau). In 1882, he accompanied Prince Arisugawa during his visit to Europe to represent the Emperor Meiji at the coronation of the Tsar Alexander III, which was postponed. After various postings he came to notice as governor of the newly established Kagawa prefecture in 1888 and of Hyogo prefecture two years later. Hayashi had surmounted the obstacle of his Tokugawa background and secured remarkable promotion as a Meiji official.

In May 1891, Hayashi's patron, Viscount Enomoto Takeaki, became foreign minister and invited Hayashi to join the ministry as vice-minister, an office he was to hold for four years. His qualification was his outstanding knowledge of English, and his ability to deal with foreigners. But he had had no experience as a diplomat overseas, apart (that is) from his membership of the Iwakura Mission and the Arisugawa Mission. At all events he served the second Itō cabinet and was attached as aide to the ailing foreign minister, Mutsu Munemitsu, who was appointed in 1892 and wanted Hayashi, for whom he had great respect, to stay on.[3]

In his vice-ministerial position he played a substantial part in the negotiations for the Anglo-Japanese commercial treaty which was eventually signed in July 1894. It was part of Mutsu's strategy that the site of the negotiations should be in London away from the frenzied anti-foreign atmosphere of Tokyo at the time. But Hayashi and Mutsu had to lobby strongly with Hugh Fraser, the British minister, before the talks in London got under way.[4]

Hayashi also played a major role during the Sino-Japanese War, especially in the peace-making process. The peace negotiations began early in 1895, first in Hiroshima and later at Shimonoseki and Mutsu went to western Japan to accompany Prime Minister Itō as plenipotentiary. From April he was forced to withdraw to Kyoto because of illness. The role of the vice-minister in Tokyo became critical because he was the channel of communication with Mutsu and with the other negotiators. Since the European powers – Russia, France, Germany – interfered in the peace process through their ministers in Tokyo, Hayashi's role became one of substance rather than acting merely as an administrator and postbox. For his shrewd handling of this international crisis, probably the first major one which the young Japan had faced, he was duly honoured. Strangely enough, he was more highly esteemed by Mutsu during this crisis than he had been by his earlier patron, Enomoto.[5]

Shortly after the conclusion of the negotiations, recriminations were made against the minister in Berlin, Aoki Shūzō, who belonged to the Yamagata faction and was not respected by Mutsu and Hayashi, for having mishandled the Germans and misinformed Tokyo. This disagreement was to play a significant part in Hayashi's later career. In October he was made a baron for his pains during the war.

As soon as the Triple Intervention was resolved, Hayashi was posted on 21 June 1895 as minister to China, his first diplomatic posting. In March 1897 he moved to St Petersburg as minister to Russia, Sweden and Norway. It is notable that, while he took on the Russian assignment, he was never posted to Berlin, where he may have felt that the main roots of the Intervention were to be found. During his Russian posting he went as Japan's representative to the First Hague Peace Conference, which had been convened at the initiative of the young tsar, Nicholas II.

LONDON LEGATION

But it was Hayashi's promotion to the Court of St James's that was the high point of his diplomatic career. He was posted to London in February 1900, taking over from Katō Takaaki who had cultivated cordial relations with Britain over the years of Russian expansion from 1895 to 1899.

Hayashi's conversion to the need for an alliance with Britain came comparatively late. In 1897 he had been an advocate of an agreement with Russia over Korea. But in 1900, when he was waiting in Tokyo prior to leaving for his new post in London, he told G.E. Morrison, *The Times* correspondent in Peking, who was in Tokyo on a short visit, of his ambition to achieve an alliance with Britain during his period as minister there.[6] The ideas, which he was to put forward in London, had their origins before he left Tokyo. This is confirmed by the evidence in his *Secret Memoirs*, where he states that he discussed the issue with the two Elder Statesmen, Itō and Inoue, and 'formed the impression that they were in favour of an alliance with Great Britain'. But he received no positive mandate to present such views to the British government.[7]

Hayashi entered the lists at the foreign secretary's diplomatic reception on 17 April 1901. He asked whether it was possible to have some lasting arrangements between Japan and Britain to safeguard their respective interests. He avoided speaking of an Anglo-German-Japanese alliance and confined his remarks to some permanent understanding between Britain and Japan alone, in order to combat the power of Russia becoming strongly entrenched in Manchuria. There had been discussions from the spring onwards for some sort of Anglo-German-Japanese understanding, but when the Germans withdrew from the 'project', it was Hayashi with the foreign secretary, Lord Lansdowne, who kept the idea in play. It is hard to say with which country the origin of the alliance lay, because diplomats are always reluctant to be seen to be taking the initiative. Be that as it may, Hayashi had a central role in keeping the alliance project alive.[8]

Hayashi's *Secret Memoirs* are a valuable source on this subject; but they convey a picture of Hayashi's own initiative which goes beyond anything which would have been allowed to a minister in his country's foreign service. They lay stress on the undoubted progress made in these informal discussions but fail to show that Tokyo took a more cautious line. Important as was Hayashi's persuasiveness with Lansdowne, he could make little headway in Japan on account of the change of cabinet and the government crises there during May and June. What rankled with Hayashi was the meeting between Prime Minister Katsura and Yamagata, Inoue Kaoru and Itō himself, representing the Elder Statesmen in August before Itō, the most senior Japanese statesman, set off from Japan on his round-the-world trip. The cabinet could perhaps not prevent Itō from going abroad or indeed prevent his including St Petersburg in his itinerary. But Hayashi felt it should not simultaneously have agreed to proceed with the British overtures.

Britain's first draft of the alliance was passed over on 6 November. Itō was by this time staying in Paris, before going on to Russia. The Tokyo cabinet decided that Hayashi should go over to Paris to obtain Itō's consent for Britain's proposals. Hayashi could not have been happier to confront Itō over what seemed an untimely idea of visiting Russia at such a sensitive time. He could not talk Itō out of going to the Russian capital, but Itō followed his advice and went straight to Russia, only changing trains in Berlin. Meanwhile, Tokyo made it clear to the Japanese Legation in Russia that Itō had no official mission but could discuss with the Russian leaders 'freely and without reservation'. Hayashi was sarcastic about this fudging by the Tokyo cabinet.[9]

By the end of November, the Japanese cabinet definitely committed itself to accepting a treaty with Britain. News of this was allowed to leak out judiciously. The foreign minister passed the Japanese counterdraft to Hayashi so that he too was made aware of the position. In order to consult Itō, Hayashi was told to send the draft agreement by the hand of some responsible person to Itō wherever he was. On 1 December, Matsui Keishirō, the first secretary at the London Legation, was delegated to take the draft to St Petersburg, where Itō was still staying. Eventually Japan replied to Britain's draft on 16 December and the negotiations went smoothly to the end, the draft being given Itō's blessing during his brief stay in London in January 1902. [See below, p. 145.]

After the treaty was signed on 31 January and duly published, Hayashi drew up his report on 'the truth behind the alliance' (*Nichi-Ei dōmei no shinsō*).[10] It amounted to a detailed and damaging account of Japan's two-headed diplomacy – of seeking to conduct private parleys with Russia while being partially committed to talks with Britain. The report was in two parts. Hayashi appears to have penned the first memorandum on the day following the signing of the Alliance on 31 January 1902. It contained serious allegations regarding Japan's true motives. On 30 March, he prepared – or, more likely, had prepared in his office – a more detailed memorandum which amounted to a historical survey of the negotiations. It was a substantial document occupying thirty pages of print. This, too, contained a damning section entitled 'The progress of the negotiations and Marquis Itō's trip to Europe'.[11] It was eventually forwarded to the Foreign Ministry by safe hand. It was to be carried by Konishi Kotarō, a junior diplomat, who was returning to Japan on board the *Bingo Maru* in the middle of May. It was not therefore available in Tokyo before Itō had returned to Japan in triumph and presented to the emperor the telegrams he had exchanged while he had been overseas.

The Foreign Ministry commissioned a young official, Ishii Kikujirō, to draw up an account of the alliance negotiations as seen from Tokyo.[12] It is not known what the motive was or whether it was a matter of political significance. At all events, it was not compiled as a matter of great urgency. According to Ishii's own account in his *Diplomatic Commentaries*, which was translated into English and published in 1936, the memorandum was written for the first anniversary of the signing of the agreement in 1903. There are serious gaps in this account of events in that it makes no mention of the councils of the Elder Statesmen and is, perhaps understandably, weak regarding events in Europe.[13]

Hayashi was duly honoured for his services to the alliance, both by Britain, which conferred the Grand Cross of the Victorian Order on him, and by Japan, which made him a viscount. He is described by one British diplomat as 'the prime mover, if not the creator, of the alliance'.[14] But for his efforts and his persistence, the alliance might not have come into being. He had to press the matter on Tokyo; and he had to intercede with Itō both in Paris and in London. But his personal success has to be set against the fact that he had a brush with Itō at this time, and while they may have made it up during Itō's visit to London in January 1902, it was damaging for Hayashi's career to lose the goodwill of an Elder Statesman.

In its early stages the Anglo-Japanese Alliance was an alliance of mutual ignorance. Perhaps this was to be expected at a time when diplomacy was secret. But whereas the Japanese government took steps to correct the British public's ignorance of Things Japanese, Britain did not particularly address the problem. It was the object of Hayashi's embassy in London to educate the great British public and to create a good atmosphere. The press, book publishers and journal publishers appear to have been the targets for the enlightenment. On the whole, there was a considerable coverage of Japanese events and Japanese culture in the 1900s.

During the Russo-Japanese War of 1904-5 Hayashi's legation became a focal point in the war effort. On the military side, the attaché, Colonel Utsunomiya, was abetting the efforts of Colonel Akashi to stimulate forces hostile to Russia in Europe and thus damage the tsarist war effort on the home front. The vice president of the Bank of Japan (later Finance Minister), Takahashi Korekiyo was present raising loans for Japan, while Baron Suematsu Kenchō, Itō's son-in-law, was actively trying to win over British and European opinion by his propaganda activities.[15] Hayashi meantime was negotiating the revised Anglo-Japanese Alliance, which was signed in August 1905 (though its existence was not immediately made known). Again the negotiation had been conducted by Hayashi in London rather than in Tokyo.

In view of these efforts – and what Hayashi described as 'the anxiety and strain' felt at the time – it was fitting that the London Legation should be given embassy status in December 1905 and that Hayashi should become the first Japanese ambassador to Britain, indeed the first Japanese ambassador anywhere in the world. However, he was recalled to Tokyo on 20 March 1906 after six strenuous years without enjoying his new status to the full. This was because Katō had resigned as foreign minister early in March and Hayashi was invited to take over at short notice.

CABINET APPOINTMENTS

In May, he became foreign minister (for the first time) in the first Saionji cabinet. He was immediately immersed in a conference on the Manchurian problem which had surfaced because of the continued occupation by Japanese armies of large parts of Manchuria following the Portsmouth Treaty. He was worried about the deteriorating international reputation of Japan after the war because of the Manchurian problem. In September he opposed the establishment of advisers to the Kwantung leased territory and took leave from the Foreign Ministry temporarily because of illness. He argued, plausibly, that he had come back from Europe to be immediately plunged into a high cabinet post and was exhausted. But in 1907 he was back, negotiating important treaties with Korea, France and Russia and thus stabilizing the East Asian situation. For his efforts he was made a count.

Alongside these successes, Hayashi had difficulties over Aoki Shūzō who was Japan's ambassador in Washington. After he had been in the United States for eighteen months, Aoki reported that he had in his personal capacity suggested an American-Japanese treaty, along certain lines, to President Theodore Roosevelt and that this had been favourably received. Hayashi noted that the project made no mention of the immigration issue, which was, in his view, the sole problem requiring attention. The matter was presented to the cabinet, who rejected Aoki's initiative. It was also considered and rejected by Itō and by Katsura who was visiting him in Seoul.[16] Hayashi, therefore, replied to Aoki, recalling him to Tokyo for taking the law into his own hands without receiving instructions. This misunderstanding over policy towards the United States was to have wider implications for Hayashi's last years.

The majority of the Elder Statesmen became critical of Hayashi. Yamagata and Katsura, who might be described as the leader of the Opposition, denounced Hayashi's Manchurian policy.[17] Eventually the Saionji ministry itself was forced into resignation and on 14 July 1908 Katsura returned to form a new cabinet. According to Hayashi's memoirs, he immediately concluded a treaty with Washington (the so-called 'Root-Takahira Pact') which 'closely resembles the draft prepared by Aoki. . . . What was the reason which made Katsura regard its conclusion as a necessity when last year he opposed it, is unknown.[18] It seems to have been one result of the bitter personal dispute between Hayashi and Aoki, in which the latter (some six years his senior and probably the most senior member of Japan's diplomatic service) was able to mobilize the support of influential clan friends whose disagreements with Hayashi were wider than the American issue. At all events, Hayashi felt thereafter a sense of grievance that he had not received due thanks and recognition from the state for his labours. After the end of his rather ineffective period as foreign minister, Count Hayashi was now able to enjoy true retirement for the first time. He had already begun working on his memoirs while he was at the London Legation. During his leisure in 1909 Hayashi began to dictate his memoirs to a reporter of *Jiji Shimpō*, to which he had contributed articles anonymously for some years past. The final version, *Nochi wa mukashi no ki*, was published in December 1910. It was generally understood that some portions had been omitted from the book as published.[19]

In August 1911, Hayashi joined Saionji's second ministry as minister for communications and for a while also acted as foreign minister. But the cabinet was short-lived and resigned in the following year when it failed to secure a consensus over increasing the army by two divisions.

On 10 July 1913, Hayashi died in Tokyo at the age of 63. But, like his friend and superior, Mutsu Munemitsu, he left an unexploded bomb behind. He opened the portion of his memoirs which had not been included in the published book, supplemented by other original material, for publication in the newspapers. Immediately after his death, his memorandum on 'The Truth Behind the Anglo-Japanese Alliance' began to be published in serial form by *Jiji Shimpō*. But the government stepped in and banned the publication because it was based on secret official documents, it still being an age of secret diplomacy. Naturally journalists were infuriated by the suppression of the series and versions became available. In particular *Jiji Shimpō*, whose proprietor Fukuzawa was Hayashi's son-in-law, brought out a four-page supplement on 21 August.[20]

Britain's attitude to the Japanese version of the documents when they appeared in 1913 is given in the Tokyo Annual Report for that year:

> The 'Reminiscences of Count Hayashi of the Anglo-Japanese Alliance'. . . which were distinguished by their indiscretion, were banned by the Ministry for Foreign Affairs, but nevertheless were published in a local newspaper. They professed to give the history of the negotiations leading up to the Alliance, as vouched for by Count Hayashi, who was himself the prime mover, if not the creator, of this compact. The reminiscences, which were, I take it, the work of a disappointed man, went to prove that the Imperial Government had been inconsistent, if not insincere, in its dealing both with Great Britain and with Russia. They did not, however, do much mischief, and were soon relegated to the category of 'back numbers'. I understand that the publication in question is only a portion of much more extensive reminiscences written by Count Hayashi, but that the Minister for Foreign Affairs has taken steps to prevent the issue of the remaining portions.

Andrew M. Pooley, the Japan correspondent of Reuters, claims that he was able to come into possession of further articles and that the remaining portions were offered to him by a Japanese in October. He duly bought them, translated them and was planning to incorporate them with the other parts of his material in a publication, despite the protestations of the Hayashi family and the Japanese government.[22] In spite of interference by the Japanese police, Pooley was able to smuggle a translation to London. But he himself was under investigation on blackmail charges in connection with the Siemens bribery scandal during much of 1914; he was later prosecuted in the courts and detained for part of the time. Thus he was not able to proceed with the publication immediately. But the assorted Hayashi materials were published under the slightly misleading title *The Secret Memoirs of Count Tadasu Hayashi, GCVO* by Eveleigh Nash late in 1915 in a remarkably elaborate wartime edition. Pooley boasts that revelations in the English language may have created no small surprise to the literary public abroad.[23] It has, however, to be said that the British government knew most of the story already. The revelations, therefore, did not come as a shock to British officials or journalists who were also aware of the background to the Itō mission in general terms.

Questions have been asked about the authenticity of Pooley's manuscript, notably by Professor Hilary Conroy.[24] It has to be said that the original manuscript on which it is based can be verified from Japanese Foreign Ministry records, and on the whole it is not inaccurate. The raw material taken from Hayashi's writing is authentic (allowing for translation difficulties), but the title 'Secret Memoirs' is misleading. Cheque-book journalism was rife in Tokyo at the time. Pooley was an exponent of it in his private capacity, though Reuter's denied all connection with it. But, while his methods may have been underhand and his book not without its inaccuracies, the general message which he conveys is accurate.

As the British chargé wrote, Hayashi was a disappointed man at the end of his official life. He felt bitterness tinged with a desire for self-justification. One of the factors in his desire to publish the truth may have been Hayashi's yearning to be a journalist – shared incidentally with his contemporary, Katō Takaaki – and an inclination to 'publish and be damned', which was uncommon among Japanese bureaucrats. But, if this was one motive behind Hayashi's desire to clear his name by publications late in his life, there was also an undertone of bitterness, of bearing a grudge against Japanese society and the ruling elite. What was the nature of his complaint? On the surface, he had been eminently successful. After a brief but brilliant diplomatic career from 1895 to 1906, he had been plunged into Japanese politics at the highest level, becoming foreign minister twice and communications minister once. Indeed, he had been a minister until a year before his death.

He had entered into the party structure, joining the Seiyūkai ministries of Saionji. But, in doing so, he had alienated the formidable coalition of forces around Prince Katsura, the Chōshū-dominated political clique associated with the name of the Elder Statesman, Field Marshal Yamagata. It followed policies which Hayashi instinctively abhorred: a continued military presence in Manchuria; a tough line towards the United States over emigration; an increase in the army in Korea; and an increase of the overall strength of the army. Into the bargain, he had alienated one of the lesser luminaries in the Chōshū coalition, Aoki Shuzō, who felt disgraced by his recall from the Washington embassy.

Hayashi claimed to be a victim of political intrigue, and to have been denied his just rewards. By manipulation his opponents apparently withheld what Hayashi sought most, membership of the Privy Council (and possibly certain retirement moneys).[25] This does not entirely explain the mystery since the publication of 'the real facts behind the British Alliance' was not only aimed against Katsura but also against Itō who had died in 1909. Hayashi had the misfortune to have alienated not only the Katsura group but also the most influential statesman of the late Meiji period, Itō Hirobumi. He was short-tempered and had a strict code of honour, which did not readily allow him to make the compromises which were sometimes needed in Meiji times.[26]

MAN OF CULTURE

Hitherto, we have dealt with Hayashi as the political man. It is now necessary to write of him as a scholar, a man of culture and, in particular, as a writer. Not unnaturally he used his talent in English to translate what seemed to be some of the nineteenth-century English classics. In 1875 he translated John Stuart Mill's *Principles of Political Economy* (*Keizairon*) and in the years that followed published in nine parts Jeremy Bentham's *Principles of the Penal Code* (*Keiho Ronko*). Much later in life he published a short novel in English *For His People* (1903). As we have seen, his reminiscences appeared in 1910 as *Nochi wa mukashi no ki*. He also wrote *Itarii-shi*, a history of Italy. Hayashi was also one of the patrons of the movement in the 1900s to replace Chinese ideographs by Roman letters – this at a time when nationalism was growing and Japaneseness was at a premium. But Hayashi in his day was a force for international trends in Japan. He was a Meiji gentleman of a special kind. He had a code of honour and propriety which he felt had been transmitted from generations past, but he was always attentive to opinion abroad. He was always ready to stand up for his beliefs.

In this composite picture of Hayashi, his contacts with Britain obviously played a large part. From his year in London as a youth to the time when he left as ambassador in 1906, he was regarded as an anglophil. Like many in Japan his idea of the Meiji gentleman had been moulded by his conception of the Victorian English gentleman. In appearance he was bearded and high-collared in the Victorian fashion. He was a consistent advocate of the Anglo-Japanese Alliance. When the third alliance came into existence in 1911, it was widely attacked because it was linked to arbitration agreements. Although he was out of government, Hayashi in *Jiji Shimpō* pointed out that this was a narrow view which did not take into account the ever-increasing tendency among civilized nations to substitute arbitration for war.[27] In the Coronation number of the *Japan Times*, 22 June 1911, Hayashi wrote that there could be no doubt about the Alliance's continuation: '. . . the only point against which Japan must guard is a wantonly aggressive policy'. Not that Hayashi's sights were solely fixed on Europe; he also had a vision for Japan as the following quotation from 1909 will show: 'The Pacific Ocean will, at a not very distant date, become one of the principal theatres of commercial and political activity.'[28]

If Hayashi had respect for Britain, Britain also had respect for Hayashi. He was much honoured. He received the Honorary LD of the University of Cambridge in 1905 and the DCL of Oxford. He was president of the Japan Society of London from 1900 until 1906 – his only rival in length of service being Ambassador Matsudaira Tsuneo in the 1930s. Lord Lansdowne, the British foreign secretary for most of his years in London, found him loyal and straightforward. After his return to Japan, Sir Claude MacDonald, the British ambassador in Tokyo, thought him, like Katō Takaaki, to be friendly to Britain, 'frank and honest, very English in his proclivities' and a source of insider information on happenings in

Japan and the Japanese court.[29] When Sidney and Beatrice Webb met Hayashi in October 1911 during their leisurely travels in Japan, they recorded their impressions of him in their travel diary thus: 'A sort of Japanese Arthur Balfour with a detached philosophic mind and delightful manners.'[30]

In Japanese circles, Hayashi has been less conspicuous. There is no major biography of him. He does not merit a mention in the *Biographical Dictionary of Japanese History*. So the lack of recognition which Hayashi sensed in the last years of his life may be said to have outlived him. And perhaps unjustly. In our eyes, Hayashi was a remarkable son of the Meiji period, combining a desire for national progress with a sensitivity to internationalism which not all of his contemporaries exhibited.

[1991]

NOTES

1.   T. Hayashi, *The Secret Memoirs of Count Tadasu Hayashi, G.C.V.O.*, edited by A.M. Pooley, London: Eveleigh Nash, 1915, pp. 1-7.
2.   S.D. Brown and A. Hirota (eds), *The Diary of Kido Takayoshi*, 2 vols, Tokyo: University Press, 1985, Vol. II, pp. 119-20.
3.   G.M. Berger (ed.), *Kenkenroku: A Diplomatic Record of the Sino-Japanese War, 1894-5*, Tokyo: University Press, 1977, p. xvii (hereafter cited as *Kenkenroku*).
4.   Hayashi, *Secret Memoirs*, pp. 8-9; Berger (ed.), *Kenkenroku*, pp. 50-3, 121.
5.   Berger (ed.), *Kenkenroku*, pp. 203-5.
6.   Diary of Dr G.E. Morrison (Mitchell Library, Sydney, NSW), 312/60, 8 March 1900, But see J.H. Gubbins, *The Making of Modern Japan*, London: Seeley Services, 1922, p. 247, who dates Hayashi's interest in the Alliance rather earlier.
7.   Hayashi, *Secret Memoirs*, p. 110.
8.   I.H. Nish, *The Anglo-Japanese Alliance, 1894-1907*, London: Athlone Press, 1966, pp. 127-34.
9.   Hayashi, *Secret Memoirs*, pp. 135-7. 'Nichi-Ei dōmei to Itō Hirobumi' in *Gaimushō no 100-nen*, 2 vols, Tokyo: Hara Shobō, 1969, Vol. I, pp. 415-29.
10. T. Hayashi, 'Nichi-Ei dōmei no shinsō', *Nihon Gaikō Bunsho*, Tokyo: Gannandō, Meiji 35, no. 25.
11. ibid.
12. ibid.
13. Ishii Kikujiro, *Gaikō Yoroku*, Tokyo: Iwanami Shoten, 1930, pp. 53-60.
14. Annual Report for the Tokyo Embassy by Rumbold 1913, p. 3 in *British Documents on Foreign Affairs*, Part I, Asian series: I.H. Nish (ed), Japan, Vol. 9. University Publications of America, 1990.
15. Cf. O.K. Falt and A. Kujala (eds), *Rakka Ryūsui: Colonel Akashi's Report on His Secret Cooperation with the Russian Revolutionary Parties During the Russo-Japanese War*, Helsinki: Societas Historica Finlandiae, 1988, pp. 56-60, 72, 93.
16. Hayashi, *Secret Memoirs*, pp. 8 and 236-41.
17. [British] Foreign Office records, 800/68 (Public Record Office, London), MacDonald to Grey, 19 February 1908: 'The Count is terribly heckled and harried in the Diet just now and being somewhat hot-tempered by nature the heckling is having a bad effect. He has several times told me that he sighs for peaceful times in England'. Also MacDonald to Grey, 13 July 1908: 'From personal experience I have found him lazy and forgetful and this has been the experience of my French, German and American colleagues. . . . Indeed he has made no secret of the fact that the work is too much for him, and he wants to get back to London'.
18. Hayashi, *Secret Memoirs*, p. 240.
19. Foreign Office 800/68, Greene to Grey, 31 August 1913.
20. Hayashi, *Secret Memoirs*, pp. 30-1.
21. Annual Report for the Tokyo Embassy by Rumbold 1913, p. 3 in *British Documents on Foreign Affairs*, Part I, Asian series: I.H. Nish (ed.), Japan, Vol. 9. University Publications of America, 1990.

22. Hayashi, *Secret Memoirs*, pp. 31-4.
23. Hayashi, *Secret Memoirs*, pp. 57
24. F.H. Conroy, *The Japanese Seizure of Korea, 1868-1910*, Philadelphia: University of Pennsylvania Press, 1960, p. 514.
25. Foreign Office 800/68, Greene to Grey, 31 August 1913: 'The reason for the publication is probably to be found, in part at any rate, in the pique which Count Hayashi felt at the way in which he was treated when he retired from office. It seems that when the Cabinet fell in which he was Foreign Minister, he was not awarded any solatium in the way of a seat in the House of Lords, Privy Councillorship or pension, so much so, in fact, that he was reduced to straightened circumstances, and had to retire to a small villa by the sea.'
26. FO 800/68, MacDonald to Grey, 13 July 1908: 'Denison who is foreign adviser to the Foreign Office here tells me he is disliked in the Office being very indolent and also very hot-tempered'.
27. T. Hayashi, 'Jiji Shimpo', in I.H. Nish, *Alliance in Decline*, London: Athlone Press, 1972, p. 76.
28. Hayashi in the Preface to Arthur Lloyd, *Every-day Japan*, London. Cassell, 1909, p. xv.
29. Annual Report for the Tokyo Embassy by Rumbold 1913, p. 3 in *British Documents on Foreign Affairs*, Part I, Asian series: I.H. Nish (ed.), Japan, Vol. 9, University Publications of America, 1990.
30. Sidney Webb and Beatrice Webb, 'Asian Travel Diary, 1911-12' (British Library of Political and Economic Science), p.f. 2863.

FURTHER READING

Matsui Akira (ed.), *Matsui Keishiro jijōden*, privately, 1983.

Hirama Yoichi, *Nichi-Ei dōmei*, Tokyo: PHP Shinsho, 1996.

Phillips P. O'Brien, (ed.), *The Anglo-Japanese Alliance, 1902-22*, London: 2004.

Collected Writings of Ian Nish, Part I, 'The Anglo-Japanese Alliance', Richmond: Japan Library, 2001.

10

INTERLUDE:
Life in the Legation/Embassy, 1884-1913

AYAKO HOTTA-LISTER

Mutsu Hirokichi (1865-1936),
1st secretary and chargé d'affaires
at the London embassy, 1905-10

In the early Meiji period, before the introduction of the entry examination into the Foreign Ministry in the 1890s, when well-trained diplomats were scarce, the best qualifications for a post as a member of the legation staff were having experience of living abroad and acquiring language proficiency and being either a Chōshū or Satsuma man. There was not much consideration of the diplomat's suitability to the profession. After the examination system started, however, a diplomat was expected to possess outstanding ability in various fields and become much more professional than before, what we now call a 'career diplomat'. In this period, which was a transitional phase in this respect, if we look at some of the staff in the London Legation with the benefit of hindsight, we can see that quite a number of eminent future diplomats and leaders were there in the making when they were young, as though London had been designated as a suitable training ground for them. Matsui Keishirō, Shidehara Kijūrō, Hayashi Gonsuke, Ijūin Hikokichi, Katō Takaaki, Mutsu Hirokichi, Makino Nobuaki, Uchida Yasuya, Hayashi Tadasu, Komura Jutarō and Yoshida Shigeru, to name but a few, were working in the London legation in different capacities, some in junior and some in the highest post as minister or ambassador. Half of them became foreign ministers and Katō, Shidehara and Yoshida later attained the highest position, prime minister. Since Britain was regarded as the most important of all nations before the First World War, a position in the London legation/embassy was highly respected.

In the 1880s, there were generally three or four Japanese staff at the legation and the number increased around the turn of the twentieth century to four or five staff. When Uchida Yasuya arrived in the London legation in April 1893, there was only three members of staff including himself, in addition to the minister and naval attaché. This suggests the Legation was still a small affair. The

Japanese officials working in London also included those at the Consulate-General, which had their own separate premises in London around Holland Road, Fenchurch Street or Bishopsgate. This office had at least three or four members of staff including the Consul-General and kept in close contact with the Japanese legation/embassy.

A noticeable development in the legation/embassy in London from the late-nineteenth century on was the appointment of usually one or two military/naval attachés (*Bukan*), often in charge of purchasing and arranging the delivery of cruisers from British shipbuilders for the home government. Notable *Bukan* included Major-General Shiba Gorō, the famous hero of the Boxer Uprising in 1900, who served between 1896 and 1897, and again from 1906 to 1908; and Naval Captain Katō Kanji between 1909 and 1911.

In general, the Japanese staff consisted of about a dozen or so at a time around the turn of the twentieth century, with frequent comings and goings, providing them with a sense of community in a foreign land.

In order to demonstrate the background to legation/embassy life, we quote from two works: the writings of Uchida Yasuya (1865-1936) who went to London as third secretary in 1893 and Mutsu Hirokichi (1869-1942) who was in Cambridge and London as a student in close contact with the legation from 1887 to 1893 and ultimately became first secretary and chargé d'affaires on several occasions between 1905 and 1910. Here follow excerpts from Uchida's biography (1969), edited by Ikei Masaru, which illustrates some features of his life as a young diplomat of twenty-nine:

> In January 1893, Uchida, now a secretary in the diplomatic service, was posted to London. Uchida who boarded the ship at Kobe went by way of Shanghai and Hong Kong to Singapore. He landed and dined at the inn (*ryokan*) for Japanese businessmen. He blundered by missing his ship because he had become gloriously drunk on his favourite sake which he had missed for a long while. He had to wait two weeks to join the next steamer. . . Uchida who was exhausted by the cruise through the Indian Ocean was shocked and alarmed by the British and French activities which he had seen in territories they had passed through like Shanghai, Hong Kong, Singapore and Colombo. Having witnessed the enormous scale of the powers' expansion, Uchida was, however, not necessarily dazzled by it. On the contrary, he came to appreciate keenly what the eastern expansion of the European powers amounted to. (p.17)
>
> Two months after leaving Tokyo, Uchida reached London on 7 April. At the time the Japanese legation was in No.8 Sussex Gardens. Its staff apart from Minister Kawase consisted of three junior diplomats including himself. Apart from that Captain Endō Kitarō of the Imperial Japanese Navy served as naval attaché. The legation did not have appropriate furniture and was short of Western cutlery and tableware. It was therefore very inconvenient for entertaining foreigners. Judging from Uchida's diary for the year between his arrival and the opening of negotiations for treaty revision (1894), the legation was far from busy. He spent his spare time observing the House of Commons, meeting friends and dining with colleagues while they discussed contemporary affairs. In the light of the actions of the powers and Japan's general situation, Uchida drew up a personal plan for Japanese foreign policy; but it did not get further than a personal note. After a while office work expanded sharply because of the discussions over treaty revision and the start of the war with China, and spare-time for contemplation

disappeared. (pp.17-8)

According to the 'grand programme' which Uchida had mapped out, he had anticipated a posting of four or five years in Britain, and hoped to study the international situation of the European powers. However, with the signing of Japan's commercial treaty with Britain (July 1894) and the Sino-Japanese War which started that month and led to peace the following year, Foreign Vice-Minister Hayashi Tadasu was appointed Minister to China. In order to assist him in negotiating a commercial treaty with China, he asked for the help of Uchida who had been involved in the treaty negotiations in London. When he was recalled, he left London on 1 June 1895. After returning briefly to Tokyo, he reached his new post in Peking on 10 September. (pp.40-1)

Not all young diplomats were as serious and high-minded as Uchida. Mutsu Hirokichi was a prolific diary writer throughout his career and presents a more relaxed view of what officials did out of office-hours in London. We include some typical extracts from *Mutsu's Diary* which demonstrate that a senior diplomat from Japan could experience an active social life and was welcome in high society in London. His diary entry on 7 October 1905 says '. . .Dined at Lyceum Club – Ladies Club – invited by Stead. "Japanese Eve[ning]". Sat between Countess of Aberdeen and Mrs John Lane, American wife of the publisher. Had to speak after dinner. Met Mrs Bennett nee Tuck. There were Hayashi, Takahashi (Korekiyo), Yamakawa, Takakusu, Hirosawa etc.' From time to time, some notable visitors were in London and, though partly on official duties, Mutsu was more than willing to meet and entertain them. On 28 October entry says, '. . .Gave luncheon to Dr. Baelz, Count Bernstorff, Edward Moon, Korekiyo Takahashi and M. Arakawa at the Trocadero.' On 30 July 1906, he says '. . .Dinner at Savoy invited by Chinese minister and met Sir Ernest Satow, Consul-General Hall of Yokohama, Townsend of Hong Kong & Shanghai Bank etc.' On 28 January 1907, 'Went to Paddington to meet Baron Kikuchi this evening arrived from Japan.' and on 13 March, 'Dined at the Nippon Jin Kwai with Baron Kikuchi. Went to the Japan Society for a few minutes this evening to take Baron Kikuchi and met there Sir Claude McDonald.'

Amongst his leisure activities, frequent visits to theatres with his English wife, Iso, are noticeable. The following are taken from the year 1907 as an example. On 30 March the entry says 'Went to Wyndham's Theatre with Iso this afternoon to see a piece called "When Knights were Bold." On 10 July, '. . . .Went to the Playhouse with Iso, Cyril Maude's Co. in "The Earl of Pawtucket" . . .' and on 12 October 'Went to Drury Lane Theatre with Iso this afternoon "The Sins of Society".' On 7 December it records 'Lunch at Grosvenor Hotel invited by General Shiba. Went to Tivoli Theatre in afternoon with Sakata. . . .' and followed by another visit to a theatre on 14 December, 'Went to St. James Theatre with Iso this afternoon – the "Thief", French play by Bernstein – George Alexander's Co. . . .' On 26 December, surprisingly, Mutsu went to the theatre twice, 'Went to Comedy Theatre with Iso in afternoon, "Anguish" – Marie Tempest etc. Gave dinner to Count Yanagisawa, Ijūin and Sakata at Ikuine tonight afterwards went to the Palace Theatre.'

One of the popular places for the Japanese residents in London to congregate was a Japanese club, called variously 'NJK', 'Nippon/Nihon Jin Kwai' or 'Nippon Club'. Since it had been founded before Uchida's time, he may well have frequented there. Many entries in the *Mutsu Diary* indicate that Mutsu and some legation/embassy staff, and sometimes other Japanese who happened to be in

London, met up at NJK for meals and to exchange views and information. He was elected as a committee member of the club in August 1892 and again in January 1906. Since Mutsu was exceptionally gregarious and seems to have enjoyed what we would now call 'clubbing' during his stay in London, he seldom ate meals on his own, but invited, or was invited by, his embassy colleagues or someone else for lunch at NJK or other popular places such as the St. James' Club. Mutsu was an active member of the Japan Society, which was established in January 1891, and during his early stay in Britain, he was elected a Council member and often reported its events to *Jiji Shimpō* as its London correspondent.

A few annual events were held at the London legation/embassy when not only the staff but also their families and other Japanese residents were invited and the number of attendants increased towards the end of this period. *Shin-nen kai* (the New Year's Celebration) at the beginning of the new year, *Kigensetsu* (the Foundation Day) on 11 February, *Tenchōsetsu* (Emperor's birthday) on 3 November were holidays for *Yōhai-shiki* (worship from afar). On these occasions, they were served with appropriate Japanese meals. On the New Year's Day in 1890, for example, Mutsu was invited by Minister Kawase and his wife and given an elaborate Japanese meal and played *Hyakunin Isshu* ('the game of the Hundred *Waka* Poems'). Many entries in the *Mutsu Diary* are filled with these events, one of which on 3 November 1891 shows that about sixty Japanese, including all the members of the legation, gathered there for the *Tenchosetsu* celebration dinner and some entertainment. Another event that took place at the legation was a monthly *Sawa-kai* (Tea and conversation meeting), attended by legation staff and other Japanese residents, where views and information were exchanged: certainly, Mutsu was interested enough to travel there from Cambridge to attend it regularly during the first half of 1893.

The situation changed when the legation became an embassy in December 1905. By this time the Japanese in London were much more confident. Britain was now Japan's ally; Japan had defeated Russia on land and on sea. As befitted a proud nation, Japan's Foreign Ministry was prepared to spend more on building up Japan's image while the British were more ready to offer entertainment to the Japanese community in Britain. This is well illustrated by the *Mutsu Diary*. On 2 December 1905, Mutsu was upgraded to first secretary on the same day that the legation was raised to embassy status, but his 'rank and salary', he lamented, 'remained the same'.

During his second stay in London, Mutsu was also deeply involved with Japan Society activities, often took the chair, and read a paper at one of its meetings. Some of the legation/embassy staff were also members and attended meetings. Interestingly, Mutsu was also a member of the China Society and often attended its meetings held at the Chinese legation, presumably developing his diplomatic skills. He also cultivated social skills with people in the business sector, going to dinners at the Mitsui Club and often having meetings with some of the Japanese banking staff. Mutsu also attended meetings and lunches at the 'Oxford and Cambridge Club', was involved with the *Mita Kai* with Fukuzawa men and often had tea at the Grosvenor Crescent Club, and other clubs. Although Mutsu was exceptionally sociable, it is quite plausible that many of the legation/embassy staff frequently used the *NJK* for meetings, eating and socialising, as well as other venues, as many Japanese residents in London still do now.

The wives of embassy staff, too, joined by other Japanese women residents, had activities other than performing their official duties accompanying their husbands. Now and then, they were invited to the *Fujin Kai* (Women's Club) held at the embassy and Mutsu's wife attended a few times while they were in London. Entries in *Mutsu's Diary* indicate such meetings on 23 March 1909 and 11 January 1910 when his wife attended. I believe that *Fujin Kai* still exists, with a continuous tradition of over a hundred years except for a break during the war.

The legation and embassy staff were most likely to experience one British tradition: being invited to 'at home' parties, which were quite commonly organised as a matter of course in this period. Mutsu and his English wife were often guests at these events and, indeed, his wife gave her own 'at home' at the 'Royal Pavilion' at the Japan-British Exhibition in White City in 1910. According to the *Mutsu Diary*, even Komura, who was not thought to be very sociable, held an ambassador's 'at home' on 3 November 1907 at the embassy and again his own private one on 27 March 1908 at Hyde Park Hotel, inviting many guests, and hiring 'Kawakami and Sada Yacco' for some entertainment.

London was a prominent theatreland then just as now and one of the leisure activities of the Mutsus was to go to see performances at various theatres, as they often took time off in the afternoon. They even took some of the embassy staff to see plays, and, indeed, on 25 October 1906, they took the recently arrived new ambassador, Komura Jutaro, to Drury Lane Theatre to see 'The Bondman'. This may have been a difficult pastime for other embassy staff and their wives due to the language problem, while Mutsu with his fluency in English and his English wife had a tendency to enjoy such cultural activities. They also went to some concerts and operas, including 'Madame Butterfly' at Covent Garden on 2 November 1905, which Mutsu found very disappointing.

London was a host to many exhibitions, large and small, then as now, and the Mutsus were frequent visitors to many art exhibitions at various galleries and museums. They included 'The Old Japan', 'The German Exhibition', and 'The Victorian Exhibition' at Earls Court; 'The Venice', 'The Electricity' at Olympia; 'The Egypt' at the Niagara Hall, Westminster; 'The Electric Wonder' in Strand, and the Franco-British Exhibition in the White City. Occasionally, some of the embassy staff either joined them or went by themselves, taking the opportunity of such privileges. Of course, Mutsu became the main Japanese organiser of the Japan-British Exhibition, so visiting exhibitions in the past must have been useful in giving him valuable experience.

Other events that embassy staff may have experienced in London during the Victorian and Edwardian periods were attending various royal functions. The *Mutsu Diary* is full of such occasions, including the regular leveé, and the state balls and the like at Buckingham Place, where Mutsu also went to write his name on some significant royal occasions such as the queen's or king's birthdays and the deaths of members of European royal families. Some other embassy staff may have done likewise. In this period, as far as British royal occasions were concerned, there were also at least two jubilee celebrations, two funerals and two coronation celebrations, for which embassy staff may have either attended or witnessed, as Mutsu and some legation staff had on the occasion of the Queen's Golden Jubilee in 1887.

Most embassy staff lived in London for an average of at least two years, which included some summers. What did they do in summer? Did they take holidays as we do now? It seems that most of them had some time off in the south of England. According to the *Mutsu Diary*, Mutsu, who suffered from chronic asthma, certainly took summer and even winter holidays at the seaside, at various towns, including Folkestone, Hastings, Seaford, Eastbourne, Bournemouth and St Leonards-on-the-Sea for one or two weeks. His diary records that other embassy staff were coming back from seaside resorts such as Bournemouth and Eastbourne, including Komura who is stated to have returned from Bournemouth on 31 August 1907 and from Torquay on 14 September 1907. Did the legation/embassy staff only go to the seaside? What about having sightseeing holidays? It is quite possible they did so in varying degrees. The Mutsus indeed travelled extensively for nine days in October 1908, visiting Warwick, Stratford-upon-Avon, Birmingham, Bristol and Cardiff, and even went as far as Ilfracombe in North Devon. At weekends, Mutsu and Embassy staff often made trips to Kew Gardens and Richmond.

For the new breed of young professional diplomats who passed the Foreign Ministry examinations, London at the time was a training ground in various ways, not only for cultivating diplomatic and social skills but also for learning the life in Britain in general at the grass roots level with acute observations to broaden the mind. The young Shidehara Kijūrō was certainly one of those who made the most of his stay in Britain. The future Foreign Minister and Prime Minister served twice in London in 1899 and 1912. His first posting in London, at the age of 27, was to the Consulate-General. He was thoroughly impressed by the common practice of ordinary British families, of strict up-bringing for their children in order to make them as independent as possible in adulthood, witnessing this in his landlord's family. He also found it hard to believe when he attended a lecture at Toynbee Hall with a packed audience, that the ordinary working-class were articulate, expressing opinions of their own, which were highly philosophical and sensible. The speaker thanked them saying that he had never spoken to such an appreciative and praiseworthy audience in his life. Shidehara was greatly impressed by the lively atmosphere of Toynbee Hall and the meaningful work it did. These experiences were totally new to him and he remembered them clearly even fifty years later, when writing his memoir: *Fifty years of diplomacy*, in 1951.

Shidehara's contemporary, Yoshida Shigeru, according to his biographer Inoki Masamichi (*Yoshida Shigeru*, 1978), left Tokyo within one week of his marriage to Yukiko, Makino Nobuaki's daughter. He arrived in London in May 1909, shortly after Ambassador Katō Takaaki had arrived, to take up a post as an assistant counsellor at the Consulate. Although his stay in London only lasted for nine months, he seems to have picked up, among other things, a few notable British characteristics. Inoki believes that Yoshida's famous sense of humour was nurtured during his stay in London from his favourite P. G. Wodehouse novels, which were hardly known in Japan. His love of the British upper-class lifestyle, which he tried to follow later, was also picked up in London at this time.

On the whole, according to the material I have examined, the legation/ embassy staff during this period appear to have led a varied social life out of official duty hours, engaging in a wide variety of social and cultural events. Finally, there was one notable point with regard to the life of the legation/ embassy staff outside official duties. In this period the members of staff were quite happy to do their own leisure activities either with their colleagues and friends or their own families, rather than with their superiors, which is quite understandable. Therefore, we seldom find the names of ministers or ambassadors in the diaries, biographies and autobiographies used for this paper, except on occasions when official duties were involved. Besides, ministers and ambassadors themselves had their own social life that may have not necessarily involved their subordinates.

NOTES

For this paper, I am greatly indebted to Mrs Sachiko Mutsu, the wife of late Mr Yōnosuke Ian Mutsu, the grandson of Munemitsu Mutsu, who kindly allowed me to read the diary of her father-in-law, Hirokichi Mutsu, relating to this period.

11

KOMURA JUTARŌ, 1855-1911
Great Statesman; Struggling Diplomat
[London, 1906-08]

IAN NISH

Komura Jutarō

INTRODUCTION

T his is an account of one of the strong characters of the late Meiji period and one of the great Japanese statesmen of the twentieth century, Komura Jutarō (1855-1911). It concentrates on his dealings as a diplomat with Britain and especially his years as ambassador to the Court of St James's (1906-8). At one level, it is a story of success, demonstrating how someone from a comparatively humble background could be promoted to a position of leadership in Meiji Japan. At another level, the paper argues that Komura who made a success of international conference diplomacy was less at home as a diplomat at one of the major courts of Europe, London.[1]

Komura came from a *bushi* (samurai) family in the small Obi clan in the south of Kyushu. In 1871, he received clan assistance to study in Tokyo and four years later went to Harvard University where entrance standards were less exacting in those days. He studied in the Law School and later worked in New York. In 1880, he returned to Japan via London where he met up with Kikuchi Dairoku and other students studying there (*ryūgakusei*). He also visited France before sailing home from Marseilles.[2]

Recruited into the Foreign Ministry in 1884, he became head of the translation bureau. But Komura was plucked from this backwater by Foreign Minister Mutsu Munemitsu who probably felt some fellow-feeling for him as the product of one of the lesser clans which had found difficulty in placing their sons in the bureaucracy since the Meiji restoration. Appointed to Peking (Beijing), he became chargé d'affaires there in November 1893. When war broke out between China and Japan, he was posted to Manchuria to act as civil administrator (*minseichō chōkan*) under the commander of the first army, General Yamagata Aritomo. In this office he got to know General Katsura Tarō, a contact which was to bring him preferment for the rest of his career. After brief experience in Korea, he served as deputy foreign minister from 1896 to 1898 while he was still only in his early forties. Komura then served briefly as minister, first at Washington (1898-1900) and later at St Petersburg (1900). At the end of that year, he was appointed to Peking to act as Japan's representative at the Peking conference which had to resolve the China problem created by the Boxer Uprising there.

FOREIGN MINISTER

In May 1901, while he was still in Peking, Komura was invited to serve as Foreign Minister in General Katsura's first cabinet at the comparatively young age of forty-five. He accepted but could not take up the assignment until the Peking conference ended in September. When he took office, he found that Japan was moving ahead with overtures for an alliance with Britain but that the country's leaders were divided over the issue. He threw his weight on the side of the alliance.[3] He had to try to persuade Prince Itō Hirobumi (then in Russia) and overcome his reluctance to make an exclusive commitment to Britain. From this time onwards, Komura tended to be aligned with General Katsura and those of the Yamagata group. He steered through the negotiations until the alliance came to fruition on 30 January 1902. He had not been the initiator of the alliance but had taken a positive line during the stalemate in November. The alliance might not have come into being but for his persistence, which was rewarded with the title of baron (*danshaku*).[4]

The next years were years of strain for Foreign Minister Komura. After the abortive negotiations with Russia, there were the diplomatic problems thrown up by the outbreak of war. It was Komura's strategy that Japan's diplomacy towards Europe during the Russo-Japanese War should be concentrated on Stockholm and London. Komura withdrew the Japanese Minister to Russia early in February 1904 and relocated him in Stockholm. Japan's purpose was for the diplomats, in collaboration with an active military attaché, Colonel Akashi Motojiro, to subvert the Russian war effort by encouraging disaffected groups inside Russia and the Russian Empire in Europe, like Poland, Lithuania, Latvia and Estonia. But Minister Kurino and Akashi had to act alongside the Japanese Legation in London, which was indispensable as a source of finance and reliable because of the British alliance. They therefore acted along with Minister Hayashi Tadasu and Colonel Utsunomiya Tarō, the military attaché. Between them they conducted a sophisticated intelligence operation throughout the war period.[5] It was perhaps fitting, therefore, that Japan should in the dying days of the war have put the finishing touches to the second Anglo-Japanese treaty which was signed in August 1905 and published the following month.

At the end of the war Komura had two difficult assignments: his appointment as plenipotentiary at the Portsmouth peace conference in 1905; and later his mission to Peking to conclude the Manchurian agreement with China. When Komura returned from the first of these on the *Empress of India* and landed at Yokohama, the people who did not know the circumstances greeted him coolly without even a welcoming flag. In their view he had been forced to make too many concessions in order to secure peace. He was greeted with curses and even told 'it is better you should go back to Russia than come here to Japan'. He faced a disappointed people who felt that they had not obtained at the negotiating table the reward for the sacrifices they had made in the war, notably an indemnity. His unpopularity was moreover unjust because Komura had been in favour of holding out for better terms at Portsmouth but was overruled by the Tokyo government who wanted the war to end without delay.[6]

Sir Claude MacDonald who became the first British ambassador in Japan reflected on the thankless task which Komura had had in Portsmouth. He wrote:

> Amongst the Japanese themselves opinions are divided in regard to Count Komura's merits, some maintaining that he is weak and timid, whilst others, and these include the greater number of those who are well acquainted with the affairs of their country, strongly support him and argue that he obtained practically the best terms possible under the circumstances at Portsmouth. I was always on the best of terms with Count Komura, and certainly never found him weak or timid. There is no doubt that he signed the Portsmouth treaty at the risk of his life of which he was only too well aware.[7]

By contrast, he came back from Peking in December with terms satisfactory to the Japanese people. These Peking talks were designed to obtain China's consent to what had been agreed at Portsmouth. The Chinese had not been involved in the war; and it required much skill – what Komura's official biography calls *kangen*, a combination of leniency and toughness – to get them to agree to the terms. Eventually, by a combination of assiduity and patience and threats, he managed to obtain their approval to the treaty of Peking in December.[8]

It has to be said, however, that that success and the security which the second alliance gave to Japan after the war were little consolation to Komura for his sense of unpopularity. It is now generally accepted that the decision to conclude the peace treaty was taken in Tokyo and not by the plenipotentiaries at Portsmouth. As Admiral Yamamoto Gombei was later to explain the position in London, 'the Japanese statesmen knew that they had a good deal to lose and perhaps not much to gain by prolonging the war'; the war had been a tremendous strain on the resources of the nation and the cabinet could not contemplate holding up the peace by standing out for improved terms. Komura obfuscated the issue by claiming that 'affairs at Portsmouth' worked out exactly as he thought they would and the terms obtained were those which he had sketched out on paper before leaving Tokyo.[9] Be that as it may, there must have been a feeling on Komura's part that he had been made the scapegoat for someone else's folly and that the Japanese people had shown ingratitude for his efforts. So Komura was bitter when his house was attacked and his person threatened.

When its outstanding business had been completed, the Katsura ministry resigned in January 1906. Komura as a reward for past services was appointed to the Privy Council, which seemed an appropriate job for a senior minister of five years' standing.

AMBASSADOR TO BRITAIN

In December 1905, it had been agreed that the Japanese Legation in London should be given embassy status. It had earned this both because of Japan's new-found reputation for defeating Russia and because of the legation's undoubted efforts for the war. The first Ambassador to Britain was Hayashi Tadasu but he returned to Tokyo on leave on 20 March 1906 and at short notice took over from the Foreign Minister who had resigned unexpectedly.[10] There is reason to believe that Hayashi hoped to return to London; but his assumption of ministerial office forced him to give up such a plan. On 23 May Komura's name was approved by the Emperor for appointment as Ambassador to London at the age of 51.[11]

It is an open question as to why Komura was willing to take on the London embassy after five years of strenuous activity as the Foreign Minister which had left him exhausted. He had never been robust in health; and it was a miracle that it had stood the test in war. The strongest motive may have been a sense that the Japanese people had been ungrateful and that a period of exile would be beneficial. Perhaps he also wanted to practise his diplomatic skills again in a more relaxed, peace-time atmosphere. His experience and diplomatic skills were readily acknowledged. MacDonald reported that:

> I have always found Komura very straight, somewhat brusque in manner and in that way a marked contrast to Hayashi. . . . He is practical and very intelligent and has a wild and irritating laugh. He is not popular in his own Foreign Office.[12]

The government was ready to send Komura to the London embassy, which was then regarded as the prime posting overseas for Japanese diplomats, in order to keep him on side.

Komura left Shimbashi station for Yokohama on 20 July 1906 and sailed on the *Empress of Japan*. He was seen off by a considerable throng including Counts Inoue and Ōkuma and Viscount Yoshikawa. He travelled via the United States and reached London on 16 August. It was the Edwardian age when diplomatic life was supplemented by – some might say, consisted of – banquets, entertainments, bridge parties and dances. Unlike the younger members of his embassy staff, Komura was not dazzled by this kind of social life. For someone who had seen how Japan had suffered during and after the Russian war, these pastimes did not hold much appeal: life was too serious. Komura had the reputation for spending many of his evenings instead in reading and relaxation.

The image of Japan in Britain was mixed at this time. MacDonald who took leave around this period commented:

> I was very much struck last spring coming from Japan (where the alliance and we are immensely popular) by the unpopularity of the Japanese and to a certain extent of the alliance. Most certainly the alliance is much more popular in Japan than it is in England and I suppose Komura coming direct from Japan has noticed the difference and reported accordingly.[13]

While there was appreciation of the gallantry of the Japanese army and navy and the hardships which the Japanese people had endured during the war, there were political difficulties between Britain and Japan. Some of these related to emigration to the British dominions. More telling was the problem of Manchuria. It seemed that Japan, which had fought the Russian war under the banner of the Open Door in China, had in the post-war period closed the markets of Manchuria to all except Japanese goods. Komura was in the eye of the storm and had to face the criticisms of the British ministers direct.[14]

It was criticism not just from British ministers but also of the British press, which was deeply interested in the Manchurian problem. Komura had had trouble in handling the world press at the Portsmouth conference: he had fought for secrecy being maintained over the proceedings whereas his Russian counterpart, Sergei Witte, had indulged in calculated leakages.[15] Britain by and large supported the need for secret diplomacy at Portsmouth. But in the post-war period the British press sought a special relationship with Komura as ambassador, expecting that disclosures would be readily made to the Third Estate of an allied country. This was not Komura's style as ambassador. Moreover, the post-war scene in Manchuria was a subject of controversy and disagreement; and it was certainly not one on which Komura was prepared to embark on a public debate.

The British perception of reasonable communicativeness was very different. It may be seen in this private letter written by the famous Foreign Editor of *The Times* of London, Valentine Chirol, a journalist who was generally pro-Japanese in his attitudes:

> It is quite useless to talk to Komura, whom I have given up seeing, as it is impossible to get a word out of him. My relations with Hayashi, on the other hand, when he was here were exceedingly friendly and he treated me throughout with a very considerable degree of confidence, and I should like to give him fair warning that the attitude of *The Times* towards Japan may have to suffer change.[16]

Komura's facility in English was not as good as that of Hayashi. That may have been an inhibiting factor. Another insight is, however, given by MacDonald who was visiting London and described how 'Komura lunched with me to-day and, after I had poured a flask of rich Falernian into him, became somewhat communicative'.[17] This is a portrait of a more relaxed Komura.

It may be argued that sociability and communicativeness were not the prime functions of the ambassador. Indeed, Komura was supported by a strong team of gregarious young diplomats: Count Mutsu Hirokichi who had exceptional ability in English, Sakata Shujirō, Honda Kumatarō, Matsudaira Tsuneo and others. The military attaché was Major-General Shiba Gorō, the hero of the Japanese legation at Peking during the Boxer Uprising. With this team it should have been possible to cope with the social contacts which were deemed to lie at the heart of Anglo-Japanese relations.[18]

There were two ways in which Japan dealt with this unpopularity. One was the mission to London in May 1907 of Prince Fushimi. In the previous year King Edward VII had sent a distinguished mission to Tokyo in order to confer on Emperor Meiji the Order of the Garter. In accordance with protocol, Japan sent to London a reciprocal mission led by a royal prince. At a practical level, there was a good deal of important negotiation which went on in the background to the Fushimi mission, including the rudiments of a military-and-naval under-standing. At the symbolic level it was an appeal to the British crown, to the ruling élite and to the people at large. It was an attempt to bring home to both peoples that an alliance could have colour and ceremonial. In spite of his reserved nature, Komura took a full part in the various ceremonies associated with the Fushimi mission.[19]

A second approach was the arrangement for the Anglo-Japanese exhibition which eventually took place in 1910. But the foundations were laid earlier during Komura's embassy. While he was in London, Komura witnessed a number of exhibitions, notably the Franco-British exhibition of 1908, which had been organized by Imre Kiralfy, an entrepreneur in this sphere. Kiralfy approached the Japanese with a similar proposition; and Komura as ambassador became one of its strongest supporters. In the view of the most recent expert in this field, he thought that the exhibition might divert Britain's attention from major points of disagreement with Japan, notably over Manchuria.[20]

The cabinet fell in Tokyo on 3 July 1908 and General Katsura was again invited to form a ministry. He immediately asked Komura to become the new Foreign Minister and obtained his acceptance. London arranged at short notice a number of ceremonies to give Komura an appropriate send-off. He had already been decorated with the GCMG and GCVO by the grateful British government. He was not just a senior ambassador going into retirement; he was the incoming Foreign Minister who would be called on to handle difficult bilateral problems. The British Foreign Secretary asked his officials whether there were any issues which should be raised in saying goodbye to him. The Office felt that 'emigration arrangements' were 'more important than all the rest put together, the possibilities being most disagreeable'. If Britain could get an assurance about numbers of Japanese seeking to go abroad, it would mollify the Canadians who claimed to be most disadvantaged by this emigration.[21]

Komura left London on 26 July 1908, being seen off by Prince Fushimi. He travelled by Vienna in order to investigate the tension in the Balkans. He then visited St Petersburg and Moscow and was feted by the Russian establishment, including Witte, his old antagonist.[22] He did not have an audience with the Tsar who was out of the capital. He travelled home in a special car of the Trans-Siberian Railway. It was 26 August before Komura reached Tokyo and took over the Foreign Ministry, an office he was to hold for almost three years.

There is naturally speculation as to why Komura left London after a period as short as two years. Though there is little evidence on this point, Komura may have felt ill at ease and unsuccessful in London. Two months after returning, he may have provided a clue. He prepared for the cabinet on 25 September a lengthy document setting out the broad lines of his thinking entitled 'Proposals for overseas policy' (*Taigai seisaku hōshin*) in which he asserted that the British alliance was at the core of Japan's policy. But in a separate memorandum on Manchuria he stated his aim as being to ensure that Japan's current stake in Manchuria should be maintained in perpetuity and to obtain the support and recognition of the world powers for Japan's 'special position' in Manchuria.[23] These had presumably been points which were central to Komura's embassy in London where he must have found the government stance uncongenial. Komura may therefore have thought that British opinion was hostile to a central theme of his policy.[24]

CONCLUSION

This is not the place to mention the important developments which took place during his remaining three years as Foreign Minister. But there were several matters which had been initiated in London which he now carried to fruition. The South Manchurian Railway Loan of six million pounds was successfully issued in London at the end of 1910. The Anglo-Japanese treaty of commerce which gave Japan the tariff autonomy she had long sought was concluded in 1911. The revised Anglo-Japanese Alliance was signed on 15 July 1911. It was favourably received by the Japanese press which saw the revision as essential in view of Japan's annexation of Korea. Komura told the British Ambassador that practically all the items on the government's programme had been carried through and that he and Katsura preferred to allow another group of statesmen to draw up a fresh programme.[25] Accordingly, Komura resigned with the Katsura cabinet on 25 August 1911, relatively content with his achievements.

Komura who had been a victim of consumption for a long time had suffered from pleurisy for some months during 1909. Indeed, it was largely due to the strength of his personality that he overcame this long-term ailment and stayed in office so long.[26] On 6 September 1911 he went for treatment for consumption to a house at Hayama, spending his time in lonely isolation. His condition deteriorated from 1 November and he finally died on 26 November at the age of fifty-six.[27]

Komura left behind him a career of remarkable achievement. He had many good bureaucratic qualities: he was efficient, conscientious and supportive of his juniors. His subordinates praised the seriousness and thoroughness of his office-work and his abnormal powers of concentration.[28] Yoshizawa Kenkichi who as head of the first political section in the Foreign Ministry had close contact with Komura, testifies to his clear-headedness and his quick brain, concentrating on the exchange of telegrams between diplomatic capitals.[29] He was an effective Foreign Minister who dominated policy-making for a decade. He was a skilled negotiator with foreign states and secured tranquillity at home by gaining consensus with the military. On the other hand, as the British ambassador wrote, Komura was 'very guarded on all occasions'.[30] He was discreet, patient and deliberately secretive. He was not good at handling the foreign press. Like most foreign ministers of the time, he found parliamentary debate and criticism very trying.

Komura was evidently happier on the Tokyo scene than in London. In this, he stands in marked contrast to his predecessor Hayashi, who after his return to Tokyo was always sighing for peaceful times in England and remembered embassy life with affection.[31] Komura was content with the hard administrative grind in Tokyo and did not put a premium on life abroad. He entered fully into embassy activities when he was required to do so but he was more at home in Tokyo.

Komura had a special confidence in the value of the Anglo-Japanese Alliance for Japan without, one feels, being a thoroughgoing Anglophile. Whereas he has the reputation of being a hard-liner in relation to policies towards China, he was at the same time the most consistent advocate of an alliance with liberal England. He had been important in steering through the first alliance in 1901 against the opposition of some of the Elder Statesmen. The 1905 revision of the alliance was equally his handiwork: it was more important for Japan because there was a real possibility of a war of revenge on the part of Russia. That did not materialize; but it was a contingency against which Komura had to provide. In the last months of his life in 1911 he devised other amendments to the alliance, which emerged weaker than before but endured longer than the earlier treaties. It was probably the alliance that brought Komura the supreme accolade of his career, the conferment of the title of *kōshaku* (marquis) in April 1911. It was a remarkable achievement for the ambitious son of a small and remote southern clan.

[1996]

NOTES

1.   An earlier version of this paper was presented at the conference held on the occasion of the 80th anniversary of Komura's death at Nichinan city, Kyushu in November 1991. This is reproduced from *Florilegium Japonicum* 'Studies Presented to Olof G. Lidin on the occasion of his 70th birthday', Akademisk Forlag, 1996.

2.   Matsumura Masayoshi. 2003. *Nichi-Ro sensō, 100-nen*, Tokyo: Seibunsha, pp. 22-36.
3.   Nish, Ian H. *Anglo-Japanese Alliance, 1894-1907*, London, 1966, Athlone Press, 1985, p.132.
4.   Nish, *op.cit.*, pp.170-2.
5.   Akashi Motojirō. *Rakka ryūsui*, Inaba Chiharu (ed.), Helsinki: SHS, p. 56ff. 1988.
6.   Okamoto Shumpei. 1970. *The Japanese Oligarchy and the Russo-Japanese War*, New York: Columbia University Press, pp. 150-5.
7.   C.M. MacDonald, 'Annual Report for Tokyo Embassy for 1907' in K. Bourne and D.C. Watt, (eds.). 1990, *British Documents on Foreign Affairs*, Maryland: University Publications of America, Part IE, Vol. 9, p. 74.
8.   *Komura gaikōshi*, 2 vols, Tokyo: Foreign Ministry, Vol. II, 242-3; Okamoto Shumpei, 'A phase of Meiji Japan's attitude toward China: The case of Komura Jūtarō' in *Modern Asian Studies*, 13(1979), 431-57.
9.   MacDonald to Grey, 29 June 1906 in Archives of the British Foreign Office, Public Record Office, Kew, FO 371/86.
10. Pooley, Andrew M.(ed.). *The Secret Memoirs of Count Tadasu Hayashi*, London: Nash, pp. 14-15. 1915.
11. MacDonald to Grey, 23 May 1906 in FO 371/86.
12. MacDonald to Grey, 13 July 1908, in Papers of Sir Edward Grey (Public Record Office, Kew), Vol. 68; *Nihon gaikō bunshō*, Meiji 40, Tokyo: Foreign Ministry, Vol. 1, pp. 140-4.
13. MacDonald to Grey, 19 February 1907, in Grey papers, Vol. 29.
14. Tsunoda Jun. 1967. *Manshū mondai to kokubō hōshin*, Tokyo: Hara Shobo, chs. 4-9.
15. Matsumura Masayoshi. 1987. *Nichi Ro sensō to Kaneko Kentarō*, Tokyo: Shinyudo, pp. 430.
16. V. Chirol to G.E. Morrison, 19 July 1907 in Lo Hui-min. 1976. *Correspondence of G. E. Morrison*, Cambridge: University Press, Vol. I, 423 [Hayashi was foreign minister at the time of this letter].
17. MacDonald (in London) to Hardinge, 11 Jan. 1907 in FO 371/270.
18. Nish, Ian H. 1966. *The Anglo-Japanese Alliance*, London, Athlone Press, pp. 346, 353-4; Shimojō Akiko. 1994. *Junai: Ethel to Mutsu Hirokichi*, Tokyo: Kodansha, p. 207. 18.
19. Nish, Ian H. 1972. *Alliance in Decline*, London: Athlone Press, pp. 11-13.
20. Hotta-Lister, Ayako, 'The Japan-British Exhibition of 1910' in Nish, Ian H. 1994. *Britain and Japan: Biographical Portraits*, Folkestone: Japan Library, pp. 146-58; Nish, *Alliance in Decline*, pp. 28-9.
21. Minute by Campbell on MacDonald to Grey, 8 June 1908 in FO 371/474.
22. *Komura gaikōshi*, Vol. II, 282-4.
23. *Nihon gaikō nempyō narabini shuyō bunsho*, 2 vols., Tokyo: Foreign Ministry, Vol. I, 305-12; *Nihon gaikō bunsho*, Meiji 41, No. 1.
24. V. Chirol to Komura, 19 July 1909 in Lo Hui-min, *op. cit.*, i, 497-501.
25. C. M. MacDonald, 'Annual Report for Tokyo Embassy for 1911', in *British Documents on Foreign Affairs*, Part IE, Vol. 9, p. 243.
26. V. Chirol (in Japanese waters) to Morrison, 7 July 1909, in Lo Hui-min, *op.cit.*, I, 490-1.
27. MacDonald, 'Annual Report for Tokyo Embassy for 1911', in *British Documents on Foreign Affairs*, Part IE, Vol. 9.
28. *Komura gaikōshi*, Vol. II, 242-3.
29. Yoshizawa Kenkichi. 1958. *Gaikō 60-nen*, Tokyo: Jiyu Ajia, pp. 40-1.
30. MacDonald to Grey, 19 Feb. 1908 in Grey papers 68.
31. Nish, Ian H., 'Hayashi Tadasu' in Cortazzi, Hugh and Daniels, Gordon (eds). 1991. *Britain and Japan, 1859-1991: Themes and Personalities*. London: Routledge, pp. 151-7.

FURTHER READING

Josef Kreiner (ed.), *Der Russisch-Japanische Krieg, 1904-5*, Bonn: University Press, 2005.

Okazaki Hisahiko, *Komura Jutarō*, Tokyo: PEP., 1998.

Matsumura Masayoshi, *Nichi-Ro sensō 100-nen*, Tokyo: Seibunsha, 2003.

12

INOUYE KATSUNOSUKE, 1861-1929
A Highly-respected Envoy
[London, 1913-16]

IAN NISH

Inouye Katsunosuke

Professor Christopher Thorne in his outstanding book on Anglo-American relations in the Asia-Pacific war described the wartime relationship of Britain and the United States as 'Allies of a Kind'. This description is true also of the relationship between Britain and Japan during the First World War. They were allies; but there were wartime issues where the national interests of the allies clashed seriously and led to great tensions. The task of presenting Japan's case to Britain and defending Britain's position in Japan fell to Inouye Katsunosuke who was appointed ambassador to the Court of St James's in February 1913 and had to steer Anglo-Japanese relations until 24 July 1916. These were difficult times and Inouye coped in a way which attracted the greatest respect.[1]

Inouye's connection with England went back a long way. Born in the Chōshū domain, he was orphaned at an early age and was sent to London for education at what the Japanese call the London School of Political Economy in 1871. He was therefore on the spot when the Iwakura Mission visited London in the summer of 1872. It was common for the early Japanese 'students' in the capital to do errands for the great men of the mission and Inouye won the special commendation of Kido Takayoshi, one of the senior members of that mission. He stayed on for some years studying in Europe and was around when Inouye Kaoru, later to become an important statesman, visited London to study economic and fiscal policies in 1878. It was there that Inouye who had only two daughters adopted this promising youngster (yōshishi) as his heir.[2]

On return to Japan, he was appointed first to the Ministry of Finance but later to the Foreign Ministry where he assisted his father when he served as the minister in charge of treaty revision negotiations. It was during this period that through the mediation of Yamagata Aritomo he married Ozawa Sueko in 1883. This was followed by his appointment to the Japanese Legation in Berlin in 1886. Returning to Japan on leave in 1892, he served in the ministry and became part of the team which went to Hiroshima with the General

Headquarters (*Dai Honei*) during the war with China and took part in the Shimonoseki talks, which brought that conflict to an end in 1895. He was then briefly posted to Seoul to help sort out the crisis created by the complicity of Japanese officials in the murder of the Korean queen.

ENVOY IN BERLIN

Inouye, now a fully-fledged diplomat, went to Berlin as Minister Plenipotentiary in 1898 and stayed there until 1902 when he returned home on leave. It is not for us to record all his doings in these years. But Berlin was at the heart of Europe and had a great influence on Japan's thinking, especially when she was looking around for support and security from European powers. There was a division between the elder statesmen over this. The senior Inouye initially wanted to explore the possibility of some arrangement between Japan, Britain and Germany. Whether this was because his son was in charge of the Berlin legation cannot be said. At any rate, the initiative failed. Next, Inouye *père* favoured some arrangement with Russia. A rather devious scheme whereby Itō Hirobumi would be sent to St Petersburg in November 1901 to test the ground was evolved. Itō had to stop in Berlin for a week on the return journey from Russia where the initiative was again unsuccessful.[3]

After leave in Japan in 1902, Minister Inouye returned to Berlin to find his legation playing an important role in the run-up to the Russo-Japanese war. When war broke out in 1904, the Berlin legation, like all Japanese legations in Europe, became a central point for military intelligence (*yōeki no jōhō*). It was one of Japan's objectives to destabilize the Russian government by encouraging dissident movements inside Russia and in the wider Russian Empire; and the legations acted as important sources of funds and information. Germany maintained a nominal neutrality during the war; but the Kaiser and his court left the Japanese with the impression that they were pro-Russian. In particular, Inouye had to lodge complaints over the use of German ports and installations by Russian warships. Inouye was awarded a senior Order of the Rising Sun for his services during the war and left in November 1907 as ambassador, much feted and decorated.[4]

During his tenure Inouye had the ceremonial duty of hosting Prince and Princess Arisugawa Takehito who came to Germany to attend the wedding of the German Crown Prince in the summer of 1905. Prince Arisugawa who had trained with the Royal Navy also visited Britain, the royal couple 'being received with special distinction and staying at York House as guests of the king who conferred on the prince the Order of GCB (Military Division)'.[5]

From 1908, Inouye was *en disponibilité*, to quote the diplomatic jargon. He then spent a period on mainly ceremonial tasks, basically a sort of retirement and recuperation. This included a trip to South America, taking in the celebrations for the centenary of Chilean independence. When his diplomatic appointment lapsed, he was transferred to the Upper House of the Diet. Inouye Katsunosuke joined the Imperial Household Ministry for temporary service in connection with the funeral arrangements for the Meiji Emperor who died in 1912.

The political order in Japan was changing. Itō Hirobumi had been assassinated by a Korean in 1909, leaving his father, Count Inouye, as senior *genrō*. Whether this made a great difference in Inouye Katsunosuke's fortunes is not clear because Inouye Kaoru had never won the favour of the Emperor Meiji and had never served as Prime Minister. But he now became in practice the leader of the Chōshū faction opposed to Yamagata.[6]

At the end of 1912, Japan's senior diplomat, Katō Takaaki, then Ambassador to Britain, was recalled to become Foreign Minister. One of his first acts after taking up office in Kasumigaseki was to appoint Inouye Katsunosuke as his successor on 8 February. In going to the London embassy, the senior post in the Japanese diplomatic hierarchy overseas, Inouye Katsunosuke had first to resign his seat in the Upper House. He was then given a farewell banquet in Tokyo by the newly-formed Japan-British Association at which the Foreign Minister proposed his good health.[7]

Inouye Katsunosuke left Shimbashi with his wife on 20 May, seen off by a multitude estimated at 2000 people. He faced another 500 at Yokohama before proceeding to Pusan and the Siberian railway. Reaching London on 8 June, he met Sir Edward Grey, the Foreign Secretary, and presented his credentials on the following day. He was happy returning to the place of his schooling. He was comfortable also in the cordial atmosphere created by the Anglo-Japanese Alliance which had been in existence over a decade and had been renewed only two years before. On the other hand, it had to be said that it was a curious appointment for someone who had for so long been identified with Germany, at a juncture when British public opinion was turning strongly against that country. Moreover, Inouye always cultivated the military moustache associated with the Prussian gentry.

Because of his good (*migoto*) English, Inouye was much in demand to give public speeches of the mammoth kind favoured in spacious pre-war days. Notably, he made the keynote speech at the Japan Society party (400 attended) at which Sir Claude MacDonald spoke on his retirement from the Tokyo embassy (19 November).[8] While Inouye stressed in these speeches the benefits of the alliance to both partners, he did acknowledge how difficult it was for Britain to understand Japan's incursions into south China. He had taken over at a time when relations had plummeted because of serious commercial confrontation over south and central China. This came to the fore over railway investment. The Japanese government wanted to obtain railway concessions in central China where Britain's existing interests were predominant. Since the Japanese had excluded British rail entrepreneurs in their sphere in Manchuria, it was argued by London that it was unreasonable for Japan to expect to have access to established British areas.[9] It was an issue on which it was difficult to secure a meeting of minds and, as the two countries slid into war against Germany, it was still an unresolved issue.

One of the new members of Inouye's embassy was Shidehara Kijūrō who joined from Washington in December 1913. Shidehara, already regarded as one of the rising stars in the diplomatic firmament, came as counsellor for a short period of six months before he was promoted to be minister to the Netherlands. In his autobiographical writings he lets us into the atmosphere of the London embassy with a cordial ambassador and his intelligent and linguistically talented wife. He was impressed by his time in London and stated his belief that the British Foreign Secretary, Sir Edward Grey, stood out as a model Foreign Minister.[10]

WARTIME TENSIONS

The fast-moving character of the early days of the European war inevitably increased the misunderstandings, already generated over China. Ambassador Inouye, like Sir Conyngham Greene, his counterpart in Tokyo, had to try to moderate relations and smooth out mutual suspicions.[11]

When the so-called 'Oshū taisen' (as the Japanese liked to describe the European war) broke out, Inouye's father Kaoru spoke of it as 'divine aid conferred on the new Taishō era for the achievement of Japan's destiny'. To seize the opportunity, Japan decided to get involved in the war, but only at the periphery. This did not suit Britain who, having initially asked Japan for assistance, wanted her not to go the whole hog and become a belligerent, bearing in mind the sensitivities of the United States, Australia and New Zealand over any attempt by Japan to take over territory. Japan went ahead and declared war on Germany on 23 August. Her action was not required under the alliance, as Katō made clear. She entered the war in order to secure her own national interests as she was perfectly entitled to do. But Japan would not agree to Britain's repeated request to send troops to the western front. The two allies had to agree to disagree over the limits of Japan's area of involvement in the war (senchi kyokugen).[12]

Early in September, the Japanese army began an attack against the German leased territory in China surrounding Tsingtao, a port where Japanese trade had for long been predominant. The port and fortress in the lease (Pachtgebiet) were expected to hold out for six months; in fact they fell to the Japanese force on 7 November in some six weeks. The campaign was a difficult but ultimately a successful one for the Japanese army. By extension it was a victory celebrated by the Entente powers. Inouye was called on to attend many congratulatory dinners, notably the Lord Mayor of London's annual banquet at the Guildhall which included speeches by Lord Kitchener and A.J. Balfour singing the praises of Japan.[13]

But Japan's popularity soon changed in the new year because of the crisis in China. Ambassador Inouye could not fail to be at the heart of it because Britain was apprehensive about China in spite of her prime preoccupation with the European front. The crisis broke very slowly, starting with the presentation of Japan's demands to President Yuan Shikai of China on 18 January. To the Western world this is known as the 'Twenty-one Demands Crisis' with its focus on Group V of the demands; but Japanese records do not show it as a crisis so much as a tidying-up operation rendered necessary by the successes of the occupying army and the need to reach some understanding on the administration of the occupied territory. In the run-up to the crisis, Foreign Minister Katō had been overwhelmed by receiving an avalanche of memoranda from a wide range of right-wing bodies, army officers and individuals including the Kokuryūkai (Amur River Society), Tōa Dōshikai and Tai-Shi Rengōkai. While they had been received from early in 1914 they became more numerous in the last months of the year and tended to emphasize the strong line which should be taken towards China during the emergency created by the European war.[14] It would appear that, while the presentation of the Twenty-one Demands was undoubtedly the responsibility of the Foreign Ministry, its role was to some extent that of coordinating ideas which came from a wide variety of pressure groups.

Ambassador Inouye became involved in the crisis at two levels, diplomatically and personally. Diplomatically, he was under instructions to pass over confidentially to the British government the four groups of demands, which had been presented to China, as a gesture between allies.[15] Gradually, other versions of the demands came out through various leakages, mainly in the press. But Inouye gave assurances to Britain that these were not true. On 6 February, therefore, Grey went on the record, with a degree of naïveté, saying that the versions circulating were 'greatly exaggerated'. It was only four days later that Baron Katō first mentioned to London that Japan had also presented the Chinese president with '*kibō jōkō*' – 'conditions hoped for' or 'desiderata' as distinct from 'demands'. These have subsequently gone down in history as 'Group V'. In Japan's view, these were distinctly of a lower priority than the 'demands'. In other eyes they were more extreme than the 'demands', implying on the one hand an attempt to impose a kind of Japanese suzerainty over China and on the other an intention to encroach on railway rights in the Yangtse valley which Britain thought her entrepreneurs had already acquired.

It is puzzling that Baron Katō should have been so secretive to his ambassador and the international community. Katō had a very high reputation for personal integrity and diplomatic frankness in the eyes of the British government, the British press and the treaty-port press in Japan. So his assurances seemed credible in these quarters. Obviously he wanted to avoid premature leakages while negotiations were going on with China. Presumably, he withheld them from London in particular because the last thing he wanted was to provoke Britain to raise again the Yangtse valley issue which formed part of Group V. It is possible that Katō himself disapproved of many of the demands, including those which had been forced on him by right-wing lobbies. As a former ambassador in London, he knew that the commercial implications would be seriously studied there.[16]

Personally, Ambassador Inouye was understandably annoyed. He may have learnt of Group V only from the press and felt that he had been badly let down by his ministry. He had given specious assurances to Britain in good faith. It is understood that he offered his resignation because he had not been treated openly by the Foreign Ministry, which had been secretive throughout. The evidence comes from the treaty-port journalist known by his pen-name as 'Putnam Weale' who wrote:

> Count Inouye had persistently denied the existence of Group V to Viscount Grey. When it transpired that there really was such a group of which he had been kept in ignorance he telegraphed confidentially over the heads of the cabinet asking that the Emperor recall him as his honour had been compromised by Baron Katō, forcing him to prevaricate in his dealings with Viscount Grey.[17]

It is not possible to confirm this. Inouye Katsunosuke's biographers quote it as a rumour. It was not implausible because this was Inouye's last post and so recall and possible resignation and retirement would not have been a great sacrifice.

Whatever the truth, Inouye stayed on in London. But the rumour was a not unimportant one, because it truly identified the sheer anger of a senior Japanese diplomat towards Katō who had earlier been instrumental in his appointment. It was his duty thereafter to negotiate an accommodation over the Yangtse interests of Britain and Japan. But Britain emphasized that Japan's demands should be consistent with the existing Anglo-Japanese Alliance which had guaranteed the independence and territorial integrity of China.[18] Some modifications were made in the light of protests like these, and the American and other governments weighed in to get Group V dropped. When Japan sent

Beijing her final ultimatum, Britain was convinced that China would not give way to such exorbitant demands and that a 'rupture' which could have a disastrous effect on the European war would ensue. Grey came close to acting as a mediator to prevent war, ultimately counselling China to give in to the more moderate terms on offer. China accepted on 9 May and signed a new treaty on 25th. It is clear that Japan's reticence was the fault of the Foreign Ministry, not Ambassador Inouye who was not taken into Tokyo's confidence. It was widely held in Japan that Katō had mishandled the crisis, forfeiting Japan's good reputation abroad and his popularity at home.

As the crisis ended, Ambassador Inouye also became involved on a personal basis because of his father. In the summer Marquis Inouye was suffering from a serious illness but was still a figure to be reckoned with. He was one of the leaders of the Elder Statesmen (*genrō*) who felt that they had not been adequately consulted during the international crisis of 1915. Foreign Minister Katō, who believed fervently in the autonomy of his Ministry, deliberately refused to circulate papers to the Elder Statesmen and acted in this instance without obtaining their prior agreement. When the crisis turned sour, he had to shoulder the blame. In mid-June Inouye Kaoru, in incandescent rage at being by-passed, wrote to the Prime Minister that Katō must be replaced. If not, he threatened to cut all political ties, call his son home from London and retire from political life.[19] Whether these were idle threats or not, they are interesting. It is unclear whether letters or telegrams passed between son and father and, if so, on what sort of scale. It suggests that Inouye, even in London, was very much implicated in Japan's domestic political scene. But it is bizarre to think of a senior and experienced diplomat being 'recalled' by his father against the wishes of the Ministry.

The issue evaporated because Marquis Inouye died on 1 September 1915 at the age of eighty-one, leaving Count Inouye to succeed to the title of Marquis. Inouye Katsunosuke asked permission to return to Tokyo; but this was disallowed by Katō on the grounds that the international crisis was by no means resolved.[20]

We cannot go into all aspects of Inouye's conduct of diplomacy towards Britain. But the delicacy of his position is illustrated by the story of the Russo-Japanese Alliance which came into existence in July 1916. The prime aim of Inouye's embassy had always been to polish the tarnished image of the Anglo-Japanese Alliance and to make clear the special relationship between the two countries. Britain, while disillusioned with Japan, could not afford to allow the alliance to lapse during the war. But many in Japan, perhaps doubtful of Britain's capacity for achieving ultimate victory, wanted to diversify their foreign relations by concluding a separate alliance with Russia. When the idea of expanding the alliance to take in war-time collaborators like Russia was mooted, Inouye, Katō and Grey were initially opposed. But, as Russia's military position weakened, Grey withdrew his opposition. He wanted to commit Japan to Russia in such a way that Russia could safely remove her troops from Siberia without fear of Japan taking over her territory. In this way the Russo-Japanese Alliance came about in July 1916. While London superficially welcomed this develop-ment, it may in reality have been less enthusiastic. Ambassador Greene from his perspective in Tokyo took a sceptical view:

> Prior to the war. . . there was a tendency to look upon Japan as a model of all international virtues. . . Today we have come to know that Japan – the real Japan – is a frankly opportunist, not to say selfish, country of

very modest importance compared with the giants of the Great War, but with a very exaggerated opinion of her own role in the universe.[21]

The time came for Inouye's recall after a fairly turbulent time in London. He left after serving over three years and received such hospitality as war-time London could muster. His Japanese biographer speaks of his popularity in Britain. He certainly was honoured by King George V on 12 July 1916, the King expressing pleasure at the friendly relations just forged between Russia and Japan: 'Inouye replied that he shared H.M.'s views on the great value of the new accord between Japan and Russia in harmonious cooperation with the Anglo-Japanese Alliance.' He was admitted to the first class of the Royal Victorian Order. Both he and his wife had been popular and made the best of a difficult job. In particular the Marchioness had been active in helping the British Red Cross during the war.[22]

Inouye finally received permission to return home. His successor was appointed on 13 June 1916. The Inouyes departed on 24 July, seen off by Lord Crewe, the acting Foreign Secretary. From the vantage-point of the London embassy, he had witnessed the first phase of an unprecedented war, the phase before the United States joined in. On 22 August, the Inouye family arrived in Japan, having travelled via Canada. Inouye Katsunosuke was interviewed by the press on arrival and made an interesting statement:

> I was deeply impressed by the universal determination [in Britain] to fight to the bitterest end. There can be no consideration of peace proposals without complete victory of the arms of the Allies. On the other hand, Germany is weakening. She will take six months to recover from her recent heavy losses in defeat in the North Sea. While Germany claims a good harvest, her supplies are diminishing and her resources are becoming more and more limited.[23]

This was a surprisingly upbeat assessment of the allied war effort at the time. His prediction in 1916 of an allied victory was in marked contrast to the view of many Japanese policy-makers who saw things differently.

END-OF-WAR MISSIONS

As Inouye Katsunosuke entered retirement, he continued to be active. He spent the next few years involved in certain state ceremonies. He was one of the hosts of the mission to Japan led by Prince Arthur of Connaught in order to present a Field-Marshal's baton to the Emperor Taishō. This was intended to be a mark of respect and friendship to the new Japanese sovereign. In view of the danger the mission faced in the Atlantic from German submarines, it was a risky war-time gesture. On 18 June 1918, Inouye welcomed them at Yokohama. They were met at Tokyo station by the Emperor himself and placed in the Kasumigaseki Palace. The baton was passed over on the following day.[24] In order to reciprocate, Prince Higashi-Fushimi was sent on a thanksgiving mission to the British sovereign. Inouye was appointed as head of the accompanying mission which consisted of ten members, including General Shiba Gorō and Admiral Oguri Kisaburō, two pro-British officers. They set off from Yokohama in the *Fushimi Maru* on 26 September, travelling via Vancouver and Halifax. They reached Plymouth safely and reciprocated by conferring a Japanese Field-marshal's sword on the British sovereign. They inspected the Grand Fleet and set off for the battlefields of the allied powers, France, Belgium and Italy, meeting Field-Marshal Sir Douglas Haig on Armistice Day, 1918. They left again via Plymouth across the Atlantic to New

York, arriving back in Yokohama on 7 January 1919. This lengthy journey of over a hundred days was to give Inouye his last sight of Britain, although he later acted as head of the committee which planned the visit of the Prince of Wales (later Edward VIII) to Japan in 1922.[25]

In his retirement, Inouye became engaged in charitable and educational works and was appointed to the Privy Council. In that capacity he intervened from time to time as over the Chinese policies of the Tanaka cabinet. But his health deteriorated and he died in November 1929 at the age of sixty-nine.[26]

During his time in the London Embassy, Inouye unquestionably tried to uphold the international reputation of Japan at a particularly difficult time. His tenure coincided with a crunch-time for the Anglo-Japanese Alliance, a time when the existence of the alliance was in jeopardy because of the competing interests of the two allies and especially because of Britain's suspicions of Japanese ambitions. It cannot be said that Inouye was exclusively Anglophil like his predecessors Hayashi Tadasu or Katō Takaaki for he had spent much of his career in Germany. But he was very professional, adapting himself to the environment in which he was placed. In many of his gestures he showed himself to be a man of probity and an admirer of British institutions and culture. Inouye was, however, far from happy with the actions of his home government. He must have felt that he had been let down by its secretiveness over the Twenty-one Demands and embarrassed by its refusal to allow him to return home after his father's death. But the fact that the Anglo-Japanese Alliance, which was central to the interests of both countries during the war years, was in the doldrums was not the fault of Inouye. He had nursed it; and it survived his departure.

[2005]

NOTES

1.   C.G. Thorne, *Allies of a Kind*, London: Hamish Hamilton, 1978. P.C. Lowe, *Great Britain and Japan, 1911-15*, Macmillan 1969, is the most thorough account of the general history of this period.
2.   *Segai Inouye-ko den*, Tokyo, 1934, Vol. 5, contains an appendix dealing with the life of his adopted son and heir, *Kōshaku Katsunosuke kun ryaku-den*, pp. 1-285. (hereafter cited as 'Katsunosuke-den'.) I am unable to reconcile this evidence about his marriage with British Embassy reports that Inouye Kaoru had two daughters and the elder one married Katsunosuke who thereafter took on the adopted family name of Inouye. *British Documents on Foreign Affairs*, Part I, Series E, Vol. 9 (Maryland: University Publications of America, 1989), p. 71 (Hereafter cited as 'BDOFA').
3.   Ian Nish, *Anglo-Japanese Alliance*, London: Athlone, 1966, chs 4 and 9.
4.   *Katsunosuke-den*, pp. 117-19.
5.   *Katsunosuke-den*, pp. 128-33; *The Times* (London), 7 July 1913 (at the time of Arisugawa's death).
6.   *BDOFA*, Vol. 9, p. 126.
7.   Ian Nish, 'Katō Takaaki' in Hugh Cortazzi (ed.), *Britain and Japan: Biographical Portraits*, Vol. IV, London: Japan Library, 2002, pp. 14-27.
8.   Inouye's speech engagements included American Independence Day at Savoy Hotel (14/7); Trafalgar Day (21/10); Launch and Visit of IJN ship *Kongo* to British ports; Guildhall (9/11); Shipbuilders' Association dinner (30/3/14); Colchester City. Details in *Katsunosuke-den*, pp. 178-84.
9.   *BDOFA*, Vol. 9, p. 363.
10. *Shidehara Kijūrō*, pp. 72-8.
11. P.C. Lowe, 'Sir William Conyngham Greene' in Cortazzi (ed.), *Biographical Portraits*, Vol. IV, pp. 64-77.

12. Lowe, ch. 6 and Ian Nish, *Alliance in Decline*, London: Athlone, 1972, ch. 7.
13. Nish, *Alliance in Decline*, pp. 128-9.
14. *Nihon Gaikō Bunshō*, Taishō 3-nen, Vol. 2, docs 595-606, pp. 865-953. (Hereafter cited as 'NGB').
15. *NGB*, Taisho 4-nen, Vol. 2, doc. 488; *Katsunosuke-den*, pp. 215-23.
16. F.R. Dickinson, *War and National Reinvention: Japan in the Great War, 1914-19*, Cambridge, Mass.: Harvard UP, 1999, p. 115.
17. Putnam Weale, *An Indiscreet Chronicle from the Pacific*, Basingstoke: Palgrave, 2002, p. 308. I have carried out a limited search to try to trace this in the Japanese and British press and through Japanese official sources but without success. *Katsunosuke-den*, p. 224. Inouye was in touch privately with Tokyo affairs through correspondence with his brother-in-law, Tsuzuki Keiroku.
18. *NGB*, Taishō 4-nen, Vol. 2, docs 609 and 635.
19. Dickinson, pp. 111-12; *Katsunosuke-den*, pp. 224-7.
20. *Katsunosuke-den*, pp. 229-30.
21. (British) Foreign Office papers, 410/65 [222589], Greene to Grey, 26 September 1916.
22. *Katsunosuke-den*, pp. 247-9; *The Times* (London).
23. *The Times* (London).
24. *Katsunosuke-den*, pp. 253-5.
25. *Katsunosuke-den*, pp.255-7; P. Ziegler (ed.) *The Diaries of Lord Louis Mountbatten*, Glasgow: Collins, 1987.
26. *Katsunosuke-den*, pp. 262-4.

FURTHER READING

Xu Guoqi, *China and the Great War*, Cambridge: University Press, 2005.

Peter Lowe, 'Sir William Conyngham Greene' in H. Cortazzi (ed.), *British Envoys in Japan*, Folkestone: Global Oriental, 2004.

Keith Neilson, *Britain and the Last Tsar, 1894-1917*, Oxford: Clarendon Press, 1995.

13

CHINDA SUTEMI, 1857-1929
Ambassador in Peace and War
[London, 1916-20]

IAN NISH

Chinda Sutemi

H istorians have a penchant for examining the origins of war. That is very proper because it is important to learn the art of preventing wars. But the aftermaths of war are equally worthy of study because it is there that things go wrong for the future and the decisions have often to be taken at breakneck speed in fast-moving situations. This requires adaptability, flexibility and vision on the part of decision-makers.

This was nowhere more needed than in the case of Japan and the Paris Peace Conference of 1919 which brought an end to the 'first world war'. In spite of the description, it had been primarily a European war; and Japan had kept herself on its fringes. She had grown prosperous as a result of it. Without doubt she had made a contribution to allied victory, mainly as a result of her naval actions. But she had not suffered many casualties which for many nations was to be the criterion by which their contribution to the war effort was judged. This left the Japanese with a seat at the top table at the Paris Peace Conference where the peace was negotiated – one of the members of the Council of Five Great Powers but outside the Council of Four in which many of the critical decisions were vested. Japan had advanced on to the world stage and had much to do to adjust to her new role.[1]

Chinda Sutemi, as Ambassador to Britain from 1916 to 1920, was one of those who had to attend the Paris conference and address these new international problems. He had a role in the preparation of Japan's peace terms, took his share in steering through the negotiations and conducted important business during the first two years after the armistice.[2]

Born in Mutsu, Aomori-ken, Chinda graduated at an American university and joined the Foreign Ministry in 1885. After a variety of consular posts, he became minister to Russia briefly in November 1900. He then returned to the ministry as vice-minister under Komura Jūtarō in 1903 and served throughout the stressful days of the Russo-Japanese War. Because of Komura's frequent illnesses and his absences at Portsmouth, New Hampshire and Beijing, Chinda was effectively in charge at critical junctures. He had close relations with the British ambassador who reported confidentially to London in 1908: 'Chinda is considered by some to be a man of exceptional ability. The Baron speaks excellent English but is very reticent.'[3]

In June 1908, he went to his first ambassadorial post, succeeding Inouye Katsunosuke in Berlin. He then moved to Washington from November 1911 where he had a long stint of five years. He enjoyed cordial relations with the British Ambassador there, Sir Cecil Spring Rice.[4]

CHINDA IN LONDON

Chinda was appointed to the London embassy in the middle of the First World War and arrived at his post at a critical juncture on 1 August 1916. It was a strange coincidence that he should succeed Inouye whom he had earlier replaced in Berlin in 1908. It was rumoured that he had turned down the post of foreign minister in 1915, a sign that he was approaching the pinnacle of his career. He came to London at a depressing time for the Allies before the United States joined them in April 1917. China, which was even more a matter of concern for Japan, entered the war in August of that year. While Britain was preoccupied by the changing fortunes of the fighting, Japan was looking ahead to the bargaining which would take place at the peace-table.

In October 1916, the Okuma cabinet resigned, making way for the cabinet led by General Terauchi Masatake. The foreign minister appointed was Motono Ichirō, the former ambassador to Russia, who had played a large part in formulating the Russo-Japanese Alliance which had just been concluded in July. Motono came to the post dissatisfied with the lack of clarity over Japanese policy towards the war. Basically, Japan was at war against the Central Powers of Germany and Austro-Hungary, and should cooperate with the Entente to the fullest degree. But the situation, Motono wrote, was full of uncertainties:

> Peace terms should include Japan's retention of Tsingtao and occupied islands in the Pacific and acquisition of rights possessed by Germany in Shantung province. . . But, if victory does not go either to the Alliance or the Entente, it is likely that Germany will reject Japan's claims. . . If the war ends in victory for the German Alliance, it will be even more difficult to get approval for Japan's claims. . . Even if the Entente are victorious, they will probably expect the country that made the least sacrifice in the war [i.e. Japan] to be modest in its demands. . . Hence we should give the Entente countries as much help as possible in materiel, finance etc.[5]

Clearly, from Japan's perspective, all contingencies were being explored. But Motono was seeking clarification and proposing a radical shift of emphasis away from a policy which would not send troops to the Western Front and hitherto had declined to send war-ships beyond Singapore. The Japanese cabinet agreed that, now that the war was finely balanced, it was desirable that Japan should more explicitly throw in her lot with Britain and her Entente partners in the hope of securing the prizes on which she had set her sights.

Such was the policy which Chinda had to apply in the months ahead. Almost as soon as he reached London, the naval situation in the Atlantic took a turn for the worse because of German submarine attacks. Britain reiterated to Chinda her appeals for naval assistance and Japan responded by requesting a number of undertakings. These included a post-war guarantee for Japan's retention of Shantung and Germany's insular possessions in the Pacific which were already occupied by Japan. Japanese naval authorities were probably itching to go beyond the confines of the China seas; and Chinda indicated that there would probably be no difficulty in securing their cooperation. On 2 February 1917, Japan agreed to make available the necessary naval assistance. The *Tsushima* and *Niitaka* were to go to Cape of Good Hope, while the *Akashi* and two flotillas of destroyers were to be despatched to the Mediterranean.[6]

The British war cabinet duly responded by confirming the necessary guarantees on 14 February. Britain agreed in rather careful language that she would support Japan's claims in regard to the disposal of Germany's rights in Shantung and possessions in the Islands North of the Equator on the occasion of a peace conference, it being understood that Japan would '. . . treat in the same spirit Britain's claims to the German islands South of Equator'. This last phrase was included in order to create the impression of parity between the two sides. But this was spurious since Britain was in this instance the mendicant, desperate to obtain Japanese naval assistance regardless. Where this formula was devised is not clear. Probably in London; but Chinda's role in this negotiation is not completely clear. He was a newcomer to the post, compared to Sir Conyngham Greene who had been Ambassador in Tokyo since 1913 and was, of course, able to lobby the naval establishment there direct.[7]

Over the next issue, Chinda took a more personal interest. A telegram from Deputy Foreign Minister Alfred Zimmermann in Berlin to Mexico on 19 January 1917 had been intercepted and successfully decoded by British intelligence.[8] The thrust of the message was that 'if war broke out between Germany and the United States, Germany would offer Mexico an alliance and try to persuade her into operations against the United States, with the ancillary suggestion that the Mexican president should mediate between Germany and Japan and request Japan to take part in their alliance'. This obscure speculation was dynamite. The intercept was passed over by Britain to Washington; by President Wilson to the press; and by the newspapers to an astonished American public. Germany was on the point of starting unrestricted submarine warfare in the Atlantic and wanted to dissuade the United States from declaring war. In April, however, the Americans severed relations with Germany because of her threat to make these submarine attacks against both enemy and neutral shipping.

The air between Washington and Tokyo was already hostile; and those suspicions were greatly intensified by the inclusion of Japan's name in the Zimmermann telegram. Chinda at Washington had had the additional responsibility as envoy to Mexico and was already familiar with the problems there. Japan had sold a considerable amount of arms to Mexico; and the arms dealers were a source of constant embarrassment to the Japanese government. Chinda was able to tell Britain with considerable authority that Japan was keeping her distance from the Mexican government. She published denials that she would have had any hand in such a deal and emphasized that there was no way that Mexico of all states could persuade Japan to make peace with Germany.

On 5 May, Viscount and Viscountess Chinda were invited to spend two nights at Windsor Castle as royal guests. During their visit the king spoke to them of the need for Japanese destroyers to sink German submarines because of the Battle of the Atlantic Ocean and the need for arranging convoys. At this stage Japan asked in return for the supply of special materials required for the construction of naval ships, in other words, steel. Britain had to say that she had none to spare and urged Japan to approach the United States where she was again refused.[9]

American entry to the war on the Entente side was succeeded by the decision of the government of China to follow the same path. This had long-term consequences for Japan as the Motono statement above has shown. It was now inevitable that China would send plenipotentiaries to the ultimate peace conference and dispute the major Japanese claim.

PARIS PEACE CONFERENCE

When the war ended in 1918, Chinda as Ambassador to Britain was chosen alongside Matsui Keishirō, Ambassador to France, and Ijūin Hikokichi, Ambassador to Italy, as Japanese delegates to the peace conference. The initial idea was that Japan would rely on those who had expertise from the Portsmouth Conference of 1905 which ended the Russo-Japanese War. Viscount Chinda arrived in Paris on 11 January 1919. On the 18th the main delegation led by Baron Makino Shinken, a former ambassador and foreign minister, arrived via the United States. For the critical first six weeks Makino conducted negotiations as de facto chief. Chinda was in effect second in the pecking order, slightly higher than Matsui and Ijūin. Chinda had some advantages over the other Japanese delegates: his English was superior; and he was 'robust in argument'. More importantly, he knew most of the American delegates who had been members of the Wilson administration and had had dealings with them and with the British. He was, in particular, familiar with Arthur Balfour who as Foreign Secretary was a chief British negotiator. When Prince Saionji arrived on 2 March to head the mission, not much changed since he was content to keep a low profile and be consulted behind the scenes.[10]

Nonetheless, conference diplomacy was a novel experience for which Japan as a whole was ill-prepared. The Portsmouth negotiations of 1905 had been no real preparation. Similarly, the international conference at Beijing of 1900-1 to sort out the Boxer problem, while it was truly international, dealt only with a limited and well-defined subject. This was a problem for the delegates who were to be pitied because their instructions were strictly laid down from Tokyo. They were formulated not only by the Foreign Ministry but sometimes by the *Gaikō Chōsakai*, an extra-parliamentary group of politicians with strongly-held views and without exposure to the arts of international negotiation.

That left much of the business of the delegation to be conducted by what one Japanese scholar calls the 'Makino-Chinda *kombi*'. That is, the two tended to combine as a team and lobby together on all substantial issues. Cooperation between Makino and Chinda was to be a special feature of the Japanese delegation's actions at Paris; and it worked well. They had a broad mandate from Prime Minister Hara to follow the line taken by the British and Americans. But this was not easy to implement because they found that Anglo-Saxon feeling was generally in favour of China and this was shared by conference participants as a whole.

Japan was negotiating as one of the victors. In the initial stages of the conference Japan lost out over the racial equality clause.[12] There was a fierce determination, therefore, not to give in over her most precious demand, the transfer to Japan from Germany of the former German-leased territory in Shantung province in China. This issue became an acute embarrassment to the

Council of Four, all the more so as Italy had already left Paris dissatisfied and in disgust. Chinda was at his most threatening at this stage, suggesting that Japan would not join the League of Nations. On 16 April he met Balfour to see if any compromise could be worked out over Shantung. Balfour told him that the United States and France were supporting China. Chinda assumed not inaccurately that Britain, while ready to act in accordance with her agreement of 1917, was endeavouring to induce Japan to reduce her demands in order to secure a compromise acceptable to other delegations. But he would not agree. When the Versailles treaty was signed, it transferred the residue of the German lease of Shantung to Japan, in spite of China's pleas. But, in order to secure her prime demand, the Japanese delegates, not least Chinda, had to give some assurances of the vaguest kind that Japan would ultimately restore some of Germany's rights to China. That assurance was probably given in good faith but it was not publicly endorsed by the Tokyo government.

The Paris Peace Conference left a lot of loose ends. This was particularly true of the Far Eastern field and the issue of Shantung. Since it had not been possible to resolve this to the satisfaction of the powers, it was left to the Foreign Office and the State Department to pursue the issue with Japan on a bilateral basis. These were awkward days for Chinda who was summoned to meet the acting Foreign Secretary, Lord Curzon, on 18 July for this purpose. Curzon reported that he had told Chinda that:

> . . . it was unwise of Japan to insist upon the technical rights secured to her by her agreement with China in respect of Shantung. I was aware that a declaration of her intentions had been made by Japan to other Allied Powers in Paris; but this action which was to a large extent a justification of the action taken by the Powers had never been published to the world. . . The whole policy of Japan was wrapt in a mist of doubt and suspicion which was creating very general alarm.

In response, the ambassador (as described in the flowery language of Curzon):

> . . . intervened with an almost impassioned defence of the action of his country and his Government, the fervour of which in no wise abated until our conversation lasted for nearly an hour and a half. . . Arguments were again and again reiterated with great vigour.[13]

Something of the personality of Chinda comes out in these exchanges. He was not inexperienced in diplomacy and was not prepared to be browbeaten by Curzon. Loyal to his government, he stood up to the imperious Foreign Secretary.

Chinda continued to be actively involved in the politics of Europe after the Versailles treaty. It was one of the consequences of Japan's enhanced role in international affairs that her representatives had to be involved in the various conferences held around Europe in order to implement and expand on the findings of the Versailles treaty. There were also meetings of the nascent League of Nations of which Japan was a founder member. For example, Chinda had to attend a special meeting of the League Council which was summoned for St James's Palace on 14 June 1920, London acting for the time being as the headquarters of the world body. The press were calling for the highest possible representation by prominent politicians so that the League of Nations could be launched strongly. Alas, 'apart from Lord Curzon for Britain and Viscount Chinda for Japan, other representatives lacked distinction', it was reported.

Chinda was punctilious in attending to these public duties. Japan wanted to be seen as cooperating in the League Council which was the prime international body of the time; and Chinda played his part.[14]

DEPARTURE: END OF THE ALLIANCE

Chinda's term of office in London was fast coming to an end. One item of business which he wanted to resolve before he left his post was the future of the alliance, the third treaty being due to lapse on 13 July 1921. There was no doubt that Hara Kei as Prime Minister was committed to the continuation of the alliance and carried his cabinet with him. But, as in Britain, there were discordant elements outside the cabinet. Some thought that Britain was a symbol of old-style imperialism which had been further displayed in the terms of the Versailles treaty and was not to be trusted by Japan. Others in intellectual circles were broadly favourable, taking the view that the United States had become so hostile to Japan during the war that Britain was the only great power that could be relied on to be moderately sympathetic to Japan.

Apart from xenophobic distrust, which is natural to all countries, what divided the two allies in 1920 was the relation of the alliance to the newly-founded League of Nations. To the Japanese the issue was simple: the alliance was stable and tested in time, while the League was experimental and its future unpredictable. British opinion-makers looked at it differently: the world had moved on from the days of alliances towards world organizations and so the alliance would have to take second place to the covenant of the League. The London embassy found it necessary to inform Tokyo of the existence of two contrasting strands of opinion within the British Empire: those for extending the alliance (*dōmei enchō ronsha*) and those opposed to continuing it (*hikeizoku ronsha*). To the Japanese, however, it was a nonsense to think of a contradiction existing between the League and the alliance; the two would complement one another in achieving stability in East Asia. The end result was that a formula had to be found which would preserve the alliance and would see the League through its teething period.[15] That formula was approved by the cabinet and the *Gaikō Chōsakai*.

One of Chinda's last acts was to sign, along with Curzon, at the Spa conference on 8 July 1920, the following document:

> '[Our agreement of 1911] though in harmony with the spirit of the Covenant of the League of Nations, is not entirely consistent with the letter of that Covenant. [The two governments agree] that, if the said Agreement be continued after July 1921, it must be in a form which is not inconsistent with that Covenant.'

In order to get this formula through the Privy Council where opposition was expected, it was necessary for the Ministry to append lengthy explanations.[16]

Before Chinda left his London post, there were a large number of farewell functions for the retiring ambassador. Of course, he was entertained by the Japan Society of London of which he had been president. But he was widely feted by the political establishment. In spite of all the doubts and dismays in diplomatic circles, the Japanese were generally popular in Britain in 1920. The Chindas were the symbolic beneficiaries of this affection.[17]

In particular, Chinda met with Britain's leaders. On 17 August, Chinda called on the British Prime Minister, Lloyd George, whom he had known well from the various post-war conferences that they had attended together. While ex-changing parting greetings, they discussed first the future of Russia and later the Anglo-Japanese Alliance. Chinda, raising the alliance issue, said that Japan wanted to continue the former Anglo-Japanese relationship which was in the interest of both countries and also in that of the world. While he was due to retire, he said he would strive for that relationship to the best of his ability. Lloyd George asked how Japanese opinion thought about continuing the alliance. Chinda said he had no doubt that the majority of the responsible intellectual classes agreed to the continuation of the alliance. The prime minister pointed out that he believed that British public opinion also favoured continuing the alliance but he had to consider the views of dominions overseas and of the United States. In his opinion, if it were possible, there would be advantages in adding the United States to the parties to the alliance. But, considering the present difficulties of the American administration, it would be absolutely impossible to attempt to negotiate on this problem. Following this, Chinda made his farewells to Curzon and found him very cordial. On the alliance he took the same view as the prime minister.[18] These views were not expressed out of politeness because they were repeating views like these to their cabinet colleagues.

Chinda, accompanied by Viscountess Chinda who had played a large part in her husband's success, sailed from Tilbury on 24 August by the *Kitano-maru*. He was succeeded by Hayashi Gonsuke. This was at roughly the same time as the arrival of Sir Charles Eliot as the new ambassador in Tokyo. So there was a change of pilots in both capitals. Exhausted after four years of wartime and post-war diplomacy, which had taken their toll on his health, the departing ambassador returned to Japan early in October.

Chinda was as good as his word to the British ministers and gave his views on the alliance in a conversation in the Foreign Ministry on 15 October, explaining how he saw British opinion:

> since the alliance had been in existence so long, it would raise all sorts of important issues for it to be abrogated without very special reasons. Besides, turning to the future of the League of Nations, the whole British nation was feeling a bit disturbed. By and large, there were no obvious objections on the part of the government to continuing the alliance. But Japan must try to avoid some cases which whipped up anti-Japanese feeling like the arrest of Shaw and the issue of Shantung and Tsingtao and make her viewpoint clearer. Britain's major problem was to take into account the opinion in the United States and the Dominions.[19]

This was a broadly accurate interpretation of British thinking. Perhaps Chinda placed undue emphasis on the views of Lloyd George and Curzon which did not wholly represent those of the people at large and the Foreign Office secretariat. But he clearly identified the intense feeling of British subservience to Washington. There was not much that Japan could do for the present while the election campaign was being fought out in the States or, in the case of the British Dominions, until the imperial conference was held during the summer of 1921. Japan should, however, avoid provocative actions which would stir up a damaging press campaign against her. This was a recognition of a new truth about the power of public opinion and the media in post-Versailles foreign policy-making in Europe. Japan could well understand that the future of the alliance would not be a simple legalistic matter such as had been the case with the renewal in July 1920 but was likely to become a major issue of international affairs.

Viscount Chinda was made a Count on 7 September 1920 for services during the First World War. Whether this was a reward for his work at the London Embassy or at the Paris and other conferences is not stated. It was merely one of a number of elevations announced at the same time.[20] Chinda was appointed to the Privy Council and in 1921 joined the Imperial Household Ministry. He played an important part in promoting the notion of international cooperation through various activities of the Japan League of Nations Association [*Nippon kokusai remmei kyōkai*], a branch of the global organization set up to win support for the cause of the League.[21]

Chinda was further honoured by his appointment to accompany the Crown Prince during his state visit to Britain commencing on 9 May 1921. It was not a political mission insofar as it was designed primarily as part of Hirohito's education and coming of age. Chinda's role was not to negotiate but to instruct him on the niceties of protocol and steer him through the byzantine rituals of the British court. He is to be seen in the photographs of the visit, a diminutive figure standing protectively close to the young prince. He only surfaces in one instance where the Prince of Wales, thinking that the Crown Prince should come closer to the British people, was alleged to have proposed that he should travel on the London underground. When, however, this madcap proposal was raised, Chinda was the one that had to veto it, or rather (to avoid lèse majesté) to discourage the enterprise. Overall, the itinerary ran smoothly thanks to Chinda; and Curzon as Foreign Secretary saluted the prince's visit as 'a uniform and conspicuous success'.[22]

The culmination of Chinda's career in London has to be measured in two respects. First, as ambassador to London. Like his predecessor, he came without early training in London or a previous London posting. By the time he left in 1920 he had been won over to Britain and, in spite of the verbal knocks he experienced at the hands of Lord Curzon, he appears to have genuinely enjoyed his last few months. *The Times* saluted him for taking his share of the heat and burden of those anxious days.[23] Second, he has to be measured against the changing face of world diplomacy. Chinda was at the centre of things at the Paris Peace Conference and in the post-war round of international conferences. Conference diplomacy required linguistic ability and political flexibility, not qualities that Japan had conspicuously shown in the past. Nonetheless Chinda, in combination with Makino, did his best at Paris in a new and difficult role. Kimura Eiichi, a Foreign Ministry official attached to the plenipotentiaries there, described Chinda as showing great fighting spirit with special reference to the Shantung question at Paris and general coolness in negotiation.[24] While Makino appealed more to foreign observers as a man of ideas ready to explore and discuss new approaches, Chinda was a more conventional bureaucrat but he emerged as a firm believer in the League of Nations. *The Times*' editorial summed up his qualities on his departure, saying that he had 'a fixed and unswerving loyalty to the immemorial traditions of his country [which went] hand in hand with a sympathetic understanding of the problems and growth of Western democracy'.[25]

[2005]

NOTES

1.   The best general treatments of the subject are R.H. Fifield, *Woodrow Wilson and the Far East*, New York: Crowell, 1952; and Bruce Elleman, *Wilson and China: A revised history of the Shantung question*, Armunk, NY: M.E. Sharpe, 1984.
2.   Kikuchi Takenori (ed.), *Hakushaku Chinda Sutemi-den, 1857-1929*, Tokyo: Kyōmeikaku, 1938.
3.   *British Documents on Foreign Affairs*, Part I, Series E, Vol. 8, Maryland: University Publications of America, 1989, p. 69.
4.   Honda Kumataro on 'Chinda and Spring Rice' in Kikuchi, p. 288.
5.   Kajima Morinosuke, *Diplomacy of Japan*, Tokyo: Kajima, 1980, Vol. 3, p. 203 (my parenthesis). See also *Nihon gaikō bunshō*, Taishō 6/3, doc. 667 [hereafter cited as 'NGB'].
6.   Professor Seki Eiji in his book *Nichi-Ei dōmei*, Tokyo: Gakushū Kenkyū, 2003, devotes chapters 2 and 3, pp. 71-179, to Japan's Mediterranean expedition and Malta experiences.
7.   There are new studies of this topic by Yoichi Hirama and Ian Gow with John Chapman, *History of Anglo-Japanese Relations*, Vol. 3, 'The Military Dimension', Basingstoke: Palgrave, 2003, while the older study by G. Nakashima, 'Japanese Navy in the Great War, 1918-20' in *Proceedings of the Japan Society of London*, 31(1917) is still useful.
8.   See C. Andrews and D.N. Dilks, *The Missing Dimension*, London: Macmillan, 1984, pp. 144 and 147. Barbara Tuchman, *The Zimmermann Telegram*, London: Macmillan, 1983.
9.   NGB Taishō 6/3, docs 106 and 110.
10. Margaret MacMillan gives a good pen portrait of Saionji and how his role puzzled foreigners. *Peacemakers*, London: John Murray, 2001, pp. 316-19.
11. Kimura Eiichi as quoted in Kikuchi, pp. 220-2. This view is generally supported by Naoko Shimazu, *Japan, Race and Equality*, London: Routledge, 1998.
12. Japan's claim for mandates over the Pacific islands which is sometimes depicted as a failure was eventually settled in her favour. The allocation, initially made at the Paris conference, was confirmed at the San Remo conference of 1920 and later by the League-Japan agreement in 1922.
13. Fifield, pp. 546-7 contains only the shortened version passed to the Americans. For the full version, *Documents on British Foreign Policy, 1919-39*, London: HMSO, 1(vi), doc. 429. [hereafter cited as 'DBFP'].
14. George Scott, *Rise and Fall of the League of Nations*, London: Hutchinson, 1973, p.56.
15. NGB Taishō 9, Vol. 3/2, doc. 882.
16. NGB Taishō 9, Vol. 3/2, doc. 884.
17. Kikuchi, pp. 214-5.
18. NGB Taishō 9, Vol. 3/2, nos 888-9; Kajima, Vol. 3, p. 427.
19. NGB Taishō 9, Vol. 3/2, doc. 986. George Shaw was an Anglo-Chinese merchant with business interests on the Yalu river. He was arrested by Japanese police in Korea on what seemed to Britain to be flimsy charges.
20. *The Times*, 7 September 1920.
21. Ogata Sadako in Dorothy Borg and Shumpei Okamoto (eds), *Pearl Harbor as History*, New York: Columbia UP, 1973, pp. 462-3. Japan League of Nations Association was formed on 23 April 1920 and grew rapidly.
22. *DBFP*, 1(xiv), docs 277 and 287. Ian Nish, 'Crown Prince Hirohito in Britain' in Ian Nish (ed.), *Biographical Portraits*, Vol. II, Richmond: Japan Library, 1997. Dealt with also in F.S.G. Piggott, *Broken Thread*, Aldershot: Gale and Polden, 1950, pp. 123-31 and Philip Ziegler (ed.), *Diaries of Lord Louis Mountbatten*, London: Collins, 1987.
23. *The Times*, 18 August 1920.
24. Kikuchi, p. 222-5.
25. *The Times*, 18 August 1920.

FURTHER READING

Teruhiko Nagao, *Nitobe Inazo: From Bushido to the League of Nations*, Sapporo: Hokkaido University, 2006.

Naoko Shimazu, *Japan, Race and Equality: Racial Equality proposal of 1919*, London: Routledge, 1998.

14

HAYASHI GONSUKE, 1860-1939
Leading the Way to the Washington Conference
[London, 1920-25]

Hayashi Gonsuke

HARUMI GOTŌ-SHIBATA

AMBASSADOR TO BRITAIN

The Japanese Ambassador to Britain from May 1920 to August 1925 was Hayashi Gonsuke. He was born in 1860[1] to a samurai family in Aizu domain (now Fukushima Prefecture). In early 1868, when Hayashi was still a child, both his father and grandfather died in the battle of Toba-Fushimi near Kyoto, one of the major conflicts fought between pro-emperor and pro-shogun forces during the Meiji Restoration. About eight months later, he experienced the siege of Aizu Castle by forces from the domains demanding the restoration of power to the emperor. Having been defeated, the Aizu samurai who were considered to be supporters of the Tokugawa *Bakufu* were punished by being expelled to northerly and infertile parts of Japan. Hayashi and his mother were among them. He later left the area to escape the hardships of life there.[2]

Hayashi was fortunate enough to come to Tokyo while still very young. In Tokyo he was looked after by a former Satsuma retainer who had known his grandfather through the Toba-Fushimi battle. This man was not a wealthy patron but was from the winning side in the struggles leading up to the Meiji restoration. Hayashi, who received financial support from several other people, graduated from Tokyo Imperial University. In 1887 he entered the Foreign Ministry. This was seven years before the examination system for admission began. Among those recruited in the same year, was Uchida Yasuya, who later became the Foreign Minister at the time of the Paris Peace Conference of 1919 and the Washington Conference of 1921-2.

By the time Hayashi became Japanese Ambassador to Britain in 1920, he had served in various overseas posts. From 1893 to 1898, he had worked in London as consul and then first secretary, and had the opportunity of observing how the British reacted to the Sino-Japanese War.[3] He then spent nine years in Korea from 1899 as Minister. This was a crucial period that led to Japan's colonization of Korea in 1910. When the Great War broke out, he was in Italy. He was also appointed as Minister to China (1916-18) and the Governor of the Guandong Leased Territory (1919-20). In these last two posts he was at odds with the military and bitterly opposed to the activities of Nishihara Kamezō (a businessman known for the Nishihara Loans to the Chinese government) and his associates. He did not enjoy these posts at all,[4] while some Japanese did not rate highly the line he took.[5]

Hayashi was a sociable person and was considered favourably by the diplomats of other countries. For example, Daniel Varé, an Italian diplomat who in 1920 attended the early meetings of the League of Nations with Hayashi, wrote that Hayashi was his 'old friend from Peking'.[6] S.P.P Waterlow, a member of the Far Eastern Department of the British Foreign Office, described Hayashi as 'a sensible and moderate man, not afraid of disagreeing with his Government'.[7] Sir John Tilley, British Ambassador at Tokyo from 1926 to 1931, in a despatch of 1927 wrote of him:

> [Hayashi] has the reputation of being a clever and able diplomatist, and was popular during his stay in England. He is friendly to foreigners and pro-English in sympathies. He speaks English well.[8]

FUTURE OF THE ANGLO-JAPANESE ALLIANCE

While Hayashi was Japanese Ambassador in London, the most significant issue for Britain and Japan was the Anglo-Japanese Alliance. In this section I propose to concentrate on Hayashi's performance between the autumn of 1920 and the summer of 1921.

As soon as Hayashi arrived in Britain, he noted that some people in the government were denouncing Japan and the alliance.[9] He thought that one of the reasons was their disapproval of Japanese policies, especially her policy towards China over the previous few years, and that hence the renewal of the alliance depended on the conduct of Japan's policy in China.

As early as 29 September 1920, he wrote to the Foreign Ministry in Tokyo and suggested that the Japanese government should take steps to solve the 'misunderstandings' which Britain and the United States had. He wrote that Japan should, first of all, abolish military rule in Qingdao which she had occupied since 1914 and withdraw troops from Jinan.[10]

Later, he wrote to Foreign Minister Uchida, repeatedly suggesting the necessity of changing Japan's China policy.[11] Although Hayashi and Uchida had entered the Foreign Ministry in the same year, Hayashi was older. He did not hesitate to express straightforward opinions to a person of higher rank.

Hayashi was not the only one in the Japanese diplomatic service who disapproved of the country's China policy. For example, Makino Nobuaki, Japan's representative at the Paris Peace Conference, stated at a meeting held by *Gaikō Chōsakai* [Advisory Council on Foreign Relations] on 8 December 1918:

> Although Japan has always claimed that her stance is fair and just, and that she adheres to the policies of open door, non-intervention into China and Sino-Japanese friendship, her actual policies have been inconsistent with what she has claimed, with the result that the powers have come to regard Japan as untrustworthy.[12]

This observation is accurate and reasonable, and seems to have received some support in the Foreign Ministry.

However, this view was not acceptable to the people who were at the centre of Japan's foreign policy-making. Itō Miyoji, one of the Privy Councillors, demanded that Makino should explain why he thought Japan was regarded as unreliable. Both Itō and another senior politician, Inukai Tsuyoshi, strongly insisted that it was necessary for Japan to possess more territory. Following their remarks, Terauchi Masatake, the Prime Minister from 1916 to 1918, claimed that Japan had never been unfair and unjust.[13] The *Gaikō Chōsakai* did not endorse Makino's opinion.

The views, which Hayashi sent from London, were not even discussed at the *Gaikō Chōsakai* meetings. Neither Uchida nor the Asian Department of the Foreign Ministry could accept the idea of abandoning Japan's existing interests without negotiations merely to fend off British criticisms.[14] Although Hayashi continued to express similar opinions, the Ministry was determined to ignore them.

In the meantime, Britain had been busy considering the views of the Dominions as well as those of the United States. She failed to take account of the sensitive feelings of her ally during the summer of 1921, when two issues made Japan doubtful whether Britain was a trustworthy partner or not. The first issue was the argument on how to interpret the Anglo-Japanese joint announcement of July 1920 and the other was Britain's suggestion that China should be invited to the Pacific Conference. Mutual distrust of the allies grew considerably.

On 9 May 1921, the British Foreign Secretary, Lord Curzon of Kedleston, met Hayashi and proposed a three-month extension of the Anglo-Japanese Alliance, which would reach its full ten-year span on 13 July 1921. This proposal was made as a result of a very complicated situation brought about by the Anglo-Japanese joint announcement of 8 July 1920.

The creation of the League of Nations in 1919 had made it urgently necessary for the two countries to define the legal relationship between the alliance and the League Covenant. In June 1920, Britain suggested to Japan that the two governments should jointly inform the League that the alliance treaty of 1911 could only be continued after July 1921 in a form consistent with the League Covenant. Japan agreed with the idea, but argued that the announcement should state that both countries wished in principle to continue the alliance. Therefore, Curzon proposed the phrase: 'if the said Agreement *be continued* after July 1921, it must be in a form which is not inconsistent with that Covenant'.[15]

It is clear from these negotiations that Japan at this point wanted to continue the alliance. Britain was non-committal, but the decision-makers did not necessarily intend to end the alliance at this stage. However, around the time the note was signed by Hayashi's predecessor and Curzon, a legal adviser of the British Foreign Office who was asked for his views indicated that the declaration was legally equivalent to denunciation of the alliance and that the alliance must either be modified or deemed to terminate in 1921. Curzon did not attempt to overrule this opinion, which became the official interpretation of the British Foreign Office.[16]

According to this legal adviser, the one year's notice necessary to terminate the 1911 agreement had been given in July 1920, with the result that the alliance would lapse automatically in July 1921. As Britain had to seek the views of the Dominions and as the Imperial Conference was due to assemble as late as the middle of June, Britain considered it desirable that the alliance should be extended for an interim period.[17] This was why Curzon proposed the prolongation by three months.

Hayashi advised that Japan should answer immediately without trying to scrutinize British intentions,[18] but the British suggestion understandably created a stir in Tokyo. Eleven months earlier, the Japanese Government had made it plain that Japan did not want the declaration to be treated as equivalent to a denunciation of the alliance. From Japan's point of view, Britain seemed to have suddenly begun to insist on a totally new interpretation that the alliance would end automatically. This inevitably led to doubts in Tokyo about Britain's true intentions.

In the Japanese view, the joint communication when it was made in July 1920 was not the equivalent of the one-year's notice stipulated to terminate the alliance. Furthermore, the idea that the alliance would lapse automatically without any negotiations taking place was considered to be especially unreasonable. Consequently, at a *Gaikō Chōsakai* meeting held on 28 May, the draft reply to Britain was approved with some amendments.[19] On 3 June, Hayashi sent an embassy official to the Foreign Office to seek clarification of the British view. When Sir Victor Wellesley, the head of the Far Eastern Department, was asked whether Britain's legal interpretation was adopted after Curzon's meeting with Hayashi in May, Wellesley's answer was affirmative.[20]

Hayashi's reaction to this situation was restrained. He did not show even the slightest doubt about what Curzon and the British Foreign Office were saying to him and his staff. He wrote to Uchida in his despatch sent on 6 June that to argue which legal interpretation was correct was not fruitful but only damaging to the good feelings between the two countries. According to him, if Britain intended to abrogate the treaty, it could not be maintained even if Japan's interpretation was found to be right. He was, therefore, of the opinion that Japan should agree to the prolongation and make efforts to negotiate and conclude a modified treaty successfully within three months.[21]

Curzon was less willing to back down than Hayashi. On 8 June, he gave Hayashi a formal letter, informing him that 'the communication of last year must be held to constitute the notification of termination required under article 6' of the 1911 treaty. Japan declined to accept this proposition.[22]

Curzon had not been unfavourable to the continuation of the alliance and continued to be sceptical of the opinions of his own legal expert. Professor Nish describes this British stance as follows: 'They stuck to their guns but admitted privately that there were weaknesses in the British case.'[23] To end the stalemate, Curzon suggested on 27 June that both sides should issue a second joint notification to the League so worded as to show that the agreement remained in force until October 1921.

In a letter to Uchida, Hayashi insisted that, although he fully agreed with Japan's interpretation, Japan should face the reality that the treaty might be abrogated in October. As long as the British strenuously insisted upon their own legal interpretation, Hayashi could not believe that working relations would be sustained, however well Japan made her case. If Britain wanted to terminate the alliance, he thought it more decent and respectable for Japan to accept Britain's wishes than go on nagging endlessly. He continued that, even if the treaty was not renewed, Japan should not show her disappointment. Rather, she should pronounce to the world with dignity that Anglo-Japanese relations had developed to the extent that a special alliance was no longer necessary.[24] By this stage, Hayashi seemed to have sensed that the British Foreign Office and its legal adviser strongly wanted to be rid of the alliance and were ready to use whatever excuses were available. Influenced by Hayashi, both Uchida and the Japanese Prime Minister Hara Takashi began to think that 'automatic lapse' might be inevitable.[25]

Actually, the British cabinet was much more favourable towards Japan than the Foreign Office. At a cabinet meeting convened on the morning of 30 June, the British Prime Minister David Lloyd George expressed the view that needless difficulties were being created by assuming that the communication sent to the League in July 1920 was tantamount to denouncing the alliance. The cabinet decided that Lord Birkenhead, the Lord Chancellor from 1919 to 1922, should be asked for an opinion. When the Dominion Prime Ministers met later that day in the afternoon, Lloyd George remarked that there had been no formal denunciation of the alliance. Birkenhead, who had been specially invited to attend this meeting, stated that it was 'a remarkable construction' to say that the communication to the League was to be construed as a denunciation. In effect, he endorsed the view taken by the Japanese lawyers.[26]

The Japanese government was relieved when the gist of Birkenhead's ruling was communicated to them.[27] The second joint Anglo-Japanese note was soon sent off to the League.[28] However, Japan's trust in Britain was shaken further by another issue.

On the afternoon of 4 July, Curzon called in Hayashi and asked whether his government would be prepared to join in a Pacific conference with the United States, and possibly with China. Hayashi said that he was strongly in favour of this conference and, although he could not speak authoritatively for his government, he entertained little doubt that they also would be in favour of it. From this, Curzon drew the false conclusion that Japan would welcome such a conference. Hayashi then sent a despatch to Uchida, suggesting that Japan should accept the Pacific conference proposal in principle in the first place.[29] Hayashi also suggested that Japan should not repeat the same mistakes as those committed at Paris. He was of the opinion that Japan should participate in the proposed conference in the spirit of Sino-Japanese friendship, should co-operate with Britain and the United States, and should aim at solving the powers' 'misunderstanding' about Japan.[30] Perhaps he was reflecting ideas he had acquired previously as Minister in Peking (Beijing).

As mentioned above, Hayashi's opinions concerning Japan's China policy were completely at odds with those of the Foreign Ministry and influential members of Gaikō Chōsakai back home. The Hara cabinet might not be in favour of a forward policy in China; but they were not inclined to see Japan's privileges there eroded. What Hayashi said to Curzon was his own opinion, and his government did not endorse it. The Japanese objected to Curzon approaching China directly without clearing their approach with Japan first. The nature of the proposals and the method of their communication deeply offended the Japanese.[31]

All through July, Britain tried to convene the Pacific conference in London and to enlist Japan's support for the idea. However, the Japanese had already lost their trust in Britain and started to think that it was best for them to make a direct arrangement and cooperate with the Americans, who were simultaneously trying to hold the conference in Washington. Both London and Washington were geographically far away from Japan, and it would make no difference for the Japanese whichever place was chosen for the conference.

Curzon laid some of the blame for this discord between London and Tokyo on Hayashi.[32] However, as mentioned above, it was Hayashi who strove to solve the problem all through the difficult period in the summer of 1921. Hayashi was pro-British and never spoke ill of Japan's ally. When the argument over the joint declaration had finally ended, Hayashi was pleased to see Curzon appearing to be genuinely relieved.[33] Furthermore, his suggestions for Japan to take initiatives in improving Sino-Japanese relations were rational. However, neither Curzon nor the Japanese Government valued the role played by Hayashi. The government did not find it necessary to ask Hayashi to travel all the way to Washington and attend the Pacific conference. Although Hayashi held the same rank as Shidehara Kijūrō, the Ambassador to the United States, he was not to play a major role during the conference.[34] This was odd considering that Shidehara was unwell at the time.

On 14 October, the instructions of the Japanese government were communicated to the conference delegates in Washington. Like Britain, Japan was prepared to give up the alliance in favour of closer ties with the United States. The alliance had been of low repute,[35] and compared with many problems relating to China on which the Japanese were less willing to make concessions, the question of how to deal with it was no longer a difficult issue for the Japanese Government. At the Washington Conference the alliance was replaced by the Four Power Pact.

Hayashi remained in London until his retirement from the diplomatic service in August 1925, and endeavoured to overcome some of the tensions which might have arisen from the break in the alliance. In 1922, he spoke at a Japan Society of London dinner insisting that the Washington conference had cleared the air: it had cut away artificial ties.[36] He certainly reacted to the end of the alliance with dignity, but most people did not know what had happened during the summer of 1921 as closely as Hayashi. There were many different reactions among the Japanese. One example is the scene described in F. S. G. Piggott's *Broken Thread*. On the day when the abrogation was discussed at Washington, he dined with his Japanese friend:

> . . . I had asked Morita to dine with us at the Racquet Club, and he brought with him Major Nishihara, private secretary to the Minister of War, who spoke English and French perfectly. I had not met him before the Conference, but had established close relations in recent weeks and considered him one of the most intelligent and forthcoming Japanese officers of my acquaintance. Morita . . . was strangely silent; Nishihara hardly said a word. It was a dull and gloomy evening, and we were all glad when the small party broke up.[37]

Some of Piggott's Japanese acquaintances felt as if they had been shell-shocked at the news of the demise of the alliance, and this feeling was to be utilized to back up an anti-British line in the late 1930s and early 1940s.

ASSESSMENT

How can we assess Hayashi as Japanese Ambassador to Britain? He had become truly internationally-minded after spending many years abroad; this is a quality that not all diplomats necessarily possess. Being sociable and outspoken, he contributed to keeping Anglo-Japanese relations as amicable as possible while he remained in London.

On the other hand, he was not in tune with the thinking of the government in Tokyo. In order to improve Anglo-Japanese relations, he placed emphasis on China, suggesting repeatedly that Japan should change her policies towards that country. Unfortunately, Japan's foreign policy was made by those who were determined to preserve existing privileges in China, and to enlarge them where possible. Hayashi's opinions concerning China were simply ignored by his government.

For Curzon and members of the British Foreign Office, Hayashi was one of the most important channels through which they could gain information on the Japanese Government, although it seems that they had lost interest in Japan by the summer of 1921. Hayashi was unwilling to be the mouthpiece of his government, and what Hayashi said sometimes lacked the backing of his government. He was remarkably independent-minded and individualistic for a Japanese diplomat, probably because he had been recruited before the examination system for admission was introduced in 1894. Hayashi's stance was fair, but he was not the best intermediary. It was probably difficult for the British who spoke only with Hayashi to realize how the politicians in Tokyo felt frustrated and had lost their trust in Britain. The blame, however, should be laid on the Japanese Government for appointing Hayashi as ambassador while pursuing policies with which he could not sympathize.

[2005]

NOTES

1.   This was seven years after Commodore Matthew Perry of the US navy had come to Japan to demand the country to open its doors to outsiders, an incident that had thrown the country into economic and political chaos.
2.   Hayashi Gonsuke, *Waga 70 nen wo kataru* [On my 70 years] (Tokyo: Dai ichi shobō, 1935), pp. 2-39. The last daimyo of Aizu was the father of Matsudaira Tsuneo, the Japanese Ambassador to Britain from 1929 to 1935.
3.   Ibid., pp. 70-72.
4.   Ibid., pp. 419-421; Ian Nish, *Alliance in Decline* (London: Athlone Press, 1972), p. 309.
5.   *Chū Ei taishi no kōtetsu to Nichi Ei dōmei no shōrai* [The change of the Ambassador to Britain and the future of the Anglo-Japanese Alliance], *Gaikō Jihō* [Revue Diplomatique], no. 374, 1 June 1920, p. 1011.
6.   Daniel Varè, *Laughing Diplomat* (London: J. Murray, 1938), p. 175; Hayashi, *Waga 70 nen*, pp. 352, 356-7.
7.   PRO, FO 371/10329, F 3834/20/87, letter from Waterlow to Anderson (Home Office), 18 Nov. 1924.
8.   PRO, FO371/12525, F8585/8585/23, 13 Oct. 1927, from Tilley, no. 541.
9.   See also Antony Best, *British Intelligence and the Japanese Challenge in Asia, 1914-1941* (Basingstoke: Palgrave Macmillan, 2002), pp. 45-8.
10. *Nihon Gaikō Bunsho* [Documents on Japanese Foreign Policy] (hereafter, NGB), Taisho 9 nen, Vol. 3-2 (hereafter, T9-3-2), No. 894, Hayashi to Uchida, 29 Sept. 1920.
11. NGB, T9-3-2, no. 899, 9 Nov. 1920; T10-3-2, no. 799, 19 Jan. 1921.
12. Kobayashi Tatsuo (ed.), *Suiusō Nikki* [Diary of Itō Miyoji] (Hara shobō, 1966), p. 333, 8 Dec. 1918. *Gaikō Chōsakai* was constituted in June 1917 to unify discussion of foreign policy, and worked until September 1922.
13. Ibid., pp. 334-42.
14. NGB, T10-3-2, No. 799, 19 Jan. 1921, Rangai chūki.
15. Nish, *Alliance in Decline*, p. 302.
16. Ibid., p. 303.
17. Ibid., pp. 324-5.
18. NGB, T10-3-2, No. 868, 25 May 1921.
19. *Hara Takashi Nikki* [Diary of Hara Takashi] (Tokyo: Kangensha, 1950), entries for 27 and 28

May 1921.
20. NGB, T10-3-2, No. 875, 3 June 1921.
21. NGB, T10-3-2, No. 876, 6 June 1921.
22. NGB, T10-3-2, No. 877, 9 June 1921; Nish, *Alliance in Decline*, p. 327.
23. Nish, *Alliance in Decline*, p. 331.
24. NGB, T10-3-2, No. 901, 28 June 1921; No. 903, 30 June 1921.
25. Hayashi, *Waga 70 nen*, p. 374; *Hara Takashi Nikki*, entry for 1 July 1921.
26. Hayashi, *Waga 70 nen*, pp. 374-5; Nish, *Alliance in Decline*, pp. 335-7.
27. *Hara Takashi Nikki*, entries for 2 and 7 July 1921.
28. NGB, T10-3-2, No. 910, 4 July 1921; Nish, *Alliance in Decline*, p. 340-1.
29. NGB, T10-3-2, No. 915, 4 July 1921; Nish, *Alliance in Decline*, p. 339.
30. Asada Sadao, *Ryō taisen kan no Nichi Bei kankei* [Japanese-American Relations Between the Wars] (Tokyo Daigaku Shuppankai, 1993), pp.104, 114.
31. Nish, *Alliance in Decline*, pp. 341-2.
32. Ibid., pp. 348-9.
33. Hayashi, *Waga 70 nen*, p. 376.
34. *Hara Takashi Nikki*, entries for 25 and 26 August 1921.
35. See for example the following articles in *Gaikō Jihō*. 'Editorial', No. 9 of 1915, 1 May 1915, p. 930; article by Ninagawa Arata, No. 5 of 1915, 1 Sept. 1915, pp. 459-460; article by Tanaka Suiichirō, No. 376, 1 July 1920, p. 7; and 'Jiron' by Hanzawa Tamaki, No. 389, 15 Jan. 1921, p. 132.
36. Ian Nish and Yoichi Kibata (eds), *The History of Anglo-Japanese Relations*, Vol. 1 (Basingstoke and London: Macmillan, 2000), p. 257.
37. F. S. G. Piggott, *Broken Thread* (Aldershot: Gale & Polden Ltd., 1950), p. 147.

FURTHER READING

Harumi Gotō, *Igirisu to Shanhai, 1925-32: Nichi-Ei no kyōchō to taikō*, Tokyo: University Press, 2006.

Robert Bickers, *Empire Made Me: An Englishman Adrift in Shanghai*, London, Penguin, 2004.

Sadao Asada, *From Mahan to Pearl Harbor: The Imperial Japanese Navy and the United States*, Annapolis: Naval Institute Press, 2006.

Ian Gow, *Military Intervention in Prewar Japanese Politics: Admiral Katō Kanji and the 'Washington System'*, London: Routledge/Curzon, 2004.

15

MATSUI KEISHIRŌ, 1868-1946
An Efficient Public Servant
[London, 1925-28]

TADASHI KURAMATSU

Matsui Keishirō

INTRODUCTION

Matsui Keishirō had a distinguished diplomatic career which included the posts of Vice-Minister for Foreign Affairs, Ambassador to France, one of the chief delegates to the Paris Peace Conference, Minister for Foreign Affairs and Ambassador to Britain, which was his last post. Despite this he has been largely overlooked and there has been no biography or study of him. His autobiography was published by his son[1] thirty-seven years after his death. For students of Japanese diplomatic history he is not known for any major diplomatic achievements. Yet a closer scrutiny reveals that he was very active in the wings, being involved at numerous important turning points in the history of Japanese external relations. He was present at the Japanese Embassy in London, when the Anglo-Japanese Alliance was signed, being deputy to the Minister, Hayashi Tadasu. When the First World War broke out, he was the Vice-Minister under Katō Takaaki. Most of his long diplomatic career, which extended over nearly forty years, was spent overseas.

EARLY CAREER

Matsui was born in Osaka on 5 March 1868. After graduating from the Osaka English School (*Osaka eigo gakkō*), which was, according to Matsui, 'the only good school in the Kansai region at the time', he moved to Tokyo and studied for two years at *Daigaku yobimon*, the forerunner of the First High School (*Dai-ichi kōtō gakkō*). He studied English Law at Tokyo Imperial University, graduating in July 1889. Upon his graduation Matsui 'did not like the idea of becoming a judge or lawyer very much' and heard that there was a position at the Foreign Ministry. He therefore consulted his international law professor at his university, Hatoyama Kazuo, who also worked in the Foreign Ministry as the head of the investigation division (*torishirabe kyoku*).[2] Hatoyama told Matsui to pay a visit to Katō Takaaki,[3] who was at the time Private Secretary to Foreign Minister Ōkuma Shigenobu and the head of the political affairs section (*seimu ka*). After visiting Katō at his house in Surugadai in Tokyo, Matsui got the job.[4]

He was assigned to the political affairs section but, the Foreign Ministry being such a small-scale operation at that time, he also worked in the translation bureau (*honyaku kyoku*). The most important issue at the time was Treaty revision. The seriousness of this issue was rammed home three months after Matsui joined the Foreign Ministry. Ōkuma was thought by nationalists to have made too many concessions to foreign powers and an attempt was made to assassinate him. In the bomb blast Ōkuma lost a leg. In December Aoki Shūzō[5] became Foreign Minister. He decided to abandon 'the multi-national approaches' and instead to concentrate on negotiating a revised treaty with Britain. The first step was to approach Hugh Fraser,[6] the British Minister in Tokyo, with 'his personal plans'.[7] According to Matsui, a legal adviser to the ministry drafted the memorandum. Matsui had to translate it into Japanese so that Aoki could present it to the cabinet for its approval.[8] In those days Matsui was mainly dealing with Korean affairs. In November 1890 he was ordered to go to his first overseas post as the Third Secretary at the Japanese Legation in Seoul.

He spent four challenging years in the lead-up to the Sino-Japanese War. He served under no less than six Chargés d'Affaires and Ministers in Seoul. The last of these was the *genro* Inoue Kaoru with whom Matsui maintained a close relationship thereafter. In December 1894, with the war going in Japan's favour, Matsui was transferred to Washington where the Japanese Minister at the time was Kurino Shinichirō, a Harvard graduate. He left Tokyo in February 1895 and stayed in Washington for three years until the outbreak of the Spanish-American War.

FIRST ASSIGNMENT IN LONDON

Matsui was transferred to London as First Secretary in 1898, arriving there in June that year to replace Hayashi Gonsuke.[9] The Minister was Katō Takaaki. In those days there were only four members of staff under Katō, Matsui being his deputy.[10] On 27 September, the Japanese Legation moved from Sussex Square to 4 Grosvenor Gardens. In the spring of 1899, Katō left London after a dispute with the Foreign Ministry, which wanted Katō to postpone his pre-arranged leave to see through the raising of a public loan on the London money market. The task fell to Matsui as chargé d'affaires. With help from staff sent from the Finance Ministry and the head of the Yokohama Species Bank London office, Matsui successfully organized a consortium of banks[11] and raised 10 million pounds.[12]

At the time, there were two issues concerning Anglo-Japanese relations: immigration and China. Discriminatory immigration laws were being considered in Queensland (in Australia), and British Columbia (Canada). The Japanese government tried to influence the Australian and Canadian governments through London. On China, Matsui was instructed to sound out the reaction of the British government to the US Secretary of State John Hay's 'Open Door' note issued in September 1899.[13] In addition, Matsui had to handle the Boxer Rebellion issue just before handing over the embassy to Hayashi Tadasu, the new minister.[14] Usually Matsui, as he was only a chargé d'affaires, met an Assistant Under-Secretary, Francis Bertie, but on this occasion he was instructed to see the Foreign Secretary to find out what action Britain would take.[15] Matsui went to see Lord Salisbury but as he was out of London for the Whitsun holiday, he saw Bertie instead.[16] Matsui reported that, according to Bertie, it would be difficult for the British government to send a large contingent until the Boer War ended.[17] Finally, Matsui met Lord Salisbury who confirmed to Matsui that because of the Boer War Britain could not send more troops at that time, but he hoped that Japan would do so.[18] On 6 July, the Japanese Cabinet decided to send the 5th Division.[19] On the same date, before he learnt the decision of the Japanese government, Salisbury sent a telegram to Tokyo, pressing for more Japanese troops to be sent as 'Japan is the only Power which can act with any hope of success for the urgent purpose of saving the foreign Legations at Peking' and offered 'financial assistance which may be necessary'.[20] It was at this point that Hayashi Tadasu arrived in London on 6 July, relieving Matsui from this responsibility.

The most important event when Matsui was in London was the conclusion of the Anglo-Japanese Alliance. The negotiations leading up to it have been studied in detail elsewhere,[21] but Matsui had his share of involvement. Nearly a month before the German Chargé d'Affaires, Eckhardstein, approached Hayashi on the subject, he had met Matsui in early February 1901 at the St James's Club, suggesting an alliance between Britain, Germany and Japan.[22] Matsui was also sent to St Petersburg with a coded telegram from Prime Minister Katsura Tarō to Itō Hirobumi, explaining the situation.[23] Because he did not succeed in having a meaningful talk with Itō, who was leaving for Berlin the next day, Matsui followed Itō to Berlin. For three days Matsui tried in vain to ascertain Itō's views on the matter. In the end he called on Itō in his room on the night before his departure for London and had a frank talk lasting over three hours while they drank Rhine wine. According to Matsui, Itō was not against the idea of an alliance with Britain *per se*, but thought that due attention should be paid to Russia and Germany.[24] Matsui wrote the official report on the negotiations leading up to the signing of the alliance. He made three copies; one for the Ministry, one for the Embassy and one for Hayashi, who later published his version of the story in *Jiji shimpō*.[25]

TOKYO, PEKING, PARIS, WASHINGTON, TOKYO, PARIS

With the alliance safely negotiated, Matsui left London in July and returned to Japan in September for the first time in seven years. Matsui was given the task of reporting to the *genro* about the alliance. After just a month in Tokyo, Matsui was sent to Peking (Beijing) to act as Chargé d'Affaires while Minister Uchida Yasuya was on winter leave. Uchida came back in April but heightening tension with Russia over Manchuria meant that Matsui had to stay on. It was only when Japan's victory looked certain that Matsui was able to come home at the end of June 1905 to cover for Yamaza Enjirō, the head of the Political Affairs Division, while the latter accompanied Foreign Minister Komura Jutarō[26] to Portsmouth (USA). One of the tasks he performed was acting as an interpreter between Prime Minister Katsura, who was acting as Foreign Minister in Komura's absence, and Sir Claude MacDonald, the British Ambassador in Tokyo,[27] the latter describing Matsui as 'a master of diplomatic English'.[28]

After another brief stay in Tokyo, he was sent to Paris as counsellor, arriving there in May 1906. Being posted to France for the first time, Matsui's time was 'mainly devoted to the study of the language'. Again, Kurino was the

Ambassador in Paris.[29] The major event during his time in Paris was the signing of the Franco-Japanese Agreement of 1907.

After two years he was transferred to Washington, DC. Matsui helped Ambassador Takahira Kogorō to conclude the Root-Takahira Agreement. The agreement safely negotiated, Takahira left Washington, DC, in August 1909 and Matsui became Chargé d'Affaires until Takahira's successor Uchida Yasuya's arrival in December 1909. [30]

Matsui arrived back in Tokyo in July 1911, starting his longest period of office work at the ministry.[31] At the end of January 1913, Katō Takaaki became Foreign Minister for the third time. He appointed Matsui to be the Vice-Minister. Although the government only lasted less than a month, Matsui stayed on in this post under the new Foreign Minister, Makino Nobuaki, in the Yamamoto cabinet. This cabinet resigned because of the Siemens scandal and Katō again became Foreign Minister in April 1914 in the new Ōkuma cabinet.

On 7 August 1914, British Ambassador Sir William Conyngham Greene[32] delivered a message from Foreign Secretary Grey requesting Japanese naval assistance against German raiders. Following the late night cabinet meeting, at which the decision was taken to go to war, Katō went to inform the Emperor who was then at Nikko. It fell to Matsui to tell the British Ambassador on the following morning and to deliver Japan's ultimatum to the German Ambassador, Arthur von Rex, on 15 August.[33] As soon as Japan entered the war, preparations for the eventual peace with Germany were started in the ministry. In September 1915, a committee (*Nichi-doku seneki kōwa junbi iinkai*) was set up, its members including the Foreign, War and Navy Ministries and the Legislation Bureau. Matsui was appointed chairman. Matsui was involved in the preparation of the notorious 'Twenty-One Demands' on China. In August 1915, Katō resigned following the Interior Minister's bribery scandal; and after Chinda Sutemi[34] declined to accept the offer, Ishii Kikujirō was brought back from Paris to take up the post of Foreign Minister.

Matsui was then sent to Paris to take up his first ambassadorial post. His voyage to France took two months because the ship had to go round the Cape of Good Hope. He arrived in Paris the day after the start of the battle of Verdun. During his time in Paris one of his most important assignments was to attend the various meetings of the Allied countries such as the Supreme War Council. After the armistice in November 1918, Matsui and all his family caught Spanish flu. Having recovered, he was appointed as one of the chief delegates to the Paris Peace Conference, the highlight of his diplomatic career. Matsui's main task was to sound out the French attitude. After all the other delegates had departed, Matsui was left to attend the Supreme Conference, which culminated in the signing of the peace treaties with Austria, Hungary, Bulgaria and Turkey. With the signature on 10 August 1920 of the Treaty of Sèvres, which effectively marked the end of the Ottoman Empire, Matsui decided that it was time to go home. His leave was duly granted and he set off in October. *The Times* Paris correspondent wrote a glowing report on Matsui's departure:

> His departure will be regretted, for during four-and-a-half years that he has been here he has shown powers of statesmanship and tact worthy of his race.
>
>   His previous varied experience, his remarkable command of the French tongue, his personal charm and intimate knowledge of French men and affairs made him an outstanding figure in Paris very soon after his arrival, and his influence in the political world has grown every day.

His work as representative of Japan at the Peace Conference and afterwards on the Supreme Council has been most fully appreciated.[35]

For his service during the war and the Peace Conference Matsui was made a baron.

It seemed that Matsui was nearing the end of his career, but he had two more assignments. In January 1924 Matsui became the Foreign Minister in the Kiyoura cabinet. It was an unexpected appointment and the British Ambassador Sir Charles Eliot[36] explained how it came about:

> The post of Foreign Minister was originally offered to Baron Fujimura, who was formerly connected with the Mitsui firm, and had no experience of service in the Japanese Foreign Office or in diplomacy. But Mr Matsudaira, Vice-Minister for Foreign Affairs, and corresponding to our Permanent Under-Secretary, protested so strongly against the appointment that Viscount Kiyoura was obliged to admit the principle that an Ambassador ought to be appointed. Baron Hayashi and Baron Ishii were mentioned, but as they were in Europe it was feared that the Cabinet might not last until their arrival. Besides Viscount Katō, who is the head of the Kenseikai party, there are two unemployed ex-Ambassadors in Tokyo, Baron Shidehara and Baron Matsui. As the former is ill, the latter was appointed by a process of elimination. He was Ambassador in Paris from 1914 to 1920, and is probably well versed in the routine work of his profession, but has not, so far as I know, any reputation for remarkable ability.[37]

The cabinet itself was not expected to last long and the British Foreign Office did not have high hopes for Matsui.[38] Following a general election, Katō Takaaki became the Prime Minister in June and Shidehara Kijurō Foreign Minister. Over six months Matsui had three issues to tackle: China, the Soviet Union and the United States. He could not make much headway on the first, but on the second he gave new impetus to the Yoshizawa-Karakhan meetings in Peking (Beijing) which led to the eventual normalization of diplomatic relations with the Soviet Union a year later. On the last issue, unfortunately the incident over the Hanihara 'grave consequences' memorandum soured Japan-US relations although Matsui did his best to calm the situation.[39]

On the surface, Matsui could not boast of any great achievements, doubtless due to the brief time he was in office. By the end of his tenure, however, Matsui impressed Eliot who stated in his memorandum reporting the change of government:

> I cannot close this despatch without adding a tribute to Baron Matsui, who now leaves the Ministry for Foreign Affairs. He came to his post with a good reputation as an efficient public servant but nothing more, and doubts were expressed as to whether he had a sufficiently strong character for the high position offered to him. He may not be a man of great originality or determination, but he won the esteem of the whole Corps diplomatique during the six months that he was in office. I have never met a Japanese official who seemed so European in speech, manners and methods of conducting business. Not only was he much more communicative than most of his countrymen, but he seemed genuinely anxious that cases brought to his notice by foreign missions in Tokyo should receive prompt and friendly attention. It is said that the Government contemplate making considerable changes in the Diplo-

matic Service before long, and that in the event of Baron Hayashi being recalled, Baron Matsui may be sent to London. I believe that he and Mme. Matsui would be well suited to the post. Baron Hanihara and Baron Ishii are also mentioned as possible candidates.[40]

Matsui was appointed to the House of Peers and it seemed to be the end of his diplomatic career. However, the new Prime Minister Katō offered him one more assignment before his retirement. In the summer of 1925, while Matsui was staying at his summer cottage in Karuizawa, Katō Takaaki came to see him and asked him to become Ambassador to Britain.

AMBASSADOR IN LONDON

Matsui left Japan in October and arrived in England in November 1925 having travelled via Canada. When he presented his credentials at Buckingham Palace King George V enquired about the Taishō Emperor, the regent (later the Shōwa Emperor) and the situation in China. The king also said that he did not like establishing diplomatic relations with the Soviet Union but accepted his government's decision. On 19 November, Matsui paid his first visit to Foreign Secretary Austen Chamberlain at the Foreign Office and talked about the Locarno Treaties (concluded on 1 December 1925), the tariff conference in Peking (Beijing) and Japanese relations with Russia.[41]

Matsui and his wife were welcomed to London by the Marquess of Salisbury, Lord Privy Seal, at the Annual Banquet of the Japan Society in January 1926, the occasion being honoured by the presence of Prince Chichibu.[42] Matsui's first considered public statement in Britain appeared in the *Morning Post*, in which, for a solution to the China problem, he suggested that:

> . . . China needs a strong man; no other government has been found possible in a country where distances are so vast and the conditions and peoples so diverse.
>
> The kind of chaos we see at present has always occurred in the intervals between the emergence of strong men; yet, it is remarkable to observe that the country has, after long years of disturbance, always come out in the end as a united whole, embracing all sections of that peaceful and industrious people. How long it will be before a single man can again achieve unquestioned supremacy none can foretell; while any other solution, such as a federation of provinces, seems equally impossible of realization.[43]

After the 30 May incident in Shanghai in 1925, the boycott of British goods spread across China and the British tried to gain Japanese cooperation. The Japanese government was pursing a 'non-intervention policy' under Foreign Minister Shidehara and was not forthcoming. Matsui thought that since Japanese goods were likely eventually to become the target of a boycott, it would be wise to show some sympathy towards the British and he sent a telegram to that effect.[44] He received such a stern rebuttal that he did not pursue the issue at the time, waiting for another opportunity. With the change of government in April 1927, Tanaka Giichi became Prime Minister and served as his own Foreign Minister. The next month, in conversation with the British Ambassador, Sir John Tilley,[45] Tanaka stressed the importance of Anglo-Japanese cooperation and even hinted at a revival of the alliance. Matsui thought this idea out of the question:

Baron Matsui then observed that English friends often remarked to him that we ought to renew our old alliance. This he regarded as out of the question. He doubted whether even written understanding was desirable. Certainly Great Britain and Japan had by far the largest share of all the foreign interests in China, but America was also interested. We could not ignore that Great Power nor ought we to do anything to arouse her suspicions. He added that, whilst it was of the first consequence that these three Powers should act together, it was also important to keep unity among the Powers as a whole.[46]

Chamberlain agreed and in reply stated:

The fullest interchange of opinion and agreement as to policy was all that I thought we should be wise to seek at the present time; possibly this might lead at a later date to some more formal agreement though not indeed to the renewal of the alliance which had been so much misunderstood in America and had, therefore, proved an obstacle to the maintenance of the friendly relations with the United States which both the Japanese and ourselves wished to cultivate. For the moment I shared his view that any attempt at a written agreement was undesirable.[47]

Ashton-Gwatkin[48] of the Far Eastern Department in the Foreign Office commented on Matsui's talk of 'unity':

Japan has done her full share in obstructing unified action by the Powers; but I do not suppose this is quite what Baron Matsui meant. He does not seem to have been very encouraging or very helpful.[49]

It was probably not fair to criticize Matsui for a lack of cooperative spirit. As we have seen he urged Tokyo to show more sympathy towards the British but never received the instructions to do so. It is interesting that when Matsui was highly praised by Eliot this was the only time he was in a position to act without instructions.

Officials in the Far Eastern Department of the Foreign Office could not agree on the real reasons for the ending of the Anglo-Japanese Alliance: some stressed American opposition, others opinion in the Dominions and still others Japan's aggressive policy in China.[50] In other words, it was a combination of factors rather than a single issue. Certainly, if there was any chance of closer Anglo-Japanese relations, even an alliance, it was from 1927 to early 1928. The Geneva Naval Conference of 1927 broke down because of Anglo-American disputes. Strong anti-American sentiments were shared by cabinet ministers.[51] While most critical of his American counterpart, the British chief delegate to the conference, First Lord of the Admiralty, William Bridgeman, reported to Chamberlain that 'one very satisfactory thing which came out of the conference was our good relationship with the Japanese'.[52] Also, during the conference Winston Churchill, the Chancellor of the Exchequer, suggested that, if the United States built more, '[t]he result might be . . . to bring Japan and Great Britain closer together. . . The alternative to building ourselves would be to renew the Japanese alliance.'[53] Furthermore, the British and Imperial Japanese Armies both perceived a Soviet threat and there was even an exchange of intelligence information between them.[54] Indeed, the revival of the alliance with Japan was considered in the War Ministry at the beginning of 1928.[55] Tilley, who did not believe that 'an alliance was really desirable for Great

Britain', thought that 'a security pact, including America and Australia, might be desirable and feasible.' However his thinking was that:

> It is also no doubt feasible to act in concert with Japan, as we are now trying to do in China, for certain particular purposes. It has always appeared to me to be well within the bounds of possibility to act temporarily in concert with Japan for purposes of aggression, which is happily not contemplated, or defence against aggression, but not within the realm of practical policies to act with Japan in making a friendly settlement with another country, China in particular, from which we each expect to draw advantage for ourselves. Our interests are not sufficiently alike.[56]

Towards the end of 1927, Matsui received a letter from the Vice-Minister Debuchi Katsuji that his appointment was only meant to be short-term and suggested he return home at the age of fifty-nine.[57] Matsui was to be succeeded by Matsudaira Tsuneo.[58]

On 3 April, Matsui paid a farewell call on Chamberlain, which the latter recorded as: 'Consistent to the last, he began the interview by stating that he had nothing in particular to say to me and enquiring whether there was anything of interest which I could say to him.'[59] Matsui left London in March 1928, his last diplomatic post, and arguably his most unrewarding. Ironically, a few months after Matsui's departure, the Japanese government began to attempt to secure British co-operation in China now that the boycott targeted Japanese goods.[60]

After attending the Shōwa Emperor's coronation ceremony, Matsui retired from the diplomatic service in 1929. In his retirement Matsui became an apologist for the conduct of Japan, adding his name to open letters and articles.[61]

Matsui lived on to see the defeat of Japan. Having seen Tokyo in ruins, he spent his last year or so in bed. Matsui said to his son, 'through the Anglo-Japanese Alliance and the Paris Peace Conference, and so on, I thought I had contributed a little to Japanese diplomacy, raising the status of Japan among the Five Great Powers but in the end I wonder what it was all for'.[62] Matsui died on 4 June 1946. It was a sad end to his life not to see Japan rise once again or to see his son follow in his footsteps as the Ambassador to the United Nations and France.

[2005]

NOTES

1. *Matsui Keishirō Jijo-den* (Tokyo, 1983) [hereafter cited as *Matsui*]. A week before his death Matsui instructed his son that the publication of his autobiography had to wait until all the people mentioned in it had passed away. His son, Akira, became Ambassador to the United Nations (1963-67) and France (1967-70).
2. It was set up in 1880 by then Foreign Minister Inoue Kaoru to investigate legal issues relating to the Treaty revision issues.
3. See portrait of Katō Takaaki by Ian Nish in *Biographical Portraits*, Vol. IV, 2002.
4. *Matsui*, pp.7-12.
5. See portrait of Aoki Shūzō by Ian Nish in *Biographical Portraits*, Vol. III, 1999.
6. See biographical portrait of Hugh Fraser by Hugh Cortazzi in *Biographical Portraits*, Vol. IV, 2002 and in *British Envoys in Japan 1859-1972*, 2004.
7. See Ian Nish, 'Aoki Shūzō (1844-1914)' in *Britain and Japan: Biographical Portraits*, Vol. III,

1999, p.133.
8. *Matsui*, pp.13-14.
9. See separate portrait in this volume.
10. Katō Takaaki haku den hensan iinkai (ed.), *Katō Takaaki*, Vol. 1 (Tokyo, 1970), p.678.
11. Yokohama Species Bank, Parrs' Bank, Hongkong Shanghai Bank and Chartered Bank of India, Australia and China.
12. *Matsui*, pp.39-42. Also see Toshio Suzuki, *Japanese Government Loan Issues on the London Capital Market, 1870-1913* (London: Athlone Press, 1994), pp.69-74.
13. Matsui to Aoki, 16 & 27 Nov. 1899, *Nihon Gaikō Bunsho* [hereafter *NGB*] Vol. 32, Doc. 76, 78, 82, pp.205-9, 213-14. Also see a draft reply from Salisbury to Matsui, 21 Nov. 1899, FO 46/521.
14. For this issue see Ian Nish, *The Anglo-Japanese Alliance* 2nd Ed. (London: Athlone Press, 1985), pp.80-95. See also Ian Nish's portrait of Hayashi Tadasu in *Britain and Japan: Themes and Personalities*, Routledge, 1991.
15. Aoki to Matsui, 9 June 1900, *NGB* Vol. 33 Supplement 1, Doc. 329, p.341.
16. Matsui to Aoki, 11 June, *NGB* Vol. 33 Supplement 1, Doc. 336, p.345.
17. Matsui to Aoki, 13 June, *NGB* Vol. 33 Supplement 1, Doc. 343 & 361, pp.352-53 & 361-63.
18. Matsui to Aoki, 6 July 1900, *NGB* Vol. 33 Supplement 1, Doc. 589, pp.570-71. For Memoranda of Matsui's conversation with Salisbury on 25 June and 5 July, see *NGB* Vol. 33 Supplement 1, Doc. 584, pp.556-63.
19. Cabinet Decisions, *NGB* Vol. 33 Supplement 1, Doc. 592, pp.572-73.
20. The offer was later defined as a million pounds for additional twenty thousand troops. Memorandum from British Chargé to Aoki, 8 & 14 July 1900, *NGB* Vol. 33 Supplement 1, Docs 605 & 618, pp.579-80, 589. In the end the Japanese government did not want it to appear that they were sending more troops because of the British request with an offer of financial assistance and tried in vain to prevent the offer being included in the bluebook. *NGB* Vol. 33 Supplement 1, Docs 638, 640 & 641, pp.610-12.
21. Ian Nish, *The Anglo-Japanese Alliance*.
22. *Nihon gaikō hiroku* (Tokyo, 1934), pp.65-7; *Matsui*, pp.47-8.
23. Hayashi to Komura, 3 December 1901, *NGB* Vol. 34, Doc. 53, p.62.
24. For the official version of Matsui's conversation with Itō, see *NGB* Vol. 35, No. 25, pp.41-3. Also see *Matsui*, pp.50-1.
25. *Jiji shimpō*, 12-17 July & 21 August 1913; Yui Masaomi (ed.), *Nochi wa mukashi no ki hoka* (Memoirs of Hayashi Tadasu) (Tokyo, 1970), pp.295-383; A. Pooley (ed.), *The Secret Memoirs of Count Tadasu Hayashi* Reprint Ed. (Basingstoke: Palgrave Macmillan, 2002).
26. See separate portrait in this volume.
27. See portrait of Sir Claude MacDonald in *Biographical Portraits*, Vol. I, 1994 and in *British Envoys in Japan 1859-1972*, 2004.
28. *British Documents on Foreign Affairs*, Asia, 1860-1914, Vol. 8, Doc. 338, p.305. The author is indebted to Professor Nish for this reference.
29. The year before Matsui married Imamura Teru, following a *miai* at *Genrō* Inoue Kaoru's place. The *nakōdo* (go-between) were Mr & Mrs Kurino.
30. According to a magazine reporting on the Japanese diplomats at the time, Matsui was described as someone well-versed in diplomatic business, but lacking flare. *Taiyō* 17(9)(15 June 1911), cited in *Gaimushō no hyaku-nen* (Tokyo, 1969), pp.569-70.
31. However, Matsui first had to go to Peking (Beijing), then on to Shanghai during the 1911 Revolution in China.
32. See portrait of Sir William Conyngham Greene by Peter Lowe in *Biographical Portraits*, Vol. IV, 2002 and *British Envoys in Japan, 1859-1972*, 2004.
33. *Matsui*, pp.78-80.
34. See separate portrait in this volume.
35. *The Times*, 25 August 1920.
36. See biographical portrait of Sir Charles Eliot by Dennis Smith in *Themes and Personalities*, Routledge 1991.
37. F473/14/23, Eliot to Curzon, 14 January 1924, F473/14/23, FO 371/10303. There was an enclosure which said: 'For his services during the war he was created a baron. He has the reputation of being an extremely efficient civil servant, and as Vice-Minister for Foreign Affairs is said to have earned the encomiums of his chief, Viscount Kato. But doubts are expressed as to his suitability for so responsible a post as that of Minister for Foreign Affairs.'
38. Ashton-Gwatkin of the Far Eastern Department wrote: 'I gather from people who knew him in Paris that he is a typical Japanese official, and not a man of outstanding character.' Note by

Ashton-Gwatkin, 8 Jan. 1924, F55/14/23, FO 371/10303. For comment on Matsui's speech in the Diet see Eliot to FO 23 January 1924 and Minute by Ashton-Gwatkin, 24 January 1924, F236/14/23, FO 371/10303.

39. For Matsui's statement issued to the American journalists at the time, see *The Times*, 16 April 1924.

40. Eliot to MacDonald, 19 June 1924, F2432/14/23, FO 371/10303.

41. Chamberlain to Eliot, 19 November 1925, F5627/3755/23, FO 371/10965.

42. *Bulletin of Japan Society*, No. 2 (October 1950), pp.10-11.

43. 'The Future of Japan' by Matsui, *Morning Post*, 15 February 1926, F694/694/23, FO 371/11707.

44. Matsui to Shidehara, 1 December 1926 *NGB* 1926 Vol. II Part 2, Doc. 962, pp.1125-6; *Matsui*, pp.142-3.

45. See portrait of Sir John Tilley by Harumi Goto-Shibata in *Biographical Portraits*, Vol. IV, 2002 and in *British Envoys in Japan, 1859-1972*, 2004.

46. Chamberlain to Tilley, 2 June 1927, F5202/201/23, FO 371/12518. For Matsui's version of the record of this conversation see Matsui to Tanaka, 2 June 1927, *NGB* Shōwa Era, Ser.I (1927-31) Part 2, Vol. IV, Doc. 4, pp.9-10.

47. As early as in May 1925 Chamberlain thought that 'close & sympathetic cooperation with Japan which, of course, must be with & not against the U.S.A.' Note by Chamberlain, 22 May 1925, F1713/19/23, FO 371/10961.

48. See portrait of Frank Ashton-Gwatkin by Ian Nish in *Biographical Portraits*, Vol. I, 1994.

49. Note by F. Ashton-Gwatkin, 3 June 1927, F5202/201/23, FO 371/12518.

50. Minute by Kenneth Johnstone, Notes by Philip Nichols and Frank Ashton-Gwatkin, 28 March & 19 April, F2779/2779/23, FO 371/12524.

51. T. Kuramatsu, 'Viscount Cecil, Winston Churchill and the Geneva Naval Conference of 1927' in T. Otte & C. Pagedas (eds), *Personalities, War and Diplomacy* (London: Frank Cass, 1997), p.115.

52. Bridgeman to Chamberlain, 7 August 1927, FO 800/261.

53. Minutes of CID 228th Meeting, 7 July 1927, CAB 2/5.

54. A. Best, *British Intelligence and the Japanese Challenge in Asia, 1914-1941* (Basingstoke: Palgrave Macmillan, 2002), p.90.

55. Memorandum on the desirability, from a Military Point of View, of reviving the Alliance with Japan, MO1(a) memorandum, Feb. 1928, WO 106/129. It states that on military considerations the revival of the Alliance 'would seem to be not only desirable but essential'.

56. Tilley to Chamberlain, 28 June 1927, F 6510/2779/23, FO 371/12524. Wellesley commented: 'Sir J. Tilley is quite right. You cannot base a policy of co-operation on diversity of interests. What you get in practice is alternate co-operation & opposition according to the circes [circumstances] of the case and the moment. That is precisely what makes our difficulties so great.' Note by Wellesley, 5 August 1927, Ibid.

57. Matsui suspected that Debuchi, being a relative of Tanaka, wanted to secure an ambassadorship while the latter was in power. Debuchi succeeded Matsudaira and became the Ambassador to the United States.

58. See portrait of Matsudaira Tsuneo by Ian Nish in *Biographical Portraits*, Vol. I, 1994. On this appointment Tilley commented that 'From what I hear of Mr. Matsudaira, I think he would be an improvement on Baron Matsui'. Tilley to Wellesley, 3 November 1927, F9000/9000/23, FO 371/12525. Ashton-Gwatkin agreed: 'Mr. Matsudaira will certainly be an improvement.' Note by Ashton-Gwatkin, 5 December 1927, Ibid.

59. Chamberlain to Dormer, 3 April 1928, F1594/186/23, FO 371/13246.

60. Harumi Goto-Shibata, 'Anglo-Japanese Co-operation in China in the 1920s' in I. Nish & Y. Kibata (eds), *History of Anglo-Japanese Relations, 1600-2000* Vol. I: The Political-Diplomatic Dimension, 1600-1930 (London: Macmillan, 2000), pp.244-46.

61. For example, see the letters to the Editor of *The Times* at the time of the Shanghai Crisis and the breakout of Japan-Chinese War. *The Times*, 27 February 1932, 6 & 28 October 1937; Keishiro Matsui, 'Anglo-Japanese Relations', *Fortnightly*, Vol. 138 (November 1935), pp.513-23.

62. *Matsui*, p.147.

16

MATSUDAIRA TSUNEO, 1877-1949

Diplomat and Courtier
[London, 1929-35]

IAN NISH

Matsudaira Tsuneo

M atsudaira Tsuneo was the longest-serving Japanese Ambassador to the Court of St James's. He presided over the London Embassy from 13 February 1929 to the end of May 1935. This was a total of six-and-a-half years and slightly exceeds the period spent by Ambassador Hayashi (1900-06).[1] Matsudaira gave continuity to Anglo-Japanese relations during a time of political instability in Japan: he was ambassador under eight prime ministers. Moreover, relations with Britain were always tense; and he had to make the best of a deteriorating situation. The Manchurian and Shanghai crises of 1931-33 destroyed many British illusions about Japan; and it was the task of the ambassador to present his country's case in Britain and in the wider forum of the League of Nations in liberal terms in order to forge a *modus vivendi* with European statesmen. When he left London in 1935, he took up an appointment close to the emperor and from this obscure position was still engaged in the exercise of damage limitation. His exploits did not prevent war but they were one strand in the complex tapestry which was being woven in the years before 1941.

Matsudaira Tsuneo (1877-1949) who was related to Matsudaira Sadanobu, a leading Tokugawa statesman, was educated at Gakushūin and Tokyo Imperial University where he studied law and politics. He entered the Foreign Ministry by examination in 1902 and was sent to London for training in the following year. The tension with Russia and the war which followed strained the legation staff of six. He married in 1906 the daughter of Marquis Nabeshima of the Saga clan. They left London with their two children in June 1911 after a happy period. Matsudaira was posted to the treaty revision section and rose steadily in the ranks of the Gaimushō. After a period in China, he became head of its Europe-American section (Ō-Bei Kyokuchō), in which capacity he served on the Japanese delegation to the all-important Washington Conference (1921-22) where he made valuable international contacts. When the Yamamoto cabinet took over in 1923 with Ijuin Hikokichi as foreign minister, he became vice-minister, a post he retained under the short-lived Kiyoura cabinet in 1924.[2]

On 18 December 1924, Matsudaira was deservedly promoted to the key post of ambassador to Washington. Relations had deteriorated because of the anti-Japanese immigration legislation introduced in 1923; and it was to be his role to continue the task which had already absorbed him as vice-minister to work for improved relations with the United States. He was warmly welcomed by the Japan Society in San Francisco and in Washington. Among the diplomatic issues taken up during his tenure in Washington, the most significant were the arrangements for the Geneva Naval Conference of 1927 and the treaty for the Renunciation of War, sometimes referred to as the Kellogg-Briand pact. The first initiative came to nothing, while the second came to maturity after Matsudaira's return to Tokyo on leave in June 1928.[3]

A month after he reached home, it was announced that he would succeed Baron Matsui Keishiro as ambassador to Britain. This was followed in September by the marriage between his daughter Setsuko and Prince Chichibu, the younger brother of the Shōwa Emperor. After the long sea journey, Matsudaira reached London in February of the following year. In the climate of the twenties London was not just a centre for sorting out bilateral issues but also a focal point for sorting out multi-national issues. The ambassadors at London and Paris were expected to represent Japan at the international conferences of the day. Matsudaira was immediately engaged on behalf of the Tanaka government in working out the preliminary details of the London Naval Conference which eventually began early in 1930. The purpose was to control and limit the extent of naval armament. Matsudaira was plenipotentiary along with Wakatsuki Reijirō, and Admiral Takarabe Takeshi, the vice-minister of the navy who travelled from Japan with Admiral Baron Abō Kiyokazu, vice-chief of the naval general staff (kaigun gunreibu jichō). It was a triangular conference, taking in Japan, Britain and the United States.

When the conference opened on 21 January, the Japanese delegates announced that they did not wish to accept the Washington ratio of 60 per cent overall applied in the case of cruisers, as the American plenipotentiaries wanted. But, by reason of Matsudaira's frankness and patient diplomacy, cordial discussions took place on this fraught issue. Compromise was difficult because Admiral Takarabe was confronted by opposition from his accompanying technical staff whom he was unable to win over. In order to prevent deadlock, Matsudaira met for a long series of sessions with Senator David Reed, one of the American delegates. Eventually, on 13 March, a formula was reached whereby Japan should have 69.75 per cent in overall tonnage and 60.02 per cent in respect of heavy cruisers. This 'Reed-Matsudaira compromise' preserved the Washington formula of 10-10-6 while allowing Japan in practice a ratio of 10-10-7.

The navalists argued that Matsudaira had not pressed the case as he should.[4] Wakatsuki, the head of the delegation, defended him and urged his government to accept the formula in order to avoid causing the breakdown of the talks. But the naval objections in London were as nothing compared to those raised in Tokyo. Nonetheless, the government, acting through the vice-minister for the navy, agreed to go ahead with the treaty on 10 April and instructions were sent to London accordingly. But Admiral Katō Kanji, chief of the naval general staff, sought an interview with the emperor and announced his resignation. Though the treaty was signed on 22 April, there was a lengthy ratification process; but eventually the ratification procedures were completed and the treaty came into force in October.[5]

The American and British leaders extended their thanks to Wakatsuki and Matsudaira. In London much had been left to the diplomacy of civilians; and Matsudaira and Reed had had to bear the brunt of finding a solution to a prickly and emotional issue. Given the high expectations in Japan, Matsudaira tried to negotiate a formula which would ensure the continuation of arms limitation while saving the face of the navy. It may be that the result was a fudge, but it was a fudge skilfully arrived at.

MATSUDAIRA AND MANCHURIA

Hardly had the crisis over the naval treaty passed than a new international crisis over 'Manchuria' developed. On 18 September 1931, the Kuantung army moved out of its Leased Territory and occupied the key cities of south and central Manchuria. The Chinese reported the dispute to the League of Nations which for two months tried to get the parties to withdraw their troops without success. The sessions of the League Council and the League Assembly in Geneva and Paris greatly increased Matsudaira's work-load as he had to travel over to the continent and coordinate policy with the ambassador to France, Yoshizawa Kenkichi, and the ambassador to Rome, Yoshida Shigeru. It is impossible to cover the vast canvas of the Manchurian crisis in this essay: we shall confine ourselves to sketching the importance of Matsudaira's role. He was important because of his wide experience at Washington and London and his relationship with the new British foreign secretary, Sir John Simon, because Britain was still assumed to have more of a role in settling the crisis than the other pillar of the League, France. After two months of embarrassing diplomatic failure, Matsudaira met Simon in Paris on 17 November and presented a memorandum. Under point 2 of the note, the Japanese offered to propose that the League should send a 'Study Commission' to examine the whole question of Sino-Japanese relations and, in particular, the relations of those two countries in Manchuria. Sugimura Yōtarō, an assistant secretary at the League, told the director-general: '. . . Mr Matsudaira was being extremely courageous in making these proposals. He would simply announce to Tokyo that he had put them forward to Sir John Simon and to General Dawes. If Tokyo refused to accept them, he would then resign, but his personal position was such that he did not believe Tokyo would take this step.'[6] Since the League Commission that emerged from this proposal was the nearest that the League came to solving the Sino-Japanese dispute, it is historically important to know how far Matsudaira was the author of the proposal.

The proposal of an enquiry committee sent by the League to China (*chōsadan*) which had been mooted by Matsudaira and Dr Sugimura on 17 November, was then presented to the Gaimushō in their reports and through the efforts of Frank Walters, a senior official of the League secretariat, who happened to be in the Far East at the time. He was travelling as secretary of the League mission of educational experts, investigating the school system throughout China.[7] He had moved to Tokyo and was in touch with Shidehara and 'high officials' [kōkan] of the ministry. It was simultaneously taken up by Matsudaira with Ambassador Dawes, Sir John Simon and Sir Eric Drummond, the League secretary-general, who had all moved to Paris for the meetings of the League Council. It was conditional on the delegates (*shisatsuin*) visiting China proper as well as Manchuria in order to investigate the anti-Japanese movement.[8] After discussion it seems to have received the endorsement of all three parties in Paris and Simon conveyed this to Matsudaira on 19 November. At the Tokyo end, Shidehara was understandably vigilant but was probably more responsive than many other Japanese leaders. So Matsudaira did not lose his job.

As the League Council drew up the mandate for the new commission, there were three weeks of bitter recriminations between Japan and China. But it was finally proposed on the motion of the Japanese delegate that a commission of five members should study on the spot and report on circumstances which had disturbed the peace in China. This was approved on 10 December with the understanding that one of the five would be from the United States.[9] So the League Commission which took shape in January 1932 was in effect the result of Matsudaira's bold initiative.

It is important to remember that Japan took the initiative to propose an international commission. It appears from Japanese documents that Matsudaira was the moving spirit. Yoshizawa and Japan's other League delegates played their part, as did Dr Sugimura of the secretariat. But it was evidently Matsudaira who carried the clout to have it adopted in Tokyo. When a similar proposal had been raised in October, Japan had disapproved of sending inspectors from Peking into Manchuria to report to the League. Now it passed because it broke the stalemate.

Foreign Minister Shidehara felt that the new private initiative (*shian*) of Matsudaira was worth a try, partly because the Chinese were threatening to ask for the dispute to be examined under Clause 15 of the covenant, partly because Japanese opinion was becoming increasingly extremist (*kyokutanka*) and needed to be held in check. I have argued elsewhere that there was also an element of party politics in Japan which entered into Shidehara's calculations because the cabinet was at that moment in disarray;[10] it would suit the Wakatsuki ministry to have a League enquiry commission (*chōsa dan*) which, being lengthy, would permit a cooling of opinion. If international opinion could be wooed away from support of China in this way, it would redound to the credit of the more moderate elements in the ministry and in the country at large. So Shidehara was able to give the proposal his blessing, even if another foreign minister might not have been inclined to do so. Hence Yoshizawa was able to report on 20 November that the Council was already considering drafts of the resolution which the representative of Japan was proposing.[11]

The League commission, generally known as 'the Lytton commlssion', in due time reported from the East to Geneva. While it was away, Japan had been fighting a backs-to-the-wall struggle at Geneva. Sawada Setsuzō, one of the Japanese delegates and head of Japan's League secretariat, explained his perspective on events:

> When the Manchurian crisis arose, Geneva became the heart of international affairs. Even Japan seems to have focused her overseas activities there. Hence our delegation gradually increased and was at one time 170-80 strong.[12]

Over Manchuria – and over the Disarmament Conference which was being held simultaneously – Matsudaira was playing a full part. When, however, the Lytton report appeared in late summer 1932, Tokyo sent to Geneva Matsuoka Yōsuke to head the delegation. This was an implied criticism of Matsudaira and his fellow negotiators who protested politely. They did not think it was necessary for Japan to recognize Manchukuo (as she had done in September) and questioned

Matsuoka's commitment to the League.[13] From November, the focus was no longer on Matsudaira. In due course the vote was taken on 24 February 1933 on the resolution to approve a report based on the Commission's recommendations. Japan alone opposed. Matsuoka beckoned to the Japanese delegates to withdraw from the floor of the Assembly. There is reason, however, to believe that Matsudaira was not in favour of such a flamboyant gesture.

The final act of the crisis was the decision of the cabinet in Tokyo to give notice of withdrawal from the League at the end of March. This was made without consultation with senior ambassadors overseas and there is every reason to believe that Matsudaira, if he had been approached, would have advised Japan to stay within the League. But it was not to be. The resignation did not take effect until 1935 and Japan was able for the time being to continue to take part in League-inspired events. Thus, at the World Economic Conference held in London in June 1933, Matsudaira was one of Japan's chief delegates. Matsudaira did not like the strategy of leaving the League and '. . . sighed from the bottom of his heart about the climate of the times, saying that Japan should build up her strength quietly and thus recover her international position'.[14]

AMBASSADOR IN A DIVIDED BRITAIN

It is not the purpose of this essay to offer a ball-by-ball commentary on the second half of Matsudaira's embassy to London. Anglo-Japanese relations were not so cordial after the Manchurian incident of 1931-33 and Japan's departure from the League as they had been before. It was hard for Matsudaira who was conscious of British opinion being generally favourable to China. It was progressively less easy for the ambassador to operate through the Foreign Office which seemed to reflect these pro-Chinese sentiments. Naturally, therefore, Matsudaira gave encouragement to a Japanophile group which came into existence in 1934 around Sir Warren Fisher, the permanent secretary to the Treasury, with Neville Chamberlain as his accessory.[15] Its avowed object was to repair 'the relation of friendship and mutual respect' with Japan. In this way, Matsudaira knew of the disagreements among British policy-makers and learnt to exploit them.

As part of his desire to broaden the range of Japan's friends in Britain, Matsudaira promoted the mission organized by the Federation of British Industries which went out in the summer of 1934 to visit Japan and Manchukuo. In Britain's perception, this so-called Barnby mission was an unofficial group which did not have the backing of the Foreign Office and was playing with fire by visiting Manchukuo. Matsudaira reported to Tokyo that it was superficially 'an industrial mission' in search of contracts but had in fact the political aim of promoting friendly relations.[16] As the result of his strong recommendation, it was given a royal reception in Japan and special treatment when it ventured on to Manchukuo. That no contracts for British industry resulted from their efforts was due to the reluctance of the nominally independent Manchukuo authorities to open their market to Britain, not to the absence of support on the part of the London ambassador.

On 14 May 1935, Matsudaira was permitted to return home on leave. There was a host of hastily improvised functions in his honour. Most prominent was the special dinner at Claridges given on 19 June by the Japan Society. The then foreign secretary, Sir Samuel Hoare, offered a eulogy of Matsudaira as president of the Society in these words:

He has in fact been one of the most distinguished members of the Corps Diplomatique. No one can better interpret the views of Japan to England and those of England to Japan. His Excellency has entered into all our interests and activities. He is as well known on the golf course as he is in Whitehall. He has taken a prominent part in all social functions and with Madame Matsudaira has made friends whose number is quite uncountable.

Matsudaira replied in a moving way, saying that his absence from his country for such a long period as six years was not necessarily desirable:

Especially in the Far East there have occurred in recent years several serious events and political and economic conditions there have altered so rapidly that I ought to have returned home before this to see them, as well as to report to my Government in person all I have seen abroad.[17]

He then set off *via* Canada and reached Japan at the beginning of August. It should be observed that Matsudaira seems genuinely to have been under the impression that he would be returning to Britain and was only going temporarily on leave. He wrote to correspondents that this was his intention. If he had returned, it would have been in contradiction to the normal practices of the Foreign Ministry: for an ambassador who stayed longer than four years in one post was almost unknown. But there was nothing to be gained by dissembling and every reason to believe that Matsudaira genuinely felt that his mission was unfulfilled and that he would return.[18]

The autumn was filled with family events. At the end of October his second daughter Masako was married to the eldest son of Tokugawa Yoshitomo, a scion of the Tokugawa house. Later on 28 December, his eldest son Ichirō, married the eldest daughter of Tokugawa Iemasa, Japan's Ambassador to Turkey. Matsudaira's aristocratic connections had been confirmed by marriage.

Despite this, matters of grave political urgency were looming. The second London Naval Conference was due to open in January. Britain as host was anxious about Japan's representation and took the bold step of suggesting to Kasumigaseki that '. . . it may prove convenient if your Government were to be represented by your Ambassador in London'.[19] London wanted Matsudaira back but, for personal reasons, this was next to impossible. It is, however, indicative of the confidence that the British authorities felt in him.

Mention should also be made of the mission of Sir Frederick Leith-Ross. The proposal to send a mission to Japan arose from China's proposal that Britain should give her a substantial loan and Britain's response that this should only be done after consultation with the United States and Japan. Leith-Ross, the chief economic adviser to the British government, by-passed Washington and reached Japan in September 1935. He knew many Japanese because of the World Economic Conference held in London in 1933. But he had a special relationship with Matsudaira, now back in Tokyo, whose cousin, Viscount Matsudaira Keimin, had been known to him at Oxford University. Leith-Ross records his meetings with the ambassador thus:

[Matsudaira] before he left London had been very optimistic about the political situation in Japan, and had expressed the view that the military faction . . . had now lost influence and were under the control of the Civil Government. Since his return to Japan I found that he had completely changed his opinion. He was evidently very nervous about the attitude of the Army to my mission.[20]

All that Matsudaira said was abundantly confirmed by Leith-Ross's Tokyo experiences. After six months of investigation in China, the question of Leith-Ross making a return journey to Japan was raised in London. The Treasury was very much in favour, while the Foreign Office reiterated its view that the China loan scheme should be dropped and he should not re-visit Tokyo.

The political climate of Japan altered after the military mutiny of 26 February 1936. A new cabinet had been set up, but it was clear that the army still had much power because they managed to veto the appointment of Yoshida Shigeru as foreign minister. It is interesting that Matsudaira who had entered the Foreign Ministry four years ahead of Yoshida in 1906, was not considered for that office. But the Lord Keeper of the Privy Seal had been murdered by the troops and Yuasa Kurahei, the Imperial Household Minister, moved over to take that job. Matsudaira agreed on 6 March to take over from Yuasa as *Kunai-Daijin*, as soon as he had given notice of leaving the Foreign Ministry. He had assumed an office which made him one of the mediators between the cabinet and the court and a figure of some indefinable influence in Japanese society. Matsudaira wrote to the Japan Society on 9 March that he found himself unable to return to England because of his appointment to this new post. The Society replied with congratulations upon this high office '. . . giving pleasure to innumerable friends and inspiring renewed confidence in all who cherish good relations between our two Empires'.[21]

This affected the debate over Leith-Ross in London. Eventually, disagreements were resolved and Leith-Ross was authorized to pay a short visit to Tokyo in June in order to assess (among other things) '. . . to what extent Japanese policy is guided by those (e.g. Mr Matsudaira) who sincerely desire a rapprochement with Britain'.[22] Leith-Ross's talks with Matsudaira took priority but he had to record that '. . . Matsudaira and the Ministry of Foreign Affairs were anxious to maintain good relations with Britain and America and to find some solution of their difficulties with China, but I sensed that many of the younger Foreign Office officials whom I met were in full sympathy with the programme of the military'.[23] It would appear from these quotations that, both in Britain and in British circles in Japan, Matsudaira was regarded as an important leader who was regarded as favourable and sympathetic towards Britain. Indeed, he was a prominent member of the *Ei-Beiha*, though he was as a member of the court precluded from taking too conspicuous a role in leadership.

It is difficult to assess Matsudaira's role as Imperial Household Minister which he held until June 1945. The secrecy in which the office was shrouded does not permit many insights. It is probable that the court, like the Elder Statesman, was 'marginalized' after 1936 and did not have much influence on the direction which affairs were following. Matsudaira's name is not to be found in the newspapers of the day. But, if we may judge from the experiences of Leith-Ross, he was still able to pull a few strings.[24] His internationalism was resented by the organizers of the anti-British movement of 1939 when an assassination attempt on Matsudaira was attempted and failed.

RETIREMENT JAPANESE-STYLE

After the war, the Matsudairas lived in their private house in straitened circumstances. Sir George Sansom, who as a member of the Far East Commission visited Tokyo in January 1946, recalled that:

The Matsudairas had lost everything and he himself [Tsuneo] was wearing his son's tidy suit, which they wear in turns.[25]

But he still had wide international interests and certain court connections. In June 1946 he was appointed to the privy council (*sumitsu komonkan*). In the first general election in April of the following year, he was elected to the House of Councillors (*sangiin*) and became its president. But his illnesses increased and he died in Tokyo on 14 November 1949 at the age of seventy-two. Sansom's account shows that Matsudaira was more than an uninvolved private citizen. He still had access to the Emperor and was clearly given assignments by the latter to act as intermediary with foreigners.

As General Piggott wrote in his obituary in the Japan Society *Bulletin*, Matsudaira came of ancient lineage but was a commoner: 'The innate conservatism of his race was blended with a streak of modern liberalism that he had acquired from the West'. He was, wrote Piggott '. . . the physical embodiment of sound, solid commonsense'.[26] He was neither brilliant nor intellectual. He was sociable, even gregarious, and made friends both Japanese and foreign, fairly readily. As a senior diplomat, he had the reputation for using 'golf diplomacy'. He tells how Sir John Simon would phone up to say that there were some troublesome points facing him in the Office and ask him whether he would take some exercise at Walton Heath or Combe Hill. As ambassador, he acquired a taste for Old Parr whisky; and it was as a connoisseur that he was affectionately remembered by his juniors in the London embassy. Like his companion in the Manchurian diplomacy, Dr Sugimura, he was rather over-weight but this gave him a reputation for bonhomie.[27]

Matsudaira had a career which went from strength to strength. Passing into the diplomatic profession in 1902, he was promoted steadily until he reached London at the summit of his career. Given his aristocratic background, it was a natural progression for him to become Imperial Household Minister. Though he was criticized after the war by opponents of the *Tennōsei*,[28] his election as speaker of the Upper House was a mark of the respect which he had earned from the majority of Japanese.

His connection with Britain was a thread running through his diplomatic career. His long first stint gave him a taste for the British way of life. The postings he had were mainly in the English-speaking section of the ministry. To end up with long stays in Washington and London was indeed good fortune. Even in the straitened circumstances of the allied occupation of Japan, he was still interested in Things British and quizzed Sansom when they met in 1946. Yet, if he was Anglophile he was also a Japanese patriot. It is not easy to assess the advice he was giving his home government from London. But there is good evidence that, at critical points in his career, he was prepared to put his career on the line and stand up to his government. Matsudaira Tsuneo, the longest-serving ambassador to the Court of St James's, seems to have accomplished that most difficult of conjuring tricks: advising his government and representing his country, while at the same time sympathizing with the country to which he was accredited and presenting its case to Tokyo. He was, in the assessment of Sir John Tilley, 'a most successful ambassador in London'.

[1994]

NOTES

1.   I. Nish 'Hayashi Tadasu', in H. Cortazzi and G. Daniels (eds), *Britain and Japan: Themes and Personalities, 1859-1991*, London: Routledge, 1991, pp.147-56.
2.   Article by Admiral Yamanashi Katsunoshin, in *Matsudaira Tsuneo Tsuisō-roku*, published privately, 1961, pp.530-2. (Hereafter *Tsuisō-roku*.) F.S.G. Piggott, *Broken Thread*, Aldershot, 1950, pp.8, 60. Because of Shidehara's indisposition, much of the work of the Japanese delegation at Washington had to be organized by Matsudaira.
3.   J.C. Grew, *Turbulent Era: A diplomatic record of forty years, 1904-45*, 2 vols, London: Hammond, 1953, Vol. I, ch. 24 passim.
4.   A. Henderson to J. Tilley, 15 March 1930: '. . . hitherto Mr Wakatsuki and Mr Matsudaira have not been able to win over their naval colleagues in the delegation', in W.N. Medlicott et al., *Documents on British Foreign Policy, 1919-39*, London: HMSO, 2nd series, Vol. I, No. 156. (Series hereafter cited as *DBFP*.)
5.   Kobayashi Tatsuo, 'London Naval Treaty, 1930', in J.W. Morley (ed.), *Japan Erupts: The London Naval Conference and the Manchurian Incident*, 1928-32, New York: Columbia UP, 1984, pp.90-4.
6.   *DBFP*, 2 (viii), No. 749.
7.   R.H. Tawney et al., *The Reorganization of Education in China*, Paris: League of Nations, Institute of Intellectual Cooperation, 1932, p.11.
8.   *Nihon gaikō bunshō, Manshū jihen*, 1/3, No. 557. (Hereafter *NGB-MJ*.)
9.   *NGB-MJ*, 1/3, No. 810.
10.   I. Nish, *Japan's Struggle with Internationalism: Japan, China and the League of Nations, 1931-3*, London: 1993, pp.50-1.
11.   *NGB-MJ*, 1/3 No. 595.
12.   Article by Sawada Setsuzō, in *Tsuisō-roku*, pp.269-70.
13.   Nish, *Japan's Struggle*, pp.171-2.
14.   Fukai Eigo, *Kaiko 70-nen*, Tokyo: Iwanami, 1949, pp.279, 295; Article by Shimazu, in *Tsuisō-roku*, pp.322-3.
15.   D.C. Watt, *Personalities and Policies*, London: Longman, 1965, pp.83-99. The most recent study is Gill Bennett, 'British Policy in the Far East, 1933-6: Treasury and Foreign Office', in *Modern Asian Studies*, 26 (1992), pp.545-68.
16.   Hosoya Chihiro, in I.H. Nish, *Anglo-Japanese Alienation, 1919-52*, Cambridge: UP, 1982, p.19.
17.   *Transactions and Proceedings of the Japan Society (London)*, 32 (1934-5), xx-xxiv.
18.   Matsudaira to Japan Society, 9 March 1936, in *Transactions and Proceedings of the Japan Society (London)*, 33 (1936), xxi.
19.   R.L. Craigie to K. Fujii, 24 Oct. 1935, in *DBFP*, 2 (xiii), No. 538.
20.   F. Leith-Ross, *Money Talks*, London: Hutchinson, 1968, p.201.
21.   *Transactions and Proceedings of the Japan Society (London)*, 33 (1936), xxi.
22.   *DBFP*, 2 (xx), No. 506.
23.   Leith-Ross, *Money Talks*, p.221.
24.   S.S. Large, *Emperor Hirohito and Showa Japan*, London: Routledge, 1990, passim. It is understood that one of Matsudaira's actions as Household Minister was to arrange the appointment of Admiral Yamanashi Katsunoshin whom he had known from the time of the Washington Conference of 1921 as president of Gakushuin in 1940.
25.   Diary of Sir George Sansom, 22 Jan. 1946, in K. Sansom, *Sir George Sansom and Japan: A Memoir*, Tallahassee: Diplomatic Press, 1972, p.151. Also Piggott, *Broken Thread*, p.365. Some writers were under the impression that Matsudaira continued as Household Minister under the occupation; but this was not so.
26.   *Bulletin of the Japan Society (London)*, no. 1 (1950), pp.7-8. Also to be found in *Tsuisōroku*, pp.456-7, where it is stated (speaking of him and his wife) that no foreign representatives were more popular, '. . . not only in the London society where they occupied a special place, but wherever they went'.
27.   Shiotani and Mushakoji Kintomo, articles in *Tsuisōroku*, pp.298-9 and 506-7.
28.   M. Gayn, *Japan Diary*, Tokyo: Tuttle, 1981, p.280.
29.   J Tilley, *London to Tokyo*, London: Hutchinson, 1944, pp.180-1.

FOR FURTHER READING

Sadao Asada, *From Mahan to Pearl Harbor*, Annapolis: Naval Institute Press, 2006.

Ian Gow, *Military Intervention in Pre-war Japanese Politics: Admiral Kato Kanji and the 'Washington System'*, London: Routledge/Curzon, 2004.

17

YOSHIDA SHIGERU, 1878-1967
Difficult Years for Anglo-Japanese Relations
[London, 1936-38]

IAN NISH

Shigeru Yoshida on arrival at
Waterloo Station, 24 June 1936

Yoshida Shigeru and his wife, Yukiko, occupied the Japanese Embassy at 10 Grosvenor Square for two significant years – 1936-8. These were unhappy and difficult years for Anglo-Japanese relations; but the affection for Britain which they both felt from previous postings in London stayed with them in these disheartening times. These feelings seem to have remained with him when he rose to great distinction as prime minister of several cabinets between 1948 and 1954.

Yoshida was born in Tokyo on 22 September 1878 as fifth son of a Tosa samurai family. He was adopted into the family of Yoshida Kenzō who had stayed in London for two years in the 1860s and later became Yokohama manager for Jardine, Matheson.[1] A wealthy banker and financier, he died prematurely, leaving Shigeru with a good sufficiency at the age of ten. After many changes of schooling, he finally entered Gakushūin Middle School, though it was soon closed with the death of the principal, Konoe Atsumaro (father of Konoe Fumimaro). In 1906 he graduated in politics from Tokyo Imperial University and, after sitting the entrance examination, was admitted to the Gaimushō. One commentator has observed that 'among eleven persons who joined the Foreign Ministry in that year, including Hirota, Mushakōji, Hayashi Kyūjirō, Yoshida appeared to be the least likely to stand out.'[2]

After a preliminary posting in China at Shenyang (Mukden), he joined the London embassy under Ambassador Katō Takaaki in 1908-9. On his return to Tokyo he married Yukiko, the eldest daughter of Count Makino Nobuaki (Shinken). Makino was the son of Ōkubo Toshimichi, the great statesman of Satsuma and Meiji Japan. He had accompanied his father, a member of the Iwakura mission, to the United States in 1872 and stayed on for further study. He was assigned to the London legation and spent over three years there. He had a varied career as a diplomat, ending up as foreign minister in 1911-12 and

1916-18. Hence Yoshida, the adopted son of a prosperous business background, had married into one of the influential families of Meiji and become a Meiji gentleman. While Makino had been minister in Italy and Austria, Yukiko had gone to English-speaking schools and become an expert in the English language and literature.[3]

Yoshida was appointed consul first at Antung and later, more significantly, at Tsinan, the capital of Shantung province. He was lucky to be invited by his father-in-law to accompany him to Paris as his personal assistant at the Peace Conference in 1919. The other senior delegates were Chinda, the ambassador in London, and (later) Prince Saionji. After he returned home, Yoshida was posted to London in 1920 as first secretary, a position he held for two years, serving for part of the time as honorary secretary of the Japan Society of London. Yoshida and his wife accordingly had a prominent role to play in receiving the Crown Prince (later to be the Showa Emperor) on his visit to Britain in May 1921.

Yoshida returned to China service as consul-general, first at Tianjin and later at Shenyang. In 1928 he successfully lobbied the new Seiyūkai leader, General Tanaka Giichi, to become vice-minister for foreign affairs under Tanaka himself. During his years in China, he had not liked the non-interventionist policy of Foreign Minister Shidehara and his party towards that country. He therefore claimed Seiyūkai membership and offered his services. In 1930, he was appointed to his first ambassadorial post in Italy; but, because Japan was embroiled in the dispute over Manchuria during his tenure there, he found himself spending most of his time attending sessions of the League of Nations. After his return he was sent on a tour of inspection of Manchuria and China in 1933. In 1934-5, he made a lengthy tour as inspector-general of legations which took him round Europe and the United States. He resigned from the ministry (*taikan*) in October 1935.

His appointment as ambassador to London was connected with the Incident of 26 February 1936 in which the army tried to take possession of the central districts of Tokyo and to assassinate key political leaders. While it was primarily an example of military insubordination by younger officers which their seniors were unable to control, it still had implications for diplomacy. The attacks on statesmen included that on Count Makino, formerly the Lord Keeper of the Privy Seal and therefore a close adviser to the Shōwa emperor. Insofar as the army officers involved believed that the emperor was being misled by his civilian advisers, they were gunning for Makino especially. Fortunately, he escaped from the inn where he was staying in Yugawara by the rear entrance, with the help of his granddaughter, Yoshida's daughter. This left the attackers so furious that they set the building on fire.[4]

The mutiny was crushed following an outright rejection of the cause by the emperor who called on loyal troops to suppress it. It nonetheless caused the collapse of the cabinet. The mandate passed first to Prince Konoe Fumimaro and, when he declined it on grounds of ill-health, was re-directed to Hirota Kōki, a former ambassador to the Soviet Union. Yoshida commented: 'I had never taken any active interest in politics and always avoided being mixed up in such matters, but on this occasion was asked by Konoe, President of the House of Peers, to prevail upon Hirota to accept the Premiership and assisted in the selection for various posts in the Cabinet.'[5] The genro's invitation was accepted by Hirota. In the formation of Hirota's government, Yoshida Shigeru was in effect his chef de cabinet (*sokaku sosambo*). It was widely speculated in the press that Yoshida would become a member of the new ministry, probably in the role of foreign minister. But the army staged an unequivocal piece of interference in cabinet-making. General Count Terauchi Hisaichi, who had been nominated by the army for the post of war minister, led a delegation of senior officers including General Yamashita Tomoyuki which declared that the army would not serve in a cabinet containing Yoshida (among others) on the ground that he had offended the military. Perhaps the fact that Yoshida was the son-in-law of Makino may have contributed to his unpopularity with the army. The puzzle for the historian is why the army which should have been in disgrace after the mutiny came out of the incident strong enough to lay down the law in this way.

AMBASSADOR TO BRITAIN

It took four days for Hirota to announce his cabinet on 9 March. He decided to appoint as Foreign Minister Arita Hachirō who had been minister to China and to look for another outlet for Yoshida's energies. Fortunately, Matsudaira Tsuneo, the ambassador to Britain then on leave in Tokyo, was appointed on that day to the imperial household and would not be returning to London. Though he was reluctant, Hirota eventually decided to send Yoshida as ambassador to London after the issue had passed over. In his writings Yoshida dismisses the issue casually as though the offer of the foreign ministership had not been made but it was public knowledge and clearly was to affect his tenure in London. On 20 March, newspapers reported the possibility of Yoshida becoming ambassador though it was not officially announced until three weeks later.[7]

Yoshida departed for London on 21 May via Washington. He had encouraging conversations before he left with the British Ambassador, Sir Robert Clive. He also met the representatives of British newspapers to present his thinking on his new mission. Thus, the reputation that he was 'intensely pro-British and believes that the only solution of the Far Eastern problem is cooperation between Japan and ourselves' reached London before him.[8] The three issues on which he would be concentrating were apparently leaked to the press who reported them as: 'The situation in China, the British Empire and naval policy'. Yoshida, however, made the point that: 'Many influential Japanese dislike the present isolation of their country, and his efforts to revive the former friendship with Britain have military as well as official and popular support.'[9]

When Yoshida arrived at Waterloo Station on 25 June, he was entering a complicated area in British foreign policy. Officials and ministers in Whitehall and outsiders differed widely among themselves in their prescriptions for the most desirable course for Britain to take on the Far Eastern scene. To simplify greatly, there was a Treasury group associated with the names of Neville Chamberlain, the chancellor of the exchequer, and Sir Warren Fisher, the head of the Civil Service, which was in the ascendant in 1936. Their attitude towards Japan was one of Realpolitik, that is, Britain's prime enemy was Germany and, being unprepared for that, she must seek accommodation with Japan which might entail offering concessions connected with naval matters or with China. In the end Britain alone could not, the group believed, be successful in any Far Eastern war. The group's first ventures – the Barnby mission to Japan (1934) and the mission of Sir Frederick Leith-Ross to China (1935-6) – had, however, been failures. The Foreign Office who had scarcely been consulted in these ventures was by contrast more inclined to be sympathetic to China and distrustful of

Japan. Its position was reinforced by the return from the legation in Peking of Sir Alexander Cadogan who became deputy under-secretary in the Foreign Office in 1936 and then permanent under-secretary on the retirement of Vansittart in December 1937. These divisions were well-known to the Japanese and to Yoshida in particular.

Another lobby which was non-official included A.H.F. Edwardes, an adviser to the Japanese Embassy in London, Howell Gwynne, the editor of the *Morning Post* and others with access to the corridors of power. These already had connections with Yoshida from his earlier official tour of diplomatic missions overseas in 1934-5. A Japanese official writing of Edwardes described him as always close to the Japanese Embassy. Gwynne, for his part, was one of the old-style editors who occupied the editorial chair for a long period (1911-37). He was one of the first hosts of Yoshida at an influential dinner party. Edwardes, writing about the event, told Gwynne: 'As you know, he was the "fons et origo" of the conversation [at] your dinner party. Although this fact is manifestly unpublishable, I think it would be an excellent idea to refer to Yoshida's definite policy as expressed by him on his departure from Tokyo.'[10] The *Morning Post* not unexpectedly carried articles about Yoshida's views.

Perhaps with a view to preparing the atmosphere, Shigemitsu Mamoru who had been vice-minister until May entered the lists. He prepared the way for Yoshida by sending a conciliatory letter in English to Edwardes which appears to have reached London on 11 July so it must have been written about three weeks earlier. Its theme was:

> In the commercial field, the conflicts of interest are certainly visible as they are real – in India, in Canada, in Egypt, in Australia and practically in all parts of the globe. The Japanese are extremely irritated under the pressure of British policy against the legitimate expansion of their trade, which is of vital necessity to their national existence and growth, and which, despite the alarm so loudly sounded, constitutes only 3 or 4 per cent of world trade. Here our grievances are justified, I believe, to a large extent. . . A general conversation between the two Governments on the subject of the Anglo-Japanese relations as a whole may be quite valuable; it may help pave the way for an amicable solution of individual questions as these are more or less inter-related.[11]

Edwardes passed on Shigemitsu's letter to Gwynne: 'I think much valuable use can be made of it if it is shown to the select few.' Gwynne replied that he could 'make good use of it quietly and confidentially'. Fisher, though he was anxious to prevent tensions from developing with Japan, wrote on 31 July:

> While we must accept a larger degree of Japanese interest [in China], it is quite a different thing to acquiesce in Japanese monopoly or to accept the view that China can for all time be dragooned into 'brotherhood', i.e. subordination by Japan against China's wishes.[12]

Yoshida for his part must have drawn much satisfaction from the views contained in *The Times*' editorial of 8 August:

> A renewal in some form of the Anglo-Japanese Alliance would be a development welcome to Japan. It is true that Japan is very far from being inherently pro-British. Granted the expediency, however, there is nothing in the temper of the country to prevent an Anglo-Japanese rapprochement; and there is much in the traditions of both parties to

forward. . . [There are serious though not insuperable obstacles], never-theless *this country would welcome the friendship of Japan, a proud and gallant young nation for whom we have always had respect*[13] (My italics)

Whether this guarded reaction was an early response to Yoshida's new broom or the cumulative effect of his predecessors like Matsudaira Tsuneo and Fujii Zennosuke is impossible to tell. But Yoshida, having met a cross-section of British opinion, wrote to his father-in-law that the atmosphere on his arrival was more friendly than he expected. But everyone was out of town and so the Yoshidas set off to Scotland to stay at Marchmont.[14]

OLYMPIC AND HIGHER DIPLOMACY

The initial issue to which Yoshida had to turn his attention was what in the annals of history may seem an unimportant one but which in national terms was politically vital: where would the Olympic Games be held in 1940? Following the Oslo meeting of the International Olympic Committee in February 1935 there had been intense competition between Helsinki and Tokyo to host the event. In June 1936, London threw its hat into the ring also – though belatedly. It became a triangular contest; and a truly Olympian struggle between the three cities began.

Like the Japanese Olympic delegation under the leadership of Count Soejima, Yoshida in London had to do formidable lobbying. He met not only government ministers but also the Lord Mayor of London to urge his case. Whether his special pleas struck a responsive chord we cannot say; but England voluntarily withdrew her application on 30 July. This facilitated Japan's success. By 36 votes to 27 it was decided by the IOC meeting in Berlin on the occasion of the Olympic Games there, to award the event in 1940 to Tokyo. When the crucial decision was announced, the Japanese press and athletes were overwhelmed with joy. Some said: 'The Japanese people's ambitions have finally succeeded. . . In Olympic history a significant "new epoch" is opening up. . . In 1940 the sacred flame will come for the first time to the East.' As an additional guarantee of success it was stated that 'the army authorities would help the organizing body (*sōshiki iinkai*) from the outside though they would not want to take a prominent part'.[15]

These preliminary efforts of Yoshida and his colleagues had secured tangible results. His embassy had started with a triumph. But, alas, the Tokyo government on 15 July 1938 announced that, because of the 'extension' of the China Incident, it would be inappropriate to hold the Olympics in Tokyo under wartime conditions.

Yoshida is often accused of using unofficial channels for influencing the British government. This was true and was resented by the Foreign Office. But it was a style pursued by his predecessor, Matsudaira, and his successor, Shigemitsu, also.[16] In any case, it was not unnatural for the Japanese ambassador to get his message over in whatever way possible in the knowledge that Britain was pursuing a dual diplomacy at this time. As long as the Foreign Office was at loggerheads with the Treasury group, the ambassador had in effect a choice of routes by which to exert influence over British elite opinion. Naturally, the Treasury group praised Yoshida, while the Foreign Office was caustic in describing him. Indeed, the Foreign Office records include a minute criticizing his suitability as ambassador to London and his handling of Anglo-Japanese relations. Another condemned his 'inefficiency' in handling affairs.[17] Surely a very extreme reaction by officials at the end of their tether!

Despite this, Yoshida persisted in putting forward his views on reconciling Anglo-Japanese differences which were of course considerable. From Yoshida's point of view there was considerable urgency because of European developments. When he reached London, Japan's negotiations for an agreement with Germany were reaching their final stages. The Foreign Ministry had taken over the negotiations from the army general staff. Under the Hirota cabinet it was decided to carry on these talks during the summer, even if the majority of Kasumigaseki officials disapproved of them. It was clearly pressure from the army which made the cabinet come down in favour of the anti-comintern pact. As a compromise, however, it decided to consult Japan's diplomatic representatives overseas. This was the special task of Colonel Tatsumi who had just arrived as military attaché. Later, his pleas were reinforced by those of Colonel Ōshima, the military attaché in Berlin, who paid a special visit to London. Yoshida records: 'I replied that I was opposed to the idea: an opinion I repeated when, later, both Eiichi Tatsumi and Hiroshi Oshima visited me in an effort to prevail on me to change my views.'[18] The pact with its accompanying documents was signed on 25 November.

Yoshida embarked on the first phase of his overtures to Britain through the Conservative party in October and they continued in dilatory fashion well into the new year. But Neville Chamberlain very properly passed his rough draft of an Anglo-Japanese agreement to the Foreign Office for consideration.[19]

Japanese scholars have made clear that Yoshida's overtures were not authorized from Tokyo and were made on his own initiative. He was careful to say that they were personal. Yoshida did not clear his actions with Tokyo because he knew that he was *persona non grata* with the military and, therefore, wanted to go as far as possible on his own. This is not unknown in diplomatic history but is a risky course. So convinced was Yoshida of the need and the opportunity that he was prepared to take the risk. But Britain by her enquiries in Tokyo and by intercepts was baffled by his actions and was privately highly critical of his tactics. There were more hopeful signs when a change of ministry took place in Tokyo in January; and both the Prime Minister, General Hayashi, and the Foreign Minister, Satō Naotake, gave pro-British speeches. During their brief tenure of office, Yoshida felt that his views were commanding support, as he wrote in his letter to Makino.[20] It seemed a good omen also when Neville Chamberlain with whom Yoshida had good relations took over as Prime Minister in May 1937.

Yoshida frequently spoke of the need for him to return to Japan to talk the matter over with his government. As late as 1 May, the press was giving publicity to a report of Yoshida's negotiations with 'a high official' of the Foreign Office for a settlement of Anglo-Japanese differences and misunderstandings.[21] But when war broke out between China and Japan in July, Yoshida's mission (as he saw it) became impossible. Once the Japanese army in China intruded into Shanghai and the Yangtse valley, it was inevitable that many issues of difference with Britain would come to the fore and many complaints would be registered. A sustained campaign from some organs of the press in favour of China resulted. Left-wing demonstrations outside the ambassador's residence were reported from 24 September – the strongest since Matsuoka's visit to London in 1933. But embassies do not invariably report such indications of national unpopularity. Commenting on this change, Mme Yoshida wrote poignantly: 'British feeling naturally went with the Chinese.[22]

GROSVENOR SQUARE

Domestic affairs are not often mentioned in diplomatic history. Yukiko Yoshida, gives us an account of these in her memoir of these years in English, entitled *Whispering Leaves in Grosvenor Square*. She had come to London for the first time as 'a young attaché's wife' of 19 with some excitement because her father was an Anglophil and often wrote letters to his daughter in English. The embassy had then moved to 10 Grosvenor Square. When she came as the ambassador's lady, she was, she writes, delighted with London but the embassy in Grosvenor Square 'was a disappointment to us as it was so neglected, having been vacant for ten months. We had to spend over a month among cleaners and painters before the house was habitable, and even now we are gradually improving it when our Government allows us the expense'. Yoshida was not partial to golf like the rest of his embassy colleagues. Instead, he took exercise during the week from horse-riding in Hyde Park. The only other sport recorded was salmon fishing.The Yoshidas travelled most weekends, either to political country-house parties or for independent sightseeing. From 1 July 1937, they rented a country cottage called Little Fishery at Maidenhead for two months. Sometimes, Mme Yoshida went her own way and had her own entertainments. She seems to have had an especially cordial relationship with Mrs Neville Chamberlain. Her interests were literary and she wrote a good deal of poetry in English about London.

The ambassador and his wife had to be observers and reporters on the British scene. They had to describe the distress felt by the people over the abdication crisis. Mme Yoshida writes: 'On the morning of 11 December I heard the sad news of the Abdication. . . I listened with emotion to the King's last speech on the radio which moved me greatly.'[23] The crisis had relevance to Japan in two respects: Edward VIII as prince of Wales had visited Japan in 1922; and Japan was also a monarchy.

The agony of the abdication was dispelled by the anticipation of the coronation. The Yoshidas were also deeply involved with the preparations for the coronation of King George VI and Queen Elizabeth. As representatives of the Japanese Emperor, Prince and Princess Chichibu arrived on 13 April and stayed at Hove for a month. The Yoshidas were partially their host, especially at the Emperor's birthday reception on 29 April. At the main ceremony at Westminster Abbey on 12 May, Prince and Princess Chichibu, representatives of one of the world's monarchies, were given precedence over the other foreign royalties. Although a farewell dinner in honour of the Chichibus was given on 24 June, the Princess suffered from the first of a series of illnesses which prevented their departure before 18 September.[24]

Mme Yoshida's health was always delicate and took a turn for the worse in August. Suddenly, she was taken to the London Clinic and operated on for hernia. During the long period of her convalescence Yoshida had to rely on his daughter Kazuko to act as hostess at embassy functions.[25] Thus, Kazuko addressed the Japan Society on 26 May 1938 on the subject of the Japanese Woman.

DEPARTURE

In August 1938, Mme Yoshida left with her daughter for Japan. Yoshida who had now come to the age of 60 was recalled from his post in London on 3 September and returned to Japan on 19 October. It is not easy to discover whether he left at his own request or whether he found it opportune to go when policies that he disliked were being followed. It certainly suited him to return at this time because it enabled him to attend the wedding of Kazuko to Asō Takakichi in November. He had appeared to get on well initially with General Ugaki who occupied the portfolio of foreign minister for four crucial months. But it was ultimately he who was responsible for his recall. Moreover, it was Ugaki who thought that his diplomatic career should be ended when he returned from London, regardless of his connections with Makino and Saionji. It may have been a factor that Yoshida had written some 60 letters to the *jūshin* which may have been resented at an official level.[26]

The Foreign Office considered the question of conferring some decoration on Yoshida on the occasion of his departure. But the consensus was against doing so. He eventually retired from the foreign service a second time in March 1939, London having been his final post. Yoshida's departure led to a general post among diplomats. Konoe, by now Prime Minister, promoted Military Attaché Oshima Hiroshi as ambassador to Berlin, while the controversial Shiratori was sent to Rome. Whatever gloss is put on these appointments, they were anathema to Yoshida who was clearly anti-fascist and a member of the Anglo-American group in the Foreign Ministry. They were clearly concessions to military opinion. This was not the scene on which Yoshida wanted to operate.

What impression did Yoshida have of his years in London? Yoshida's biographer, Professor Inoki, says that he appreciated especially the attitudes and style of Sir Robert Craigie and Neville Chamberlain. Yoshida highly valued what he regarded as Chamberlain's policy of reconciliation with Japan as also his tactic of reconciliation with Germany by the Munich settlement. As a student of diplomatic style, he found Japan's diplomatic style too rigid and unyielding, but found England's to be flexible and pragmatic.[27]

John Dower writes that Yoshida was more Anglophile than pro-American. He was not put at his ease during visits to the United States either in 1934 or in 1936. It is hard to reach either a contemporary assessment of his thinking because of the rhetoric in which an ambassador has to indulge. It is also hard to believe all that was said after 1945. Dower goes on to say what is unquestionably true: Yoshida belonged to the 'Ei Bei riyōha', the group which believed in using Britain and America for the solution of Japan's problems. He was opposed to Japan's German leanings and opposed the suggestion of a full alliance. He was in touch in his retirement in Tokyo with both Joseph Grew and Craigie and was in favour of peace and against the continuation of the war.[28] It is probably true that Yoshida was greatly impressed by the aristocratic style of the upper levels of British politics.

Yoshida was notoriously inconsistent and opinionated. He was a man of action rather than a political philosopher. We need not be too swayed by the vindictive and savage criticisms made of his personality by Foreign Office bureaucrats. In a sense Yoshida was a businessman in diplomatic garb. He had assumed the clothes of his father-in-law Makino happily enough but he did not really fit into the pinstripes or at least the conventions and courtesies of diplomatic protocol as practised in Europe.

It was Yoshida's misfortune to be ambassador at the Court of St James's for two years and four months at a time when relations were deteriorating. When Yoshida was in London, as he later wrote in his autobiography: 'Japan reversed its stance, making enemies of Britain and the United States and forging ties with the more distant Germany and Italy. This was not only inept strategically but truly deplorable in that it lost Japan the good faith of the international community.'[29] Yoshida Shigeru was to live on until happier days and to become prime minister, the highest officer of state under the post-war constitution. In his contacts with General MacArthur he looked a sort of English figure from the past with his spats and his outsize cigar. When the general was planning reform of the police system, Yoshida argued unsuccessfully for the adoption of the system of London bobbies on the beat.

Yukiko, whose memoir of London was full of prayers for peace with China, was not to survive beyond 1941. Touchingly, Yoshida dedicates his memoirs to Yukiko: 'the memory of whose constant faith in her country and her people strengthened me during the years of crisis'.

[1997]

NOTES

1.   Yoshida's period in London has been comprehensively covered in Inoki Masamichi, *Hyōden Yoshida Shigeru*, 4 vols., Tokyo: Yomiuri, 1981, Vol. 3, pp.7-111; Hosoya Chihiro, *Nichi-Ei kankeishi, 1917-49*, Tokyo: Todai Shuppankai, 1986, pp.8-13; *Ningen Yoshida Shigeru*, Tokyo: Chuo Koron, 1991; Ono Katsumi, *Kasumigaseki gaikō*, Tokyo: Nihon Keizai, 1985; Haga Toru, 'Gaikokan no bunsho', in *Gaiko Forum*, 82-4(1995). I have published some studies of the subject in 'Ambassador at Large: Yoshida and his Mission to Britain, 1932-7' in Sue Henny and J.P. Lehmann (eds.), *Themes and Theories in Modern Japanese History*, London: Athlone, 1988, pp.195-212; 'Mr Yoshida at the London Embassy, 1936-8' in Japan Society of London, *Bulletin*, 4(1979), pp. 1-7.
2.   Watanabe Akio in *Nihon Gaikoshi jiten*.
3.   Ian Nish, *Japan's Struggle with Internationalism*, London: KPI, 1993, p. 49.
4.   John Dower, *Empire and Aftermath*, Cambridge, Mass., 1979, ch. 5; Ben-ami Shillony, *Revolt in Japan*, Princeton, 1973, p. 132.
5.   Yoshida Shigeru, *Memoirs*, London: Heinemann, 1962, p. 13; *Kaiso 10-nen*, 4 vols, Tokyo, 1957, Vol. I.
6.   Yoshida, *Memoirs*, pp. 13-14.
7.   [London] *Times*, 20 March, 9 April 1936.
8.   Ian Nish in Saki Dockrill (ed.), *From Pearl Harbor to Hiroshima*, London: Macmillan, 1994, p. 21.
9.   [London] *Times*, 22 May 1936.
10. Miyake Kijirō in *Kasumigasekikai kaihō*, 1968; Dockrill, p. 21; Inoki, III, 39.
11. For the text of this letter, see Dockrill, pp. 19-20.
12. E. O'Halpin, *Head of the Civil Service: a biography of Sir Warren Fisher*, London, 1989, p. 237. Also Gill Bennett, 'British Policy in the Far East, 1933-6: Treasury and Foreign Office' in *Modern Asian Studies*, 26(1992), pp. 545-68.
13. [London] *Times*, 8 Aug. 1936.
14. Yoshida to Makino, 7 Aug. 1936 in Inoki, III, 29.
15. *Tokyo Nichi-nichi Shimbun*, 1 Aug. 1936.
16. Miyake in *Kasumigasekikai kaihō*, 1969, p. 12.
17. John Dower, *Japan in War and Peace: Selected Essays*, Cambridge 1995, p. 209.
18. Yoshida, *Memoirs*, p. 15. Inoki, III, 17-20i quotes Tatsumi, III, p. 45.
19. Bennett, p. 568.
20. Yoshida to Makino, May 1937, in Inoki, III, 45.
21. Inoki, III, 53.
22. Arthur Clegg, *Aid China, 1937-49: A Memoir of a Forgotten Campaign*, Beijing, 1989, pp. 74, 81-2. Inoki, III, 64-5.
23. Yuki Yoshida, *Whispering Leaves in Grosvenor Square, 1936-7*, private, 1938, p. 28. (Reprinted, Folkestone: Global Oriental, 1997)
24. Yuki Yoshida, p. 55. Princess Chichibu, *The Silver Drum: A Japanese Imperial Memoir*, Folkestone: Global Oriental, 1996, pp. 129-37.

25. Yuki Yoshida, p. 70.
26. Inoki, III, 115.
27. Yoshida, *Memoirs*, pp. 16-17, 118.
28. Inoki, III, 111; Ono, *Kasumigaseki gaiko*, pp. 4-5; Dower, *Japan in War and Peace*, p. 216.
29. Yoshida, *Kaiso 10-nen*, I, 34.
30. Richard B. Finn, *Winners in Peace: MacArthur, Yoshida and Postwar Japan*, Berkeley: University of California Press, 1992.

FURTHER READING

A. Best, *Britain, Japan and Pearl Harbor: Avoiding War in East Asia, 1936-41*, London: Routledge, 1995.

A. Best, *British Intelligence and the Japanese Challenge in Asia, 1914-41*, Basingstoke: Palgrave Macmillan, 2002.

18

SHIGEMITSU MAMORU, 1887-1957
Critical Times in a Long, Ambivalent Career
[London, 1938-41]

ANTONY BEST

Shigemitsu Mamoru

S higemitsu Mamoru was Ambassador to Britain in the critical period from 1938 to 1941 but his earlier career had many British connections. He is known to those interested in Japan's foreign relations in the twentieth century as one of the most influential diplomats of the Shōwa era and possibly as the most difficult to categorize. To some Shigemitsu is a figure to be vilified as an expansionist and a collaborator with the Imperial Japanese Army; to others he emerges as an enlightened figure keen to expand Japan's links with the West and fighting a rearguard action against the army's excesses.[1] Part of the difficulty in coming to any understanding of Shigemitsu is that his career was so long and varied: he was the Minister to China (1931-2), the Vice Minister for Foreign Affairs (1933-6), the Ambassador to the Soviet Union (1936-8). Following his embassy in London, he became the Ambassador to the Nanking regime (1942-3), and Foreign Minister on three separate occasions (1943-5, 1945, 1954-6). In addition, one might note that he was the hobbling, almost anachronistic figure (dressed in top hat and tails) who signed the surrender document on the USS *Missouri* on 2 September 1945 and that, at the end of the Tokyo War Crimes Trial in 1948, he was sentenced to a seven-year term in prison.

The wide range of Shigemitsu's responsibilities means that it is difficult to follow the continuities in his thinking, but an assessment of his role in Japanese diplomacy is important because his continued proximity to the decision-making process allows us to illuminate some of the motivations behind Japan's actions. This is particularly the case in terms of the development of Anglo-Japanese relations from 1934 to 1941. In analyzing Shigemitsu's impact on this relationship it is important to bear in mind a number of constant themes in his thinking. It is clear, for example, that he considered relations with China to be the most significant axis in Japan's foreign relations, and that he consistently sought to find a means of reconciling the rise of Chinese nationalism with

Japan's domination over East Asia. In addition, like many of his peers he was profoundly suspicious of the Soviet Union and wanted to form bonds with other countries in order to contain communism. Indeed, one may go further and state that he was uneasy with any of the new 'progressive' thinking that affected international relations in the inter-war period. He was opposed to the League of Nations and had little time for American moralizing.

One of the major problems that Shigemitsu faced in his diplomacy was how to reconcile his desire for a strong Japanese influence in Asia with the need for Japan to remain on good terms with a global power such as Britain. Clearly, Japan could not afford to alienate Britain, which was the world's leading financial and naval power and a major trading partner. The problem was, however, whether Britain would be willing to accept an expanded role for Japan in China. If Anglo-Japanese relations had remained as cordial as they had been at the height of the Alliance, this might have been possible but, as far as Shigemitsu was concerned, British attitudes had changed for the worse after the end of World War I. Indeed, a central element in Shigemitsu's thinking towards Britain from the time of the Washington Conference onwards was that it was Britain, not Japan, which had changed the nature of the bilateral relationship. Like others of his generation he regretted the ending of the Anglo-Japanese Alliance, but his disquiet with British policy was greatly exacerbated by the famous memorandum issued by Austen Chamberlain, the then Foreign Secretary, in December 1926 which announced that Britain would pursue a more liberal line towards Chinese nationalism. As far as Shigemitsu was concerned, Britain in this memorandum changed from its previous policy of seeing Japan as a collaborator to viewing it instead as a competitor; this justified Japan's move towards a more forthright policy in East Asia in order to defend its own interests.[2] The problem facing Shigemitsu in his dealings with Britain in the 1930s was whether it was possible to reverse this emergence of competition and return to a more convivial relationship.

Both as Vice-Minister for Foreign Affairs and as Ambassador to Britain, Shigemitsu contended that such a change was feasible, and he was encouraged in this belief by some of his British contacts who expressed both their dismay at the decline in Anglo-Japanese friendship and their lack of faith in the pro-Chinese and pro-American policy favoured by Britain since 1926. The most important contact Shigemitsu had was Arthur Edwardes, whom Shigemitsu had known in China when the former had worked as Acting Inspector-General of the Chinese Maritime Customs in 1927, and who in 1932 became the London-based adviser to the Manchukuo government, and later the adviser on world affairs to the Japanese embassy in London.[3] Edwardes was well-connected; he had friends in the media such as the pro-Japanese editor of the *Morning Post*, H.A. Gwynne, and contacts in Whitehall like Sir Warren Fisher, the Permanent Secretary at the Treasury, Sir Maurice Hankey, the Chief Secretary to the Cabinet, and Sir Horace Wilson, the Chief Industrial Adviser to the Government. Through these channels Edwardes was able to communicate his own and Shigemitsu's views to the very highest levels. The problem was, however, that, while it was relatively easy to influence the Treasury, the Foreign Office tended to remain impervious to these unofficial blandishments; indeed Edwardes was virtually *persona non grata* as far as the latter ministry was concerned.[4]

The opposition of the Foreign Office to an improvement of relations with Japan was seen by those like Shigemitsu as a result of its being steeped in enthusiasm for the new thinking in international relations epitomized by the

League of Nations. As far as Shigemitsu was concerned, this interest in the League was evidence of a disturbing tilt leftwards in British politics under the influence of pro-American internationalists, such as Winston Churchill, allied with radical left-wing groups who favoured the Soviet Union. Disturbingly, this leftist influence, he believed, was even felt in the Conservative party due to the prominence of Winston Churchill and younger politicians such as Alfred Duff-Cooper and Anthony Eden. The problem facing Shigemitsu was how to outflank this radical group. The obvious answer was that Japan should attempt to appeal to the British government not through the Foreign Office, but through sympathetic mandarins such as Fisher and Wilson, and by appealing directly to the 'orthodox faction' within the Conservative party, led by figures such as Neville Chamberlain, Sir Samuel Hoare and Lord Halifax, who, it was hoped, would welcome a return to the traditional Tory policy of friendship with Japan. This was the motive for the myriad unofficial contacts made by Shigemitsu and his predecessor, Yoshida Shigeru, which so antagonized the Foreign Office during this period, although it is worth noting that, increasingly, Edwardes was able to find one sympathetic contact at the Foreign Office, the Parliamentary Under-Secretary, R.A. Butler, who was a protégé of Chamberlain's.[6]

Shigemitsu's superficial perspective on British politics raises a number of problems; in particular by painting pro- and anti-Japanese sentiment as a simple right-left divide it greatly underestimated the sense of genuine outrage in Britain towards Japan which was apparent across the whole political spectrum. For example, Shigemitsu noted in 1952 in his book *Gaikō Kaisōroku* (Diplomatic Memoirs) that at the time of the Tientsin Crisis in the summer of 1939 anti-Japanese feeling in Britain had been provoked by the activities of the pro-American faction and by left-wing propaganda; in reality it was simply abhorrence at the Japanese army's treatment of British civilians which caused a wave of protests to be sent to the press and to the Foreign Office – it did not need to be stirred up by the left.[7] Again, it is significant that in 1940, when Britain proposed a temporary solution to the Burma Road crisis which met Japan's wishes, Shigemitsu's interpretation of this decision was that it was the traditionalist high Tory, Lord Halifax, who had persuaded the pro-American Prime Minister, Winston Churchill, to accept this measure of appeasement, when in fact it had been the other way round. Indeed, Halifax was consistently from the start of the Sino-Japanese War one of the figures in the Cabinet who argued for tougher measures against Japan, a stance which appears to have been influenced by his disgust at Japan's propensity for bombing civilians in China.

Another, perhaps even more significant, problem was that, putting the moral issues aside, the belief that a traditional Conservative government free of pro-American and pro-Soviet influences would necessarily try to establish a new relationship with Japan which would be acceptable to both sides was clearly misplaced. The fact is that during this period neither Britain nor Japan was willing to allow the other a dominant position in East Asia, it was rather the opposite as each sought to expand its own influence. Shigemitsu was, in fact, one of the key figures on the Japanese side who was pushing for the diminution of the Western stake in China and the establishment of a new Sino-Japanese understanding which would enhance Japan's standing. Obviously, it was extremely unlikely that a British government would enter into a new arrangement with Japan in which it would agree to any such sacrifice of its own position in China, and therefore the result was that Shigemitsu's policy towards China directly contradicted the aim of achieving better relations with Britain.

PROBLEMS AS FOREIGN VICE-MINISTER

A clear example of this disparity of interests came during 1934-5 when Shigemitsu was Vice-Minister at the Gaimushō. As Vice-Minister, Shigemitsu was aware of the advantages that could accrue to Japan from an improvement of diplomatic relations with Britain, since this would allow Japan to escape from diplomatic isolation and to avoid a major crisis over the collapse of naval limitation. He was not, however, prepared to see any *rapprochement* which would impinge upon Japan's interests in East Asia and instead wanted British recognition of Japan's paramount position in China. This essential qualification was not clear in the vague overtures that Shigemitsu and the Foreign Minister, Hirota Kōki, made to Britain during this period, with the result that those in Britain who sought a *rapprochement*, such as the Chancellor of the Exchequer, Neville Chamberlain, and Sir Warren Fisher, felt that the Gaimushō's soothing words were sincere and augured well for Anglo-Japanese cooperation in China.[9]

The problems which led to this misunderstanding began in the autumn of 1934 when Shigemitsu created much interest in the British Treasury by enthusiastically welcoming to Tokyo the Federation of British Industry mission led by Lord Barnby which was due to visit Manchukuo to assess the possibilities for British trade. Even more significant was the series of talks he held with Arthur Edwardes, who travelled to Tokyo with the FBI mission. Edwardes informed Fisher on his return to London that Shigemitsu had informed him that the Japanese people were 'pro-British' and that the 'Japanese Government would greatly welcome a gesture of friendship from this country'.[10] These hints encouraged Chamberlain and Fisher to believe that an understanding could be reached if only the right means could be found, and they hoped that better relations with Japan would allow for the recovery or even expansion of Britain's economic position in China. Such thinking could not have been further from Shigemitsu's intentions. In a memorandum of 20 November 1934 Shigemitsu recorded his view that, if Japan was to accomplish its aims in East Asia, this meant 'the expelling of politically influential countries and foreigners from China' and specifically the withdrawal of Western garrisons and the destruction of the British-dominated Chinese Maritime Customs Service.[11]

The British Treasury's misinterpretation of the Gaimushô's thinking helped to lead to the plan in 1935 to send Sir Frederick Leith-Ross, the Chief Economic Adviser to the Government, to East Asia to try to arrange a Sino-Japanese settlement through the medium of a joint Anglo-Japanese loan to China in return for Chinese recognition of the independence of Manchukuo, a development which, it was hoped, would ease Anglo-Japanese tensions and advance the cause of British trade in the region. Leith-Ross arrived in Tokyo in September 1935 and held a number of talks with Shigemitsu and other prominent figures, but found little enthusiasm for his ideas. Shigemitsu later claimed in *Gaikō Kaisōroku* that the Gaimushō's response had been lacklustre because they had been caught off guard by Leith-Ross's proposals having failed to receive any forewarning of his plans through Sir Robert Clive, the British Ambassador in Tokyo, or Matsudaira Tsuneo, the Japanese Ambassador in London.[12] Such an explanation seems at best disingenuous, for in reality Shigemitsu stood opposed to any plan that would have involved Anglo-Japanese political cooperation in China; the most he was willing to tolerate was a British economic presence. At the very time that Leith-Ross arrived in Tokyo the Gaimushō was involved in the formulation of Hirota's 'Three Principles' for relations with China which, it was hoped, would reassert Hirota's control over Japanese foreign policy in the face of army activism and which dealt with China solely in terms of the Sino-Japanese relationship. The proposals brought by Leith-Ross were an unwelcome diversion.[13]

The failure of the Leith-Ross mission to elicit a positive response from the Japanese government was a severe blow to Anglo-Japanese relations, for even though Shigemitsu and Hirota had decided by December 1935 that it was necessary to restore Britain's trust in order to avoid alienating the Treasury, it blunted the cause of the pro-Japanese lobby in London and strengthened the scepticism of the Foreign Office.[14] It is significant, however, not just for its short-term effects but also for the light it sheds on the fundamental incompatibility of Anglo-Japanese interests in China. Unfortunately, Shigemitsu was never able fully to come to terms with this. Later, as Ambassador to London, he continued to press Britain to accept only an economic role for itself in China and to accept Japanese political domination. In December 1938, just after his arrival in London, Shigemitsu approached the Conservative MP, Sir John Wardlaw-Milne, who was chairman of the House of Commons China Committee, to suggest a scheme that would break the deadlock in relations, a central element in this plan being recognition by Britain of 'Japan's unique position in China'.[15] The proposal did not prosper. Later, in October 1939, he again pressed for Britain to change its stance towards war in China, convinced with the start of the war in Europe 'that there were the conditions for an appropriately fair settlement of the China problem, and that Britain would exhibit its traditional statesmanship and recognize Japan's position in East Asia and China'.[16] For a brief moment he believed that he had made a breakthrough when he reported to the Gaimushō that the Foreign Secretary, Lord Halifax, had informed him that 'His Majesty's Government had no intention of pursuing political designs in China, their interests being limited to commercial and financial considerations'.[17] This was, however, a misreading of the British position; the Foreign Office had no intention of starting a British retreat from China. It was only at the end of his time in London that Shigemitsu admitted that perhaps Japanese policy and he himself had been misguided, when he noted in a conversation recorded by Leith-Ross that:

> [Japan] had made many mistakes in her policy towards China, but now both the civilians and the military were agreed that peace should be made without territorial gains and without indemnities. . . [H]e regretted that collaboration with us had not been arranged at the time that I went out to China.[18]

This was, however, too little and too late.

China was not the only area of policy in which Shigemitsu felt that progress could be made; he was also keen to see a settlement of commercial tensions, but believed that here, too, it was for Britain to make concessions and allow Japan greater access to markets within the British Empire. The importance of these commercial issues was one of the reasons why Leith-Ross was invited for a second visit to Japan in June 1936. In addition, in a letter that Shigemitsu sent to Edwardes at this time he argued that this was one of the major areas of concern and observed that:

The Japanese are extremely irritated under the pressure of British policy against the legitimate expansion of their trade, which is of vital necessity to their national existence and growth, and which, despite the alarm so loudly sounded, constitutes only 3 or 4 per cent of world trade. Here our grievances are justified, I believe, to a great extent.[19]

His stress on this area of relations was, however, not so great when he was in London, as the start of the Sino-Japanese War had the initial effect of lessening trade tensions outside East Asia, although over the longer term the issue was to re-emerge in the different form of protest against British sanctions towards Japan.

A more significant policy area which Shigemitsu, both as Vice-Minister and Ambassador to London, hoped could be used to construct a new Anglo-Japanese understanding was to stress the advantage of Anglo-Japanese cooperation against Soviet activities in East Asia, in the hope that this strategy would appeal to those on the traditional wing of the Conservative party who were deeply antagonistic towards the Soviet Union. The effort to play on British fears began shortly after Leith-Ross's visit to Tokyo in September 1935 and can be seen in part as an effort to repair the damage: it was, however, also an element in a wider attempt by the Gaimushō to construct a 'Defence against Communism' policy which would help to rein in the Japanese Army in north China and push them from anti-Chinese into an anti-Soviet direction. In January 1936 Shigemitsu informed the British Ambassador in Tokyo that recent events in north China had to be seen in the light of Soviet machinations and that it was necessary for Japan to construct a barrier against communism.[20]

AMBASSADOR TO LONDON

In London, after two years of service in Moscow from November 1936 to October 1938, Shigemitsu's willingness to use the anti-Soviet card became much more marked, as his animosity towards Soviet communism had grown with acquaintance. In his talks with Halifax and Butler he consistently emphasized the threat that the Soviet Union posed to other states and that Stalin would be the only one to gain from the differences that existed among the non-communist countries. This line of attack became particularly noticeable following the conclusion of the Nazi-Soviet Pact in August 1939 and the subsequent opening of hostilities in Europe. Clearly, Shigemitsu hoped that Britain's experience of Soviet duplicity after the Anglo-French-Russian talks of the summer of 1939 had been a bitter lesson and would lay the basis for Anglo-Japanese collaboration. In the spring of 1940 he informed Butler that 'the determination of Japan to keep on terms with us against Russia was undiminished' and warned that 'the ardent desire of the . . . Soviet Union was to keep everyone in trouble and gradually getting weaker'.[21] Here again, however, he was misjudging the climate of British opinion, for while there was little love for Russia there was even less for Japan.

Although his efforts to engineer an overall improvement of relations with Britain came to nought, Shigemitsu was able as Ambassador in London to ease some of the tensions in relations. He worked well, for example, in the first six months of 1940 to deal with some of the economic problems that arose from the start of the European war, and was able to lay a basis for a policy of 'gradual cooperation', a policy aided by the relationship between Butler and Edwardes.[22] All of this began to change with the Burma Road crisis in the summer of 1940.

Shigemitsu first became aware of this crisis when he called on the Foreign Office on 21 June 1940 to explain the demand made to the British Military Attaché in Tokyo by a representative of the Japanese Army that Britain close the Burma Road or face war. Shigemitsu was initially taken aback by this news, but soon recovered his composure to argue that Britain was wrong to take seriously warnings emanating from unofficial channels. This approach was, however, quickly undermined when two days later the demand for the closure of the Burma Road became official policy. Despite this setback, Shigemitsu tried to turn the crisis in relations to Japan's advantage so that Japan could gain the dominant position in East Asia but without risking war with Britain.[23] As with other prominent Japanese policy-makers, Shigemitsu realized that the conditions in South-East Asia following the defeats suffered by Britain, France and Holland in Europe favoured an increase in Japan's political and economic influence in the region, but in addition he believed that Britain's insecurity could lead it to back a Sino-Japanese peace settlement. He was therefore enthusiastic about the settlement of the Burma Road issue negotiated by Foreign Minister Arita Hachirō and the British Ambassador in Tokyo, Sir Robert Craigie, which stated that the Burma Road would be closed for three months while Japan sought a 'fair and equitable' solution to the China problem.

In London, Shigemitsu did his utmost to try to forward what he saw as this 'great opportunity', as he believed that there had been 'a major conversion of its [Britain's] policy towards Japan and the obstacles to the East Asian problem'.[24] He visited the Foreign Office frequently for talks with Halifax and Butler and once again used Edwardes as a vital but unofficial conduit of information. Shigemitsu also sought to persuade the Gaimushō to adhere to his policy and take a firm line towards Britain designed to push the latter towards a recognition of Japan's interests. On 25 July he explained that at this time:

> . . . it was necessary for Japan to consolidate her position in East Asia. As a result Japan should encourage England to get herself out of the position she has got herself into, & help her towards her policy of promoting peace in China, in the hope that the U.S. will follow suit.[25]

In a further telegram to Tokyo on 5 August Shigemitsu observed that Japan should proceed with 'scrupulous consideration and prudence in our relations with Britain' and noted that, if Japan carried out its 'Greater East Asian policy with a responsible, fair and square attitude, we may properly expect Anglo-American obstacles to be removed in the natural course of events'.[26]

By this time, however, Shigemitsu's cautious policy for expanding Japanese influence was being undermined by the incoming Konoe government with Matsuoka Yōsuke as Foreign Minister. The first act of the new administration in regard to relations with Britain was at the end of July to arrest over twenty British civilians in Japan and Korea on charges of spying. Shigemitsu was furious at this flagrant insult to Britain which he believed would undermine all he had been trying to achieve. Worse was to follow, for within a month Matsuoka initiated a drastic purge of the Gaimushō which included orders for Shigemitsu's trusted deputy, Okamoto Suemasa, to return to Tokyo. Shigemitsu began to fear that the diplomatic service was being handed over from mature, cautious professionals like himself to young, inexperienced and hot-headed reformers, and confirmation that this was so came on 27 September when news arrived at the Embassy in London that Japan had signed a Tripartite Pact with Germany and Italy.[27]

For Shigemitsu the conclusion of the Tripartite Pact was a mistake of the greatest magnitude, and in hindsight he declared that it set Japan 'on the road to the death of the nation'. His opposition to any anti-Anglo-Saxon combination with the Axis powers was long-standing, as in the winter of 1939, he had mobilized opinion among the majority of the Japanese ambassadors in Europe to any strengthening of the Anti-Comintern Pact. In the early autumn of 1940, he was still of the same opinion, despite the series of German victories since April of that year which had convinced most Japanese observers that Britain was on the verge of defeat. Shigemitsu believed by late September that Germany had missed its chance for victory over Britain; it had failed to defeat the Royal Air Force and could not launch an invasion. Britain, meanwhile, was increasing its production of armaments and Churchill was manoeuvring to win over American opinion. Moreover, Shigemitsu was struck by Britain's resolve in the face of the shock fall of France and the German bombing of British cities. This was not merely an abstract observation as Shigemitsu himself had personal experience of the Blitz; he had remained in London in September and thus witnessed at first-hand how Britain had coped with the German onslaught without buckling. The experience, one might postulate, did not endear Germany to Shigemitsu, as during this period the Embassy buildings in Portman Square were half-destroyed and the farewell party for Okamoto was disturbed by an air-raid.[28]

Following the arrival of this new pro-German line in Japanese foreign policy, Shigemitsu was tempted to resign, but after reflection he decided to remain in London to do what he could to mitigate its effects and avoid direct Anglo-Japanese confrontation. In *Gaikō Kaisōroku* Shigemitsu noted of this period that:

> Tokyo's position was simply to persist in an extreme way with the destruction of Britain, but I thought privately that in their moves in international relations they were virtually blind to the course of the war in Europe. I felt I had no choice but to become a pillar and support the nation. That is to say that, to make sure a sudden break in relations did not occur, it was necessary to support Anglo-American relations in London. This was the first point, next was also to give accurate reports about the outlook for the course of the war in Europe, this point would show that Tokyo had made a mistake (it was in vain, they did not take this news into consideration at all). I decided to be as resolute as I was when I did not flinch in the middle of a bombing raid, I would harden my determination to fight alone in this extremely difficult period.[29]

It was, however, very difficult for Shigemitsu to make any positive impact on Anglo-Japanese relations. By the autumn of 1940 many of the pro-Japanese figures of the mid-1930s were marginalized and those such as R.A. Butler that did remain were now much cooler. In his conversations with Butler, Shigemitsu's argument that the Tripartite Pact was analogous to British support for China cut little ice and his efforts to revitalize talks about a payments agreement met with little enthusiasm. Shigemitsu did try once to use unofficial channels to stem the tide and held a series of talks with Lord Hankey, the Chancellor of the Duchy of Lancaster, and Lord Lloyd, the Secretary of State for the Colonies, in an attempt to arrange a ministerial visit to Tokyo. These efforts were in vain, as the Foreign Office was now interested solely in the containment of Japan in league with the United States; the time for talking had ended.[30]

The seriousness of the situation was brought home to Shigemitsu when on 7 February 1941 he was called to the Foreign Office for a meeting with Eden who had recently replaced Halifax as Foreign Secretary. At this interview Shigemitsu was, without warning, faced with a tirade from Eden about Japan's ambitions in South-East Asia and its confrontational policy towards Britain. Shigemitsu tried to argue that the crisis in Anglo-Japanese relations had been exaggerated by Eden and that he was relying too much on inaccurate newspaper reporting. He also attempted to demonstrate that Japan's ambitions for East Asia were not any different to the spheres of influence controlled by the British Empire and the United States and asked, in the light of Japan's claim that 'it possesses the greatest economic and political interest in East Asia', whether Britain was opposed to the 'assertion of the United States that it has the greatest interest in the Western Hemisphere'.[31] Despite this bravado, Shigemitsu was deeply concerned at the appearance of the 'war-scare' in East Asia and his fears were not calmed by the subsequent correspondence that took place between Churchill and Matsuoka in which he acted as postman.

During Matsuoka's visit to Europe in March-April 1941, Shigemitsu tried to arrange a meeting with his Foreign Minister in Berne in order to bring to the latter's attention his own interpretation of the prospects for Anglo-Japanese relations and his own predictions for the future of the war in Europe. Shigemitsu worked through Butler and Hankey to arrange transport to continental Europe, but in the end the meeting never took place. It is, however, interesting to note that the British government was enthusiastic for Shigemitsu to make this trip and that the chartering of a plane for him was approved at the War Cabinet level. This interest in Shigemitsu resulted from the realization that the Japanese ambassador had what Butler referred to as 'a proper view of the British war effort and the state of Europe', that is, that Shigemitsu believed Britain would eventually win.[32]

This understanding of Shigemitsu's thinking came not only from his comments to British ministers and officials but also from the fact that since February 1941 (and possibly before) British codebreakers were regularly deciphering Shigemitsu's telegrams home. These revealed that, while the ambassador was not an outright Anglophile, he did perceive that Japan would be making a very rash move indeed if it should enter the war on Germany's side. In one of these telegrams Shigemitsu noted, as a comment on the last of the messages sent by Churchill to Matsuoka, in which the British Prime Minister declared that the United States was in effect already a combatant in the European war, that:

> If America enters the war the Tripartite Pact comes into operation whereby Japan may be involved. It is not, however, quite clear as to whether when the Pact has failed in its objective of preventing America's entry into the war, Japan is bound to come in immediately. The moment of Japan's entry must be very carefully chosen in the interests of the Axis & it might be best for Japan to remain neutral until she is able to clarify the situation by entering the war after Britain and America's strength is exhausted.
>
> In fact careful thought should be given to the point that those who enter the war precipitately will finally exhaust their national resources & will be unable to move if non-belligerents such as the U.S.S.R. then decide to establish themselves in advantageous positions.[33]

This carefully weighted message was clearly intended to play on the fears of Japan's policy-makers and reveals once again Shigemitsu's own concerns about

Soviet ambitions. As such one can presume that it was read with interest in Whitehall.

With the failure of his plan to meet Matsuoka in Switzerland, Shigemitsu's time in Britain drew to a close. The exact circumstances of his return to Japan are not clear. Shigemitsu always claimed that it had been his decision to withdraw from London in order to report his views in Tokyo in person, but one of the intercepted telegrams from Matsuoka to Shigemitsu suggests that the Foreign Minister was behind this decision.[33] Whatever the case, it is clear that, before Shigemitsu left, he was feted by many members of the War Cabinet and by top Whitehall officials. The idea was to buttress his belief in British victory and to provide him with ammunition for his forthcoming struggle with Matsuoka. In fact, by the time of his return to Tokyo, Matsuoka had resigned; but this did not make Shigemitsu's task any easier as the army and navy were set on the path to war. Shigemitsu did try in September 1941 to put pressure on Craigie to push London into taking a role in the Washington talks, but once this effort failed he slipped into the background and played no further part in averting confrontation.

To assess Shigemitsu's impact on Anglo-Japanese relations in his time as Vice-Minister for Foreign Affairs and as Ambassador to London is not an easy task. It would clearly be a mistake to view him as an Anglophile, as contemporaries such as Lord Hankey, Major-General F.S.G. Piggott and even Shigemitsu's secretary, Kase Toshikazu, did in their memoirs, but it is also difficult to paint him as anti-British. What does emerge from a study of his career is that he was prepared to see Japanese cooperation with Britain as long as the latter was willing to accept a reduction of its influence in East Asia and recognize the economic and political paramountcy of Japan in the region. This, as far as Shigemitsu was concerned, was only accepting the reality of the situation, and he appears to have believed that, if Britain followed its traditional diplomatic practice, it would have recognized this. His diagnosis was that British opposition to Japan was due to its new 'left-inspired' adherence to the principles of the League of Nations, and that Britain would only see sense when the orthodox wing of the Conservative party asserted its control. To a degree, this assessment has the ring of truth, as it was quite clear in the 1930s that much of British public opinion objected to Japan for moral reasons, but it ignores the fact that this morality extended to both right and left. Even more, it also misunderstood the intentions of those in Whitehall and the Conservative party who favoured closer relations with Japan, failing to acknowledge that their wish was for a revival of British interests in China rather than a retreat. Shigemitsu may have argued in his last year as ambassador for a cautious policy that would avoid a direct Anglo-Japanese clash, but it is difficult to escape the judgement that it was his earlier policies that had contributed to lay the roots for this confrontation.

[1997]

NOTES

I would like to thank Saho Matsumoto and Philip Best for their help with this essay.
1.   For favourable contemporary views of Shigemitsu, see Lord Hankey, *Politics, Trials and Errors*, (Oxford, Pen in Hand, 1950), F.S.G. Piggott, *Broken Thread*, (Aldershot, Gale & Polden, 1950), and T. Kase, *The Eclipse of the Rising Sun*, (London, Jonathan Cape, 1951). For a more critical assessment of his career see K. Usui, 'The Role of the Foreign Ministry' in D. Borg & S.

Okamoto (eds), *Pearl Harbor as History: Japanese-American Relations 1931-1941*, (New York, Columbia University Press, 1973) pp. 127-48, and K. Usui, 'Japanese Approaches to China in the 1930s: Two Alternatives' in A. Iriye & W. Cohen (eds.), *American, Chinese, and Japanese Perspectives on Wartime Asia, 1931-1949*, (Wilmington, Scholarly resources, 1990) pp. 93-115. For more neutral views, see A. Best, 'Shigemitsu Mamoru as Ambassador to Great Britain, 1938-1941' in I. Nish (ed.), *Shigemitsu Studies*, (LSE STICERD, International Studies Series, 1990), pp. 1-44, and T. Sakai, *Taishō Demokurashi Taisei no Hokai: Naisei to Gaiko* (The Collapse of the Taishō Democracy System: Domestic Politics and Diplomacy), (Tokyo, Tokyo University Press, 1992), passim.
2. M. Shigemitsu, *Gaikō Kaisōroku* (Diplomatic Memoirs), (Tokyo: Mainichi Shimbun, 1978), pp. 201-2.
3. On Edwardes, see ibid, pp. 190-3, and I. Nish, 'Anglo-Japanese Alienation Revisited' in S. Dockrill, *From Pearl Harbor to Hiroshima: The Second World War in Asia and the South Pacific, 1941-45*, (London: Macmillan, 1994), pp. 19-22.
4. Shigemitsu, op. cit., p. 192.
5. Ibid., pp. 203-7.
6. Ibid., p. 192.
7. Ibid., p. 205.
8. Ibid., p. 212.
9. On Treasury thinking, see G. Bennett, 'British Policy in the Far East 1933-1936: Treasury and Foreign Office', *Modern Asian Studies*, 26, (1992) pp. 545-68.
10. Public Record Office (PRO), T172/1831, Edwardes to Fisher, 26 November 1934.
11. Sakai, op. cit., p. 59.
12. Shigemitsu, op. cit., p. 159.
13. Sakai, op. cit., p. 128.
14. Ibid., p. 129.
15. PRO FO371/22052 F13642/12/10, Howe minute, 19 December 1938. See also Best, op. cit., pp. 5-8.
16. Shigemitsu, op. cit., p. 209.
17. PRO FO371/23534 F11827/6457/10, Craigie (Tokyo) to Halifax, 11 November 1939.
18. PRO CAB96/3 FE(41) 111, Shigemitsu/Leith-Ross conversation, 11 June 1941.
19. Shigemitsu to Edwardes, 11 July 1936, in Gwynne Papers, Bodleian Library, Oxford, Ms. Gwynne 18.
20. PRO FO371/20227 F209/34/l0, Clive (Tokyo) to Eden, 13 January 1936. On the 'Defence Against Communism' policy, see T. Sakai, 'Nichi-Bei Kaisen to Nichi-Soren Kankei' (Soviet-Japanese Relations and the Outbreak of War Between Japan and the United States) in C. Hosoya, N. Homma, A. Iriye and S. Hatano (eds.), *Taiheiyō Senso* (The Pacific War), (Tokyo: Tokyo University Press, 1993), pp. 133-61.
21. PRO FO371/24724 F2072/23/23, Shigemitsu/Butler conversation, 18 March 1940, and FO371/24708 F3174/193/61, Shigemitsu/Butler conversation, 26 April 1940.
22. Shigemitsu, op. cit., p. 210.
23. Ibid., pp. 212-3. See also Best, op. cit., pp. 14-18.
24. Ibid., p. 212.
25. The contents of this telegram are taken from a British decrypt, see PRO WO208/862 BJ.082394 Shigemitsu to Matsuoka 25 July 1940, (no decryption date).
26. Shigemitsu to Matsuoka 5 August 1940, in R.J. Pritchard and S.M. Zaide (eds.), *The Tokyo War Crimes Trial*, Vol. IV, (New York: Garland, 1981), p. 9713.
27. Shigemitsu, op. cit., pp. 220-1.
28. Ibid., pp. 216-17 and p. 220.
29. Ibid., p. 222.
30. See A. Best, *Britain, Japan and Pearl Harbor: Avoiding War in East Asia, 1936-41*, London: Routledge, 1995, pp. 153-4.
31. Shigemitsu, op. cit., p. 230.
32. Best, *Britain, Japan and Pearl Harbor*, p. 155.
33. PRO WO208/862 BJ.090111, Shigemitsu to Matsuoka, 18 April 1941, decrypted 23 April 1941.
34. Best, *Britain, Japan and Pearl Harbor*, p. 157.

FURTHER READING

James E. Auer (ed.), *From Marco Polo Bridge to Pearl Harbor*, Tokyo: Yomiuri Shimbun, 2006.

Keith Neilson, *Britain, Soviet Russia and the Collapse of the Versailles Order, 1919-39*, Cambridge: UP, 2006.

19

INTERLUDE:
SNAPSHOTS OF THE LONDON EMBASSY IN THE 1930s

Madame Yoshida and daughter Kazuko
in court dress, leaving for the
Presentation Ball, 1936

YUKI YOSHIDA

EDITOR'S NOTE: Mme Yuki Yoshida, the wife of Ambassador Shigeru Yoshida (1936-8), left a manuscript published privately in 1938 about life in the London embassy entitled *Whispering Leaves in Grosvenor Square*. It was reprinted by the publisher, Global Oriental, in 1997. Readers who wish to read about her journeys outside the Southeast of England, her descriptions of English countryside and her poems should consult the full book.

The passages from the book published below are selected at random but the general objective is to illustrate the kind of life that the wife of the ambassador led. We start with her arrival in the United Kingdom:

'We left the *Berengaria*, on which we had enjoyed five days' voyage [from the United States] among British and American passengers, and alighted at Southampton on British soil after so many years. [She had been resident in London in the early 1920s.] I came here for the first time when I was nineteen years old as a young attache's wife, and I fell in love with England and her people, and have never recovered from it since. So I was overcome with pleasure just to be in England again, only I wished I had come as a private individual, to have and enjoy a carefree life among English people.

Many kind people were at Waterloo Station to welcome us. It was Alexandra day and all the people wore roses, which looked like cherry-blossoms. We drove straight to Grosvenor Square, which is a dignified square but our Embassy was a disappointment to us as it was so neglected, having been vacant for ten months. We had to spend over a month among cleaners and painters before the house was habitable, and even now we are gradually improving it whenever our Government allows us the expense. . . .

Mrs McEwen [the daughter of Sir Francis Lindley] kindly invited me to come and stay a week-end with her at Marchmont [near Duns], and though I knew I ought to stay and supervise the cleaning of the house I could not resist the call from beautiful Scotland of which I had been dreaming so long. So I set off by the express 'The Flying Scotsman' one Saturday morning. . . .

On 22 July [1936] there was the Royal Party at Buckingham Palace, and King Edward VIII was to receive 500 debutantes besides the Diplomatic Corps and the dignitaries of the nation. In the tent a Court official approached and said something to the King, then His Majesty said in an undertone 'Oh, some new Japanese are there?' and kindly gave us his hand and said a few words to us. I felt so grateful as I noticed how tired he already looked after receiving countless people.'

We take up the story with the preparations for the coronation in the spring of 1937.

'We came back to our London home just in time to welcome Their Imperial Highnesses Prince and Princess Chichibu. On 10th April our aeroplane 'Kamikaze' (Divine Wind) sent by the newspaper 'Asahi', bearing with her messages of congratulation for the Coronation of King George VI safely arrived. We went to Croydon to welcome it. When I first noticed it, it looked as small as a dove in the softly lit pearl grey sky. It made two circles over the aerodrome and came down smoothly, but I was so struck by the smallness and shabbiness of it compared with the other machines there. I was so happy to find the two young men so simple. Lord Sempill, who was the first to extend to them a warm welcome, was the first teacher of the art of flying in Japan. He is a true friend of mine.

Kreisler came over to give his annual concert about this time and we went to hear him at the Albert Hall. I was overcome by the beauty of his performance, which stirs souls. He could give pleasure to those who are happy and consolation to those who are in need. He is more than a king. I met him again at Lady Cory's next day and he was just as I expected, so simple and child-like.

Their Imperial Highnesses Prince and Princess Chichibu arrived on 13th April. We drove down to Waterloo Station to meet them. The road-side trees dressed in new green smiling under the morning sun, looked as if they joined us in welcoming them. We were so happy to see that their Highnesses arrived in such good spirits. They went to stay at the Princes Hotel at Hove for one month before the Coronation. Their rooms looked so bright and cheerful facing the sea.

Soon after, our Ambassador to Moscow, Mr. Shigemitsu, came for a visit to London, so we gave a dinner for the Soviet Ambassador and Madame Maisky and the Chinese Ambassador and Madame Quo Tai-chi. After dinner I remember telling the Chinese Ambassador that I had lived seven and a half years in different places in China, and how I loved the vast scenery of inland China, consisting of an immense sheet of brown earth and sky, and when spring waves her wand the new greens come out all at once, intoxicating the air. Mr. Quo appreciated my taste and said I must have a poetic mind. I found him so easy to talk to and Madame Quo so sincere.

April 29th being our Emperor's birthday we gave a dinner and a reception in celebration of the day. Their Imperial Highnesses Prince and Princess Chichibu presided at both the dinner and the reception. We asked the presence of Their Royal Highnesses the Duke and Duchess of Kent, an invitation which the Duke of Kent very graciously answered himself. We shall always keep his precious letter as our family treasure. Our dinner guests besides Their Royal Highnesses were the Prime Minister and Mrs. Baldwin, Mr. and Mrs. Anthony Eden, Mr. Malcolm MacDonald and Mr. and Mrs. Walter Runciman, Lord and Lady Cromer and some others. The table looked rich with crimson and cream roses and the charming presence of the Duchess of Kent and our young princess enhanced its beauty. The stately dinner mellowed into a friendly atmosphere as the courses went on. Over seven hundred guests came to the reception which followed and all were received by Prince and Princess Chichibu. I can still picture the Duchess of Kent in a beautifully cut white satin dress, and her broad diamond bandeau looked so proud to be adorning such a handsome head. It was after one o'clock when everyone left. I thought the party was a success and I did hope our guests enjoyed themselves.

As my husband had a cold I went to the Marchioness of Londonderry's reception alone. Just after I was received by the host and hostess I saw Mrs. Chamberlain standing and she so kindly suggested taking me round as her husband also was not there, attending a men's dinner. As it was just a short time before Mr. Chamberlain became the Prime Minister the guests greeted her all the more. Mrs. Chamberlain so kindly and patiently introduced me to each one saying, 'As we are both without our husbands to-night we are going round together.' 'I am taking her round,' a less gentle and cultivated person might have said. I admired her so much that I made some poems to express my feelings.'

[After the many dinners and receptions of the coronation season, the Yoshidas boarded the *Strathmore* to witness the coronation Naval Review at Portsmouth.]

'I remember sitting at the same table with Sir Robert and Lady Craigie and the American Ambassador and Mrs. Bingham. The day was a little misty, but we could see the Review beautifully. It was a grand sight. All the British warships and those of most of the other nations were of a grave grey. I do not like the purpose of warships but I do admire their appearance, so dignified and composed. Looking at all the magnificent men-of-war I could not help thinking if each country could keep the wealth spent on them, those nations could be richer enriching their people. We unfortunately could not stay for the illuminations at night and had to come back to London the same evening.

A garden party was given in honour of Their Highnesses Prince and Princess Chichibu at Hurlingham Club. About sixty Japanese children performed some athletic sports in front of their Highnesses. At the opening of the sports they formed huge British and Japanese flags by holding different coloured cloths, which was very cleverly and well done. Afterwards we all assembled on the lawn, gathering round the Prince and Princess and were photographed together for a souvenir. As we still had a warm sun we got off at a meadow on our way home. The soft green grass was sprinkled with daisies and young-leaved beeches spread their boughs above. A roof of lapis lazuli and a floor of agate would fade away in front of nature's beauty.

Mrs. Ronald Greville gave a dinner in honour of the King of Egypt and for our Prince and Princess. There were over forty people present. The pleasant string band was playing in one of the parquet floored drawing-rooms, but no one danced. The guests sat round in groups and chatted comfortably.

The Caledonian Ball given on 28th May was a grand spectacle. I felt so sorry that our Prince and Princess could not come owing to their colds as they would have enjoyed it so much. The floor of the vast hall was of polished ivory coloured wood which gave a clean yet mellow appearance to the hall. The little boy bagpipers were sweet, all of them looking so proud of their performance. I was told that the pipers had taken such pains to learn the Japanese anthem for Their Highnesses.

However, I only realized the tune after it was too late! But I felt the cordiality of our hosts very much. The men were in kilts and the ladies also wore sashes of different tartans, which made the scene very decorative. The Scotch dances were very exciting with their occasional yells. It was a remarkable entertainment altogether.

We picnicked in a wood near Henley one day. After the chaotic lunch the others left for a walk and I lay on the fallen leaves in the wood. The blue sky could be seen luminous between the young foliage and the occasional sharp notes of birds startled me. I could also see afar the glistening meadows sleeping under the young summer sun. We took tea in a restaurant on the Thames. The gay parasoled boats, followed by the swans were passing the shining river, telling us that summer had really come.

On the 24th of June we gave a farewell dinner in honour of Prince and Princess Chichibu. The table was decorated with lotuses then in bloom, a flower at once elegant and remote. The guests were Mr. and Mrs. Neville Chamberlain, Mr. and Mrs. Anthony Eden, Viscount and Viscountess Hailsham, Sir Samuel and the Lady Maud Hoare, Earl and Countess of Bessborough, Earl and Countess of Airlie, Marquis and Marchioness of Londonderry, Mr. Hore Belisha and Mr. Duff Cooper and Lady Diana Cooper, and some others.

Lady Airlie who also gave us the pleasure of having her as one of our guests will always live among my treasured memories of England. She is just like a portrait of an oil painting or of a more delicate miniature of a French Court lady come out of a frame with all the charms and the spirit of an English one. It was such an opportunity for me to dine with these people and I shall remember them all my life. . . .

We took a little house on the river at Maidenhead for the summer, and moved there on the 1st of July. The Little Fisher was the name of the house which I loved. The little house was much better equipped than our Embassy in Grosvenor Square, having more spare bedrooms in a smaller space. We could see the shining river through the bright geraniums on our verandah, which scene reminded me of my friend's poem from Santiago saying that her young, happy days were reflected in the geraniums blooming in masses everywhere there.

I could hear the rustling of beech leaves when I often lunched alone in the quiet dining-room with the faint scent of roses coming in through the window. I loved to read in my study facing the river, and often when I looked up from my book I saw a black or a cobalt coloured bird hopping round the lawn.

The swans passed in front of our garden. One morning I took some bread and hopefully threw it to one. To my delight the swan deigned to stop and pick it up. Thus we made friends, and by and by they used to come from afar whenever I called to them. The ladylike swans looked so defenceless when the north wind made waves on the grey river. Whenever I saw them pass I used to run with a bag of bread. I came to know two mother swans with a group of young ones each. The mothers never took the bread, giving it all to the youngsters. One of the swans came alone one evening. I fed her, asking her where her mate was, and when I looked up from her I saw a full moon rising over the fir tree.

My quiet life was broken one morning by the news in the papers that fighting had begun between Japanese and Chinese soldiers near Peking, but no one knew then what large proportions it was to take.'

20

INTERLUDE:
A DIPLOMAT'S DAUGHTER IN THE 1930s

AYAKO ISHIZAKA

Baroness Hide Tomii, Ayako Tomii and
Baron Shu Tomii on board the SS
Normandie, Southampton, April 1938

EDITOR'S NOTE: Some characters in this essay have been renamed to conceal their identity.

I was six when I first saw London in 1936 and eight when I left. A happy childhood, even that of a diplomat's daughter, is filled with ordinary pleasures of school and home. Too young to understand important events, my memories are filtered through the eyes of one child.

My father, Shū Tomii, was stationed twice in London, from 1924 to 1927 as 2nd and then 1st Secretary and from 1936 to 1938 as 1st Counsellor. This was in the days before the Japanese Foreign Ministry started balancing desirable with hardship postings. Thus father, besides his two tours in Britain, had three postings in the United States (New York, Washington and San Francisco) and was sent twice to Ottawa, once to Berlin and finally to Buenos Aires.

PREPARATIONS AND THE VOYAGE

There was a flurry of reunions and packing before my father sailed for London in 1936. Although he travelled by ship through Suez to Marseilles, he transferred there to a train and went on to Calais, where he took a ferry to England. He was always an advocate of speed.

Mother and I were to join father three months later. I had an eleven-year-old brother who was born in London during my parents' first stay there, and they had named him 'Masahide' or 'British statesman.' By the time he reached school age, he had been to Ottawa and Berlin and spoke fluent English and German. In Tokyo, he first entered the Peers' School kindergarten to improve his halting Japanese. There, my mother was summoned and told that, as her son spilled his food, she should pack a spoon in his lunchbox instead of chopsticks. It was extremely rude to be messy in the presence of his classmate Prince Kaya. After graduating from kindergarten, Masahide enrolled in the less formal atmosphere of Seikei School, where he became a well-adjusted student.

Masahide was to be left in Japan, like most boys of school age then, for it was all-important to have a completely Japanese education. Were not British boys also expected to be educated in their homeland? Unlike England, boarding schools for small boys were not prevalent, and, as the only son of the eldest son, my brother was expected to stay with his paternal grandparents. Grandfather Tomii had passed away by 1936, but grandmother Tomii was very much alive, and Masahide would stay with her. An uncle and aunt, and an orphaned cousin completed the household.

Sailing for England was preceded by the search for a maid. Fusa was chosen with great care as mother had previously failed with Ura, the maid we took to Father's previous posting in San Francisco. Ura had become homesick and depressed, had to be sent back to Japan after a year, and always blamed her year in America for her lack of a husband.

Fusa's father was a country teacher and wanted his daughter to see the world. She herself also wished to go to London and promised to work hard as a maid. Already twenty-nine, she was past marriageable age and was very homely looking.

Streamers still clung to the handrails, as our Japanese ship sailed from Yokohama to Southampton with mother, Fusa and me. Our cabin was filled with the fragrance of flowers from friends, who wished us a 'bon voyage', a voyage that began with frequent lifeboat drills. Sometimes I wished the ship would sink so that I could show off how quickly I could put on my life jacket, run to my station and jump into my boat. I had never done the jumping part yet, but it did not seem improbable as we soon ran into a typhoon. A steward tied the drawers and cupboards in our cabin after we took out what we needed. At mealtimes, mother and I weaved our way to the dining room, where the large windows showed the ship rolling left, on a swell, then right on another swell, then left again. All tables were chained to the floor, the tablecloths dampened to prevent dishes and glasses from slipping. One waiter lost his balance with a full tray. As the meal progressed, the dining room became emptier and emptier. Mother and I, both seaworthy, had healthy appetites, but poor Fusa had retired to her cabin hours long before.

Good weather came again and I discovered shipboard pleasures. After all, we were to be on board for two or three months, with all the ports of call, and we had to be kept happy.

It was a good idea to be on deck around 10.00 a.m. That was when a steward walked up and down the deck in his white jacket, alerting passengers on his xylophone-like instrument that they would be fortified with beef broth. With the bracing sea air, no ice-cream tasted better than this 10.00 a.m. consommé.

There was deck golf and ping-pong and costume parties. For *sukiyaki* parties, the A-deck was covered with straw mat *tatamis*, the portholes and walls camouflaged with red and white striped awning. We sat on cushions at low tables, and to make the Japanese setting complete, the purser and younger officers wore *geisha* costumes, complete with wigs and rouge.

The stopovers provided a welcome and exotic change. At Penang, apple-green snakes slithered along a temple's floors, walls and ceilings, and I never saw mother look so afraid. At Port Said mother went off to view the pyramids and to ride on a camel, while Fusa and I remained on board, portholes and door tightly locked, for it was supposed to be a dangerous port. Marseilles was a gustatory adventure. A Mr Tanaka took mother, Fusa and me to a seafood restaurant in a noisy, smelly seafront quarter. There were fishing boats, and swarms of excitable people milling around. Mr Tanaka himself was more excitable than most of the Japanese gentlemen I was used to seeing. A burly man stood outside the restaurant; he dipped his hands into a bucketful of sea urchins, threw them onto a chopping board and cracked them open with a knife. Inside, we woofed down fresh sea urchins on bread and asked for more.

THE HOUSE ON BAYSWATER ROAD

At Southampton, father was waiting for us, smiling and handsome. He had thought we would never come, why had we not taken the train from Marseilles? Mother was pleased, and not pleased, that father looked so well taken care of in her absence. But that was thanks to Ada, our new cook-general, someone who cooked and helped with the general housework. She had come with strong recommendations from the former manager of the Yokohama Specie Bank; she was good-natured and willing, and said she loved working for Japanese. That attitude in itself, said father, was a rare jewel in 1936 London where anti-Japanese sentiment ran high.

Father had also found us a place to live. He had not been keen on its location on Bayswater Road, but the house had central heating, for it used to belong to an American. Remembering the long, London winters of his first posting from 1924 to 1927, father decided to protect us from any dampness or cold. When mother chided that San Francisco had spoiled him, father laughed that weatherwise maybe, but that he still loved that house at St Petersburgh Place where Masahide had been born and where the family could walk over to Kensington Gardens. Those were the years of pro-Japanese sentiment in London. Their old friends still remained true; they had been most decent and welcoming; he could well understand why so many Japanese who had lived in Britain became Anglophiles.

Our house had three storeys plus a basement, and was dark, comfortable and roomy. It had a grand piano, overstuffed furniture, and a fireplace in every room. I loved the fireplaces from the start; there was nothing like being tucked into bed, watching the flames, and listening to a story. In the garden, stripes seemed to flow back and forth on a lawn as smooth as water.

ADA AND GOVERNESSES

If the rest of the house was dark, the basement was positively black, it was like going down steep, dark steps into a cavern. The huge kitchen resembled dungeons found in fairy tales, despite the small windows near the ceiling. Even the Aga was black. And yet this would become the sunniest place in the house for me, a far cry from a witch's hole, and all because of cheerful Ada.

Ada was short and fat, standing only a head higher than I did, but with ten times my girth. She huffed and puffed as she waddled up the stairs with trays and brooms. 'Oh, me legs' she'd puff with a laugh. I had become used to being shoved out of the kitchen by Gotō in San Francisco and the maids in Tokyo. It seemed that young ladies shouldn't go into the kitchen. Ada was different. She always welcomed me, and she was at her best in the afternoons, as she sat in a corner of the darkness, gaily sipping tea or something stronger, eager to talk about her own childhood, a childhood so unlike mine.

I did not go to school for the first year to avoid a repeat of my San Francisco experience. There, I had been sent to a kindergarten attached to a nearby state school, as the best way to learn English and make American friends. Some of the children, especially the black girls who themselves suffered, played nasty tricks on me, and I was frustrated at not knowing enough of their language to tell them off. It was a good thing I did not understand the taunts of 'dirty Jap'. As my English improved, I adjusted better, but coming down with chicken pox was a good excuse to leave the kindergarten. In London, a governess was to tutor me until I became fluent enough to make friends with my classmates. I did not like the idea of someone who was also to teach me how to act like a well behaved English girl.

The first three governesses left no impression on me, except that mother was upset each time one left. Miss Robins had muttered that she did not want to stay with a child who was rude and talked back. Ada claimed Miss Gibbons was unclean and, on the few occasions she bathed, left dirty rings around the bathtub. Miss Walker said that her living arrangements were too cramped and that it had been a mistake to work for a Japanese family.

The fourth governess I immediately liked. Miss Warner was young and pretty, with shoulder-length flaming hair and pretty dresses instead of sensible skirts and blouses. She was also easy-going and a skilful weaver of romantic tales. I spent many happy bedtimes staring into the fire and listening to Miss Warner read from her own copy of *True Romances*. But Miss Warner was sent packing after she was caught going through mother's handbag.

Was there to be no Mary Poppins? Mother lost confidence in her judgment, even as she interviewed more candidates. I was pleased to be on my own again.

My rejoicing was premature, as Miss Hamilton became my next and last governess. She had been governess to Fiona Leith-Ross. Sir Frederick Leith-Ross was on most cordial terms with my father, who appreciated the friendship but did not wish to take advantage of it by asking such a personal favour. Many Englishmen were put off by Japan's war in China, and were pro-Chinese, father used to tell mother. He did not wish to embarrass Sir Frederick.

Mother had been lamenting her governess problem with Lady Leith-Ross, who said she knew just the right candidate. Since daughter Fiona did not need a governess any more, Miss Hamilton might be interested in tutoring a Japanese girl. I was taken to Lady Leith-Ross who was most gracious, and Fiona was a ray of sunshine as she joined us. Fiona let me play with all her dolls, asked me about my life and was the perfect hostess; being on her best behaviour came naturally to her. Impossible that any number of governesses could so transform my own grudging best behaviour.

My parents doubted that our arrangements would be grand enough, but Lady Leith-Ross must have been persuasive, because Miss Hamilton came for an interview. She and I sized each other up. She saw a sallow, six-year-old Oriental child with sullen mouth and an insecure look. I saw a woman with calm brown eyes who dressed sensibly, like my first three governesses, and carried herself with an air of complete confidence. It would be hard to get rid of her.

Miss Hamilton took the smaller attic room. No thank you, she needed no sitting room as she would be returning to her home at weekends. Lessons started at once, and I had to read and write every day. There were not too many stories, but there was a lot about what nice girls did not say or do.

'I've got a dog called Prince. He's got black hair and black eyes.'

'Yes, Prince has black hair and black eyes, but "got" is American and not good English. Use "have" and "has". Repeat: "I have a dog called Prince. He has black hair and black eyes."'

'All right.'

'"Yes, Miss Hamilton", please. That is what will be expected at school.'

'Yes, Miss Hamilton. "I have a dog called Prince." It's hot here, I'm sweating. Can I open the window?'

'Yes you may. I was thinking of doing it myself, because it is rather warm, but ladies do not sweat,' Miss Hamilton said as she wrinkled her nose in disgust, 'they perspire. Even then, you need not *say* it. Just say it's warm, not hot, and that you'd like to open the window.'

'You're so fussy, I hate you!'

'Young ladies never hate, they *dislike*.'

'Hate, hate, hate!'

'We'll have no more of this nonsense. I am here to teach you English and English manners. Your mother wants you to be a well-behaved young lady.' There was something in Miss Hamilton's dry voice and disapproving eye that checked me more than her anger could have. She was not cold or unkind; she was disappointed and pitied me. I could not bear to be pitied.

Miss Hamilton was a great believer in walks, where she often told stories, though never about her own life or about Lucinda and the tall, blonde stranger as in *True Romances*. I heard about Peter Rabbit, Winnie-the-Pooh and Alice's Adventures in Wonderland, stories that we would read later in our warm house. The wind and the rain stung my face. A little bit of rain never hurt anyone, in Miss Hamilton's view, it was the way to put some colour into my cheeks. The English girl's peaches and cream complexion came from fresh air and exercise.

I quite liked to walk in Regent's Park and Hyde Park in fair weather, but more often than not, we tramped the streets. This was so that I could get my bearings by the time I was ready for school. Some streets were crowded and noisy. We walked past stores, crossed intersections and were deaf to comments like 'Hello, dearies. Wet 'haint it for a mite of fresh air?'. Mostly it was raining – I cannot remember ever being hot (warm?) and sweating (perspiring?). I guess the months she tried to make me into a nice English girl were mostly in wintertime.

We returned with rosy cheeks and sparkling eyes for tea in the playroom. Miss Hamilton poured tea, as I practised curtseying to mother's friends 'not like a chambermaid's bob, nor the way your mother will be curtseying to the Queen'.

By the time I was ready for school, I had become quite attached to Miss Hamilton. Her eyes twinkled as she said goodbye, reminding me to sit up straight like Queen Mary the Queen Mother as if I were wearing tight corsets, and never speak to strangers.

I was ready, I would not even shame a Henry Higgins.

THE CORONATION

For some time there had been talk around our house of King Edward VIII and 'that Simpson woman,' and, more recently, a buzz about his abdication and the coronation of King George VI.

One evening, father told mother that the members of a club had been talking about the abdication when he walked in. He could guess by the way they all clammed up and looked glum. On leaving, after a pleasant lunch, father sympathized with his host for the loss of such a popular King, and was thanked for understanding that this was a dark time. They had been so proud of their King Edward, and now he was abdicating for an American divorcee.

I looked at newspaper pictures of the Simpson woman. She was a vivid contrast of black and white: dark hair, white face, dark eyes and lips, white shoulders, dark dress, and a full smile. She was quite glamorous, and the Royals looked washed out in comparison.

Then the days became more and more festive, with streets garlanded for the coronation of King George VI. My parents were quite excited by the prospect of seeing this historic event, and there was much hustle and bustle in the house. From Japan, Prince and Princess Chichibu were to represent the Emperor and Empress, and father headed the organizing committee for the visit to England. The Prince was an avid sports lover and had studied in England. The Princess had lived in London as a child, and spoke perfect English. Well-loved members of the Imperial Family, they hoped by their visit to bring much needed friendship.

Ada was given the Great Day off 'to catch a glimpse o' me new King and Queen' and only Fusa and I remained at home. 'How was it, how was it?' I wanted to know the details the next day, and pored over the pictures in the special section of the papers. Father beamed. It had been magnificent, nobody could surpass the British in pomp and pageantry, and it was a welcome change to rejoice. Mother thought King George looked much more reserved than his predecessor King Edward, but Queen Elizabeth had smiled and waved all the time. And weren't the two princesses sweet, dressed identically in their crowns and ermine-trimmed capes? It was said that Princess Margaret Rose wanted the same dress as her sister, and that King George could deny his younger daughter nothing.

I looked at the pictures of the two princesses waving from the balcony with the King and Queen. Princess Elizabeth was frowning slightly, but they were very pretty, especially Margaret Rose (what a nice name.) Princess Elizabeth was exactly the same age as Masahide, and Margaret Rose was my age.

Ada had caught a glimpse of the Cinderella coaches and some of the royal guests 'from Japan too'. Later, she had danced in the streets and went on to the White Hart for a celebration. There was laughter and singing and everyone was treated to a pint.

I caught a glimpse of Prince and Princess Chichibu at the Hurlingham Club, when I took part in a tug-of-war with other Japanese children. We were told to be on our best behaviour, which was difficult in a tug-of-war. At the end, Their Imperial Highnesses came down from the stands to talk to us. Princess Chichibu remarked how much I resembled my mother, as I curtseyed, forgetting to bow as I had been taught, too flustered to glance up. Later, I took a long look at the Prince and Princess in the photograph on our piano. Framed in silver, the sports-loving Prince was in uniform, and looked studious and frail. The Princess, with a semi-smile, appeared calm and gentle, and reminded me of the Duchess of Kent.

Some time afterwards, mother was presented at court. She had been practising curtseys before the mirror, deep curtseys. All diplomats' wives were presented at court soon after their arrival, but mother waited till after the coronation, and although she had been presented before, back in the 1920s, her curtseys were rusty. She looked like a queen herself as she left the house, wearing a long white and silver lace dress embroidered with beads and pearls, with a matching train, a pearl tiara, long gloves and an ostrich fan. There had been several fittings, and at the first one, the train was thrown out, beads and all, as being too short. There was no altering or scrimping there. Tall and slender for an Oriental woman, she had long legs and the double-lidded eyes so coveted now by young Japanese women. Queen Elizabeth had been smiling and gracious when Ambassador Yoshida's wife presented mother, who was so nervous she could not remember a word that was said.

FRANCES HOLLAND SCHOOL

There were not many Japanese children of my age to play with, but I made many friends once I started going to school. I entered Frances Holland School at Clarence Gate on the recommendation of Lady Leith-Ross.

Ada, who was inclined to forget her hat, took me on the bus to school. Sometimes it was Fusa when Ada was busy. Fusa had adjusted well, liked working in London and was learning English, but she was not fluent and felt selfconscious about using it.

Classes were quiet, long and dull. My English accent was praised, but I was told to read more in order to increase my vocabulary.

Outside the classroom, things were livelier. Lunch was a welcome break despite the formal setting in the refectory: a large, dark room where we sat at long tables and benches to ensure we would not lean back. The teachers ate at the ends of each table, so there was always a scramble to sit in the middle next to a good friend, and I almost elbowed others aside to be next to Amy who told wonderful stories, and was pretty and popular. Amy's mother was American and very glamorous, like 'that Simpson woman', but very nice too, with a different accent. Amy herself didn't have any accent; she'd never been to America.

It was Katya who complicated things by wanting to sit next to me. She and her parents had fled Czechoslovakia a year ago, she spoke perfect English because of an English governess in Prague, but she did not have many friends..

Lunch itself consisted of soup, boiled meat, vegetables with a generous helping of potatoes, bread and finally dessert. Amy chanted: 'Mondays rice pudding, Tuesdays stewed apricots and prunes, Wednesdays bread pudding, Thursdays rhubarb, and Fridays trifle.' Miss Temple, faraway at the end of the table, heard everything she wanted to hear above the chatter of voices, and Amy was reminded that it was vulgar for young ladies to be talking so much about food.

I also looked forward to our walks in Regent's Park. The locker room was a flurry of anticipation before we marched in pairs. Change your shoes, put on your blazer, gloves, and hat in a hurry in order to line up and choose your partner: first ready, first to choose. If a shoe was forgotten under a bench, you had to go back to put it away and you lost your place.

There were girls like Amy whom everyone wanted as a partner, then there were others like Louise and Carol who remained unchosen till the end. Louise was fat and dour, Carol had rough manners and a twangy accent. Sometimes Miss Temple asked one of us beforehand to choose Louise or Carol.

One afternoon, during our walk, I heard Carol's nasal twang and another girl's imitation, then laughter. Carol was Canadian, and she demanded why Ayako wasn't made fun of, when she was Japanese. 'Ayako speaks English, and you speak funny' was the answer.

Another afternoon, as we were playing 'drop the handkerchief' in Regent's Park, I spotted father, and he joined us in our games, running and laughing, business suit and all. 'I wish my daddy would play with me like that' my friends said, and I fairly burst with pride.

At school, you could take piano lessons and dancing lessons 'to become graceful young ladies', according to Miss Temple. I took both, but by now found piano boring, with its Czerny and finger exercises. Dancing was livelier, and our dance performance would be something very special, we had been told over and over again. We were one of several schools to appear for charity in a real theatre, and Princess Margaret Rose would grace us with her presence. In our specially made tunics, we Grecian maidens sat stiffly backstage.

'Posture, young ladies, posture!' our dance mistress Miss Warren said, and she wanted to know how many of us remembered to sit up straight at home like the Queen Mother. Queen Mary again!

Many groups danced, and our piece was over in minutes, receiving enthusiastic applause from the parent-packed audience. Nobody cared whether we slouched or not. Squinting for a glance at Her Royal Highness, we only saw darkness; but afterwards, she came backstage and we all curtseyed deeply. Princess Margaret Rose wanted to have everything the same as her sister, mother had said. We were all presented with a gold medal with 'for service' inscribed, and I placed mine as my greatest treasure in my trinket box. I have the medal to this day.

MOTHER AND FATHER

Mother and father seemed to have even more friends than I did, both British and Japanese. My parents, having lived before in London, felt very much at ease with their English friends; my father enough to joke with them. And with fellow Japanese, there was the special bond of sharing the English experience.

There had been foreign influences in my father's home since childhood. Grandfather Tomii was one of the men who studied abroad after Japan was opened to the world in 1868. He read law at the University of Lyon and later talked about his experiences to his children. They also saw his exotic dining table: coffee, wine and Roquefort cheese, a cheese that disgusted my grandmother so much, that once she buried 'that rotten thing full of mould' in the garden.

Father decided that he, too, would see the wider world, and help bring different people together. He loved his work and the diplomatic life. Mother, though she enjoyed meeting different people, sometimes yearned for a settled life with the four of us in our own little house. Dinner parties were frequent. In winter, mother liked to entertain on three consecutive evenings because it was so expensive to fill the rooms with flowers.

The scent of rosewater eliminated any cooking signs from the basement, as Ada prepared her wholesome fare. A butler served, and Fusa helped in black uniform, lace cap and apron. The guests arrived in formal attire, the men with full decorations. Did they come for friendship and the quality of the conversation, as well as for a little diplomacy? Certainly, it was not for the quality of the food. The drinks, however, were excellent except on one occasion. At breakfast, my parents often talked about the previous evening. Sir John, a dinner guest, had flinched after a sip of brandy, but only commented 'most interesting.' Puzzled, father lifted his own glass to his lips and found that

Ada had mistakenly placed cooking brandy on the tray instead of the Courvoisier.

Sometimes, mother and father dined at a Chinese restaurant when they hankered for Oriental food, as being the nearest thing to Japanese cooking.

After English friends invited my parents to a preview of *Gone with the Wind*, my mother was ecstatic. The colour, the setting, Clark Gable and Vivien Leigh . . . at intermission, the viewers had toasted the two stars with champagne. It was the start of a new era in cinema.

SHADOWS OF WAR

Of course, all was not sunshine and laughter, for it was now 1938. Even an 8-year-old felt, though she could not understand, the shadows of war. In our class, besides Katya from Prague, we now had Elsa from Vienna and Anna from Warsaw.

Heather Baines and Fiona Smith never played with me, but one day they came up, noses held high, saying that their fathers had told them not to play with a Japanese girl. Japanese were bad, because they were murdering the Chinese. All the Nips with slanty eyes should be killed.

Father said that Heather and Fiona were just repeating what they heard at home, and shouldn't be blamed. Why were the Japanese not liked? Well, it was very complicated. Japan was becoming a modern country, like England, and needed more resources, more land. But there was no space that did not already belong to someone else, so there was fighting. And when there was fighting, lots of bad things happened: people lost homes, people were killed. The Japanese were in China, not the Chinese in Japan. But that was a long story, Father sighed.

Mother and father had been excited for weeks and I soon learned why. We were moving to Canada and they were pleased at the prospect of seeing their friends in Ottawa again. In 1928, they had also sailed to Canada from their posting in Britain. I wondered where Ottawa was, whether we would all be speaking like Carol. Fusa, now more confident, wished to accompany us to another foreign country. Several years later, after returning to Japan, she surprised us happily by marrying a widower, a local landlord and one of the most eligible men in her hometown.

I did not wish to leave Amy or Margaret or Sarah or Ann or Nellie or Frances . . . Ada . . . not even Louise or Katya. Neither did my parents want to say goodbye to England, but 'the way things were in Europe', it was not a bad time to take a child to Canada.

Mother sighed at the thought of my brother being left again in Tokyo. It was not possible for him to 'come during the holidays' when travel was by ship. Japan was nearer to Canada than to England, but father said that with the fighting in China, people in Japan led a Spartan life. Going abroad for a vacation at such a time was too selfish, even if it was to see family. Perhaps, if duties permitted, mother could make a short trip from Ottawa to Tokyo. There was always family business to attend to, and the Tomii and Nakamura graves to be visited. Father himself sailed from Canada for brief consultations with the Foreign Ministry in 1939, but mother's personal visit was put off in the worsening political climate.

I went to Amy Howard's house one last time to play before I left. It was a small but pretty place, light and airy. Mrs Howard was wrapping ornaments in newspapers and putting them in a big crate. They were moving to America.

Why? Because she was American, and because of 'the way things were in Europe.' Amy whispered that there was going to be a war. Japan and China were fighting. And 'the way things were in Europe' there might be fighting here too. What did all this mean?

POSTSCRIPT

Father became ambassador to Argentina in 1941, and World War II was a painful period for my Anglophile parents. We were repatriated in 1947, and they never saw England again. Father, however, kept in touch with Britain through its envoys to Japan, and one, Sir Esler Dening, had been a tennis partner at Niko Senior High School, where Sir Esler's missionary father used to teach. My father died in 1958, before it was easy for Japanese to travel abroad again.

Mother, who lived until 1983, stayed for some of her later years in the United States and Germany, but she was content with the England of her memories. Masahide, the 'British statesman', enjoyed several visits to England, now so quickly reached by air, and I spent seven happy years in Surrey from 1973. I was returning to my second home.

NOTES

The names of classmates, teachers, governesses and domestic help are fictitious.
1.   Baron Shū Tomii (1890-1959) Japanese diplomat. Joined the Ministry of Foreign Affairs in 1915 and was posted to New York, Washington D.C, London (1924-1927), Ottawa, Berlin, Tokyo, San Francisco, London (1936-1938), Ottawa again, with his final posting being as ambassador to Argentina (1941-1946) and concurrently minister to Uruguay and Paraguay. *Records of the Ministry of Foreign Affairs, Tokyo.*
2.   Hide Tomii (1901-1983). Daughter of Zeco Nakamura, Manchurian Railways president and mayor of Tokyo, and his wife Chiyo. Hide married Shū Tomii in 1923.
3.   Masahide Tomii (1926-). Professor emeritus of Kyushu University, Structural Engineering Department. He was left in Japan from kindergarten onwards, graduated from Seikei elementary school, Seikei high school and Tokyo Imperial University before starting his academic career at Kyushu University. He is married with two daughters.
4.   The Peers' School kindergarten used to be attached to the Peeresses' School, which was located at the site of today's Prince Chichibu memorial rugby stadium at Gaien in Aoyama, Tokyo.
5.   Seikei Gakuen, 3-3-1 Kita-machi, Kichijoji, Musashino-shi, Tokyo 180-0001.
6.   Baron Masaakira Tomii, often called Seisho Tomii (1858-1935). Drafted the Meiji period Civil Code and Commercial Code (1895) together with Nobushige Hozumi and Kenjirō Ume. *Ministry of Posts and Telecommunications, commemorative stamp 1999.* Professor, Law Department, Tokyo University and Hosei University. President of the Maison Franco-Japonaise, and adviser to the Emperor. *Masahide Tomii.*
7.   Sir Frederick Leith-Ross (1887-1968). British civil servant and authority on finance. In 1935 he visited China via Japan, to successfully work out a plan to change the Chinese currency from the silver dollar to paper. *DNB 1961-1970.*
8.   Prince Chichibu (Yasuhito) (1902-1953) was a younger brother of the late Emperor Showa. Prince Chichibu studied for a brief period at Magdalen College, Oxford, loved sports, especially mountaineering, skiing and sculling and was considered a friend of Britain.
Princess Chichibu (1909-1995) née Setsuko Matusudaira. She was born in England and graduated from high school in Washington, D.C. where her diplomat father was Japanese ambassador.
For an excellent account on the Prince and Princess, cf. Dorothy Britton, 'Prince and Princess Chichibu' *Biographical Portraits* Vol. V, pp. 23-32.
9.   Sir Esler Dening (1897-1977) was the first post-war British Ambassador to Japan (1952-1957). He was born in Japan of missionary parents.

21

ASAKAI KŌICHIRŌ, 1906-1995
High-ranking Envoy Reconnects with Britain
[London, 1951-54]

TOMOKI KUNIYOSHI

Asakai Kōichirō (left) with colleague
unfurls the Japanese flag at 32
Belgrave Square

EDITOR'S NOTE: A Japanese Government Agency was set up in London at the end of August 1951 with Asakai in charge.

This essay discusses the life of Asakai Kōichirō, the former Japanese diplomat, with special focus on his days in London during the years 1951 to 1954. Although he was never ambassador, Asakai ranks highly among Japanese envoys because of the critical task he had to perform in setting up the first diplomatic mission and re-establishing relations with Britain after the Asia-Pacific War.

Having studied banking and monetary theory and graduated from the Tokyo College of Commerce (now Hitotsubashi University) in 1929, he entered the Foreign Ministry. His good English-language skills which he had learnt at Hitotsubashi from Edward Gauntlett, an English language teacher from Wales, were further improved during a period spent studying law at the University of Edinburgh from 1929 to 1931. He then became attaché in London for two years and was posted to Nankin before returning to the Ministry.[1]

After Japan's surrender, he was appointed section head of the Central Liaison Bureau (*Shusen renraku jimukyoku*) in March 1946. In this capacity he had direct contact with American personnel and communicated the Japanese Government's views to GHQ, the headquarters of General Douglas MacArthur, Supreme Commander, Allied Powers (SCAP). He attended meetings of the Allied Council for Japan in the first three years of its activities as an observer and claimed to have attended all its meetings.[2] He was the sole diplomat who was permitted, along with a number of journalists, to watch its deliberations. He later published his diaries of the experience. From this he came to realise the nature of the relations between the great powers, in particular the confrontation developing between the US and the USSR.[3]

After attending an international conference in Geneva, Switzerland in 1949, Asakai came to London. Describing this sentimental journey, he wrote that he walked round Grosvenor Square where the embassy had formally been located and also Portman Square where its offices used to be found. He noticed many changes brought about by bombing raids during the war. He found that strict rationing of food was operating. He visited a famous restaurant in Piccadilly called Scotts, where he was told that meat was available on a first-come first-served basis and only for the first thirty customers. He was, therefore, aware of Britain's economic difficulties and publicly praised British morale, commenting that there was not any obvious black market. He also managed to fit in a visit to Edinburgh where he met his teachers from university days. He does not seem to have met any British officials during his stay.[4]

ASAKAI IN LONDON

Asakai arrived in London as the first head of the Japanese Government Overseas Agency in UK (its Japanese title being *Nippon seifu zaigwai jimusho: Eikoku chūzai*) at the end of August 1951, a few days in advance of the signing of the San Francisco Peace Treaty. From his past experience his appointment was not unnatural. But the reaction of Prime Minister Yoshida to the proposal by the Foreign Ministry was hostile, according to Asakai.[5] At some point in 1949 Satō Eisaku, the then Chief Cabinet Secretary, read the record of one of his conversations with a GHQ official to journalists which then appeared in newspapers, to the annoyance of the occupation authorities. Asakai took joint responsibility with Satō and was dismissed as Director of the General Affairs Bureau. Having suffered under this 'Y section purge', as it was known, he was not favoured by Yoshida for the London post, for which the Prime Minister's preference was for Shirasu Jirō, who had studied at Cambridge University during the 1930s, was close to Yoshida and was very fluent in English. But Asakai's appointment was more acceptable to Britain.

On arrival in August 1951, Asakai took accommodation for himself and his office at Grosvenor House. While the task he faced was difficult, he benefited from the existence of the Japan Society of London which had been set up at an Extraordinary General Meeting on 28 September 1949. As soon as the Agency opened on 30 August with consular status, the Society arranged a reception in honour of Asakai's team at the Criterion in Piccadilly. The reception was attended by Nara Yasuhiko from the Gaimushō and Ihara Takashi from the Finance Ministry. Asakai could rely on the support and cooperation of a group of English well-wishers. From his rooms in Grosvenor House, the search began for a new embassy to replace 10 Grosvenor Square. The Agency eventually set up its offices at 32 Belgrave Square. In his New Year's broadcast to Japan through the BBC, Asakai reported that he could not help feeling deeply moved, seeing the Japanese flag flying outside the new Japanese offices. On his way to the studio that morning, he had visited the Agency's office, gone up to the first-floor balcony overlooking the street, and put out the Japanese flag.[7]

British public opinion was indifferent, if not positively hostile, and government attitudes were unpredictable. This is illustrated by an incident towards the end of 1951 when the Agency asked for the use of cipher and diplomatic bag facilities. In response the London government agreed to the withdrawal of previously imposed limitations on the functions of the Agency, and at the same time agreed to its being permitted to discuss with the various government departments 'all subjects of mutual concern'. But other major powers like the US, France, Canada, the Netherlands and Italy had preceded Britain in giving Japan these diplomatic privileges. Another case arose on the death of King George VI in February 1952. The Japanese royal family instructed the Agency to visit the palace to express condolences; but its car was not initially allowed inside Buckingham Palace. While the incident was rectified, it seemed to be a symbol of Britain's uncertainty as to protocol and Japanese touchiness at this delicate time. Asakai described the government attitude on this and a number of other issues as 'correct but not kind'.[8]

It was urgently necessary to find a residence for the ambassador shortly due to arrive, to arrange for the furnishing of these new premises and to buy a new car. These were not easy tasks in the economic climate of the day. On 28 April 1952, when the San Francisco treaty came into effect, the Agency became a diplomatic mission; and Asakai became Chargé d'Affaires. On the following day, the first reception celebrating the birthday of the Showa Emperor was held. Asakai's speech at the reception stressed that a new relationship had to be established and that he was starting from scratch. He added:

> There are many difficulties, I realize, between our two countries. I am sure extreme tact and patience will be necessary, on both sides, to solve some of the problems, as I have myself experienced already. During the eight months of my tenure of office as Chief of the Japanese Government Overseas Agency I have never felt disheartened with the task of restoring relations between the two countries. I have always been warmly received, encouraged and supported by distinguished people . . .
>
> We have lost the Embassy, and with it, maybe, valuable Japanese pictures and porcelains; such things may have gone, and we have to start from scratch to build up the Japanese Embassy. However, I do not regret this too much, because, although we have lost these material assets, we still have one asset that cannot be assessed in terms of money, namely, the unchanging friendship towards Japan of the distinguished guests here to-night.[9]

On the arrival of Matsumoto Shunichi as the first post-war ambassador on 8 June 1952, the premises at No 32 Belgrave Square became an embassy and Asakai became minister, tending thereafter to specialize on economic affairs. One special task which he undertook was to lay the preparations for the forthcoming visit by the Crown Prince of Japan who was being sent to Britain in response to the invitation to attend the coronation of Queen Elizabeth II. Asakai and General F.S.G. Piggott, representing the British government, travelled in advance over the route to be followed by the Prince in Scotland and Northumberland and arranged the various functions he would attend. This involved Asakai driving 1200 miles in five days around England and Scotland.[10]

Asakai was moreover deputed to join the Prince's mission in Washington and attend him all the way to Britain on the *Queen Mary* in order that the general situation in Britain could be explained to the Prince. On 27 April, when the liner docked at Southampton, Nara from the Agency in London arrived in order to brief the Prince on the most up-to-date situation and explain the ongoing anti-Japanese feeling.[11] On 30 April, soon after his arrival, the Prince was invited to a dinner party at No 10 Downing Street. Asakai who attended as interpreter for the Prince described the favourable impression given to the Japanese in attendance. Churchill talked to the Prince with his ear very close to the latter's face (presumably because of the prime minister's defective hearing) – like a grandfather having a conversation with his grandchild. When the Prince was leaving, Churchill expressed his wish that the Prince's visit would be a happy one, adding that, if any unpleasant noises were heard, he should 'take no notice of them'. From the illustrious people who were invited to the dinner, Asakai deduced that the British government was anxious to contain the growing anti-Japanese sentiment which some journalists had been stirring up.[12]

The main friction between Britain and Japan in this period which Asakai had to deal with concerned cotton spinning and pottery. Backed by the Americans, Japan took a tough line in negotiations with the pressure group from the cotton industry led by Sir Raymond Streat which insisted on a certain quota being imposed on Japanese spinning. As regards the complaint by the pottery industry in Stoke-on-Trent against the unfair copying by the Japanese of pottery made in England, Asakai contributed to the easing of tensions by mediating between the industries on both sides. On the pottery issue Asakai was critical of the Japanese side.[13]

When Asakai's departure from Britain was first announced, he was given a warm send-off by the members of the Japan Society at the Café Royal on 2 November 1953. Britain. In his speech at the reception he said:

> One of the difficulties between Japan and Great Britain is the economic problem. Since I came here I have discussed this question with many business men in Manchester, and often they have complained about Japanese unfair competition and I have naturally denied it. . . Anglo-Japanese relations were most difficult when I arrived here before the Peace Treaty was signed. When I was instructed to take up this post in 1951, I expected that I would encounter many unpleasant and disagreeable incidents here, unavoidable after that terrible war. . . But if there is one thing of which I can boast [during my tenure of office], it is that I have done my best. . . to re-group and consolidate friends of Japan who have long lost their contact with Japan and the Japanese.[14]

He is justified in claiming that he had presented Japan's case to British businessmen, even if they were far from convinced, and that he had effectively re-created a group of well-wishers who had their roots in pre-war Japan. All in all, he gave the impression of a man who liked and respected Britain.[15]

Because of the negotiations over the sterling area treaty, in which Asakai was Japan's main negotiator, his departure was reprieved, and he did not leave Britain for another half-year. There had been difficulties over the sterling payments agreement, which was due to expire at the end of December 1953. The Japanese were experiencing an acute shortage of sterling and were arguing that the reasons for the shortage were the restrictions imposed throughout the British Commonwealth but especially Britain's African colonies. Though it was under pressure from Lancashire which feared the consequences of relaxing restrictions on Japan's textile imports to African colonies, the British government showed itself willing to receive a high-level delegation at the end of the year from Japan.

Hitherto, the talks had been handled at the London end by Ihara of the Ministry of Finance (Okurasho) who had originally come over to London with Asakai. Difficult negotiations lasted for two months. But at the end on 28 January 1954, a new Sterling Payments Agreement was signed by Ambassador Matsumoto and Foreign Secretary Selwyn Lloyd, with an accompanying protocol signed by Asakai among others. Although this bureaucratic framework for trade had been formulated, it has to be admitted that the paucity of orders for Japan's goods in British colonies was more due to the absence of local demand than to state interference.[16]

Asakai owed much to his team. He was especially helped by Nara, a fellow Hitotsubashi graduate who ultimately became ambassador to Vietnam and Canada. He was also much assisted by his wife. She was the daughter of Debuchi Katsuji, the former Japanese ambassador to Washington who was himself a graduate of Hitotsubashi. There was universal praise among the British diplomatic establishment for Asakai Yoko. John Pilcher thought that Asakai was 'much helped by a particularly charming and forthcoming wife, who speaks excellent English'[17] and this sentiment was agreed by most of his colleagues.

For a while before he left London, Asakai tells us in an autobiographical note that he went to theatres almost every night to watch plays, including Agatha Christie's *The Mousetrap* which was even then long-running. He commented that the purpose of this theatre-going was not only to enjoy plays themselves but also to watch 'ninjō' (humanity) and learn the language. In the case of Shakespeare's plays, he read the text of the plays before attending.[18]

LATER APPOINTMENTS

Asakai spent a few days on the continent on his way back to Japan, leaving Europe finally from Rome on 7 April. He wanted to leave Britain inconspicuously and to arrive in Tokyo even more quietly in order not to surface for a week or two. He took up his new post at the Economic Bureau of the Gaimushō.[19] But only five months later he was ordered to accompany Yoshida on his visit to Britain, being specially recommended as the person with the most up-to-date information on Britain. One of the interesting episodes which Asakai later recalled was how, during Yoshida's not very successful mission, he acted as interpreter during a speech at the Inter-Parliamentary Union on 26 October. Yoshida's speech which, in referring to the Anglo-Japanese alliance, emphasized the need for close cooperation between Britain and Japan to deal with the threat of communism, proved unpopular. Asakai had not agreed with the contents of the draft speech; and Yoshida indeed received a number of hostile questions. Faced with such unexpectedly aggressive questions from the MPs, Yoshida in the end lost his patience, and Asakai was told by the prime minister to deal with any 'insignificant' questions. In response, Asakai urged Yoshida to answer for himself, while the former tried to translate accurately.[20]

During Yoshida's mission Asakai seems to have attended most of the formal meetings, including the dinner party at No 10 Downing Street on 27 October. He also partnered Satō Eisaku, one of the politicians on Yoshida's team, for a game of golf.[21]

Although Asakai wanted to stay longer in Tokyo, he was appointed Ambassador to the Philippines in August 1956. There it was his role to promote greater economic relations with the Philippines, with which there existed a trade gap with Japan having an excess of imports. After this involvement with Japan's Asia policy, he was appointed Ambassador to the United States in the spring of 1957, just after Kishi Nobusuke became prime minister. He was initially expected to deal with Kishi's forthcoming visit to the US which was of great significance. At first, he was not too keen on this appointment to Washington, where the previous incumbents had only stayed for a short period; he had no wish to follow in their footsteps by ending his career in a short-term posting. In actual fact, his ambassadorship proved to be the longest of all Japan's post-Pacific War embassies to the US. Moreover, Asakai's career reached its peak in Washington, dealing with bilateral negotiations over several important issues, notably the revision of the US-Japan Security Treaty in 1960 and the growing examples of trade friction.[22]

Immediately after he resigned as Ambassador to Washington in 1963, he retired from the Foreign Ministry but continued to act as adviser. In this capacity, he took part in several international conferences, including the Geneva Disarmament Conference, 1969. After his retirement from the post, he was invited to serve in various commercial capacities for the Bank of Tokyo, for Obayashi-gumi, the construction company, and for Pfizer Japan Inc, the pharmaceutical company.[23] He died in 1995. His funeral took place at St Ignatius Church, Yotsuya, Tokyo.[24]

CONCLUSION

In line with Britain's original expectations, Asakai left a pleasing impression of frankness in British diplomatic circles throughout his two-and-a-half years of laborious work in London, being much helped by his cheerful wife. As he himself indicated later, Asakai's quick promotion within the Foreign Ministry in the early postwar period was largely due to the lack of relatively young first-rate diplomats as a result of the purge imposed on the Japanese government.[25] But, to be fair to Asakai, his frank and pleasant personality, and his ability as a diplomat, including his first-rate language skills, were a great asset to him and the Gaimushō. His strength also lay in his relatively moderate manner and his lack of partisanship, unlike some other diplomats at the time such as Ambassador Matsumoto. This was reflected in the Japanese government's appointment of Asakai as first chief of its Overseas Agency in London rather than the more assertive and openly pro-Yoshida Shirasu.

Being non-partisan vis-à-vis the Japanese political scene, Asakai loyally tried to occupy the mainstream of post-war Japan's foreign policy stance, a mainstream which tended to side with the US Cold War position. This position entailed the acceptance of Japan's temporary breaking-up of her political relationship with the People's Republic of China. Asakai and the Japanese Embassy staff did not agree with Yoshida's stance which was to seek political cooperation with Britain in order to influence American policy in East Asia, in particular her China policy.[26] This lack of keenness on the part of the Embassy and also the British government over such practical cooperation led to postwar Anglo-Japanese cooperation being limited mainly to economic fields. Given this consensus, Asakai played an important role in negotiations with the British mainly over trade issues, notably in the trade and payments talks. Japan's failure to seek any other political partner in the post-war world and her reliance upon the US Cold War stance led to the shock she suffered over the sudden rapprochement between the US and China in 1971; the so-called Asakai nightmare came true.[27] In this sense, the appointment of the pro-Yoshida Shirasu rather than Asakai as Japanese envoy might have constituted a slight trigger in preparing for a more intensive exchange of views between Britain and Japan over political issues in East Asia. For Britain, Asakai proved to be a safe choice, causing no trouble regarding Britain's re-building of the post-peace treaty relationship with Japan and her relationship with the US over East Asian policy.

Like diplomats everywhere, Asakai had a dual function in London. He was presenting the case for Japan, both culturally, emphasizing Japanese traditions, and economically, stressing the rapid progress which Japanese industry and trade were making. But he also had the responsibility for interpreting Britain to the Japanese. He undertook several broadcasts to Japan, in which he explained that Britain too was suffering since the war, that there was rationing of food and clothing, that British industries were finding it hard to modernize and perform to the level they had been used to before the war, and that the structure of British society had radically changed as the result of the war.

From the British perspective, the Foreign Office perception was that Asakai came in 1951 as one well-disposed towards Britain and continued to be generally impressed by his stay there and 'is as pro-British as a foreign service officer can be'.[28] He was popular on the tennis-court and the golf-links and from his university days had an enthusiasm for boating. He was naturally sociable, 'well-known in the drawing-rooms in London and the country'. He had to take on a task which was not easy because there was much popular resentment in Britain over POW and trading issues. It was his duty to defuse these issues as best he could. He won over the Japan Society which cooperated in his endeavours. He developed cordial relations with the Foreign Office. But it was to take a decade and more to win over the British public as a whole. As he himself put it, 'Britain always maintained a certain distance' rather than being fully sympathetic towards Japan.[29] During his years in Britain as the first of Japan's postwar envoys, he worked hard to set up an effective administration in London. Later, as Minister Plenipotentiary, he loyally supported Ambassador Matsumoto's endeavours to improve relations.

NOTES

Asakai is one of the few Japanese whose portrait is kept at the National Portrait Gallery, London.
1. Asakai, 'Watashi no rirekisho', *Nihon Keizai Shimbun*, 1988, from which much of the information in this essay is derived. For Gauntlett's teaching at Hitotsubashi, see *Hitotsubashi Daigaku Gakumonshi*, Tokyo, 1986, p. 1094.
2. 'Asakai Kōichirō and Occupied Japan' in *Collected Writings of Gordon Daniels*, London: Japan Library, 2004; Asakai, *Shoki tai-Nichi senryō seisaku*, pp. 21-2.
3. Richard B. Finn, *Winners in Peace*, Berkeley: University of California Press, 1992, pp. 37, 71; Takemae; pp. 265-70.
4. Asakai, 'Igirisu to Igirisujin' in *Kosei Torihiki*, Vol. 13 (1951), pp. 8-9. Also Asakai, *Gaiko no reimei*, pp. 145-64.
5. Asakai, 'Rirekisho', No. 11, 11 March 1988.
6. Dening to Eden, 14 July 1952, 'Leading Personalities in Japan, 1952' in FJ 10 12/I, Foreign Office papers, 410/104. [Hereafter 'Foreign Office' is cited as 'FO'].
7. Transcript Mr Asakai: New Year Broadcast translated by BBC, 1952, attached to Nara (JOA) to Roberts (FO), FJ 1051/I, FO 371/99411.
8. Asakai, *Tsukasacho*, pp. 158-60.
9. Japan Society of London, *Bulletin*, 1952 [Hereafter cited as 'JSL *Bulletin*'].
10. For further details about this visit, see Sir Hugh Cortazzi, 'Crown Prince's Visit in 1953' in H. Cortazzi (ed), *Biographical Portraits*, Vol. V, Folkestone: Global Oriental, 2005, pp. 33-45; JSL *Bulletin*, June 1953, p.26.
11. Asakai, *Tsukasacho*, pp. 163-9.
12. H. Cortazzi, 'Prime Minister Yoshida in London, 1954: The First Visit to Britain by a Japanese Prime Minister' in *Biographical Portraits*, Vol. VI, Folkestone: Global Oriental, 2007.
13. Asakai, *Tsukasacho*, pp. 179-82.
14. JSL *Bulletin*, Vol. I, No. 12 (1954).

15. Noriko Yokoi, *Japan's Postwar Economic Recovery and Anglo-Japanese Relations, 1948-62*, London: Routledge, 2003, pp. 8-10.
16. John Weste, 'Facing the Unavoidable – Britain, the Sterling Area and Japan: Economic and Trading Relations, 1950-60' in Janet Hunter and Shinya Sugiyama (eds), *History of Anglo-Japanese Relations*, Vol. IV, 'Economic and Business Relations', Basingstoke: Palgrave, 2002, p. 295ff.
17. Minute by Pilcher, 28 April 1952, FO 371/99529.
18. Asakai, 'Rirekisho', No. 16, 16 March 1988.
19. Asakai, 'Rirekisho', No. 18, 18 March 1988.
20. Asakai, *Tsukasacho*, pp. 185-90. Hugh Cortazzi, 'Yoshida's visit to London, 1954' in Cortazzi (ed.), *Biographical Portraits*, Vol. VI, Folkestone: Global Oriental, 2007.
21. *Sato Eisaku nikki* [Sato Eisaku diary], Tokyo 1998, p. 191 [24 Oct. 1954].
22. For Asakai's Washington years, see T. Kuniyoshi, 'Nichi-Bei Ampō Joyaku Kaitei no shiteki kenkyū, 1955-60', an MA thesis for Hitotsubashi University, 1998.
23. Asakai, 'Rirekisho', No. 30, 31 March 1988.
24. Enomoto Masahiro, *Kaisei to Kirisutokyō* (Kaisei and the Christian Religion), Tokyo: Enomoto jimusho, 1996.
25. Finn, op cit., pp. 82-6.
26. For Yoshida's approach to Britain over China policy, see Tanaka Takahiko, 'Anglo-Japanese Relations in the 1950s: Cooperation, Friction and the Search for State Identity' in Ian Nish and Yoichi Kibata (eds), *History of Anglo-Japanese Relations*, Vol. II, Basingstoke: Macmillan, 2000, ch.9. See also Tanaka Takahiko, 'Yoshida gaikō ni okeru jishū to Igirisu, 1952-4: Yoshida Mission wo chushin ni' [Britain and Japan's quest for autonomy, 1952-4, especially the Yoshida Mission] in *Ikkyo Ronsō*, Vol. 123 (2000).
27. Asakai, *Tsukasacho*, pp. 226-9. Also Michael Schaller, *Altered States: The United States and Japan since the Occupation*, Oxford: University Press, 1997, p.225 and p.228.
28. Brain to Churchill, 18 August 1954, with enclosure 'Leading Personalities in Japan' in FJ1012/1 F0410/106.
29. Asakai, *Tsukasacho*, p. 162.

ASAKAI'S WRITINGS

Asakai Kōichirō, *Gaikō no reimei: Geneva Kaigi ni shishite* [The Dawn of Diplomacy: as delegate to the Geneva Conference], Tokyo: Yomiuri Shimbun, 1950.

Asakai Kōichirō, *Shoki taiNichi senryō seisaku: Asakai Kōichirō Hōkokusho* [Early Occupation Policy toward Japan: Reports by Asakai Kōichirō], 2 vols, Tokyo: Iwanami, 1978.

Asakai Kōichirō, *Tsukasacho Kanwa: Gaikōkan no kaisō* [Idle Talk at Tsukasacho: Memoirs of a Diplomat], Tokyo: 1986.

Asakai Kōichirō, 'Igirisu to Igirisujin' [England and the English] in *Kosei Torihiki* [Fair Trade], no. 5 (1951).

Asakai Kōichirō, 'Watashi no Rirekisho' [My curriculum vitae], nos 1-30, in *Nihon Keizai Shimbun*, 1-31 March 1988.

22

MATSUMOTO SHUNICHI, 1897-1988
First Post-war Ambassador
[London, 1952-55]

IAN NISH

Matsumoto Shunichi

Matsumoto Shunichi was the first post-war Japanese ambassador to the Court of St James's (1952-5). This was no easy assignment since there had been no ambassador since the departure of Shigemitsu Mamoru (1887-1957) on 29 June 1941. When Matsumoto arrived in June 1952, Japan was re-emerging after the trauma of the Asia-Pacific war and was showing signs of becoming the leading industrial country in Asia. In Tokyo's eyes London was still one of the major embassies overseas. Britain, by contrast, was by no means so close to Japan as she had been in prewar days or as the United States had become. She still wanted to have a moderating influence on East Asian affairs: she had been a signatory to the San Francisco Peace Treaty, had sent troops to the Korean War, and had taken the serious step of recognizing the People's Republic of China. For the incoming ambassador, the task of establishing a new balance in the relationship between Japan and Britain and adjusting to a very different balance of power from the thirties was by no means inconsiderable.[1]

Matsumoto was born in Taiwan, Japan's first colony. When his family returned to Japan, he finished his primary and middle school education in Kure, Hiroshima prefecture. He graduated from the Law Faculty of Tokyo Imperial University in 1921 and, after a brief stay at the Finance Ministry, entered the Foreign Ministry. He served in Belgium in various consular roles (1923-5) and at the Paris embassy (1930-3). He had a temporary assignment on the staff of the Japanese delegation to the World Economic Conference which met in London in 1933. This was followed by a long tenure in Tokyo mainly in the treaty bureau, until he became vice-minister in 1942 after some of the functions of the Foreign Ministry were passed to the newly-formed Greater East Asia Ministry. He served for three years until September 1945.

EARLY CAREER

But this period was interrupted by a period as special envoy to French Indochina when Shigemitsu Mamoru as foreign minister sent him there as successor to the veteran diplomat, Yoshizawa Kenichi. When he reached Hanoi in November 1944 and met up with Yoshizawa, he found that this was going to be no easy assignment. The army there was expecting an American invasion of the French colony from the Philippines at any minute (which did not come) and was already planning an amalgamation of the French forces with its own, if necessary by a *coup de force*.[2]

The supreme French authority was the Governor-general, Admiral Jean Decoux, who had been appointed by the former Vichy government but was in communication with the government of General Charles de Gaulle, which now formed the provisional government in Paris. Matsumoto, either on his own or in line with Ministry policy, disliked the army's plan for the coup and recommended that the status quo should prevail: 'even if a coup became inevitable, occupation by force and establishment of a military government would cause great harm and no advantage would accrue from it.' His recommendation was for non-interference, though 'help should be given towards the independence of Annam, Cambodia and Laos'.[3]

It was not possible, however, for any short-term appointee to overrule the planning of the army command. When Decoux moved from his headquarters in Hanoi to Saigon on 24 February 1945, it was agreed that a brief ceremony for the signing of a rice supply agreement should take place on 9 March. But Matsumoto used the occasion to present fresh demands on behalf of the army: strengthening the arrangements for joint Franco-Japanese defence which had existed since the mutual defence agreement of July 1941, calling on Decoux to defend Indochina in cooperation with the Japanese army and asking him to make available facilities, transport, munitions etc to Japanese forces throughout the country. Decoux who was under instructions from Paris to remain neutral in any emergency sent a reply which called on the Japanese themselves to undertake the defence of the territory though he promised not to hamper the Japanese in their defence and expressed willingness to continue negotiations. When Matsumoto passed this to the army commander, he found it to be a refusal of the terms of Japan's ultimatum and unacceptable. But, even before the French reply was received, the coup had in fact been started by local army commanders.[4]

This was an unsavoury episode in which the diplomats had to present and argue for an ultimatum of which they probably did not approve, the authority of a 'special envoy' on a warfront being limited. Matsumoto was uncomfortable as the agent of the coup of 9 March. In Japanese terms he was doing his duty. But the French would never forgive this comparatively senior diplomat for what they saw as 'executing his mandate inconsiderately and for spurning the option of further negotiation.'[5]

Matsumoto asked for recall and resumed his role as vice minister on 13 May under Foreign Minister Tōgō. Japan's situation could not have been more gloomy. In Europe, Japan's ally, Germany, had surrendered. In the west Pacific Okinawa had been taken by the Americans. When the allies presented their peace terms following the Potsdam conference in July, the Foreign Ministry had to be consulted and Matsumoto as its administrative head had to play a major role in translating documents, advising, drafting and communicating Japan's policy. During the crisis over the so-called Potsdam Declaration, in which the allies insisted on unconditional surrender, Matsumoto was at Tōgō's right hand. There was immediately a major split between the army/navy on the one hand and civilian ministers and the court on the other. According to the testimony of Matsumoto to the International Military Tribunal for the Far East (IMTFE), he took the lead in converting his Foreign Ministry colleagues to adopt a firm line to accept the Potsdam terms and then to negotiate: 'The only way Japan could end the war was by accepting the Potsdam terms as they stood'. It was he who drafted the reply to Potsdam saying that Japan is 'ready to accept the terms . . . with the understanding that the said Declaration does not comprise any demand which prejudices the prerogatives of His Majesty as a sovereign ruler'. This particular ploy was rejected by the allies. But the struggle in Tokyo between those who sought peace and those who wanted to carry on the war was to continue for some weeks against the background of the two atomic bombs being dropped on Hiroshima and Nagasaki. Matsumoto seems to have played an essential role in giving the harassed Tōgō confidence in standing firm in dealing with members of the cabinet and other leaders and, particularly, in outflanking the military.[6]

Matsumoto was subject to purge restrictions from 1947 to August 1951. But he became an adviser to the Foreign Ministry at the end of that year. Many former bureaucrats were tempted at that time to enter politics, because of the greater powers which the new constitution conferred on members of the Diet. Matsumoto seems to have involved himself in politics, particularly in the Progressive party [Kaishintō] which had been led by Arita Hachirō and was coming to be led by Shigemitsu Mamoru. It was for a while the leading opposition party in the Diet. Shigemitsu had been foreign minister for part of the time Matsumoto had served as vice-minister; and they had formed a bond of sorts. At a time of great turmoil among conservative politicians, Matsumoto may have let it be known that at the forthcoming general election, which was due to take place in 1952, he wanted to contest his local constituency of Hiroshima where he had been educated. Rumour has it that Prime Minister Yoshida's Jiyuto thought this was undesirable, since Ikeda Hayato who was being groomed by Yoshida for high office was planning to stand for that seat.[7]

One way out of the dilemma was for Matsumoto to be persuaded to resume his diplomatic career by being offered the post of ambassador in London. Relations between Britain and Japan had been re-established in 1951 with the arrival in London of Asakai as Agent [see Chapter 21]. Britain had signed the San Francisco Peace Treaty, ratified it and arranged for the Royal Assent to be given. Diplomatic relations officially began when the San Francisco treaty came into force on 28 April 1952. Slightly before that, Asakai asked London for agrément for Matsumoto as ambassador. The Foreign Office received advice from many diplomats abroad, some of whom reported that French opinion was still hostile. Ambassador Esler Dening in Tokyo, however, thought the criticisms 'seemed a little unjust'. After due consultation the Foreign Office reached the not ungenerous conclusion 'that any Japanese diplomat of the war period who was faithfully carrying out the instructions of his Government was bound to have created a bad impression on any representatives of the Western powers with whom he came into contact.' For this reason, Whitehall concluded that there were insufficient grounds for withholding agrément which would in any case have stalled the improvement of Anglo-Japanese relations which it wanted to reinvigorate.[8]

AMBASSADOR IN LONDON

Matsumoto arrived in June to take up his post. He did not have the advantage of having been posted previously in London apart from the short exposure during the World Economic Conference of May-June 1933 and came indeed from the Francophone branch of the Gaimushō. It appears to have been in part a political appointment. At a function which the Japan Society gave to welcome the new envoy, Sir Robert Craigie, the chairman, said that he faced a challenging assignment:

> In a diplomat's life there is no more difficult task than to preside over the resumption of diplomatic relations after a break.[9]

Relations had been disrupted for over a decade and, however cooperative the British government was to Japan, sections of public opinion were hostile. Matsumoto presented his Letters of Credence on 24 June.

Matsumoto presided over a good team. Assistant Under-secretary Rob (later Sir Robert) Scott of the Foreign Office expressed the view that the new embassy had

> a good staff headed by three outstanding men – the Ambassador himself, obviously an extremely intelligent and able person; Asakai who knows this country very well and who is very frank and approachable; and Ihara the Financial Counsellor, who has gained the respect of the Treasury and who is recognised in Whitehall as a most efficient and cooperative person.[10]

It certainly was not an easy task to address all the issues which divided the two countries in 1952. Reflecting on it later, Matsumoto said that when he first arrived in Britain, 'the bad feeling which the British people retained against their former enemy country was still noticeable.'[11] He had to deal with several issues on which there were vocal lobbies. The most pressing was that of former prisoners-of-war detained by the Imperial Japanese Army. Article 16 of the San Francisco treaty had laid down a formula of compensation whereby Japanese funds in neutral countries were to be divided among the sufferers. But the complaint was that the amount was small and Japan had been slow to implement the article. This led to discontent and agitation.

There were also suspicions about trade in which British industrialists recalled Japan's commercial practices before the war. British industry had an intense fear of unfair competition, especially in pottery, textiles and shipping. It complained of government subsidies for shipping and the copying of textile designs. There was certainly alarm at the prospect of the renewal of intensive commercial competition in world markets. The Board of Trade was not in favour of showing a liberal attitude to Japanese imports. Some steps towards normalization were taken. The first Sterling Payments Agreement was signed in 1951. As a result of lengthy negotiations a fresh treaty was signed by Matsumoto and Foreign Secretary Selwyn Lloyd on 29 January 1954, being countersigned for Japan by Asakai. Year-by-year arrangements were limited in their value; but the trade between the two countries was relatively small and never exceeded five per cent of Japan's imports or exports. Nevertheless, the debate in the House of Commons on the renewed Sterling Payments Agreement was highly-charged and showed how deep-seated British suspicions were.[12]

During the two-and-a-half years of his tenure, Matsumoto had to deal with two special events which were designed to counteract the decline in relations between the two countries. He acted as host to the Crown Prince on the occasion of his visit to UK for the coronation of Queen Elizabeth II in 1953. The Crown Prince who had now reached twenty years of age was to travel overseas in any case as his father had done when he was Crown Prince in 1921. Matsumoto went to Japan in February 1953 in order to plan the visit to the United Kingdom with the Imperial Household. Unlike the itinerary of 1921, the Prince travelled first to the United States, the country with which Japan had closest connections overseas. Matsumoto was present at Southampton on 27 April in order to greet him off the *Queen Elizabeth*. Two days later, he celebrated the Shōwa Emperor's birthday in the newly-decorated and furnished Residence at 23 Kensington Palace Gardens 'in the presence of the Crown Prince'. This is not the place to list the various functions the Prince attended or the sightseeing tours arranged for him. Suffice it to say that his schedule included receptions by Prime Minister Churchill and the Queen. Thereafter, his itinerary in May covered visits to Scotland, the borders and Pitlochry and ended with extensive tours in London and the south. It followed the pattern of his father's trip in 1921. On his journey south it was planned that he should visit the city of Newcastle upon Tyne but the city council opposed the holding of a civic reception in his honour so the event had to be cancelled. But the Prince spent seven happy days at Cragside, Rothbury as the guest of Lord Armstrong, the shipbuilding magnate. Matsumoto was present for part of this time of rest and relaxation. The Prince attended the Coronation on 2 June. He then travelled to the continent from Folkestone in order to visit France and Germany and especially to re-establish relations with monarchies that survived on the continent. He returned from Geneva by air on 7 September, eventually leaving British shores by BOAC Stratocruiser for the USA.[13]

Some of the success of the Crown Prince's visit redounded to Matsumoto. At the royal level, it was an opportunity for restoring relations between the British and Japanese royal families through his attendance at the coronation. At a government level, a visit from the heir-apparent to the throne was welcome and symbolized the return of Japan as an acceptable sovereign power in world affairs. The British press and general public were, generally speaking, favourable to the presence of a young and innocent prince on such a festive occasion as the coronation. The Crown Prince did not put a foot wrong during his five weeks' stay in the UK and it was an outstanding personal and social success. Naturally Matsumoto as the ambassador was depressed by the boycott at Newcastle and the complaints of some of the Japanese pressmen. But these incidents only confirmed his own view that there were in Britain small pockets of irreconcilable opposition to Japan which it was vital for politicians in Tokyo to understand.

By comparison with the Crown Prince's leisurely visit, the second event was rushed. This was the visit to the United Kingdom of Prime Minister Yoshida between 21 and 28 October 1954. Yoshida Shigeru (1878-1967), who was a prewar ambassador to Britain [see Yoshida chapter], had been head of five cabinets since 1948. He had a longstanding ambition to make a foreign trip and had been planning one for several dates in 1953-4. But in the prevailing turmoil of conservative politics he could not leave Japan and it had to be postponed. Britain's view of Yoshida was that, though his shortcomings were many, his was the best available government for Japan at the time. It was important, therefore, that he should be made welcome and treated with respect since this journey was an attempt by Yoshida to establish his reputation as an international statesman. This in turn might assist him in dealing with the approaching political crisis.

On 21 October, Yoshida arrived from Italy where he had been ambassador in the 1930s. It was given out that it was not a state visit; and he stayed at Claridge's at Japanese expense. It was intended as a goodwill mission. Yoshida told the London *Times* that his object was to repair the damage inflicted upon Anglo-Japanese friendship by the war and to solve several difficult and delicate issues. He was paid due honour, being entertained by Prime Minister Churchill, by the Queen, by the foreign secretary and by the Japan Society of London. He was also involved in various public appearances. There were some public relations disasters but not of a serious kind. Yoshida created some goodwill for Japan, stirred up some nostalgia by reminding his audiences of the Anglo-Japanese alliance and conveyed an image of personal geniality. He was applauded for his undoubted courage during the war years. Yoshida's visit was historically notable for being the first to Britain by a prime minister of Japan in office.[14]

Britain had some matters to raise and Yoshida was genuinely responsive. It had originally been hoped that the British ambassador in Tokyo, Sir Esler Dening, would be able to take up with Yoshida and Matsumoto in London various points of discord. Because of the repeated postponements of Yoshida's trip, a meeting in London was not feasible. But Dening and Yoshida managed to meet up in Vancouver where the former raised the most pressing problem, that of the implementation of Article 16 of the San Francisco treaty over compensation to British prisoners-of-war. His account stated: 'Yoshida took action and was very fair. Sir Norman Roberts was sent to Tokyo to negotiate the actual settlement and Yoshida managed to implement it just before he fell from power. . . . That particular source of friction was removed'.[15] Yoshida also met members of the Far East Prisoners-of-war Association while he was in London. Trade matters were discussed but it was agreed that these were best left to the industries concerned to resolve direct. Some other substantive issues were raised. But since the prime minister was forced to resign almost as soon as he returned to Tokyo from the United States, many of the items on Britain's agenda were left unresolved. The visit took place too late in his premiership to improve Anglo-Japanese relations greatly.

Yoshida had also his own personal agenda to pursue in London. He was not sure that the diplomats in the Foreign Ministry were putting over his ideas on China policy wholeheartedly. He wanted to detach the People's Republic of China from the Soviet Union and thought that opening her to trade with the Western world would assist. Clearly, such a policy would have ancillary advantages for Japan which wanted to re-open the China market she had developed in prewar days in a way that the Americans would not allow. Yoshida wanted to test Britain's attitude on possible cooperation before he proceeded to Washington and took the matter up with Secretary of State Dulles. But the foreign secretary, Sir Anthony Eden, was disappointingly non-committal over this issue.

Matsumoto was reminded by Yoshida's visit that Britain's position vis-à-vis the United States was similar to that of Japan. Yoshida regarded Britain as a country increasingly at odds with the US and having sufficient clout to stand up to Washington. Professor Tanaka tells us: 'Matsumoto once wrote that he recognized that the US was not almighty, implying that she could not always control the diplomatic conduct of her allies. Matsumoto was influenced by his experience as ambassador to London during which the British government sought a diminution in international tension.'[16] Nowhere was this more evident than at the Geneva conferences of 1954 where the Korea armistice and the

Indochina questions came up for discussion at a forum where the chairmen were Anthony Eden and Vyacheslav Molotov. The United States was represented by a delegation but preferred not to play a prominent role. It emerged that, in spite of the Cold War, Russia and China were prepared to discuss significant international issues constructively at a conference. This was to influence Matsumoto's thinking on world affairs. He may well have agreed with British newspapers which asked why Japan was not represented at Geneva. This may have prompted Matsumoto to consider whether Japan should not be taking up outstanding issues with the Soviet Union which was now more open.[17]

DEPARTURE

Shortly before Matsumoto's departure from London on 12 January 1955, the Japan Society gave him, his wife and daughter Mikiko a warm send-off. In his opening remarks, Sir Robert Craigie as chairman said: 'Our two countries have everything to lose from the nursing of old grievances and everything to gain from closer cooperation and a better understanding of our respective problems.'[18] In reply, Matsumoto gave an overview of his stay in London, arguing that the Anglo-Japanese relationship was beginning to show slow but steady signs of improvement. On the critical issue affecting public opinion regarding compensation for prisoners-of-war, he stuck to the Yoshida line. He hoped 'that the compensation which we pledged to pay in the Peace Treaty, and which will be paid very shortly, will, though small in amount, help to obviate their natural enmity against us in due course.' Alas, the San Francisco formula was thought by British opinion to be inadequate and for some decades the resentment persisted until the British government itself announced *ex gratia* payments in 2000.

On the positive side, Matsumoto emphasized that economic ties between the two countries were being strengthened year by year and 'a sympathetic understanding of Japan's position, both political and economic, is beginning to be reflected in British public opinion through the editorials and reports of newspapers and weekly magazines in this country'.[19] Certainly this was apparent in the writings of the influential journal, *The Economist*:

> There can no longer be any doubt that Japan is on the way to re-emergence in world affairs, not merely as the strongest industrial power in Asia after the Soviet Union but also as a considerable military power. . . Britain is not isolated from Japan in another world, but is involved over a wide range of export markets in a commercial competition which is likely to become more intense. Britain cannot avoid having relations with Japan and, if they are not good, they will be bad. . . It is most undesirable that war-time feelings should be permitted to influence British policy towards Japan at a time when it is being rearmed as a part of the defensive structure of the free world.[20]

On his return from Britain, Matsumoto resigned from the Foreign Ministry. He witnessed a changed political scene. On 24 November 1954, the Democratic party had been established through an amalgamation of the Minshutō and Kaishintō with Hatoyama Ichirō as president and Shigemitsu as his deputy. On 10 December, after the collapse of the Yoshida administration, Hatoyama formed a cabinet and Shigemitsu, Matsumoto's associate in the Foreign Ministry, became foreign minister and deputy premier. It was in these circumstances that Matsumoto entered politics and was elected as a Democrat at the general election for the Lower House held on 27 February 1955.

Thus he fulfilled the forecast that he had made in his valedictory speech in London :

> Upon my return to Japan, it is my intention to enter into the political life of my country. It is my sincere belief that the friendship, knowledge and experience I have gained here will give me an insight into the promotion of even closer relations between our two countries. I should like to take this opportunity to assure my friends of the Japan Society that this will be one of my principal aims *in my future policy*.[21] (my italics)

The portion marked contains an odd choice of words. Can it be that Matsumoto was merely giving an undertaking to promote Anglo-Japanese relations in his new role as legislator? Or had he higher ambitions?

The new prime minister was anxious that Japan should not find herself a victim of American-Soviet rivalry in the Cold War and thought that the time was ripe for Soviet-Japanese relations to return to normal now that Stalin had died. Hatoyama turned to Matsumoto as one of his advisers. The choice of a neutral venue for the talks presented some difficulty. London was more the Soviet choice than Japan's. But Matsumoto, because of his term of office there, was very content to negotiate there.[22] The Soviets agreed to start negotiations and Matsumoto was appointed as plenipotentiary to open talks with Malik, the Soviet ambassador in London, which began in the British capital in June 1955. Two phases of the talks were held in London but they ran into difficulties and dragged on into March 1956 when they were finally postponed [see Nishi chapter]. In the third phase Foreign Minister Shigemitsu decided to take a personal hand and travelled to Moscow in July with Matsumoto as his assistant. Although that phase of the negotiations was also unsuccessful, Matsumoto accompanied Hatoyama himself to the Russian capital and was present on 19 October 1956 when Japan and the Soviet Union signed a joint interim declaration ending hostilities and restoring diplomatic arrangements. Japan did not secure the desired peace treaty with Russia or any agreement on the territorial dispute over the Northern Territories. She achieved normalization without total satisfaction.[23]

Thus Matsumoto remained in the public eye after he left Foreign Ministry service at the age of fifty-eight and enjoyed a fruitful career as a politician, retaining his seat on several occasions and becoming Chief Cabinet Secretary in 1958. His past experience as a diplomat was called for when he accompanied Prime Minister Kishi to the United States in June 1957. He was sent by the Foreign Ministry as a special envoy to the three states which constituted Indochina in 1965, twenty years after his first experiences there which he had come to regret. His public reports published in the *Asahi* newspaper attracted wide interest. He was broadly in sympathy with the *Asahi* line which was critical of the United States position on the Vietnam War.[24] Matsumoto continued to be connected to the family construction business.

In reflecting on Matsumoto's performance in London, which is the prime purpose of this essay, one has to conclude that he followed a policy of caution and reticence, thinking that British public opinion was still sensitive and could not be won over in a day. During the 1950s, Japan was inclined to boast of her low-posture foreign policy, preferring to concentrate on commercial development rather than take conspicuous global, or indeed regional, initiatives.

Matsumoto in some ways reflected this. It may be that his reserved and cautious personality was well attuned to the Tokyo line. Perhaps a man of reticence like Matsumoto was needed in Britain to sit out the storms. He did not make much impression at the Foreign Office, made few public speeches and gave few newspaper interviews. In approaching his task, Matsumoto was assisted by his minister, Ōda Takio, and very talented junior staff.

It was perhaps too much to expect that the suspicions of the British public would disappear overnight. But Matsumoto could always rely on the goodwill and cooperation of an inner core of Japanophiles associated with the Japan Society of London. Its chairman, Sir Robert Craigie, was probably just in praising him for his 'quiet dignity and balanced judgement which won universal esteem'.

NOTES

I have been greatly assisted in writing this essay by fellow-contributors, Hugh Cortazzi, Tomoki Kuniyoshi and Eiji Seki and by Peter Lowe.
1.   For general reading on this period, see Tanaka Takahiko, 'Anglo-Japanese Relations in the 1950s: Cooperation, Friction and the Search for State Identity' in Ian Nish and Yoichi Kibata, *The History of Anglo-Japanese Relations, 1600-2000*, 2 vols, Basingstoke: Macmillan, Vol. I. 'The Political-Diplomatic Dimension, 1931-2000', pp. 201-34; Peter Lowe, *Containing the Cold War in East Asia: British Policies towards Japan, China and Korea, 1948-53*, Manchester: University Press, 1997.
     The journal *Ekonomisto* in November/December 1971 featured a series of interviews with Matsumoto in which he reviewed his career quite frankly.
2.   *Documents diplomatiques francais, 1945-54*, '1944, tome II (Sept.-Dec.)', Paris: Imprimerie Nationale, 1996, pp. 15-16, 264 (hereafter cited as DDF). Yoshizawa Kenkichi, *Gaiko 60-nen*, Tokyo: Jiyu Ajia, 1958, pp. 278-80.
3.   Louis Allen, 'The Japanese coup of 9 March 1945 in Indo-china' in *International Relations*, STICERD, LSE, 1985/I, pp 1-29. Also L. Allen, *The End of the War in Asia*, London: Hart-Davis, 1976, pp. 96-110.
4.   DDF, '1945, tome I (Jan.-Juin)', Paris: Imprimerie Nationale, 1998, p. 60. In retrospect, Matsumoto described his assignment in Indochina as 'bimbō kuji', a piece of ill-luck, a case of drawing the short straw. *Ekonomisto*, 14 Dec. 1971, p.93.
5.   Kajima Morinosuke, *Nihon gaikōshi*, Vol. 22, 'Nanshin mondai', Tokyo: Kajima, 1973. Matsumoto Shunichi and Andō Yoshiro were the joint editors of this volume but do not include mention of this issue.
6.   R.J.C. Butow, *Japan's Decision to Surrender*, Stanford: UP, 1954, pp. 192-7; Matsumoto Shunichi and Andō Yoshiro (eds), *Nihon gaikōshi*, Vol. 25, 'Dai Tōa sensō shūsen gaikō', Tokyo: Kajima, 1972, pp. 231-8; Matsumoto Shunichi and Sakomizu Jirō, 'Dai 1-kai dai 2-kai rinji kakugi' in Gaimusho (ed.), *Shūsen Shiroku*, 6 vols, Tokyo: Hokuyosha, Vol. IV, 1977; Hasegawa Tsuyoshi, *Racing the Enemy: Stalin, Truman and the Surrender of Japan*, Cambridge, Mass.: Harvard University Press, 2005, pp. 165-6.
7.   On the general political background, Nakakita Koji, *1955-nen taisei no seiritsu*, Tokyo: University Press, 2002, pp. 18-22.
8.   Graves (Saigon) to FO, 27 April 1952 in FJ1905/14 in Foreign Office papers (National Archives, Kew) 371/99529; Pilcher (FO) to Graves (Saigon), 13 May 1952 in FJ 1905/21 in FO 371/99529. (Hereafter cited as FO).
9.   *Bulletin of Japan Society of London*, No. 15 (February 1955), p.5. (Hereafter cited as BJS).
10. R.H. Scott to Dening, 29 January 1953 in FJ 1051/3 in FO 371/105374. Ihara had served under Asakai and returned for a second tour.
11. BJS, no 15 (February 1955), p. 5. In newspaper interviews before leaving Japan, he had said that relations could not be improved overnight.
12. Noriko Yokoi, *Japan's Postwar Economic Recovery and Anglo-Japanese Relations, 1948-62*, London: Routledge/Curzon, 2003, pp. 94-5.

13. Hugh Cortazzi, 'Crown Prince Akihito in Britain' in Cortazzi (ed.), *Biographical Portraits*, Vol. VI, Folkestone: Global Oriental, 2007.
14. Hugh Cortazzi, 'Prime Minister Yoshida in London, 1954' in Cortazzi (ed.), *Biographical Portraits*, Vol. VI, Folkestone: Global Oriental, 2007.
15. Ian Nish (ed.), *Collected Writings of Richard Storry*, Richmond: Japan Library, 2002, p.267.
16. T. Tanaka, 'The Soviet-Japanese Normalization and Foreign Policy Ideas of the Hatoyama Group' in P.C. Lowe and H. Moeshart (eds), *Western Interactions with Japan*, Folkestone: Japan Library, 1990, p. 110.
17. Ibid.
18. BJS, 15 February 1955, p.5.
19. Ibid.
20. *The Economist*, 14 November 1953.
21. BJS, 15 February 1955, p. 5.
22. Takahiko Tanaka, *NisSo kokkō kaifuku no shiteki kenkyū*, Tokyo: Yuhikaku, 1993, pp. 94-5. Mayumi Itoh, *The Hatoyama Dynasty*, Basingstoke: Palgrave, 2003, pp. 134-6.
23. Tanaka, *NisSo kokkō kaifuku*, ch. 8; Nakakita, op. cit., p. 263; Mayumi Itoh, *The Hatoyama Dynasty*, Basingstoke: Palgrave, 2003, pp. 134-6.
24. *Asahi Shimbun*, 6 April 1965.

23

NISHI HARUHIKO, 1893-1985
Conscientious and Patriotic Bureaucrat
[London, 1955-57]

IAN NISH

Nishi Haruhiko

Nishi Haruhiko had the onerous responsibility of becoming ambassador in London in 1955 at a difficult time when the Asia-Pacific War was still very prominent in British memories. He was a conscientious and patriotic bureaucrat. But, like many of his contemporaries, he had not had a straightforward career as a professional diplomat because of the disjunction of the war and the allied occupation of his homeland which followed. These external events moulded his career which culminated in London but also affected his thinking deeply.

Born in Kaseda, Kagoshima-ken, in April 1893, Nishi completed his education at the Imperial University in Tokyo. He graduated in German Law in 1918 and passed the Foreign Ministry entrance examination. He joined the office just as Japan took a controversial initiative in the Siberian intervention in which British troops were also involved. He then had junior postings in Hongkong and New York. During his period in the US as a young consular official, he got to know the eldest daughter of Nomura Yōzō, a prominent samurai entrepreneur from Yokohama, while she was a student in the US, because of a passport application. On her return to Japan, she persuaded her parents to let her marry Nishi and the wedding took place in 1920.[1] Nishi had his first posting to Moscow from 1925 to 1928 as 2nd secretary. During these early phases of his career, he experienced conference diplomacy at the Washington Conference (1921-2) and the Geneva Naval Conference (1927). He returned to Tokyo to work in various departments and devoted much effort to the purchase of the Chinese Eastern Railway from the Soviet Union.[2] He then moved to Tsingtao, China, as consul-general and to Moscow as counsellor in 1936, working with Ambassadors Shigemitsu Mamoru and Tōgō Shigenori, associations which were to prove invaluable to him later in his career.

At the outbreak of the Second World War in Europe, he became director of the Europe and Asia Bureau where he was responsible for dealing with the aftermath of the Nomonhan incident (1939) where the Japanese army in Manchuria suffered a serious defeat from the tanks and aircraft of the Soviet Union. In 1940, he was appointed minister to Russia to assist the new ambassador, General Tatekawa, whose remit it was to cultivate good relations with Moscow and possibly work towards a German-Russian-Japanese compact. This did not get off the ground. But Nishi witnessed the historic visit of Matsuoka Yōsuke to Europe in April 1941 when Japan's foreign minister signed a Neutrality Pact with the Soviet Union. Nishi returned home after a clash of views with Tatekawa.

Nishi's service in Moscow had an indelible effect on his thinking as his memoirs show. Reflecting on his three prewar postings there, he later wrote:

> [I] will never forget my bitter experiences there when the Anti-Comintern Pact was signed between Japan and Germany [25 Nov. 1936]. . .After it was concluded, the Soviet government took the stance that Japan and Germany were potential enemies and made life extremely difficult for us.
>
> To start with, it refused to complete the revised draft of the Soviet-Japanese Fisheries Treaty which was awaiting signature at the very moment the Anti-Comintern deal was clinched. The consequence was that Japan had problems thereafter : year after year we had the difficulty of negotiating on an annual basis a temporary fisheries treaty valid only for one year.
>
> . . .We were placed under increasingly tight security and our embassy was encompassed by barbed wire. Travel by our diplomatic staff was subject to severe obstruction. The majority of our consulates throughout Soviet territory had no option but to close.[3]

When Tōgō was appointed as foreign minister in the Tōjō cabinet, Nishi was recalled to serve as vice-minister in October 1941 and was thus in office at the outbreak of the Asia-Pacific War. But he and his minister did not survive long. In 1942 Tōjō created the Great East Asia Ministry in order to 'remove China from the clutches of the Foreign Ministry' which were deemed to be too timid. Tōgō clashed with the prime minister over the prospect of his ministry being either emasculated or rendered subservient to the other ministry; and Nishi resigned with his superior in September. Later in the war, he became envoy to Manchukuo and member of the Japan-Manchuria Economic Cooperation.

Under the allied occupation from 1945, Nishi was 'purged', that is, he was not permitted to hold public office. He became adviser to the Shell Oil company (*Shell Sekiyū*). He served also as one of the Defence Counsels for Tōgō who had been arraigned as a major war criminal at the International Military Tribunal for the Far East where he worked under Ben Bruce Blakeney, a prominent American lawyer. Nishi who had accumulated great experience in his dealings with the pre-war Soviet Union played a large part in the Russian phase of the trial.

When Japan recovered her sovereignty, Nishi was appointed as the first post-war ambassador to Australia.[4] The embassy was opened in December 1952 and Nishi arrived in Canberra in January of the following year. He writes that this was a difficult time because Japanese were not made welcome. The Returned Servicemen's League (RSL) felt that there were many old scores to settle, including the sensitive POW issues. When the RSL heard that Japan had been invited to be represented at the annual ANZAC Day ceremony, it threatened to boycott the parade. Eventually, a compromise was reached whereby only British Commonwealth diplomats laid a wreath and other governments were not required to do so. A poignant photograph in his autobiography shows Nishi and his wife (dressed in kimono) being escorted to the front row at the parade (as protocol dictated).[5] Nishi had to deal with a host of economic problems such as wheat and wool purchases, sterling balances and GATT accession. He also worked actively as the delegate of the Japanese government responsible for negotiating over fishing for pearl oysters in the Arafura Sea off the coast of Australia's Northern Territories. At the end of his term in 1955, it was generally acknowledged that Nishi had successfully promoted Australian-Japanese relations and had performed well in an uncomfortable posting. The Australian foreign minister, Richard Casey, saw Nishi at his departure and wrote: 'he has done very well here in many ways and Australian-Japanese feeling is a great deal better than it was when he arrived 2½ years ago'.[6]

LONDON: THE SOVIET CONNECTION

Nishi was invited to become ambassador to the Court of St James's to succeed Ambassador Matsumoto Shunichi who resigned after the end of the fifth Yoshida cabinet (see Chapter 22). The reasons for the appointment are not clear. It seems that one factor was the success of his Australian mission since he had had no previous British posting (though he had visited UK in 1952, arriving on the same plane as Matsumoto). Another factor was Japan's determination to tidy up her relationship with the Soviet Union which had not signed the San Francisco Peace treaty. The government felt that it was opportune to open negotiations with the Soviets and that no more suitable place could be found than London. Matsumoto was commissioned to conduct the negotiations in the British capital although he was not a Russian specialist. He may have wanted the presence there of Nishi who was acknowledged as a foremost authority on the Soviet Union and knew the Russian negotiators. Ironically, therefore, it may have been Nishi's knowledge of Soviet affairs that enhanced his prospects for the London post. Whether he played a significant role in the talks is not clear. He was certainly present at many of the social events but Nishi himself admits that his input was slight.[7]

The Soviet-Japanese talks for normalization of relations opened on 7 June 1955 between Matsumoto and Jakob Malik who was ambassador to Britain. The London talks ran into many difficulties. After a four months' recess was arranged in late August, they reopened in January. But they were suspended again in acrimony two months later. After a year the negotiations were switched to Moscow in July with the foreign minister, Shigemitsu Mamoru, himself in attendance. Again the talks were 'temporarily suspended'; and Japan was relieved to accept an invitation to a London conference on the Suez Canal which was convened at very short notice. While Shigemitsu attended the sessions of the Suez Canal Users Association (SCUA) at Lancaster House during his stay in London (16-28 August), much of the later work on the Canal crisis devolved on Nishi.[8]

The Japan-Soviet parleys ended in Moscow on 19 October with a joint declaration which ended the state of war between the two powers and reestablished trade links. The agreement was duly ratified. But many in Japan were dissatisfied with the outcome. Nishi for one had distinct reservations about the settlement that Japan had accepted largely on domestic political grounds. In this he reflected the scepticism of the Foreign Ministry and the friction which existed between it and the politicians of the day. It was a time of extreme turbulence in Japanese politics which was only cured by the merger of the Liberal party (which Yoshida had earlier led) and the Democratic party.[9]

THE COURT OF ST JAMES'S

In Nishi's first speech after he reached London, he prophesied that it would be easier for him in Britain than in Australia. As his predecessor had found, the support of the Japan Society of London was a great help to an incoming ambassador where his country faced some degree of unpopularity. When Nishi took up his post, Japan had made progress in world diplomacy and gained international confidence, thanks to American support. There had been a relaxation of tension in East Asia, resulting from the armistices in the Korean War (1953) and the first Indochinese War (1954). Japan was already associated with the Colombo plan and sent representatives to the Bandung Conference of Afro-Asian states. She was also being admitted to the United Nations.

But trade was an immediate stumbling-block for Nishi. In September 1955 Japan completed her accession to the General Agreement on Tariffs and Trade (GATT). Japan now deprived of the trade with China on which she had relied in pre-war days had sought unconditional membership of GATT. Britain voted in favour of Japan's accession but reserved the right to invoke Article 35, thereby declining to apply GATT rules to trade between the two countries. In this she was followed by others and was running against American wishes. To resolve the problem, both the British and Japanese governments wanted to carry on bilateral negotiations for a commercial treaty which continued for the next five years. Throughout his stay Nishi was to be confronted by complaints about pre-war dumping practices by Japan and allegations that her economy was being revived on the basis of underpaid workers.[10]

On another front, the House of Representatives passed a resolution in February 1956 calling for an end to the testing of nuclear weapons. This was endorsed by the House of Councillors, the Upper House of the Japanese Diet. It was a cause which had widespread support among the Japanese public and press. Like the United States, Britain was a nuclear power and had no intention of stopping the testing of such weapons without some form of international agreement. Hence Nishi inevitably had a stormy ride, as he passed on his government's frequent protests. The Tokyo government continued to be so worried about tests in the Pacific area that it sent Professor Matsushita, the Rector of St Paul's University, Tokyo, on a personal mission to UK and USA in April 1957. But the mission had no success in either quarter.

Nishi was much involved in arranging the first visit to Japan by a British cabinet minister while in office. Lord Selkirk (1906-94), the Chancellor of the Duchy of Lancaster in Harold Macmillan's cabinet, went there in September 1956 in the course of a visit to Hongkong and South Korea. It was a goodwill mission and there were to be no formal talks. Understandably it was not intended to resolve outstanding issues, some of which were very prickly. In the view of Britain's Tokyo embassy, Selkirk was not greeted with an excess of cordiality, the Japanese government 'confining itself to the minimum of courtesy required by the occasion'. Japan had been spoilt by some of her other visitors at the time and was evidently disappointed by the limited agenda of the Selkirk mission. But the visit broke down the atmosphere of reserve which had existed on both sides; and at a dinner which Nishi gave on 5 December on Selkirk's return, the speakers described it as a great success.[11]

In February 1957, Kishi Nobusuke became prime minister and made drastic cabinet changes. He had himself served as foreign minister in the preceding cabinet and continued to act as his own foreign minister for the time being.[12] This was probably not much to the liking of the Japanese people or indeed to Nishi who had worked with him over Manchukuo during the war. Kishi was anxious that Japan should, in spite of all her balance of trade and financial problems, have a global role and undertook a strenuous series of tours in Asia and the world generally. He also encouraged goodwill missions in order to cultivate a better image for his country.

The United States had privately urged Britain to invite Prime Minister Kishi on an official visit to Britain. This proposal was not well received because of Kishi's wartime record as a member of Tōjō's cabinet. Eventually, the British government decided to invite Fujiyama Aiichirō who took over as foreign minister from Kishi in July. Fujiyama, an influential businessman and president of the Japan Chamber of Commerce, was a newcomer to active politics and was not even a member of the Diet. The idea of inviting the new foreign minister who had spent a year of study in England in the 1920s blossomed in August; and he visited London the following month as the guest of the British government on his way to the United Nations General Assembly. Thanks to Nishi, his brief visit was productive. The minister was able to have individual talks with most members of the Macmillan administration and laid the foundations for improved relations.[13] On 27 September, Nishi gave a reception for Fujiyama at which cordial sentiments were expressed. At the instance of his government, he extended a counter-invitation to Prime Minister Harold Macmillan to visit Japan – an idea supported by the British embassy in Tokyo – but the latter could not afford the time and had to decline.

The Selkirk and Fujiyama missions brought Anglo-Japanese relations on to a new plane. Britain was concerned that she had been neglected in Japan for a decade. She was relieved that she had now been restored to the map there. But on 17 November, shortly after Fujiyama's visit, Britain carried out another in the series of nuclear tests in the Pacific around Christmas Island. This was naturally a matter of profound disappointment for Nishi.[14]

Nishi toured widely inside and outside Britain. In August-September 1957 he was instructed to travel by air round Africa and called on the new leaders in Lagos, Accra, Kano, Leopoldville, Brazzaville, Livingstone, Salisbury, Nairobi, Entebbe, Khartoum and Cairo. The intention of this whirlwind tour was to observe conditions on the African continent with the approach of independence and to plant the seeds for future good relations with Japan which had hitherto neglected her relationships there. This entailed having discussions with most of the leaders of these rapidly decolonizing territories.[15] On a more modest scale were his tours of Britain by car around Wales, the north of England and Scotland (of which more anon).

Nishi announced his intention to leave London at the end of the year. At the Japan Society of London farewell dinner on 12 December, tributes were heard from many, including Sir Robert Craigie, speaking for the Japan Society, and Richard Storry of St Antony's College, Oxford, who spoke words of appreciation on behalf of the academic community. In his speech, Sir Esler Dening who had retired as ambassador to Tokyo six months earlier, said that Nishi's job in London had been much more difficult than his own. While they had shared common problems as Cold War diplomats, complicated by post-war problems of adjustment, the difficulty lay in the hostility of British public opinion. Nishi in conclusion said that he had been conscious of having 'to bridge a diplomatic gap resulting from the war both in Australia and Britain' and wanted his success to be judged by that criterion.[16]

Special tributes were paid to Mme Nishi Fukiko who spoke in reply on her own behalf, in what was a rare practice among English ladies at the time. Nishi in a later essay entitled 'Tsuma no omoide' paid tribute to the role of his wife in London for building up goodwill between Japanese and British women and cultivating a community spirit among the womenfolk of Japanese businessmen in the London area whose numbers were estimated to be as low as 200 in the 1950s. As the result of her efforts, Fukiko became the founding president of the *Fujinkai* (1956) which was intended to be dedicated to charitable work in the London community. She also planted the idea of the *Nichi-Ei Otomodachikai*, another of the thriving and long-lasting women's organizations in the capital. A strong character, she had played a vital role in Nishi's objective of creating goodwill on a personal basis.[17]

In view of 'the improving tone of our relations with Japan', the foreign secretary, Selwyn Lloyd, decided to give a farewell luncheon for the departing ambassador. In his speech Lloyd jocularly remarked that for a change it was now Britain's turn to make a protest. This acknowledged that Nishi had spent much of his time in London making protests about nuclear tests and trade matters. Now Britain had to protest against the Japanese decision to recall Nishi after only 2½ years in post! While this remark was made in jest, it reflected Britain's surprise and disappointment that Nishi's time had been cut short. It was a view widely held by his embassy colleagues.[18] It is possible that Nishi's advice on global affairs to his home government may not have been pleasing to them. He was deeply suspicious of the US as he was of the USSR from his past experience; he did not disguise his view that both were dangerous and lacking in diplomatic skill; he was pessimistic about the way the world was going and especially about China.[19] Among his recommendations to Tokyo he stressed that his successor should be someone younger who would be able 'to serve out his full term'. This suggests that Nishi thought that his stay in London had been too short and should have been extended.[20]

The years 1955-7 were a period of lull, while the comprehensive treaty of commerce was being slowly and cautiously negotiated. Nishi and his wife gradually restored good relations with the help of the Japan Society; but it was an uphill job. Thanks to the Nishis' natural charm, social relations greatly improved. But the nuclear issue was politically sensitive for the Japanese; and Japan's adverse reaction over Suez increased the difficulties.

RETIREMENT

The Nishis left London from Waterloo station on 18 December and travelled home by the P & O liner *Chusan*. They landed at Yokohama on 21 January 1958. Nishi had now reached the age of sixty-five and retired from the *Gaimushō* in February, having no expectations of a further posting. In his autobiography he writes of relishing the opportunity of becoming plain John Citizen.[21] He had returned to a Tokyo preoccupied with relations with the United States and the revision of the American-Japanese Security Treaty which was due to lapse at the end of the fifties. In Nishi's view it was a grave mistake that the Kishi government should be taking the initiative to seek a renewal and prolong the alliance.

It was not long before he produced a memorandum of advice for his government which he reproduces at length in his autobiography:

> To revise the Security Treaty will involve much danger for Japan in view of her relations with Russia and Communist China. Soviet Russia has regularly argued that, when the San Francisco Treaty was signed [in 1951], the Security Treaty was forced on Japan by the US. Accordingly Moscow has not blamed the Japanese for its existence. But, inasmuch as Japan is now herself asking for the proposed revisions, she must be ready to face the consequences which the Soviet Union and China may blame her for, even if [we know that] these changes are the result of compromises reached mutually between Japan and the US.[22]

In practical terms he was worried that American forces would operate from bases in Japan, whether or not they had consulted the Japanese government and obtained its agreement in advance. He had a real concern that the result would be a deterioration of Japan's relations with Russia and, by extension, with the People's Republic of China. The Kishi government nonetheless went ahead with the signature and ratification of the extended Security Treaty in 1960. Nishi's was a prescient view which continued to be relevant for the most of the sixties.

On the surface Nishi's memorandum appeared to be a courteously worded piece of advice to the Kishi government. But Nishi made the matter personal with criticism of Foreign Minister Fujiyama's emphasis on 'economic diplomacy'. He blamed the government for not appointing as foreign ministers specialists in international affairs. Until the time of Shigemitsu in 1955 governments could rely on foreign ministers having diplomatic experience; but with the periods at the Foreign Ministry of Kishi and Fujiyama, expertise in crisis management had been lost. One suspects that behind this criticism lay Nishi's dissatisfaction with the settlement which had been made with the Soviet Union in 1956 on the basis of 'political interests rather than rational discourse'.[23] Underlying this was the discord between Hatoyama and Shigemitsu and the long-standing question of Kasumigaseki autonomy. The Foreign Ministry, Nishi claimed, had lost its autonomy and standing. Governments were not appointing specialists trained in diplomacy so there was the danger that the country's policies would be ill-advised. But he was critical also of the Ministry mandarins for not learning the lessons from the fight which he and others had put up during the war. This continued to be his theme throughout the 1960s, first in his book *Kaisō no Nihon gaikō* (1965) and in his numerous articles and interviews in *Asahi Shimbun*. Now a popular commentator in the press, he called for further revisions of the new Security Treaty which held within it the seeds of war.[24]

THE BRITISH THREAD

It was the British perception that Nishi and his wife were, as their valedictory speeches suggested, admirers of Things British. Certainly Britain was not forgotten in Nishi's last years. He was appointed KBE in 1963. He returned to his advisory role in the Shell Oil Company, all the more important as oil crises approached. Among other appointments Nishi became chairman of the board of the Grand Hotel, Yokohama, which belonged to his wife's family. Nishi was also connected with the Tokyo-based Japan-British Society as director (*riji*) and later chairman (*kaichō*). He included in his address to its meeting on 4 March 1958 the following story:

> Upon assumption of my duties in London, I was told by a senior member of the Diplomatic Corps: "for five years after you arrive in London, you will be called by the name of your predecessor". . . If we assume this analysis to be correct, I shall be remembered, I am afraid, by almost none of the London community.[25]

This remark suggests again that Nishi's early recall from London rankled with him.

Nishi's wife who as a gracious hostess had sustained her husband's career and shared his enthusiasms died in 1961. We are told by their daughter, Madame Hirahara Kiyoko, who as the wife of Hirahara Tsuyoshi followed in the footsteps of her mother as ambassadress in London from 1982 to 1985, that on her deathbed she had expressed the hope that *Fujinkai* in London would grow and thrive, that is, she was conscious of having laid the foundation of something positive for Japanese residents there.[26]

After his wife's death, Nishi revisited Britain, especially in autumn 1976. At Oxford, he stayed in the home of his old friends from Canberra days, the Storrys. To mark the occasion, Dorothie Storry whom he had met in Japan and accompanied to Izu earlier in the year dedicated a poem to him:

> Old Friend whose youthful spirit I so admire,
> Whose independent spirit has no peer,
> While timeless lives the all-enlivening fire
> Which warms the winter of our later years.
>
> Since first we met afar in southern lands
> A quarter of a century slipped away.
> In Spring by Izu's shores we clasped our hands,
> In Autumn's breezes Oxford's dreamy day
>
> Of spires and domes and softly leafy trees,
> Returns our minds to other happy days.
> Two countries lapped by their historic seas
> Girdle our friendship with their white-edged waves.[27]

As these stanzas confirm, Nishi was recognized as a man of culture. In particular he composed poetry. On 1 April 1957, he wrote a poem for Lord Hankey, one of the stoutest friends of Japan in the prewar and postwar periods, on his eightieth birthday.[28] Again, during one of his trips to Scotland he visited Culloden, the Scottish battlefield where the Duke of Cumberland's armies destroyed the Highland clans. The carnage which they suffered impressed him greatly, because of his Satsuma origins. He was a Satsuma man at heart and reflected on how Japan's new model army of early Meiji times had attacked the samurai of Kagoshima in 1877 and decimated them. He was moved to write a poem in Japanese for the occasion, dedicated again to Lord Hankey:

Lament on the Old Battlefield

I   This ground, that year, the wardrums rolling:
Many moss-covered tablets now,
Clan-names in rows:
Kinsfolk the blade laid low:

Sorrow is endless.
Tears I shed here make me think of my own province.

II [Drumossie moor, Drumossie day,
A waeful day it was to me]
And a bad day for Dai Saigo
On the top of Castle Hill!

This ground, that year,
The pipes skirling:
Now the names of the broken clans in rows!

Those near to me slain:
No end to the sorrow,
[for there I lost my faither dear,
My faither dear, and brethren three]

Laid low by the sword:
There is no end to the sorrow,
[for e'en and morn she cries, Alas!
And aye the saut tear blins her ee.]

Sat at Culloden, my heart is at Shiroyama:
Tears I shed here make me pine for my own province.
(Japanese translated by George Fraser)[29]

Like all men of Satsuma Nishi regarded Saigō Takamori – the Dai Saigō of the
above poem – as one of his clan's great heroes. He was one of the leaders of the
rebellion against the Meiji government in 1877 and, when the remnants of the
retreating Satsuma forces took up their position on the heights of Shiroyama
(Castle Hill) in Kagoshima city, they were slaughtered by the imperial troops. In
this conflict, Saigō met his death, whether by wound or by suicide is not clear.
Nishi was much moved by this incident of 1877 and saw in it a parallel with the
experience of the Scottish clans : Satsuma leaders were reluctant to give up their
local autonomy like the Scots of the '45. Nishi was intensely proud of his
Satsuma connection. One of his major writings in English was on the war
between Britain and Satsuma (*Satsu-Ei sensō*).[30]

Nishi lived on to a ripe old age in an apartment close to the British Embassy
with which he was in frequent contact. He had a respect for British institutions,
including the Foreign Office. He is described as an affable old man, modest and
friendly, always well-informed and independent-minded, frank and ready to
indulge in open discussion.

Nishi died in 1986 at the age of ninety-three, having led an active life as
diplomat, commentator on international affairs and publicist until his dying
days. As a diplomat he had lived a many-sided professional life. His career was
one long 'hard-posting'. His contribution to Anglo-Japanese relations was, as the
Foreign Office remarked, the distinct improvement in the tone of relations. It is
not that he presided over spectacular achievements. But the climate between the
two countries improved markedly and stood his successor in good stead.

NOTES

For generous help with this paper, I am grateful to Eiji Seki.

226   JAPANESE ENVOYS IN BRITAIN

1.   For further details, see Nishi's account in *Kaisō no Nihon gaikō* (Reminiscences of Japanese Diplomacy), Tokyo: Iwanami Shinsho, 1965, pp. 8-10 [Hereafter 'Nishi, *Kaiso*'] and *Waga gaikō to zuisō*, Tokyo: Southern Cross Associates, 1985. Also Nishi Haruhiko, 'Tsuma no omoide' and 'Nomura Yōzō' in *Japan Quarterly* (October 1966).
2.   Nishi, *Kaisō*, p. 183. On the sale of the Chinese Eastern Railway, *Nihon gaikō bunsho*, Showa II, 2-2, Tokyo: Gaimushō, 1998, p. 491 and 'Kita-Man tetsudō', pp. 501-63.
3.   Nishi, *Kaisō*, pp. 148-9.
4.   Alan Rix, *Australia-Japan Political Alignment, 1952 to the present*, London: Routledge, 1999, pp. 11-12. Neville Meaney, *Towards a New Vision: Australia and Japan through 100 years*, Sydney: Kangaroo Press, 1999, p.111.
5.   Nishi, *Kaisō*, pp. 148-9.
6.   Extract from Casey's Diary, 24 May 1957 in *Documents on Australian Foreign Policy*, 'Australia-Japan Agreement on Commerce, 1957', Canberra : Dept of Foreign Affairs and Trade, 1997, doc. 103.
7.   Donald Hellmann, *Japanese Foreign Policy and Domestic Politics: The Peace Agreement with the Soviet Union*, Berkeley: University of California Press, 1969. Mayumi Itoh, *The Hatoyama Dynasty*, Basingstoke: Palgrave, 2003, p. 133ff. Nishi, *Kaisō*, p. 164.
8.   Lees Mayall, *Fireflies in Amber*, Salisbury: Russell, 1989. Nishi, *Kaisō*, p. 164.
9.   Nakakita Koji, *1955-nen taisei no seiritsu*, Tokyo: University Press, 2002, p. 247-51. Itoh, op. cit., pp. 129-30.
10. Robin Gray (ch. 22) and Hanaoka Sosuke (ch. 23) in Ian Nish (ed.), *Britain and Japan: Biographical Portraits*, Vol. II, Richmond: Japan Library, 1997.
11. Japan Society of London, *Bulletin*, No. 20 (1956). [Hereafter 'JSL *Bulletin*'].
12. Tanaka Takahiko in Ian Nish and Yoichi Kibata (eds), *History of Anglo-Japanese Relations, 'The Political-Diplomatic Dimension'*, Vol. 2, 1930-2000, Basingstoke: Palgrave, 2000, pp. 216-17. John Allison, *Ambassador from the Prairies*, Tokyo: Tuttle, 1973, pp. 272-3.
13. *Gaimushō no 100-nen*, Tokyo: Gaimushō, vol. 2, p. 977.
14. Tanaka, op. cit., pp. 218-20.
15. Nishi Haruhiko, *Afurika ryōkō hōkoku*, Tokyo: Gaimushō, 1957. JSL *Bulletin*, 22(1958), 11. See also Nishi, *Kaisō*, pp. 178-80.
16. Dorothie Storry, *Second Country*, Woodchurch: Paul Norbury, 1986, p. 94. JSL *Bulletin*, 22 (1958), 11.
17. Nishi, 'Tsuma no omoide'. *Eikoku Nihon Fujinkai: 40-nen no ayumi*, London: Sato Graphics, 1996, pp. 12-13.
18. Note by Peter Dalton, 30 October 1957 in National Archives, Kew, Foreign Office 371/127587, FJ1905/28. [Hereafter 'NAK, FO'].
19. Note by David Ormsby-Gore, 17 December 1957 in NAK, FO 371/127587, FJ1905/29.
20. Oscar Morland to Daniel Lascelles, 23 October 1957 in NAK, FO 371/127587, FJ1905/25. Nishi, *Kaisō*, p. 181.
21. Nishi, *Kaisō*, pp. 181-4.
22. Nishi Haruhiko, *Watashi no gaikō hakusho*, Tokyo: Bungei Shunju. Nishi, *Kaisō*, pp. 183-8.
23. Sado Akihiro, 'Nishi Haruhiko no onnen' (grudge) in 'Showa no gaikōkan' in *Hosho geppan* (1988), pp.9-11.
24. Nishi, *Kaisō*, p. 200.
25. Retold in JSL *Bulletin*, 25 (1958), p. 7.
26. Hirahara Kiyoko in *Fujinkai: 40-nen*, pp. 15-16. Nishi, *Kaisō*, pp. 200-1.
27. Storry, *Second Country*, p. 183.
28. JSL *Bulletin*, 22(1958). Maurice Hankey, *Politics, Trials and Errors*, Oxford: Pen-in-hand, 1950, pp. 112-13.
29. JSL *Bulletin*, 22 (1958), 10-11. The portion in square brackets comes from the poetry of Robert Burns, which Nishi incorporated in his poem. The remainder was translated from the Japanese by G.S. Fraser.
30. Nishi Haruhiko, 'The Anglo-Satsuma Hostilities' in JS *Bulletin*, 38 (1962), 2 and in *St Antony's Papers*, 'Far Eastern Affairs', London: Chatto, 1962. Charles Yates, *Saigō Takamori*, London: KPI, 1995, pp. 168-70.

24

OHNO KATSUMI, 1905-2006
A Mission to Renew Anglo-Japanese Relations
[London, 1958-64]

Ohno Katsumi

EIJI SEKI

Ambassador Katsumi Ohno left Tokyo on 28 April 1958 and arrived in London on 4 May by British Overseas Airways after visiting New York and Washington. He was imbued with a sharp awareness of his mission. In his own words:

> . . . to defreeze Anglo-Japanese relations and to repair them. If by good fortune the defreezing goes well then to bring into being a new treaty of commerce between the two countries. It would be impossible to bring back the Alliance of 1902 into life, but it was my fervent desire to revive the traditional relations of amity and friendship and to promote commercial and economic relations followed by expanded cultural exchange.[1]

Six years later, he boarded a plane for home satisfied with his accomplished mission, inter alia, the signing of the Anglo-Japanese Commerce, Establishment and Navigation Treaty in 1962. Indeed, he deserved great praise for his achievements. His footprints were not confined to economic and commercial fields but extended to all other areas of the relations between Japan and Britain. At the grand farewell dinner given at Westminster by members of the Anglo-Japanese Parliamentary Union who were from both Houses, he stated in reply:

> My assignment in London consisted of days and evenings of continuous engagements but I really enjoyed it. I now have to leave before I have fully grasped the rules and the joys of cricket. It is an irreplaceably important experience in my life to have come to learn something about the splendid British way of politics thanks to the kindness of all my friends at Westminster.[2]

Katsumi Ohno, fourth son of Seijirō and Fuku Ohno, was born in 1905 in a small town called Kiritappu on the southeast Pacific coast of Hokkaido. Seijirō was a wholesale merchant dealing in marine products but his main interest lay in the research of Buddhism, thus more or less leaving his business to other family members to look after. He was also an accomplished calligrapher known in the academic circles of Kyoto. Katsumi was the youngest of Seijirō's offspring of four boys and one girl. Though they all enjoyed longevity, he in particular was endowed with such superb health that remarkably ensured he never experienced any sickness in adulthood. He was an energetic little boy often coming home without his kimono sleeves lost in tussles with boys of his age.

Finishing his primary and secondary schools in Kiritappu, Katsumi Ohno went to Tokyo to join his brother Shinzō Ohno five years his senior. Shinzō was already studying there at St Paul's University. Katsumi then continued his studies at Kyoto Imperial University where he majored in economics. This led to his good fortune in later years when he was favoured by Prime Minister Hayato Ikeda who was from the same University. Ikeda highly valued Ohno's ability, in particular his flair for economics. He was successful in the diplomatic service entrance examination in 1928 and joined the Ministry of Foreign Affairs (the Gaimushō) upon graduation the following year. He was immediately posted to Berlin and then Hamburg in 1932. In 1930, he married Misako Kikuchi, daughter of Dr Yōzō Kikuchi, physician in Shizuoka. Misako travelled on the Siberian Railway to join him in Berlin. They had their son Kiyoshi in 1933. Their stay in Germany was a happy one.[3] But at that time Japan was experiencing political and social upheaval following the rise of militarism and the 1931 Manchurian Incident, whilst in Germany Hitler succeeded in seizing power in 1933.

DIPLOMATIC SERVICE

Ohno spent his six apprentice years in Germany where Nazism was in the ascendancy. He watched closely the country's political and social turmoil but Nazi ideology and practices failed to endear themselves to him. Back in Japan, he kept his distance from the group of Nazi sympathizers within the diplomatic service. He would not talk nor write about those days. For it was painful to him that Japan got on the bandwagon of the Axis and the Gaimushō failed to forestall the Tripartite Treaty, the root of all the troubles. He tried to avoid the subject of the behaviour of his pro-German colleagues, the so-called *Kakushin-ha* (Reformist Group), in the days of the Alliance with Germany and Italy. It would have been impossible for him to reminisce about those days without referring to the people involved. It seems that his relationship with them in the post-war period was not particularly good. At the same time it appears that he made efforts, especially after he reached the pinnacle of the Gaimushō as Administrative Vice-Minister for Foreign Affairs (equivalent to Permanent Under-Secretary in Britain), to pay more attention to placing former pro-German diplomats in senior positions in order to put their ability to use and keep the Gaimushō unified. Ushiba Nobuhiko (Ambassador to the US, 1970) and Uchida Fujio (Ambassador to West Germany, 1965) were examples of this.

After he returned from Germany in 1935 he held various jobs in the Commercial Bureau of the Gaimushō before he was posted to the US in 1939-40. He returned to the American Affairs Bureau in February 1941. He was with the Embassy at Nanking, China in May 1943 following a brief stay in Burma. In June 1945 he became Private Secretary to Foreign Minister Shigenori Tōgō. Though short, it was the crucial period leading up to the surrender of Japan in August 1945. He had to arrange day-to-day temporary lodgings/hideouts for Tōgō in order to keep him safe from the threat of assassination by the extreme rightists who, in alliance with the hardliners in the Army and Navy, opposed Japan's overtures for peace. He followed Tōgō every night to the pre-arranged secret hiding places taking with him a small packet of rice or hard biscuits and a tin of salmon for the stay overnight.

In an attempt to extricate herself from the hopeless situation in the summer of 1945, Japan misread the true intentions of the Soviet Union despite the notification of abrogation of the Neutrality Pact in May the same year, and other unmistakable indications; she made her last desperate approach to the Communist country supposed to be its traditional arch-enemy. By so doing Japan played 'straight into Stalin's hands, since he found himself in the position of being able to allow the Japanese to continue their wishful thinking for as long as it suited his purpose, which was, if time allowed, to participate in the war and therefore re-establish Russia's position in the Far East lost in 1904'.[4] It was tragic that two precious months had been wasted leading to the annihilation of Hiroshima and Nagasaki by the successive atomic bombs. The same military historian considers that 'since Japan held the mistaken view until 9 August that Russia might be prepared to act as a mediator, it is most probable that her reaction to a declaration issued in June would have been no different from that to the Potsdam Declaration at the end of July'.[5]

Nevertheless, it is still very much a moot point why Foreign Minister Shigenori Tōgō did not first broach the subject of surrender to the United States and Britain when feelers were being put out in the radio messages broadcast by Captain E.M. Zacharias, US Navy which began on V-E Day, 8 May 1945. Some important Japanese including Gaimusho officials were already on air putting out their own feelers to Zacharias, Official Spokesman of the US Government. Additional channels were also available through Sweden and other neutral countries. Ohno threw some light on the issue in his memoirs. From what he saw, he thought that Tōgō may have believed it would be better to seek the mediation of a big power rather than powerless neutrals or the Vatican to bring the global conflict to an end. He also thought that mediation by the Soviet Union would be conducive to harnessing the recalcitrant Army considering that the Japanese Kwantung Army was no longer able to defend Manchuria against the Soviet forces. In addition, Tōgō entertained a sort of wishful thinking towards the Soviet Union in the illusory belief that V. Molotov still held him in the same respect from the days when they worked out an agreement for the termination of the Nomonhan Incident, an armed border clash in which the Japanese army suffered a severe setback from the mechanized Soviet forces in May-September, 1939. It was then widely known in diplomatic circles in Moscow that Molotov admired the logic of Tōgō's arguments and the outstanding tenacity that matched his own. Ohno believed that deep in his heart Tōgō must have been confident that Molotov would respond favourably to his request.[6]

Whilst assisting Ambassador Masayuki Tani in Nanking, Ohno developed a deep respect for Wang Ching-wei, leader of the regime of collaborationist Reformed Kuomintang, and his successor, Chen Kung-po, through his frequent personal contacts with these Chinese leaders. When Japan surrendered, Chen Kung-po and his party of six escaped to the Japanese naval air base at Miho on a Japan China Army air transport on 25 August. It was just in the nick of time before a total ban was imposed by the Allied forces on all Japanese air flights that same day. Though somewhat bewildered on hearing the news, Ohno was of the strong view that, though defeated, Japan should extend whatever help to Chen for as long as circumstances permitted, even at the risk of incurring the censure of the Allied Occupation Forces. Foreign Minister Mamoru Shigemitsu approved without fuss a plan Ohno quickly improvised to give Chen asylum. Shigemitsu said that 'one must protect a hunted bird flying into one's bosom for refuge'.

With the cooperation of the Municipality of Kyoto, Mr and Mrs Chen and their suite were kept in hiding at Kinkakuji (Golden Pavilion Temple) in Kyoto. Thanks to the arrangements made by Ohno, they lived in comfort even in those days of severe shortage. In particular, they were well fed out of the special rations for foreign diplomats made available by the Kyoto Municipality. But it was not long before the Chinese Government of Chiang Kai-shek sniffed out the whereabouts of Chen and his party. The Gaimushō could not ignore the repeated requests from the Chinese Commander-in-Chief He Ying-chin that they be returned to Nanking. The Gaimushō had no alternative but to plead with the Chinese Government for leniency for Chen. But Shigeru Yoshida who succeeded Shigemitsu was not at all enthusiastic at the idea of pleading in his own words for 'the Chinese people's traitor'. Ohno was determined to plead for Chen to the extent of irritating the old man who finally caved in, angrily initialed the draft cable to the Embassy at Nanking and pushed it back to Ohno. Yoshida told him 'I can't agree to what you say but I will let the cable be dispatched since you will never withdraw your arguments and it is of no use continuing talking'. The story is interesting as it indicates not only Ohno's compassionate nature, but his willpower once his mind was set on what he believed right. The wind, however, would not always blow his way. In Yoshida's time quite a few diplomats fell out of his favour and were shunted away to minor posts by the so-called 'Y-Clause Purge'.[7] Ohno was no exception. But eventually Yoshida would restore him to the mainstream.

Chen Kung-po and his followers were flown back to Nanking on 3 October 1945 aboard a Chinese aircraft dispatched by General He. In 1946, he faced a firing squad in Soochou as a traitor to his country. Before his departure from Kyoto, Chen Kung-po wrote Fumimaro Konoe intimating that he could not but be worried about the expansion of Communist power in China; that the US way of dealing with the Communist party was immature and naïve; that they were not aware of the troubles to come; and that in future it would be more desirable for Japan to respect Britain's judgment because of her rich experience in Asia. The tragic fate of Chen always remained a matter of deep sorrow to Ohno.[8]

After Japan forfeited its independence, all the ruling powers were placed under the control of the Supreme Commander of the Allied Forces in September 1945. The Gaimushō inevitably ceased to perform its normal diplomatic functions. It was drastically restructured into a setup the main activity of which was transferred to its subsidiary organization, the Central Liaison Office in charge of liaison activities with the General Headquarters of the Allied Forces. The CLO signboard was larger and more conspicuous than that of the Gaimushō. It well illustrated the unmistakable fact of life in Japan under the Occupation. Care had been taken, however, to preserve diplomatic human resources for the future resumption of national independence. As Ohno learned from West German Deputy Foreign Minister Walter Hallstein when he became Ambassador at Bonn in 1956, the situation was in sharp contrast to the German Foreign Office which had to be rebuilt from scratch when West Germany gained independence. Ohno continued to be promoted in the mainstream during the Occupation.

With the restoration of independence in 1952, he was appointed Chief of the Japanese Mission in the Philippines in October 1953. His assignment there was to promote the negotiations for a reparations agreement with the Philippines in accordance with the wishes of Prime Minister Yoshida. He considered Japan's obligations under Article 14 of the San Francisco Peace Treaty of September 1951 to pay reparations to Asian nations as a means to improve Japan's international status in Asia. It was a reinterpretation of the nature of the obligation from the punitive to the positive. He believed it would now provide diplomatic opportunities. Ohno was the right man for the job in view of the expertise on reparations issues he had already accumulated in his first post as Chief of Reparations Division of the Gaimushō.[9] The appointment was evidence of Yoshida's keen interest in the negotiations. At that time, the negotiations were not progressing as desired.

In January 1954, Ohno threw himself energetically into preliminary negotiations with Vice President and concurrently Foreign Affairs Secretary Carlos Garcia. They managed to produce a joint Memorandum setting forth the framework of an eventual reparations agreement. The Ohno-Garcia Memorandum could not survive in its original form and substance as it was sucked into the political tug of war in the Philippines, but it helped start the ball rolling towards the conclusion of the final agreement in May 1956 by which time Ohno had moved on to Austria. Years later Ohno confided to Masamichi Hanabusa (Ambassador to Italy, 1993), his son-in-law, that he put his heart and soul into the negotiations, and that he had learned the lesson that the outcome of diplomatic negotiations should not be a clear-cut victory for one side alone.[10]

LONDON ENVOY

After a short tenure at Bonn following Vienna, Ohno was placed in the post of Vice-Minister for Foreign Affairs from January 1957 till March 1958, when he was appointed Ambassador to Britain. However, the path to London was somewhat rocky. The recall of his predecessor, Ambassador Haruhiko Nishi, was made with no successor in sight. The gap this created gave rise to a situation embarrassing to both governments. Substantiated and unsubstantiated rumours concerning the names of candidates and the interventions by politicians were rife in the press. In particular premature leakages to the press of the names of would-be appointees upset the British Foreign Office. As Ohno told Ambassador Lascelles, in the end he was asked by Prime Minister Nobusuke Kishi himself to go to London.[11]

In those days, the atmosphere in Whitehall was anything but kind to Ohno's application. He was considered to have 'not always been helpful' while he was Vice-Minister. His relationship with Ambassador Dening and then Ambassador Lascelles had been difficult – even acrimonious at times. When Lascelles was summoned to the *Kayū-Kaikan* (the social club for Gaimushō staff) to hear Ohno's explanations concerning the question of Japanese ships to Indonesia, Ohno told Lascelles that he loved all the British except his 'abominable predecessor![12] So it was not a pleasant occasion for either side. Undoubtedly, the situation coloured the atmosphere in London making the Foreign Office rather reluctant to give an immediate answer to the Japanese request for the agrément for Ohno made on 21 February 1958. It was Lascelles' sound and wise advice that helped avert a tricky situation when he endorsed the Foreign Office's assessment by saying that 'our case against the person named is not sufficient to justify withholding agrément; though in view of bad leakage a delay of some weeks in replying to the Chargé d'Affaires would, I think, have a salutary effect on the Japanese authorities.'[13] The agrément was given on 12 March.

The whole episode can possibly be explained as a personality clash between Ohno and the British ambassadors, Dening in particular. Both were strong characters and tended not to mince their words in expressing their views. Naturally, stand-offs are not always easy to avoid in such cases. To make the matter worse, the relations between their two governments in 1957 remained at a low level. In September the same year, W. Harpham in charge of the embassy reported 'Our relations with Japan, though friendly, are lacking in warmth. There are many reasons for this: geographical distance, language, the feeling created by the war, Lancashire's obsession with "unfair" competition, Suez and the agitation over nuclear weapons.'[14] The British Embassy Annual Review for 1958 repeated that the relations 'were superficially better than in the previous year, but they remained somewhat tepid and there is little of major importance to record'.[15]

It ought to be borne in mind that in those difficult circumstances both Dening and Ohno had to consider and follow the positions of their respective Governments and the feelings of the people they represented. Most British still felt bitter about the unjustified and brutal treatment of POWs during the war. They were not yet prepared to let bygones be bygones. But the severity of the anti-Japanese feeling in Britain was often lost on the Japanese. With the lapse of time and more confidence regained through their remarkable economic expansion, they were tempted to be oblivious to the fact that many countries still did not feel strong ties with their country as pointed out by Dening in his lecture at the Imperial College in London.[16] Both British and Japanese governments lamented the lack of interest in each other.[17]

When they were together in London, however, Ohno and Dening (now in retirement) buried the hatchet leaving all their unpleasant memories behind so that they could work together for the common cause of promoting Anglo-Japanese relations. At the joint reception welcoming Prime Minister Ikeda on 14 November 1962, Dening paid 'tribute to the wonderful contribution which His Excellency Ohno, ably assisted by Madame Ohno, has made during the past four and a half years to the strengthening of the ties which bind our two countries – so we owe them a great deal'.[18] Those sentiments were not confined to Dening alone but were shared by many British people. Ohno's continuous hard work and all his achievements had been finally recognized and his reputation as an able and effective Ambassador was now commonly accepted in Britain. It is officially on record that Ohno 'has done well.'[19]

The Kishi Cabinet's foreign policy was directed to strengthening Japan's relations with major European powers. With Britain in particular there was an urgent need to conclude a treaty of commerce and navigation to rectify the anomalous situation brought about by Britain's invocation of Article 35 of the General Agreement on Tariffs and Trade (GATT) nearly six months before Japan's entry into the organization in September 1955. Being denied most favoured nation treatment, Japan had to endure disadvantages in international commercial dealings not only with Britain but also with the sterling bloc countries. In the 1950s and early 60s, the enthusiasm with which Japan grappled with the trade barriers symbolized by Article 35 was intense, almost a reminder of the days of national aspiration for the revision of the unequal treaties in the Meiji era.

In October 1955, the British Embassy at Tokyo presented to the Gaimushō the British draft of the Treaty of Commerce, Establishment and Navigation together with its related protocols and revealed its wish to exchange opinions on the draft. The Gaimushō quickly responded to the move and a preparatory but extensive exchange of views took place between the two sides. Both governments decided to keep these diplomatic demarches secret for the time being in view of their delicate nature.[20] The discussions, however, progressed far enough for two Gaimushō officials to be sent to London in May 1956 to assist the embassy in fully-fledged negotiations for the conclusion of the Treaty that started in the following month but took six more years to finish.

When Ohno arrived in London in May 1958, the negotiations had not yet passed the midway mark. Anglo-Japanese relations had barely recovered from the low ebb of 1945. Wondering what Japan would be like in the hour of her defeat, D. MacDermot, Acting Consul General at Manila, had left for Japan aboard HMS *Whelp*, the first British ship to enter Yokohama since 1942. As the first British government representative to set foot on Japan after the war, he landed at Yokohama on 1 September, the day before the surrender at Tokyo bay. He reported 'the only living things in the harbour were themselves and an American hospital ship.' He went ashore with caution, suspicion and harsh feeling against the Japanese, armed with a gigantic revolver and attended by a bodyguard of Royal Navy Commanders, similarly armed.[21] Thus began post-war Anglo-Japanese contacts auguring ill for many years to come. At the time of the San Francisco Peace Treaty, the official British attitude was still 'cold and suspicious'.[22] Deep-rooted British suspicions of Japan's pre-war unfair trade practices and wartime brutality made it difficult for the British people to accord Japan entry to the comity of nations. Japan continued only to be a sad but scenically beautiful country as Ian Nish described in 1946.[23] Such a state of affairs existed right up to the time when Ambassador Ohno arrived in London.

Ohno found the air in Britain was far from friendly with the main cinema in Leicester Square boasting a full house for months on end showing a film entitled 'Knights of Bushido' depicting nauseating scenes involving Japanese soldiers. The bookshops were stacked with books of stories of horrendous barbarity committed by the Japanese. A Japanese businessman who went to see the movie out of curiosity was spotted by young men and thoroughly roughed up. Many Japanese residents experienced open protestations of anti-Japanese feeling in different ways.[24] Undaunted Ohno lost no time before he channelled all his energy into the hard task of helping ameliorate the situation. He was fully aware that there could be no return to the days of the Anglo-Japanese Alliance but he was determined to improve the overall environment and to make it conducive to the successful conclusion of the Commerce and Navigation Treaty as a cornerstone for the future relations between the two countries.

As the first and surest way he was determined to try to make as many friends as possible, taking advantage of every opportunity that might come his way. For that he opened wide the doors of his residence at Kensington Palace Gardens (KPG). He never missed a chance to accept all the invitations that came his way. He was meticulously careful in selecting guests to KPG bearing in mind their backgrounds, predilections, their mutual relationships and all the other factors that would make dinners and luncheons a success. He enjoyed meeting people and learning something about his host country on occasions such as the annual dinners of the various trading Guilds. The more outgoing he and Misako became, the more the invitations started to arrive. Ohno always accepted invitations to any events organized by British government departments, even ones for other countries such as trade fairs. He was found right there greeting the Minister or senior officials in charge. In fact, Ohno's social activities were phenomenal in frequency and intensity.[25] He could bear the physical and mental pressure arising from such activity solely because he was blessed with excellent health. Once one Japanese newspaper described him as an achiever (*shigoto-shi*) who works twenty-five hours without knowing fatigue and tired-ness.[26]

'They entertained regularly several times a week at KPG, all catering for luncheons and dinners being prepared by Madame Prunier of Maison Prunier in St. James's Street. They personally would choose from two or three sample menus. Most invitations to his carefully selected guests often in consultation with his staff were extended by a letter bearing his signature. Ohno was a prolific letter writer. The Ohnos had many friends throughout the UK and he wrote regularly to most of them – and received replies – to which a follow-up letter would invariably be sent. Ohno worked extremely hard at establishing relations between Japan and the UK by forming friendships and working relationships with many members of the Foreign Office, other government departments, as well as with leading businessmen, academics and others. Letters were on file signed by Winston Churchill, Anthony Eden and politicians.'[27]

Among the many British friends he acquired, his friendship with Sir Alec Douglas-Home was the most fruitful. Indeed, it was extremely good luck for him to have Home at the helm of the Foreign Office and 10 Downing Street for the majority of his time in London. The admiration and respect in which he held Home was genuine and deep. This is known by the fact that in retirement Ohno translated Home's book *Letters to Grandson* into Japanese in 1984. In the foreword for the Japanese edition, he praised Lord Home stating that he renewed his respect for Home's great personality and views and that he could feel the British statesman's strong will and self-reliance. He also commented that Home's chapters which set out a powerful apologia for the truer understanding and fairer assessment of Prime Minister Neville Chamberlain were very touching. Ohno was always grateful to Home for the immeasurable under-standing and assistance constantly extended to him in their joint efforts to improve the relations between their two countries:

> Mr Ohno was always very conscious of the convenience of his guests. Therefore a Buffet Supper for the Anglo-Japanese Parliamentary Group (later known as the British-Japanese Parliamentary Group) was held at the Savoy Hotel, it being closer to the Houses of Parliament. Receptions were held at various venues – KPG was not so accommodating of larger groups of people, although The Emperor's Birthday Reception was always held there, under an enormous marquee in the garden. When the Ohnos were not entertaining at home, they were invariably being entertained by their friends and colleagues. They were very sociable, both together and separately. They were both very well liked and respected by their British friends and colleagues including those in government circles. There was genuine regret amongst their British friends when they departed for Japan.[28]

Press and mass media was another important area Ohno tried hard to cultivate. He wanted to improve the image of Japan's trade and industry by providing more up-to-date information to the British media. He was looking for a suitable personality to manage an institute to improve Japan's image in the UK. The idea was definitely launched by Ohno himself. Moriyuki Motono (Ambassador to France, 1984) who was on his staff, and his close friend George Bull, then an editor of the *Financial Times*, introduced Reginald Cudlipp to Ohno. He was editor of the *News of the World* from 1953 to 1959 and belonged to the legendary family triumvirate which dominated Fleet Street newspapers in the 1950s. Ohno asked him to accept the task of Director of the newly established Anglo-Japanese Economic Institute (AJEI).

One of the immediate tasks for Yoshio Ōkawa, Second Secretary, Commercial (Ambassador to Canada, 1985) who arrived in London in mid-August 1961 was to look after the incipient Anglo-Japanese Economic Institute under the directorship of Reginald Cudlipp who had just accepted the appointment. Ōkawa took over the work from his predecessor Motono. The AJEI played an enormous role in presenting a convincing picture of Japan's economy and trade which were undergoing great changes after the war, thus paving the way to a better understanding between the two countries.[29] Cudlipp worked hard exercising all his journalistic expertise at the AJEI, but the last thing he wanted was to be regarded with any suspicion because he was in the pay of the Japanese Government. In fact, the British Foreign Office came to consider the role played by the AJEI as useful to Britain as well as to the Japanese.[30]

The main thrust of Ohno's diplomatic endeavours was directed towards exposing the Members of Parliament and the British government to the changes taking place in Japan in all spheres since the end of the war. Ohno believed this was an important step in improving Anglo-Japanese relations though he was realistic enough to know that the wounds wrought by the war were too deep to heal. An outstanding and successful example of this line of approach was the visit to Japan in 1961 by Sir Norman Kipping, Chairman of the Federation of British Industries. Fortunately, things were improving. During 1960-61 the consensus was emerging between the British Government and the Federation of British Industries that 'some revision of Anglo-Japanese trading relations must be foreseen. The discrimination exercised by the UK and some other European countries against Japan could not, it was felt, continue indefinitely: but its termination must be met by Japan with a reciprocal liberality, leading to a growth of two-way trade between the two countries.'[31] In close consultation with Reginald Maudling, then President of the Board of Trade, and Taizō Ishizaka, Chairman of the Federation of Economic Organizations of Japan, Ohno carefully prepared the ground for a visit to Japan by Sir Norman and J.R. M. Whitehorn in October the same year.

The report of the visit entitled 'A Look At Japan', written after the in-depth studies of Japanese industries, was hugely instrumental in transforming the images of Japan held by British industry. It helped improve enormously the environment for the conclusion of the Commerce & Navigation Treaty. Ohno himself was impressed by British fairness as represented in the Kipping Report. The Treaty was finally signed by the Earl of Home, K.T., Principal Secretary of State for Foreign Affairs, and Frederick James Erroll, M.P., President of the Board of Trade, and Ohno at Lancaster House in London on 11 November 1962, in the presence of Prime Minister Harold Macmillan and Prime Minister Hayato Ikeda. Because of his own close interest in the Treaty, James Erroll became a co-signatory, the negotiations having been carried out by the Board of Trade.[32] The

Japanese Parliament approved the Treaty on 29 March 1963. The treaty came
into force on 4 May.

PERSONAL

Ohno was an avid reader and his brain was constantly seething with fresh ideas.
At the same time, he was a man of action. Yutaka Nomura (Ambassador to
Sweden, 1985), on Ohno's staff in 1962-65, says that Ohno was considered the
prime power in rebuilding the Gaimushō in those difficult years following the
Peace Treaty. His strong leadership was felt throughout the Gaimushō and well
recognised even before he became Vice-Minister. The vast number of drafts and
papers he produced was legendary requiring his fountain pen to be refilled
several times a day. His main efforts were directed towards achieving a unified
approach in diplomacy, with the Gaimushō as the sole channel, so that national
interests would not be disrupted by petty rivalries and ambitions.[33] He had
strong views and did not mince his words. He was an awe-inspiring figure. But
he was a gentleman of integrity, diligence and fairness. Furthermore, Ohno was
meticulous when amending or correcting the papers submitted for his signature.
When he was Vice-Minister, there were some Division Chiefs who would be
nervous about entering Ohno's suite to obtain his signature. Motono, then his
Personal Assistant, often had to advise and help smooth their way.[34] Certainly,
he gave the impression of being a stern disciplinarian. At the same time he was
strict with himself. In London it was also usual for his staff to become tense
before approaching his desk.[35] He used to exhort his embassy staff to improve
their English in their spare time instead of playing cards or mahjong.[36] Indeed,
he took every chance to train his staff. Sometimes it was in the form of relaxed
and casual talks over drinks at his residence after he had initialled the cables
brought in by the staff. These talks were thought-provoking and often valuable
for their future careers.[37]

At the same time, however, shafts of definite warmth and kindness shone
through the crust of hardness and he would often respond to the greetings of
junior staff in the embassy corridors. Ohno was generous with his own money
but strict with public funds as expected of any public servant.[38] Indeed, in the
common Japanese way of characterization, he was of the 'soft inside but hard
outside' school. To Ōkawa Ohno was 'a great and very senior and prestigious
officer in the service' and indeed remained 'a venerable ambassador'; he recalls:

> . . . entering his office at the Embassy alone needed a certain amount of
> courage, but I have no recollection of being scolded or reprimanded. He
> would quietly listen to what I had to say and then give his own views and
> the most appropriate advice. I was impressed by the way he would go up
> the staircase two steps at a time and never use the lift. His vitality was
> contagious, so to speak, and at the same time he was broadminded and
> willing to listen to views of his younger colleagues.

Ōkawa also remembers being summoned to his office one day and told to
represent the embassy at an economic officers' meeting at Nairobi. When he
went into the ambassador's office to take leave, Ohno took a small bottle of
antidiarrhoeal pills out of his desk drawer and handed it to him telling him to be
careful during the African trip. Ohno knew he was far from robust. Deeply
touched, Ōkawa accepted this little gift with gratitude. The kind gesture remains
in his mind to this day.[39]

At the invitation of Lord Home, Ohno visited Castlemains in Lanarkshire accompanying Foreign Minister Masayoshi Ōhira who flew in to Renfrew from Copenhagen on 3 September 1963 for the first Anglo-Japanese annual ministerial meeting. After official talks in the afternoon and after dinner, they were invited to the grouse shoot and a picnic on the moors the following morning. Ohno was dressed in a full British shooting outfit for the occasion. It was a little known secret that he had taken shooting lessons beforehand. The result was that he was the only Japanese who had any success. Again, this episode casts some light on Ohno's meticulous personality. Nothing was left to chance. He was always faithful to basics. Certainly it was one of the important elements that helped him to achieve so much in his career. Ohno would relish his unique experience of the shoot at Castlemains and naturally it often found its way into the casual talks he had with his staff over drinks.

Prime ministers or foreign ministers for that matter immediately recognized the qualities Ohno possessed and kept him in major posts. Ohno enjoyed the trust of Mamoru Shigemitsu, Shigeru Yoshida, Nobusuke Kishi, Hayato Ikeda, Masayoshi Ōhira and others. Though he often became *persona non grata* to Yoshida, Ohno respected the old man for his leadership in the rebuilding of Japan after the defeat. When he retired, Yoshida used to pop into Ohno's office for a chat when Ohno was Vice-Minister. His admiration of Yoshida could be attested by the large number of pages he allotted to Yoshida in the very first part of his memoirs. Yoshida twice visited London during Ohno's tenure. Ohno was very close to Ikeda too, as already mentioned. There was also a firm relationship of mutual trust between Ohno and Kishi.[40]

He was helped hugely by Misako who was truly gentle, kindhearted, sociable and charming. She offset her husband admirably. He was strict with his children but he used to help them learn German in Vienna and English in London. He did not hesitate to spend his own money when it was necessary to perform his job properly. He was always proud of himself as a diplomat. He was careful about how to dress and eat as suited his profession. He demanded the same of his family. He never neglected replying to letters received. He was a typically traditional diplomat. He often took his family out for a drive at weekends and holidays. He was serious about anything that interested him. Before he went to an opera, he read the story and told it to his family. He truly felt at home in Britain. Undoubtedly, he and his family enjoyed their life more in London than in any other post.[41] Ohno retired from the Gaimushō in 1964 after leaving Britain.

In his retirement his inexhaustible energy and interest in life knew no diminution. He became Vice President of the Arabian Oil Company in 1967 and President of the Imperial Hotel in 1972. It was in the latter capacity that Ohno was very much in the forefront of the warm welcome extended to the Queen and Prince Philip at the time of their visit to Japan in 1975. His continued intense interest in diplomacy and foreign affairs was shown by his assuming in 1975 the chairmanship of the Japan Institute of International Affairs. Throughout his retirement he never ceased to hold Anglo-Japanese friendship close to his heart and was always ready to correct skin-deep or mistaken conceptions of the British way of life, whether political, economic, social or cultural. He never missed any chance to speak up for the importance of Anglo-Japanese relations. In his view it was most essential for preserving the peace and prosperity of Japan.

Anglo-Japanese relations have undergone positive changes from the days when Ohno was at such pains to foster a friendlier atmosphere. Britain and Japan are now in a much closer relationship. Contacts between British and Japanese people are much wider in every sense. Mutual understanding has improved though scars from the War still remain. The prospect, however, is bright when one looks at the growing contacts between the younger generations of the two countries. These contacts are now more penetrative and encompassing. Hopefully, they are ushering in an entirely new phase in the relations free from cultural, racial and historical impediments. Ohno was one of the most active participants in laying the foundations for all these developments. In that sense he achieved a lot. He deserves to be remembered as one of the most remarkable ambassadors in the post-war diplomatic history of Japan. As early as 1948, Ohno was, along with eight others in the Gaimushō including Katsuo Okazaki (Foreign Minister, 1952), among the three hundred future leaders of Japan selected from all walks of life by a group of *Asahi* newspaper reporters. He was considered to have the makings, though rough-hewn as yet, of being a big force in the future: toughness with which to bounce back out of difficulties, diligence for self-improvement, clever talking, gift for politics, attention and care for his younger staff, etc.[42] There is no doubt that Ohno fulfilled their prophecy.

NOTES

1. Katsumi Ohno, *Diplomacy at Kasumigaseki, Its Tradition and People*, Tokyo, Nippon Keizai Shimbun, 1978, p. 149.
2. Ibid., p. 110.
3. Masamichi Hanabusa, *Interviews & Written Recollections*, August 2005.
4. S. Woodburn Kirby, *The War Against Japan*, Vol. V, p. 435.
5. Ibid.
6. Ohno, op. cit., pp. 66-7.
7. Ibid., pp. 2-3. Coined by the Gaimushō staff to mean being relegated to minor posts by incurring displeasure of Foreign Minister Yoshida. They took their cue from GHQ's purge of military officers, politicians, business and mass media leaders from public life as provided in Clause G of the Supreme Commander of Allied Powers (SCAP) directives of 4 January 1946.
8. Ibid., pp. 71-99.
9. Yohko Yoshikawa, *A Study of the Japan-Philippines Diplomatic Negotiations on Reparations 1949-56*, Keiso Shobo 1991, pp.129-30.
10. Hanabusa, op. cit.
11. Ohno, 'Talk to Oxford University United Nations Association on Anglo-Japanese Relations in Retrospect and Prospect', Japan Society of London *Bulletin* 42 (February 1964) p. 21.
     Also Ambassador Lascelles reported to Foreign Office on 21 February 1958 that Ohno informed him 'on instructions from his Prime Minister (sic, not Foreign Minister)' that 'agrément for himself was about to be sought by Japanese Chargé d'Affaires In London.' Actually, the step for the agrément was taken the very same day. TNA:PRO F0371/133644.
12. Lascelles to Morland, 30 December 1957, TNA:PRO F0371/133578.
13. Lascelles to Foreign Office, 24 February 1958, TNA:PRO F0371/133644.
14. Harpham to Lloyd, 10 September 1957, TNA:PRO FO371/127523.
15. *Annual Review for 1958*, 12 March 1959, TNA:PRO FO371/141415, p. 9.
16. Esler Dening, Lecture at the Imperial College in London, 28 June 1957 in which he said 'It cannot be said, beyond the superficialities uttered by statesmen in the course of exchange visits which have become so fashionable nowadays, that any country feels any particularly strong ties with Japan. The one exception is the United States where however it is probably true to say the tie is one of policy rather than of sentiment'. TNA:PRO F0371/127521.
17. Selby to Dening, 7 June 1957, TNA:PRO FO371/127521. 'Nothing has occurred in the last few weeks to improve Anglo-Japanese relations, which have continued to deteriorate, at least in

outward appearance. Mr Kishi's Government shows no sign of being at all interested in them.'
18. Japan Society of London, *Bulletin* 39 (February 1963) p. 24.
19. Foreign Office paper, TNA:PRO FO371/176049.
20. The Gaimusho Diplomatic Record Office, 27 October 1955, Nichiei-Tsūshō-Kyojū-Kōkai-Jōyaku-Ikken, 12 Vol. 1/B'0095/2148.
21. Memorandum of D. MacDermot, 26 September 1945, F0371/46430
22. Edited and Compiled by Hugh Cortazzi, *British Envoys in Japan, 1859-1972*, p. xviii.
23. Ibid., p. 34.
24. Ohno, op. cit., p. 102. Also Hanabusa, op. cit.
25. Moriyuki Motono, Interviews, September 2005.
26. The Asahi newspapers, 4 April 1954.
27. Elizabeth Wright, Secretary to Ambassador Ohno in June 1963-April 1964 period, Written Recollections, July 2005.
28. Ibid.
29. Yoshio Ōkawa, Written Recollections, August 2005.
30. De la Mare to Tokyo, Cable No. 190, TNA:PRO FO 371/164996.
31. Federation of British Industries, '*A look at JAPAN*', Report of visit made by Sir Norman Kipping and Mr J.R.M. Whitehorn, October 1961, p. 1.
32. A. J. de la Mare, Memo recommending the Secretary of State invite the President of the Board of Trade to join with him in signing the Treaty, 25 October 1962, TNA:PRO FO371/165003.
33. Yutaka Nomura, Written Recollections, 15 September 2005.
34. Moriyuki Motono, *Oral History*, National Graduate Institute for Policy Studies, May 1999, p. 58.
35. Ōkawa, op. cit.
36. Masataka Ōkura, *Nippon Keizai Shinbun*, 8 June 1988, Morning Edition.
37. Nomura, op. cit.
38. Susumu Yamagishi, Interviews, August 2005.
39. Ōkawa, op. cit.
40. Motono, op. cit., p. 59.
41. Hanabusa, op. cit.
42. Group of Political/Economic Reporters, *Nihonwo-Ugokasu-Sanbyakunin*, Nyūsu-sha, October 1948, pp. 153-4.

Appendix I

List of Ministers / Ambassadors with Dates

MINISTERS

[Sameshima Naonobu]

Terashima Munenori, 1872-4

Ueno Kagenori, 1874-9

Mori Arinori, 1879-84

Kawase Munetada, 1884-93

Aoki Shūzō, 1894

Katō Takaaki, 1895-9

Hayashi Tadasu, 1900-5

AMBASSADORS

Hayashi Tadasu, 1905-6

Komura Jutarō, 1906-8

Katō Takaaki, 1908-12

Inouye Katsunosuke, 1913-16

Chinda Sutemi, 1916-20

Hayashi Gonsuke, 1920-5

Matsui Keishirō, 1925-8

Matsudaira Tsuneo, 1929-35

Yoshida Shigeru, 1936-8

Shigemitsu Mamoru, 1938-41

Asakai Kōichirō in charge of liaison office 1951-2; minister 1952-3

Matsumoto Shunichi, 1952-5

Nishi Haruhiko, 1955-7

Ohno Katsumi, 1958-64

LATER AMBASSADORS

Shima Shigenobu, 1964-8

Yūkawa Morio, 1968-72

Mori Haruki, 1972-5

Katō Tadao, 1975-9

Fujiyama Naraichi, 1979-82

Hirahara Tsuyoshi, 1982-5

Yamazaki Toshio, 1985-8

Chiba Kazuo, 1988-91

Kitamura Hiroshi, 1991-4

Fujii Hiroaki, 1994-7

Hayashi Sadayuki, 1997-2001

Orita Masaki, 2001-04

Nogami Yoshiji, 2004-

Appendix II

A Concise History of Japan's Ministry of Foreign Affairs

EDITOR'S NOTE: It is important to set the biographical portraits of Japan's diplomats in the context of the Foreign Ministry in Tokyo. The envoys were appointed by it, instructed by it, reported to it and were ultimately recalled by it. Just as they seemed to be in a state of perpetual flux, the institution to which they were responsible was also undergoing changes as Japan moved from being a post-feudal society to being a modern one.

The Dajōkan (or Supreme Council of State) presided over government institutions from the Meiji restoration until the formation of a Cabinet-type government in 1885. The ordinance governing the Foreign Ministry was first issued in 1868 and was revised every year in the early post-Restoration period. From that time Japan had a Gaimukyo (Foreign Minister). Only in 1885 did the present titles of Gaimushō (Foreign Ministry) and Gaimu Daijin (Foreign Minister) come into use. In this period of a quarter-century the Foreign Ministers enjoyed high status, since they had generally played some role in the civil war or the imperial restoration that followed it. In a way, many of them were statesmen and enjoyed a prestige second only to the Prime Ministers of the day. In some cases they possessed an exceptional knowledge of foreign countries by virtue of having travelled abroad. Of the early Foreign Ministers the following had visited overseas before taking up office: Inoue Kaoru; Saionji Kimmochi; Mutsu Munemitsu; Enomoto Takeaki; and Aoki Shūzō. Certainly the Ministry had prestige, and it attracted men of drive, ambition and talent, many of whom were to become Prime Ministers later in their careers – like Katō Takaaki, Prime Minister from 1924 to 1926, and Hara Takashi (Kei), Prime Minister from 1917 to 1921.

Under the Meiji constitution of 1889 the authority for foreign affairs was designated as one of the supreme powers of the Emperor. This gave the Foreign Minister a relatively independent position. In practice, however, he acted in consultation with the Cabinets of the day who accepted joint responsibility for foreign policy.

The organization in Tokyo was on a small scale at this stage. But business was still limited and depended on the personal wishes of the Minister. By 1873 there were nine overseas legations in existence. They were located in Great Britain, the United States, France, Germany, Austria, Holland, Russia, China and Korea. There was a shortage of qualified people to fill these posts and the incumbents were sometimes very young. Thus, in 1879 Mori Arinori was appointed minister in London at the age of thirty-two, having previously held the post of envoy in

Washington at the age of twenty-three.

Recruitment to the Foreign Ministry seems to have been haphazard and personal. Much depended on the patronage of the Meiji oligarchs who were the rulers of the country. They would take on, or recommend, a promising youngster as an official; and he would tend to move round the ministries following his master. Part of that patronage depended on clan influence; and some former *daimyō* were appointed as diplomats overseas. But it was also possible for young aspirants to enter the school set up by the Foreign Ministry; and entry to the profession was by no means confined to those from aristocratic families. There are cases also of older persons entering the foreign service from the ranks of journalists and merchants.

Japan was ready to learn what it could from foreign advisers. The Foreign Ministry was no exception to this. The earliest of its advisers (from 1871 to 1880) was E. P. Smith, a graduate of Columbia and Harvard. The next was Henry Willard Denison (from 1880 to 1914). Born in Vermont in 1846, he became legal adviser to the Foreign Ministry at the comparatively early age of thirty-four. He continued in the service of the Ministry until his death at the age of sixty-eight and received the highest Japanese honours for his service. He had an influence on two young officials in particular: Ishii Kikujirō and Shidehara Kijūrō. The latter was particularly close to Denison who taught him English style as well as diplomatic method and practice. Denison so effectively won the confidence of the Japanese diplomats that they allowed him a major role in the drawing up of documents and sometimes a voice in negotiations, as is alleged to have happened during the Portsmouth peace negotiations in 1905.

Among foreign employees in Japanese government service (*o-yatoi-gaijin*) Denison was not unique. Especially at the time when the law codes were being modernized in preparation for the revision of the treaties there were many legal advisers around, such as Gustave Boissonade and Sir Francis Piggott. But Denison out-served them all, and had special qualities that endeared him to the Japanese. He influenced a generation of officials and had a hand in drawing up most of Japan's treaties in these times. In an age when the language of diplomacy was increasingly becoming the language of the telegraph – English – Denison was an invaluable expert to have attached to the Ministry.

The policies in the early Meiji period, though important enough, were on a modest scale. Important business tended to be conducted in Tokyo rather than in legations abroad. The most conspicuous issue was that of Treaty Revision, which was initially settled with the signing of the Anglo-Japanese commercial treaty of 1894. In general, the spirit of the day that was reflected in the Foreign Ministry was that of '*Datsu-A nyū-Ō*', an expression that implies turning the back on things Asian and welcoming things European or Western. This goes some way towards accounting for the remarkably internationalist attitude adopted by most Japanese leaders very soon after they had taken their country into the modern world.

1894 to 1913

Great strides were taken during this period towards the modernization and rationalization of the Foreign Ministry. Its buildings were improved, though they were not reconstructed until after the damage sustained in the Great Kantō Earthquake of 1923. The Foreign Ministers tended to be drawn from among professional diplomats. As the Diet had come into being under the constitution, politicians lacked the foreign experience of their predecessors and were less well qualified to act. The Prime Ministers on election called on one of their representatives overseas to become Foreign Minister. This meant that there was little doubt about his subordination to the Premier and the Cabinet when it came to policy-making. On the other hand, policies were often influenced by and sometimes altered by the elder statesmen (*genrō*) – a group that had guided the nation's affairs in the 1870s and whose members were able, by virtue of being consulted by the emperor on an extra-constitutional basis, to express their views and often to carry the day. Important instances of their interventions are to be found in the negotiations of the British alliance in 1901 and in the run-up to the outbreak of the Russo-Japanese war in 1904.

Within the Gaimushō a political affairs bureau and commercial affairs bureau were created to cope with the increasing flow of business. The vital change abroad came in 1906 at the end of the successful Russo-Japanese war, when Japanese legations were raised to embassies in London, Washington, Paris, Berlin, Vienna, Rome and St Petersburg. The appointment of ambassadors was important to the Japanese for prestige reasons and had been considered so for many years. Minister Aoki proposed as early as 1893 that Japan should start appointing ambassadors to European courts. When he again became Foreign Minister, he proposed in 1898 the appointment of six ambassadors to coincide with the settlement of Treaty Revision, arguing that 'The prestige of our country is somewhat lessened as a great power in diplomacy. In other words, Japan is regarded in diplomacy as a second-rate country among the powers. Among countries with populations of more than thirty millions, only Japan and China do not yet exchange ambassadors.' But for technical reasons the matter was allowed by his Cabinet colleagues to rest.

With the greater role, both political and commercial, that Japan was playing in the world, it was necessary for the Foreign Ministry in 1894 to begin special training arrangements for both diplomatic and consular recruits. Until then appointments had been in the main personal. The Japanese had introduced qualifying entrance examinations for the civil service in the 1880s. In 1894 the same principle was extended to the foreign service. The intake was initially small but included some of the great names in the service later on. Thus Shidehara Kijūrō passed the examinations in 1896, Matsuoka Yōsuke in 1904 and Satō Naotake in the following year, Hirota Kōki and Yoshida Shigeru passed together in 1906 and Arita Hachirō in 1909. All of these were to become Foreign Ministers in the critical decade after the Manchurian crisis, except Yoshida, who became Foreign Minister only in 1945 and Prime Minister in later years. There seems to be little doubt that the examination system and the testing methods worked well and ensured an intake of high calibre.

Great pains were taken over the systematic admission and training of the new officials for the foreign service. The prime object was to create one service covering both bureaucrats in the Tokyo office itself and diplomats overseas, who were to become naturally interchangeable. The scheme for legation and consular officials laid down that recruitment should be by special examination, which should be separate from the ordinary civil service examination. These examinations should test the candidates' knowledge of foreign languages, especially English, French and German, and of such academic subjects as the constitution, administrative and international law, economics, finance and diplomatic history. Examinations of a lower standard would be set for those wishing to qualify for special language training as translators and interpreters and for clerkships. The intention underlying this system of recruitment was to prevent the country's diplomacy being monopolized by clan influences on the one hand and by the new academic influences (*gakubatsu*) of Tokyo Imperial University, founded in 1886, on the other. In general, it succeeded in the first of these objectives but failed to exclude the influence of Tokyo University. At a personal level, the Foreign Ministry hoped that the examination system would ignore the native place and the *alma mater* of the applicant but insisted that he should possess above average intelligence and knowledge of foreign languages.

These reforms of 1894 have held good ever since. There have of course been changes of procedure. Thus in 1918, at a time of large-scale recruitment into the foreign service, the special examinations for diplomatic and consular officers were absorbed into the general structure and it became necessary for candidates for the foreign service to take the ordinary higher civil service examinations, together with special tests to meet the needs of the Ministry. But the spirit of the reforms has been accepted. Under them, fifty-three candidates entered the Ministry between 1894 and 1903, seventy-four between 1903 and 1917, and 121 between 1918 and 1921.

In later life it was the year in which he passed the examination that was critical for the diplomat. It was this that determined his seniority; and this was important because of the strong hierarchical sense within the Japanese bureaucracy. An entrant from the class of 1906 expected to reach higher office before one from the class of 1907. They were also very conscious of their contemporaries. Thus Hirota and Yoshida, who came out of the class of 1906, remained close for the rest of their careers.

Other factors that affected the careers of those who entered the Ministry were linguistic skills, marriage, family wealth and connections, and luck. From the earliest times it was English that was the key language; recruits tended to be posted to an English-speaking post, generally the London embassy, for a spell spent on language study. Some, such as Shidehara, became specially adept and owed their advancement to language ability. A good marriage, too, was an advantage. Katō Takaaki and Shidehara married daughters from the Mitsubishi family; and the question is often asked how far their attitudes and policies were moulded by this. Yoshida came from a wealthy shipping family and married the daughter of Count Makino, who was from 1925 to 1934 an important official at Court, the Lord Keeper of the Privy Seal. Regarding connections, there were, of course, those from noble families such as Tokugawa Iyemasa and Matsudaira Tsuneo. Less important in Foreign Ministry circles was the influence of clans, which was still an important factor in the army and navy elites. But diplomats seem to have come in the main from former samurai families.

For aspiring diplomats, the summit of their ambition was the posts of vice-minister and minister, which were normally bureaucratic appointments. Even in the case of a political party Cabinet, the appointee was not a party man. He was generally drawn from an embassy overseas so that, when he returned to Tokyo, he was in the main out of the political hurly-burly. He was not generally around pulling strings for his own preferment. The post of vice-minister was generally an administrative office, the head of the office who kept the machine running, a sort of permanent under-secretary.

1914 to 1931

The Foreign Ministry reached its highest peak after the First World War, when its staff was increased in numbers and improved in training. Japan had been recognized at the Paris Peace Conference as one of the 'big five' and had a competent, professionalized delegation of sixty members. In the years that followed Japan was pushed into world affairs and had, among other things, to take an interest in Europe. The pattern of diplomacy of the time was that of high-level conferences and Japan, by virtue of being a world power, had perforce to be represented, even if its own interests were not at issue.

It was a period also of 'Kasumigaseki autonomy', that is, a time when Kasumigaseki, the place where the Foreign Ministry was located, was able to formulate policy without too much overt outside interference. The influence of the elder statesmen was on the wane as they became older or died. Thus Yamagata died in 1922, leaving as sole survivor of the Genrō Saionji who, while he had the task of advising the Emperor on the choice of Prime Minister, rarely interfered with the formulation of individual policies. This left the Foreign Ministry with greater freedom of action than it had either before or after.

'Kasumigaseki autonomy' also applied to the appointment of Foreign Minister. Except for the brief period when Tanaka Giichi, the Prime Minister, acted as his own Foreign Minister, the position of Foreign Minister was always held by an ex-diplomat. From 1919 this office was held by a product of the 1894 examination system. He was competent, reliable, efficient; but he was not a world leader, lacking in political muscle in Japan itself, retiring rather than a demagogue who was used to making popular public speeches.

There were important reforms to improve the efficiency of the office. In 1920 the Political Affairs Bureau was divided and the Bureaux of Asian Affairs and of European-American Affairs were set up. This was a sign of the shift of emphasis that was taking place in Japanese thinking over foreign policy and the vital needs of the nation. Later, in May 1934, the Bureau of European-American Affairs was broken up into its constituents: the Bureau of American Affairs and the Bureau of European and Asiatic (later East Asian) Affairs. A new specialized agency was the Cultural Work Division, created in 1923, which became an independent bureau in 1927.

With the Paris Peace Conference in 1919 the Japanese set up a temporary peace treaty office to deal with matters relating to the German and other peace treaties, the League of Nations, and other international agencies such as the International Court. These affairs were transferred *en bloc* to the Treaties Bureau in 1924. Even after Japan announced its secession from the League in 1933, the Bureau still continued to cooperate technically with the League until the League declared sanctions against Japan in 1938.

A change of emphasis was to be noted in the overseas postings of young diplomats. In the 1910s a budding recruit would commonly be posted to London, Washington or some European capital. In the 1920s it became increasingly common for him to go instead to one of the numerous consular postings in China. The balance of the service was gradually being redressed from the days of *Datsu-A nyū-Ō* (see p. 242 above).

Such was the Kasumigaseki establishment. It had *esprit de corps* and high bureaucratic standards, operating in the twenties in a basically political party atmosphere. The phrase 'Kasumigaseki orthodoxy' means the liberal inter-nationalist attitude that tended to be adopted during the 1920s by the officials and diplomats trained by the Foreign Ministry. It came to an end with the Manchurian incident of 1931-3.

The Foreign Ministry was responsive to the opinions of outside academic advisers in the field of international law. Since most recruitment was from the Faculty of Law at Tokyo Imperial University and since diplomatic history and international law were firmly rooted there as academic disciplines, it is reasonable to assume that much of the legal advice would come from that quarter also. The law professors who appear to have exerted some influence by giving advice on legal problems were Dr Suehiro Shigeo, Dr Shinobu Jumpei, himself a former diplomat, Dr Tamura Kōsaku, another diplomat of some standing, Dr Yano Jinichi, Dr Ariga Nagao, who served as legal adviser to President Yuan Shih-k'ai of China, and Dr Tachi Sakutarō, perhaps the most influential of all. The diplomats came under both the general intellectual influence of the books and articles written by these scholars and the specific advice of consultants preparing position papers for the Ministry. One has the feeling that the Japanese Foreign Ministry was greatly under the influence of experts in international law; and this may account for the slightly legalistic approach that Japanese officials were inclined to take on many problems, such as the Sino-Japanese treaties of 1915 and 1918.

A word should also be said about academic journals specializing in the study of diplomacy. The most prominent was *Kokusaihō Gaikō Zasshi*, published by Tokyo University, which was the academic medium for the professors mentioned above. A more popular journal dealing with all varieties of diplomatic issues was *Gaikō Jihō*. It was thought to have been a kind of forum for the ideas of the Foreign Ministry and the War Ministry at different times. It moved during the 1920s from an emphasis on Japan's need for international cooperation to an emphasis on Japan's need for 'autonomous diplomacy' (*jishū gaikō*). This was to take sides on one of the great debates of the day, and was equivalent to an attack on Kasumigaseki orthodoxy.

The Foreign Ministry sought a foreign adviser as a successor for Denison, who had died in 1914. Eventually Dr Thomas Baty (1871-1954) was chosen. He was a native of Cumbria, England and a graduate in law from both Oxford and Cambridge universities. He was a prodigious author of studies in the field of international law and a highly qualified barrister. He took up his appointment as legal adviser (*hōritsu kōmon*) in 1916. After a career spanning almost forty years he died in Japan in 1954. He was the author of an autobiography in English entitled *Alone in Japan: The reminiscences of an international jurist in Japan* and published posthumously in Tokyo in 1959, and wrote another reflective volume *International Law in Twilight* (Tokyo, 1954).

In describing the evolution of the Foreign Ministry, it is appropriate to record some of the criticisms that were made overseas about Japanese diplomatic methods and competence. In the twenties there was still assumed to be goodwill on both sides; but there was generally a feeling abroad that the Japanese were extremely hard to tie down. One frequent complaint was the difficulty of getting to grips with the Japanese government itself through discussions with an official overseas, because of the subordination of its foreign representatives to Tokyo head office. Even when approaches were made to Tokyo, decisions were often long delayed. Japan had the reputation of vagueness and avoidance of commitment: the ordinary response was one of the need to refer to higher authority or being without instructions. Part of the vagueness may justly be blamed on the Japanese language, and there were also problems connected with the knowledge of English. In diplomatic parleys faulty interpretations were often a source of much trouble, while progress could be slow if no interpreters were present. It was still true that Japanese diplomats were slow in conversation as a general rule, though they were often highly competent at reading English; there were of course distinguished exceptions. The Foreign Ministry was itself not immune from language problems: in an age when messages between embassies and Tokyo took the form of telegrams in English, they often arrived in badly garbled form and served as yet another obstacle to communication.

1932 to 1945

This was a time of collision between the Foreign Ministry and the military. They pursued a foreign policy in parallel, though with connections. The main disagreements were over policy towards China, Germany and the United States. There were even differences between the foreign policy standpoints of the army and navy. The Foreign Ministry was not the only westernized section of Japanese government, but was probably more so than any other department of state.

Kasumigaseki orthodoxy and Kasumigaseki autonomy were brought to an end after the crisis over the London Naval Treaty (1930) and the Manchurian incident. From 1932 the Foreign Ministry assumed the role of international defender of Japanese policies, which were often not of its own making. Indeed, it sometimes defended in public causes that it fought against in private. From 1936 onwards it lost out further; a struggle between Ministry and military became a normal factor of policy-making.

This tension led to the growth of factions within the Foreign Ministry itself. Some diplomats, such as Yoshida, deliberately antagonized the army, both at overseas stations and in the Ministry. This was their privilege. Others found that a more cautious stance was more opportune, in view of the increasing power of the armed services in the state. In the background there was always the threat, or blackmail, held out by the cases of assassination of important political figures that occurred in Japan with increasing frequency from 1931 onwards.

The consequence of this was that from 1938 onwards the Foreign Minister increasingly came to be chosen from the ranks of the services. Examples of this were the selection in May 1938 of General Ugaki Kazushige (Konoe Cabinet I), in September 1939 of Admiral Nomura Kichisaburō (Abe Cabinet), and in 1941 of Admiral Toyoda Teijirō (Konoe Cabinet II). These men were not in any sense nominees of their service. They were just exceptional outside appointments, showing that the civilians were not too ill-disposed towards appointing moderate service leaders. These appointments were, however, resented by the Foreign Ministry bureaucracy – as was the appointment of Nomura in 1940 to the then senior diplomatic post of ambassador to Washington. But the Ministry did not carry enough weight to prevent such appointments; indeed, their protests only emphasized their weakness.

It is difficult to be specific about the factions that operated. At one level, it was a question of renovation against conservatism. At another, it was a question of affiliation: with which country or group of countries should Japan cultivate relations? Thus there was the Anglo-American faction (sometimes described as the European-American faction), opposed to the China faction and, later in the 1930s, to the Axis faction. The existence of these factions affected both the Ministry itself and the embassies abroad. In the Ministry there was immense in-fighting (and bitterness) over appointments to key posts. In embassies abroad there was also some impact. Thus the military attaché in London, at the request of other military attachés in Europe, tried to convince Ambassador Yoshida in 1937 that there was merit in Japan's anti-Comintern pact with Germany. Later, by prior arrangement as members of the Axis faction, Ambassador Ōshima in Berlin and Ambassador Shiratori in Rome gave to governments to which they were accredited undertakings that were not authorized by the Foreign Ministry. This was gross defiance, and the Emperor had to step in and administer a reprimand.

This faction-fighting resulted in gradual encroachment on the Foreign Ministry monopoly of overseas affairs. It took the form of a whittling away of the responsibility of the Ministry in various areas. The first of these was the new state of Manchukuo. It was laid down that a single person would hold the positions of ambassador to Manchukuo, governor of the Kwantung leased territory and commander of the Kwantung army. The Ministry's control over the ambassador became very restricted. In December 1934 a Manchukuoan Affairs Board was established under the Prime Minister, but it seemed to be an offshoot of the War Ministry. The next instance was the creation of the Kō-A-in (Asian Development Board or China Board). The army followed up its Manchukuo success by urging the necessity for something along the same lines to cover Chinese affairs and the China Board was set up in December 1938, despite the opposition of the Foreign Ministry. Since the Nationalist Government was not officially recognized by Japan, the Ministry had only minimal responsibility for Chinese affairs. In September of the following year there was a proposal to set up a Ministry of Trade (Bōeki-shō) that would combine the commercial sections of the Foreign Ministry with those of other ministries. The Foreign Ministry officials rallied round and with a great show of solidarity offered their resignations – a keynote of Kasumigaseki orthodoxy was that commercial relations were an essential part of the diplomat's duties. Faced by this mutiny, the Cabinet had no alternative but to withdraw its proposal. But this was a hollow victory. In August 1942 the Tōjō Ministry wished to establish the new Great East Asian Ministry in order to take over dealings with the various territories occupied by the Japanese armed forces. The Foreign Ministry argued that to deal with East Asian countries through a ministry different from that which handled the rest of Japan's diplomacy would be to place on these countries a stigma that they would resent. Prime Minister Tōjō was not prepared to tolerate rebellion and in any case met with less solidarity over this issue. Accordingly, he called for the resignation of the Foreign Minister, who had been impeding his schemes and after the appointment of a more amenable successor instituted the new ministry.

This protracted campaign of 'wing-clipping' left the Foreign Ministry demoralized. Yet it was a sign of the supremacy of the army in the Japanese state. There were none more critical of Kasumigaseki orthodoxy than Matsuoka, the wayward Foreign Minister of 1940-41, who dismissed any trusted retainers of the Ministry who disagreed with him and more importantly, General Tōjō, who had much of the simple soldier's prejudice towards the diplomats whom he regarded as far too clever. Thus Tōjō wanted the Foreign Ministry to confine itself to 'pure diplomacy', which he defined as the reception of envoys and the signing of treaties; he described the Foreign Minister as 'the mouthpiece of the national will as decided upon by the Cabinet'; he had a low opinion of diplomats, taking the view that what the soldiers had acquired for the nation was generally lost by weak diplomacy.

Even if the Foreign Ministry was sunk low, it could claim to have mounted high towards the end of the war. Though the diplomatic service overseas was on a limited scale during the war, and existed only in friendly and neutral capitals, it was an essential factor in the search for a peace settlement. The endeavours of Satō Naotake, ambassador to the Soviet Union, to find a peace formula through Moscow were one of the highlights, while the Ministry came back into its own in dealing with the situation created by the Allied conference at Potsdam. Many of its officials were reserved from military service though older diplomats also helped out.

1945 to 1952

These years of occupation were a unique part of Japan's experience. Embassies and consulates overseas were closed and the diplomatic staff repatriated; foreign policy was conducted on Japan's behalf by the Supreme Commander Allied Powers (SCAP), General Douglas Macarthur; the purge of those ministers and officials who had had special responsibility for the war applied to the Foreign Ministry and reduced its ranks for the period of the occupation. The International Military Tribunal for the Far East (IMTFE) charged several Foreign Ministers, especially Hirota (who was condemned to death), Shigemitsu, Matsuoka and Tōgō. While all this might suggest that the Foreign Ministry would have only a diminished role, this would be a misapprehension. It was in a position to control what became an essential part of occupation bureaucracy, the Central Liaison Office.

The Liaison Office dealt with negotiations for terminating the war and was responsible for direct negotiations with SCAP at a time when there was a genuine shortage of those with a knowledge of English – a skill that was in particularly short supply and belonged especially to the diplomats. It was therefore the Foreign Ministry that was closest to the United States. The fact that a former diplomat, Yoshida Shigeru, was Prime Minister from 1947 to 1954 and Foreign Minister from 1945 to 1947, gave a certain additional cachet to the Foreign Ministry.

As the occupation ran its course and peace was being negotiated by John Foster Dulles, public opinion felt that the Foreign Ministry was too close to the Americans and was lacking in a spirit of independence. Some of the unpopularity of the Americans was inevitably reflected onto the Ministry, especially when the problems of China, the peace conference, and the security arrangements associated with the peace treaty threw up many issues that became subjects of sharp public controversy.

There were few structural changes of note in the Ministry during this period. As diplomatic activities were suspended after 1945, there was no need to divide the work by regions; it was divided instead into general, political and economic affairs. A more important change was in the legal status of the Ministry, when the Meiji constitution of 1889 was replaced. By Article 78 of the new constitution of 1947, diplomatic affairs were placed in the hands of, and under the responsibility of, the Cabinet rather than the Emperor; and the Foreign Minister had to acknowledge the authority of the Prime Minister. The constitution does not, however, require that every minister of state has to be a representative in either house of the Diet.

After the San Francisco Treaty (1951)

Since the San Francisco peace treaty Japan has operated within a democratic system of political parties. The Foreign Ministry has been influenced in the following ways: the Foreign Minister and the parliamentary vice-minister and ministers of state have generally been party politicians and members of the Diet; foreign policy has had to be argued before the relevant party committees and justified in debates in the Diet that have often been acrimonious, which has meant that bureaucratically arranged policies of pre-war days are subject to new checks. One result of this is that much more information has been published about foreign policy than was the case before the war, though even then it was not inconsiderable. A genuine attempt has been made to follow an open diplomacy with due process of consultation. Clearly the new system has had its critics. Within the Ministry there are those who claim that politicians are amateurs, not widely travelled enough and not experienced in overseas affairs; that party influence has been detrimental and unduly influenced by lobbies; and that debates in the Diet have contributed little but steam. Similar views have also been expressed in academic circles. Nevertheless, democratic control of foreign policy has been accepted.

From the time that Ishibashi became Prime Minister in 1956 there has been political party diplomacy. The Foreign Ministers of the period have been politicians rather than bureaucrats and have generally been household names. Many Prime Ministers since 1952 have served for some time as Foreign Minister as part of a Liberal-Democratic party strategy of circulating the ministers around the various departments of state in order to give them breadth of experience. Kishi, Miki, Fukuda and Ōhira have all acted as Foreign Minister. Clearly this is a healthy convention in circumstances where so much of foreign relations is now closely related to summit meetings and the Prime Minister is inevitably involved. It has the disadvantage that the Foreign Minister tends to be a bird of passage who is merely flying around in order to get a broader vision, and his stay in the Ministry is inevitably short. Since 1956 Japan has not had any Foreign Ministers who have spent the greater part of their lives as career diplomats. Yoshida and Shigemitsu were virtually the last of the old-style bureaucratic Foreign Ministers who came to office after a long diplomatic career.

Accompanying the new-style political Foreign Ministers, there were the parliamentary or political vice-ministers (*seimu jikan*), generally one for each house of the Diet. These men were required to answer questions on the floor of the house or in committees. They were therefore go-betweens between the politicians and the Minister and his officials. The administration of the office was handled by career diplomats as administrative vice-ministers (*jimu jikan*) Alongside them were the officials known in official translation as deputy vice-ministers (*gaimu shingi kan*) who are in effect consultative officials. The Foreign Minister's personal staff led by his private secretary completes his headquarters.

The technical interruption in the activities of the Foreign Ministry during the occupation period necessitated the adoption of new recruitment policies. The Foreign Service Training Institute (*Kenshūjō*) was set up after the war to test entrants to the profession. It has greatly extended the range of universities from which entrants are drawn. In pre-war days four-fifths of recruits came from Tokyo Imperial University; entrants now come not only from national but also from private universities, not only from metropolitan but also from provincial universities. They have studied many disciplines but the majority have specialized in the core subjects of law, politics and economics. The Foreign Ministry also encourages those recruited to spend time overseas by studying at a foreign university before their first posting. Between 1940 and 1950 most career diplomats were not able to avail themselves of the opportunity to go overseas as part of their training in the way their predecessors had done but this shortcoming has now been overcome. The kinds of families from which foreign service recruits are drawn have again been widened, though there still seem to be 'Foreign Ministry dynasties' – that is, names in the lists of the 1970s that echo those familiar in pre-war days. But perhaps this is not unexpected in a department that has in recent years gradually increased the number of its employees to over 3300 (1978 figures). Yet it is a specialized service and its numbers are smaller than those of government departments concerned with internal affairs, such as finance, agriculture, commerce and industry.

The Foreign Ministry has retained basically the same shape as it has had over the years. But the complexity of the organization has increased with the complexity of international affairs. It has been moulded and remoulded on countless occasions in the post-war years in order to meet the prevailing needs of foreign relations. Diplomatic establishments overseas have undergone a vast post-war expansion, largely created by the decolonization of the world and the growth of Japan's commercial interests in all parts of the globe. The economic ingredient in Japan's post-war foreign policy decision-making has far exceeded that of pre-war Japan. In economic terms Japan pursued bilateral trade agreements in the 1950s in order to re-establish its pre-war trade relations. The first success was when Japan joined GATT in 1955, though many countries continued to reserve their position over 'most favoured nation status'. That hurdle was passed with the signing of the Anglo-Japanese treaty of commerce and navigation in November 1962. It was a natural consequence that Japan joined the OECD in 1964. Its successful trade promotion reached a symbolic climax with the International EXPO at Osaka in 1970. This process of integrating Japan into the world economic community, which culminated in the presence of her Prime Minister at G7 and G8 summits, has clearly taxed the resources of the Foreign Ministry. Naturally the Ministry has shared these negotiations with other ministries; but it still places a premium on those diplomats who studied economics or have specialized in economic questions.

The Japanese Foreign Ministry, like the country itself, has had a variegated experience over the past century and more. It has built up a modernized, professional service with great shrewdness and skill. By the 1920s that service had acquired traditions and could look with some pride at its Kasumigaseki autonomy. In the 1930s the autonomy and independent position of the Ministry were challenged by the armed services. It was not the case that the Foreign Ministry sold itself out to the army, rather that the army pursued an independent foreign policy, using loopholes in the constitution and in the administrative system, which had seriously broken down. There was a hiatus from 1937 to 1952, during which Foreign Ministry officials were often assigned to other duties. In the post-war period it is still the bureaucracy that has a major steering role in foreign policy-making.

The Japanese Foreign Ministry has developed proud traditions over the years. There is among its diplomatic representatives overseas a strong tradition of observation and reporting, of loyalty to Tokyo and of conscientious service. Because of the turbulent history of Japan over the past century, the diplomats have had a changing and subtle role to play abroad. Because of the unstable domestic background within Japan itself, the careers and prospects of diplomats have been more than normally subject to difficulties and anxieties. Now that Japan has greater stability than it has enjoyed since the Meiji restoration, it has the unusual status of a great economic power with little military muscle. It is no mean task to be the guardian of foreign affairs of such a country.

INDEX